INTERNATIONAL BUSINESS ORGANIZATION

THE ACADEMY OF INTERNATIONAL BUSINESS

Published in association with the UK Chapter of the Academy of International Business

Titles already published in the series:

INTERNATIONAL BUSINESS AND EUROPE IN TRANSITION (Volume 1)
Edited by Fred Burton, Mo Yamin and Stephen Young

INTERNATIONALISATION STRATEGIES (Volume 2)
Edited by George Chryssochoidis, Carla Millar and Jeremy Clegg

THE STRATEGY AND ORGANIZATION OF INTERNATIONAL BUSINESS (Volume 3)
Edited by Peter Buckley, Fred Burton and Hafiz Mirza

INTERNATIONALIZATION: PROCESS, CONTEXT AND MARKETS (Volume 4)
Edited by Graham Hooley, Ray Loveridge and David Wilson

International Business Organization

Subsidiary Management, Entry Strategies and Emerging Markets

Edited by

Fred Burton

Malcolm Chapman

and

Adam Cross

First published in Great Britain 1999 by
MACMILLAN PRESS LTD
Houndmills, Basingstoke, Hampshire RG21 6XS and London
Companies and representatives throughout the world

A catalogue record for this book is available from the British Library.

ISBN 0–333–73442–4

First published in the United States of America 1999 by
ST. MARTIN'S PRESS, INC.,
Scholarly and Reference Division,
175 Fifth Avenue, New York, N.Y. 10010

ISBN 0–312–22371–4

Library of Congress Cataloging-in-Publication Data
International business organization : subsidiary management, entry
strategies and emerging markets / edited by Fred Burton, Malcolm
Chapman and Adam Cross.
p. cm.
A selection of revised papers presented at the 1997 Annual
Conference of the UK Chapter of the Academy of International
Business held at the Leeds University Business School on April 4–5.
Includes bibliographical references and index.
ISBN 0–312–22371–4 (cloth)
1. International business enterprise Congresses. I. Burton,
Fred, 1938– . II. Chapman, Malcolm, 1951– . III. Cross, Adam.
IV. Academy of International Business. UK Chapter. Conference
(1997 : Leeds University Business School)
HD2755.5.I5367 1999
658'.049—DC21   99–18872
                                                CIP

This book is printed on paper suitable for recycling and made from fully managed and sustained forest sources.

10   9   8   7   6   5   4   3   2   1
08   07 06 05 04 03 02 01 00 99

Printed in Great Britain

Contents

List of Figures

List of Tables

Preface and Acknowledgements

This book has its origins in the 1997 Annual Conference of the UK Chapter of the Academy of International Business (AIB) held at Leeds University Business School, on 4–5 April 1997. Fifty-one competitive and workshop papers were presented at this conference. All submissions were subjected to a double-blind review process, with referees drawn mainly from the UK AIB membership, and the most outstanding papers were selected for inclusion in this volume. These contributions were further honed by their authors, a process which benefited from lively discussion between the participants and session chairs at the Conference and from the reviewers' reports and comments. The editors extend their gratitude to all concerned. We would also like to thank Sheila Fordham of the Centre for International Business, University of Leeds (CIBUL), for her secretarial and administrative help with the Conference, and Jeremy Clegg and Peter Buckley, also of CIBUL, for generously sharing with us their expertise. We are also grateful to Susan Clegg and Sarah Brown of Macmillan for their guidance and support throughout the editorial process.

FRED BURTON
MALCOLM CHAPMAN
ADAM CROSS

List of Contributors

Margreet Boersma Researcher, University of Groningen, The Netherlands

Keith D. Brouthers Reader, East London Business School, University of East London, UK

Lance Eliot Brouthers Associate Professor, Division of Management and Marketing, University of Texas at San Antonio, USA

Trevor Buck Professor of Business Policy, Leicester Business School, De Montfort University, UK

Fred Burton Senior Lecturer, Manchester School of Management, UMIST, UK

Mark Casson Professor of Economics, University of Reading, UK

Malcolm Chapman Senior Lecturer, Centre for International Business, Leeds University Business School, University of Leeds, UK

Chong Ju Choi Professor, Department of Strategy and International Business, City University Business School, London, UK

Edward Coyne Academic Dean and Professor, American College Dublin, Ireland

Adam Cross Lecturer, Centre for International Business, Leeds University Business School, University of Leeds, UK

John H. Dunning State of New Jersey Professor of International Business at Rutgers University and Emeritus Research Professor of International Business at the University of Reading, UK

Igor Filatotchev Senior Lecturer, University of Nottingham Business School, University of Nottingham, UK

Peter Chi Ming Fu Senior Lecturer, Division of Commerce, City University of Hong Kong, Hong Kong

Pervez Ghauri Professor, University of Groningen, The Netherlands

Keith Glaister Professor of International Strategic Management, Leeds University Business School, University of Leeds, UK

Soo Hee Lee Lecturer, Department of Management, Clore Management Centre, Birkbeck College, University of London, UK

Carla Millar Director, Flexible Master Programme, Department of Strategy and International Business, City University Business School, London, UK

Ram Mudambi Associate Professor, Weatherhead School of Management, Case Western Reserve University, USA, and Reader, ISMA Centre, University of Reading, UK

Marina Papanastassiou Lecturer, Athens University of Economics and Business

Robert Pearce Reader, Department of Economics, University of Reading, UK

Hugo Radice Lecturer, Industrial and Labour Studies, Leeds University Business School, University of Leeds, UK

Richard Schoenberg Lecturer in International Business Strategy, Imperial College Management School, University of London, UK

George Sharpley Researcher, University of Delaware, USA

Wilfred Sleeman Magnus Management Consultants, Naarden, The Netherlands

James Taggart Senior Lecturer, Department of Marketing, University of Strathclyde, UK

Monir Tayeb Senior Lecturer, Heriot Watt University, Edinburgh, UK

Nigel Wadeson Department of Economics, University of Reading, UK

Mike Wright Professor, University of Nottingham Business School, University of Nottingham, UK

Mo Yamin Lecturer, Manchester School of Management, UMIST, UK

List of Abbreviations

AIB	Academy of International Business
AVP	Average Variable Product
CEO	Chief Executive Officer
CG	Corporate Governance
CR	Cost Reduction
EBRD	European Bank for Reconstruction and Development
EC	Employee Control
EEC	European Economic Community
EJV	Equity Joint Venture
EMU	Economic and Monetary Union
EO	Employee Ownership
EPRG	Ethnocentric, Polycentric, Regiocentric, Geocentric
ES	Economic Sociology
ESOP	Employee Stock-Ownership Plan
EU	European Union
FDI	Foreign Direct Investment
FI	Financial Intermediary
GDP	Gross Domestic Product
HCM	Host-Country Market
HRM	Human Resource Management
IAP	Investment Attraction Package
IIA	Inward Investment Agency
ISO	International Standards Organization
JV	Joint Venture
M&As	Mergers and Acquisitions
MITI	Ministry of International Trade and Industry [Japan]
MNB	Multinational Bank
MNC	Multinational Corporation
MNE	Multinational Enterprise
MVP	Marginal Variable Product
NAFTA	North American Free Trade Agreement
NIS	National Innovation System
OLI	Ownership–Location–Internalization
OLS	Ordinary Least Squares
OECD	Organization for Economic Cooperation and Development
RM	Raw Materials
RTS	Russian Trading System
TCE	Transaction-Costs Economics
TNC	Transnational Corporation
UNCTAD	United Nations Conference on Trade and Development

1 Introduction: International Business Organization

Fred Burton, Malcolm Chapman and Adam Cross

The global business environment today is characterized by increasing complexity and change. Few firms can avoid these trends. Selection processes operate that constantly test existing organizational methods and approaches. Some firms have proved adept at successfully coordinating vast networks of resources and capabilities across national boundaries, to become true transnational corporations. Other firms, however, continue to struggle with inadequate or redundant approaches and need to develop fresh solutions to the problems of global coordination and control. Indeed, for many firms, the ability to devise and implement feasible solutions to problems constitutes an important competitive advantage.

As markets become increasingly globalized and regionalized, change becomes ever more pervasive. Volatility in the global business environment means that researchers investigating the organization and management of business are also presented with special challenges. New methodologies, analytical tools and paradigms are required in order to comprehend better the dynamics of this change, and to inform the decision-making process of managers as they respond. It is not surprising, therefore, that research on the multinational enterprise (MNE) permits the development and testing of theory and procedures that have wider managerial relevance. This research can serve as a benchmark for organization theory applicable in restricted, national or domestic contexts, as well as in the international economy (Hedlund, 1996).

The contents of this volume, a selection of outstanding papers from the 1997 UK AIB Conference, at the Leeds University Business School, takes a further step in advancing our understanding of the organization and management of international business. The papers are grouped into three sections: subsidiary management, entry strategies and emerging markets. Each section begins with an introduction that briefly reviews the state of the art in the academic study of the area and provides a context for the chapters that follow.

John Dunning sets the context for the volume in Chapter 2. Dunning

1

contemplates four paradoxes in the modern world economy that have emerged as a consequence of globalization (by which is meant the integration of product, financial and – to a far lesser extent – factor markets, on a global scale; see Buckley, Clegg and Forsans, 1998). Each of these paradoxes is represented in some form in this volume. These contradictions are evident in the spatial (global vs local) distribution of economic activity, the (interventionist vs non-interventionist) role of government and the human consequences (affluence vs unemployment) of globalization. Perhaps of greater importance, in the context of this volume, is Dunning's fourth paradox, which can be seen in the nature of cross-border business relationships. While firms today are experiencing increased competition in their factor and final goods markets, there has also been a proliferation in cooperative, interfirm alliances and networking arrangements, especially in firms' non-core activities. These arrangements have multiplied in response to, *inter alia*, the accelerating rate of technological obsolescence, the interrelatedness of much cutting-edge technology, and the lowering of the transaction costs of interfirm cooperation. It is clear that competition and cooperation are no longer antagonistic but have become mutually reinforcing organizational forms. Dunning argues persuasively that, in order to formulate appropriate policy, national government and the wider international community have much to learn from the strategies and practices adopted by leading multinational companies in response to the problems of globalization.

SUBSIDIARY MANAGEMENT

Part One, which is introduced by Fred Burton, explores aspects of the organization of headquarters–subsidiary relationships. The field of headquarters–subsidiary relationships remains a fertile one because of the increasing degree of autonomy, in both scale and scope, now experienced by many subsidiaries. As the authors of the contributions in this part demonstrate, the local experience, knowledge and strategy of the most innovative and influential subsidiaries can to a considerable degree influence the evolution and success of the entire multinational firm.

In Chapter 3, Jim Taggart shows how the degree of autonomy observed in subsidiaries can vary depending on the nationality of the parent, with UK subsidiaries of US multinational firms tending to enjoy greater independence than those whose parent firms are headquartered in the European Union (EU). By focusing on the technology transfers that occur in collaborative projects with local scientific institutions, Marina Papanastassiou and Robert Pearce (Chapter 4) analyse the mutual dependence of subsidiaries on the host country economy and on the multinational as a whole. In a similar vein, Mo Yamin, in Chapter 5, examines 'reverse' transfers and the diffusion of technology from innovative subsidiaries to the parent firm. Ram Mudambi (Chapter 6) investigates whether and to what extent an MNE's experience of operating at a particular location, in terms of the duration of operations, influences the likelihood of sequential investment, after allowing for portfolio risk considerations. In Chapter 7, Monir Tayeb uses a case-study approach to consider the factors which managers of multinational firms should bear in mind in order to successfully implement the introduction of centrally-imposed policy to a local workforce.

ENTRY STRATEGIES

Organization theorists have tended to undervalue the multinational enterprise as a unit of analysis (Buckley, Burton and Mirza, 1998). There has been much valuable theorizing and empirical study, however, regarding the boundaries of the international firm and the structures used to develop non-domestic markets, which has contributed much to our understanding of organizations in general. Part Two of this volume, which is introduced by Adam Cross, further advances this line of enquiry.

The first two chapters in this section are theoretical pieces that consider the role and flow of information in organizations. Both have resonances beyond the context of international business. In Chapter 8, Mark Casson and Nigel Wadeson apply information cost analysis to gain insight into the origins of procedures and routines in the firm, and how these are planned and memorized. Peter Fu, in Chapter 9, concentrates on one type of firm – the international bank – and uses transaction cost analysis to show why such firms internalize markets for intermediate inputs across national frontiers. Issues relating to the establishment and operation of two methods for servicing foreign markets are addressed in the next three chapters. Keith Glaister, in Chapter 10, examines the strategic motives that firms have for entering an equity joint venture (EJV), and the criteria used for selecting a suitable partner. In their review of an often controversial literature, Margreet Boersma and Pervez Ghauri (Chapter 11) catalogue the variety of measures and indicators employed by empiricists to gauge the performance of EJVs, and highlight the methodological limitations associated with their use. In Chapter 12, Keith Brouthers, Lance Eliot Brouthers and Wilfred Sleeman show how a firm that uses contractual means – in this case franchises – to establish much of its foreign operations is still able to implement the internal mechanisms and external relations required to become a transnational corporation. There is clearly much scope in exploring the alternatives to internalization as an international expansion strategy.

EMERGING MARKETS

The emergence of markets previously closed to the MNE witnessed in the last decade presents many new research opportunities. The chapters in Part Three, which are introduced by Malcolm Chapman, illustrate the eclecticism in the issues raised by this subject. These papers have as a general theme the cultural and organizational problems in international business.

In Chapter 13, Hugo Radice explores the phenomenon of globalization and further develops themes and issues introduced by Dunning in Chapter 2, particularly in regard to policy implications. Focusing his analysis on global capital markets, the location of R&D activity, and systems of corporate governance, Radice describes the significance and extent to which national differences have been eroded by the fusion of national business systems. Chapter 14 uses as a laboratory the Russian privatization programme to test theoretical propositions regarding the effect of greater employee ownership and employee control on the behaviour and performance of enterprises. In Chapter 15, Chong Ju Choi, Soo Hee Lee and Carla Millar consider the growing importance of emerging markets in the context of a comparative analysis of national business systems. In their review of business exchange and enforcement issues, these authors show why counter-trade continues to have a facilitating role in conducting business with these economies. Ed Coyne, in Chapter 16, assesses how the effectiveness of investment incentives offered by Caribbean countries may vary depending upon the MNE's motive for investing. In Chapter 17, Richard Schoenburg criticizes existing research on the impact of cultural compatibility on the management and performance of firms following international acquisition.

CONCLUSION

This collection of works on the organization of international business demonstrates the vigour and vitality of the subject. This owes as much to the cross-fertilization (long overdue) between traditional discipline and area study boundaries as it does to events in the global economy. The subject of international business has a key role in integrating conventionally separate academic topics. This is essential if we are to understand the challenges that face firms as national barriers are broken down across a wide range of markets. At the heart of this is the issue of how international business organizes itself. This collection represents a timely contribution to this heavy – but exciting – research agenda.

2 Some Paradoxes of the Emerging Global Economy: The Multinational Solution[1]

John H. Dunning

INTRODUCTION

In approaching the end of the twentieth century, one cannot but be struck by both the similarities and differences of circumstances to those faced by our forefathers one hundred years ago. Then, as now, was an era of dramatic and widespread technological change.[2] Then, as now, a new generation of telecommunication advances was shrinking the boundaries of economic activity. Then, as now, the organizational structures of firms and the socio-institutional framework of countries were in a state of flux. Then, as now, the cartography of political space was being reconfigured. Then, as now, the jurisdiction of national governments was being questioned, and the locus and composition of civic responsibilities were being redefined. Then, as now, new relationships and alliances were being forged between, and within, private and public institutions, and among different ethnic, religious and social groups.

But, to a more discerning observer, the differences between the two ages are more marked than the similarities. Key among these is that, while, for the most part, the events of the late nineteenth century occurred *within* a well-established and widely accepted social and political order,[3] those now occurring seem to be challenging long-cherished ideologies and values – and, in some cases, the very cohesiveness of society. At the same time, contemporary events are moulding a very unpredictable future – both for individuals and for institutions – and, more often than not, they are as divisive as they are unifying in their consequences. Our contemporary world is in a state of transition and turmoil. Some may view this as a form of creative destruction – of ideas, of technologies, of institutions and of cultures. Others fear that it is the beginning of an era of social and political unrest, the like of which we have not seen for many generations. The order of hierarchical capitalism which, as a wealth-creating system, has served much of the world so well over the past century, is being increasingly questioned; but no one is quite sure what is going to replace it – or indeed what should replace it.

Part of our increasing sense of bewilderment and insecurity, I suggest, arises because many of the events now occurring are paradoxical, if not antithetical, in both their characteristics and implications. Indeed, we may well be moving out of Eric Hobsbawm's *Age of Extremes* into an 'Age of Paradoxes'.[4] Nowhere is this more clearly seen than in the globalization of economic activity. Few can surely deny that alongside an impressive array of opportunities and benefits offered by deep cross-border economic interdependence, it is demanding enormous and often painful adjustments, not only of corporations and governments, but of the working lives, leisure pursuits and mind-sets of ordinary men and women. One political scientist, in a book published last year,[5] avers that our planet is simultaneously 'falling apart and coming together'; while William Greiber (1997), in a new polemic with the intriguing title *One World, Ready or Not* writes about 'new technologies enabling nations to take sudden leaps into modernity, while at the same time promoting the renewal of economic barbarisms' (p. 12).

In this chapter, I shall consider just four paradoxes or contradictions of our emerging global economy – or what the Chinese might prefer to call the 'yin' and 'yang' of globalization.[6] I believe that the ways in which these paradoxes are approached and reconciled – if, indeed, they are reconciled – will determine the shape of our planet's political and economic future; and the social well-being of each and every one of us. I shall also suggest that hints of how the paradoxes may best be resolved by the international community are already contained in the strategies and actions of some of our more successful multinational enterprises (MNEs); just as, a century ago, the emergence of large domestic enterprises helped point the ways in which national governments might best respond to the then emerging phenomenon of hierarchical capitalism.

COOPERATION AND COMPETITION: THE PARADOX OF RELATIONSHIPS

At the end of the last century, the main form of interface between firms was competition. Most transactions between buyers and sellers were at spot or 'arm's length' prices, and adversarial in nature. Apart from the conclusion of mergers, combines and other business agreements to restrict competition, rival firms perceived little need to cooperate with each other. In most advanced industrial nations, free enterprise was perceived 'to rule OK'; and where markets failed, either firms or non-market entities intervened by internalizing these markets – viz. by an 'exit', rather than a 'voice', response. Governments, like private corporations, were at best suspicious of, and at worst downright hostile to, each other. To the 'yin' of competition there was no counterbalancing 'yang' of cooperation.

By contrast, yet at the same time, the economic policies of national administrations were predicated on the belief that unimpeded international trade was beneficial because it enabled each country to produce goods and services which were *complementary*, rather than *substitutable*, to each other's needs. This, after all, is what the principle of comparative advantage is all about. True, there were some interventionist actions[7] – particularly by governments of later industrializing nations, but the dictum 'Firms compete but countries cooperate – and both obey the dictates of the marketplace' was widely upheld. This was the deeply implanted order of things, which the events of the second industrial revolution of the late nineteenth century did little to disturb.

As we approach the new millennium, interfirm and inter-nation state relationships are taking on more complex, pluralistic and contradictory forms. The last decade, in particular, has witnessed a spectacular increase in collaborative agreements between firms, both to penetrate new markets and to share the costs and speed up the process of innovation. Paradoxically, at a time of increased competition between firms in the factor and final goods markets, there has been a shedding of non-core activities by firms along and between value chains; and a replacement of them by a range of closely monitored interfirm alliances and networking arrangements. This movement has also led to another paradox – viz. the renaissance of small to medium-size firms at a time when giant multinational enterprises continue to engage in international mergers and acquisitions (M&As), and dominate the markets for technology-intensive and branded goods and services.

The reasons for the emerging 'yin' and 'yang' of the organization of economic activity are many, but most reduce to the emergence of knowledge-capital as the main resource for upgrading the competitiveness of firms; an accelerating rate of technological obsolescence; a closer interconnection between many cutting-edge technologies, and the growing integration between different stages of the value-added chain (especially between the R&D and the manufacturing departments of firms). Such events, together with the lowering transaction costs of many kinds of interfirm cooperation, have encouraged multinational and other enterprises to specialize in activities based on their core competencies, while, at the same time, forging new and ongoing relationships with firms – both domestic and foreign – supplying complementary inputs to these activities.

National governments, too, are finding that globalization is leading to new, and incongruous, cross-border relationships. Increasingly, in a world in which trade and foreign direct investment (FDI) are within rather than between industrial sectors, unemployment is unacceptably high, human resource development is at a premium, and firm-specific assets are more easily transplanted across national borders, governments are increasingly and openly competing with each other for similar resources, as well as seeking to advance their own particular social agendas. As the economic structure of countries tends to converge, so institutional and organizational factors are becoming more important location-specific endowments. Foremost among these are the actions of governments, which I will consider in more detail a little later. For the moment, I would simply note that in contrast to the late nineteenth century scenario, where the policies of national administrations were either independent of, or tended to complement, each other, those of today are a mixture of the 'yin' of competition and the 'yang' of cooperation.

Even the most cursory review of now-emerging relationships between firms and governments suggests that, far from being antithetical, cooperation and competition each has its unique and mutually reinforcing role to play in a dynamic market economy. In and of themselves, each is a neutral concept. However, each may be deployed in a market-distorting or a market-facilitating way. There is an unacceptable face of cooperation and an unacceptable face of competition. One of the challenges of the globalizing economy is to manage and resolve the apparent contradictory nature of these two organizational forms.

In its 1997, *World Development Report*,[8] the World Bank calls for a rethinking of the role of the state in economic affairs, so that it can be a more creditable and effective partner to the private sector in upgrading the productivity of the resources and the competitiveness of the firms within its jurisdiction. 'Good government', the report concludes, 'is not a luxury but a vital necessity for economic prosperity' (p. 15). Clearly, the decision of *when, with whom,* and *how* to cooperate, and *when, with whom,* and *how* to compete is partly determined by firm, industry and country-specific characteristics. Because of this, it is difficult to lay down any universal guidelines. But, in the last two decades or so, Western firms and nations have learnt a great deal about the 'yin' and 'yang' of commercial relationships and institutional arrangements practiced in East Asia. The knowledge so gained is now being assiduously revamped and adapted to Western norms and needs – so much so that the expression 'alliance' capitalism is now being used to describe a new trajectory of market-based socioeconomic systems. A feature of this trajectory is that it is reconstituting the concepts of competition and cooperation, from being exclusive alternatives to being mutually reinforcing organizational forms.

In seeking to manage and reconcile the paradox of relationships, I would like to suggest that nation states have much to learn from the behaviour of MNEs. Such corporations – at least the successful ones – are 'masters of the paradox'. They are well-experienced both at translating the horns of dilemma of economic change into virtuous circles of growth and profitability; and of using both competition and cooperation as strategies to obtain their long-term objectives (Baden-Fuller and Stopford, 1992). While, in the last resort, most MNEs are subject to the discipline of the global marketplace, an increasing number are forming alliances with other firms to innovate new products to reconstruct their value chains and seek out new markets. The key to achieving the right balance between competition – a 'go it alone strategy' – and coopera-tion – a 'do it together strategy' – seems to rest on the perception of managers about the nature and strength of their distinctive or core com-petencies; and that of the other assets which need to be combined with these competencies if they are to effectively augment and exploit them.[9] Research suggests that firms are most likely to cooperate with each other where they perceive this will help them reduce their resource commitments in acquiring or utilizing these complementary assets; but, that they are less eager to do so when this requires cutting-edge intellectual capital, and learning experiences about their critical competencies. Once this balance of options is achieved – and this is a constantly moving target – compe-tition and cooperation need no longer be seen as mutually exclusive alternatives, but rather as reinforcing avenues for advancing competitiveness.

GLOBALIZATION VS LOCALIZATION: THE PARADOX OF SPACE

As the late nineteenth century witnessed the extension of local into national markets, and the emergence of foreign direct investment as a burgeon-ing of international commerce, so the late twentieth century is seeing the regionalization and globalization of economic activity. However, the difference between these two events is not just one of the size and char-acter of markets – but the fact that, while a century ago economic transactions were largely conducted between independent buyers and sellers, today between a third and one-half of all non-agricultural trade in goods, and between one-half and three-fifths of cross-border capital and technology flows, are undertaken by and within the same company or groups of related companies.[10]

The extension of geographical space has not affected all activities to the same extent. While the markets for some goods, for example Coca Cola, fast food, Levi jeans, Gucci handbags and some kinds of services (for example, financial assets, music, television and sports) span the globe; others are restricted by the specificity of local supply capabilities, customs, tastes and government regulations. Similarly, while some parts of the value chain, for example those involving the electronic transmission of standardized data, are spatially unanchored; others, in which trust-based relations, personal interface and complex, but non-codifiable, knowledge are at a premium, are having to pay more heed to distance-constrained capabilities and needs. Hence, we have the paradox of what the geographer Ann Markusen (1994) has referred to as 'sticky places within slippery space'. At the same time, the imperatives of much of contemporary product and production technology and the lowering of natural and artificial barriers to traversing space, have most certainly enabled firms to take a more holistic stance to their foreign and domestic operations.

The liberalization of markets, more outward-looking development policies, and the current attractions of regional economic integration have all helped to push out the territorial boundaries of firms. While FDI is the main route by which this extension is being accomplished, increasingly, as I have already mentioned, cross-border alliances – varying from international subcontracting and 'keiretsu' type relationships, to R&D consortia among rival firms – have become more significant in the last decade, and seem likely to be a major feature of the capitalism of the twenty-first century.

If we can think of the spatial widening of economic activity as the 'yin' of globalization, the 'yang' is surely the increasing pressure on individuals, firms, nations and localities to reassert their distinctive traits and values. The paradox of regional economic integration – albeit often market-driven – is that it introduces an economic uniformity or universality into people's lives, which they frequently wish to offset by emphasizing other, and more distinctive, characteristics of their individuality. In some cases – although we would hesitate to suggest this has been caused by the emergence of the global economy, however much it may facilitate it – it leads to ethnic and ideological schisms and to political disintegration and fragmentation. Just as there can be little doubt that the merger movement among corporations is going on alongside a reinvigoration of medium and small businesses, so as countries group together to better advance their common economic aspirations, they, or their peoples, are reasserting their singular cultural and ethnic heritages. As John Naisbitt (1994) has put it 'there is a rising conflict between universalism and tribalism, and between regional unification and fragmentation'.

As the global economy favours the growth of the large MNE, so many of its spatial units are becoming smaller. The same may well be true of the 'body politique'. The concept of subsidiarity is gaining widespread acceptance at all levels of governance; and the role of subnational economic entities is becoming more, rather than less, influential. Certainly this is the view of Kenichi Ohmae, who, in his latest book (Ohmae, 1995), argues persuasively that, in a borderless world, region states may well come to replace nation states as the ports of entry into the global economy and the centerpiece of knowledge-based economic activity.[11] And, certainly, there is accumulating evidence of the benefits of the increasing spatial concentration of the higher order of value-added activities, in spite of the tremendous advances in all forms of telematics (Storper, 1997).

Once again, however, I would suggest that the contradiction between the globalization and the localization of economic space is more apparent than real, and that this is well-demonstrated by the activities of the more successful MNEs. They know full well the axiom 'think globally but act locally'; and of the need to balance the gains offered by the coordination of scale-related technologies with those stemming from the adaptation of world product mandates, production techniques and work practices to local situations. They also appreciate that the ability to recognize these latter needs, and to efficiently coordinate them, are important competitive advantages in their own right. At the same time, the *kind* and *degree* of adaptation required in the late 1990s is very different from that of a century ago. Then, it was mainly based on the availability (and quality) of natural resources and of national consumer tastes. Now, it is based on the flexible use of created assets (viz. of innovations, production technologies and organizational structures); and on an acceptance of the fact that in a variety of quite subtle ways, the kind of product improvements sought by consumers reflects national and subnational, as well as international, physical and spiritual values.

In short, globalization is leading to a spatial reconfiguration of economic activity – and also the governance of such activity. In some cases, this is resulting in a harmonization of technical standards, of the functions of firms and of the harmonization of consumer tastes the world over. In others, it is increasing the value of close spatial linkages between firms (such as that fostered in business districts and science parks) at a subnational level, and stimulating individuals and nations to differentiate themselves from each other and emphasize their discriminating characteristics. The 'yin' of slippery space is then going hand in hand with – indeed some would say giving rise to – the 'yang', or sticky place; and to a reevaluation of local cultural religious and ethnic mores. As long as these trends of globalization are treated as complementary rather than substitutable for each other, then, I believe, there is no real paradox of geographical space. And, as I have already suggested, the more successful MNEs are already demonstrating some of the ways in which spatially related tensions can be minimized and used to promote their global objectives. I accept, of course, that this task is a good deal more challenging for national and regional governments, but grapple with it they must if the full benefits of globalization are not to be destroyed by intercountry social and cultural strife. I shall return to this point later.

THE ROLE OF GOVERNMENTS: THE PARADOX OF 'LESS, YET MORE'

A century ago, there was comparatively little dispute about the role of national administrations – at least in Western economies.[12] The spiritual heritage of Adam Smith and the founding fathers of the American Revolution was very much alive. In economic matters, at least, the invisible hand of the market was thought superior to that of the visible hand of extra-market planning and government intervention. The duties of government were to defend the realm, to maintain internal law and order, to combat the unacceptable face of capitalism, to provide the legal and commercial framework in which property rights were respected and unfettered markets might flourish, and to alleviate unavoidable social distress.

There was no conflict in performing these tasks; they were not even regarded as competitive to those of other organizational forms. The fact that in some countries (for example, France and Germany) governments pursued more paternalistic policies and were more interventionist than others (for example, the UK), was accepted to reflect their particular institutional heritages or their stages of economic development, rather than any differences in their political philosophies. In any event, because of the immobility of resources and absence of any cross-border structural integration of economic activity, national administrations were able to follow largely independent economic and social strategies. Even what international commerce there was at the time was largely determined by a world order, viz. the gold standard; although restrictions on some kinds of trade, and other forms of government intervention, were beginning to emerge.

Today, the optimum or appropriate role of government is hotly debated. In particular, the last twenty years have seen a blurring of the boundaries of the role of the private and public sector in capitalist economies; while globalization has led to an intensification of the 'yin' and 'yang' of government intervention. On the one hand, as markets have become more liberalized and central planning has become discredited, the interventionist role of governments has lessened. On the other, as the economic prosperity of firms and nations has become more dependent on the continual upgrading of indigenous created assets – notably intellectual capital and physical and commercial infrastructure – then, insofar as it has the power to influence (for example, by its educational and technology policies), the role of the state has become more critical.

I believe that, for the most part, globalization is *not* leading to a hollowing out of the responsibilities of national governments. But it is changing their *raison d'etre*, and their content. And it is doing so within the context of deepening structural integration; the growing importance of public goods, for example crime prevention, health care, education and the environment; and the increasing ease with which corporations can avoid unpopular actions by their national or regional authorities by relocating their activities outside their jurisdiction (that is, by 'voting with their feet').[13]

Another feature of globalization and economic change is that it is leading to a greater coincidence of interests between governments and the private sector in market economies. The 'yin' of a policing and um-piring, but otherwise non-interventionist, stance of governments is being supplemented by the 'yang' of governments as builders and monitors of economic systems and supportive institutions; as facilitators of efficient markets; as catalysts of dynamic comparative advantage; and as managers of social conflict. Hence, the paradox exists that a free market needs strong and effective government – a paradox which scholars are only able to resolve by constructing a theory of state involvement which, in the words of the Cambridge economists Ha-Joo Chang and Robert Rowthorn, 'takes full account of uncertainty and innovation, institutions and political economy' (Chang and Rowthorn, 1995, p. 46).

To date, the need for a reconstituted role of governments in the age of alliance capitalism has only been fully acknowledged – and put into practice – by some East Asian governments (Wade, 1995). The competing or adversarial relationships between governments and private enterprise, which was (and is) a feature of hierarchical capitalism, remains strongly embedded in Western – especially US – cultures. But, the phenomenon of the globalizing economy, the growing recognition that a nation's com-petitiveness rests as much on its ability to supply the location-bound assets necessary to attract or retain firm-specific mobile assets, as those assets themselves; and the acceptance that, *de facto*, governments *do* compete with each other for these latter assets, are combining to foster a 'sink or swim together' philosophy among all except the most extreme free-market administrations.

Of the three paradoxes so far identified, that of the 'less' or 'more' of governments may be the most difficult to resolve. This is not only be-cause of entrenched ideologies and institutional rigidities, but also because the costs and benefits of non-market intervention are extremely difficult to measure. So, if and when markets do fail, it cannot necessarily be presumed that government intervention will improve the situation, as the costs of such intervention may be greater than the benefits. Such evidence as we have, for example Bradford (1994) and Wade (1995), suggests that the interaction between national government fiat and mar-kets in countries such as Korea, Taiwan and Malaysia has led to a virtuous circle of growth and efficiency, while that in many parts of Latin America, at least until recently, has led to a vicious circle of low economic growth and social unrest.

Although there has been some research done on the kinds of government action which are most likely to improve economic performance,[14] for the most part our knowledge is woefully inadequate. Once again, however, there are some hints from the responses of MNEs to market failure and to the demands of globalization. In particular, there are major changes now taking place in the organizational structure of firms. Pyramids of hierarchies are being increasingly flattened as more heterarchical (and horizontal) relationships are being forged between decision-takers and line managers. Nowhere is this being more clearly demonstrated than in the Swedish/Swiss MNE Asea Brown Boveri (ABB).[15] In this changed organizational scenario, the job of top management is less to control and take decisions, and more to orchestrate strategic vision and set performance standards, to nurture organizational values and to encourage down-the-line entrepreneurship. The 'yin' of a centralized corporate strategy and the setting of targets is being accompanied by the 'yang' of decentralized responsibility for achieving these goals, that is, subsidiarity in action.

Are there not lessons to be learnt by governments in this respect? At the same time, globalization is leading to a re-layering of some of the traditional tasks of national governments to subnational (that is, regional or district authorities); while others, for example, the harmonization of trade, FDI and competition policies, and a variety of technical and environmental standards are increasingly becoming the responsibility of regional or supranational regimes. One wonders, indeed, whether in the course of the next decade or more we shall see, as Charles Handy (1994) has put it, (and I quote his words) 'the disappearing middle of national administrations'.

THE HUMAN CONSEQUENCES OF GLOBALIZATION: THE PARADOX OF BENEFITS AND DISBENEFITS

Perhaps the most perceived, and currently the most hotly debated effects of globalization – or more accurately the economic forces associated with it – are those on the everyday lives of people the world over. While the 'yin' of closer economic interdependence and the liberalization of markets is undisputedly raising average living standards, offering new job opportunities, popularizing new technologies and skills, widening consumer choice, and in a whole variety of ways improving the lifestyles of large numbers of people; the 'yang', or downside, of globalization is no less dramatically portrayed in terms of disturbingly high levels of unemployment – particularly among the younger unskilled workers; a personal sense of insecurity and foreboding associated with rapid technological change; the division of societies into new islands of conflicting economic interests; the breakdown of traditional social conventions; the resurgence of ethnic conflicts; and, not least, the easier cross-border movement of tangible or intangible *disbenefits*, for example organized crime, drug trafficking, international terrorism and unacceptable patterns of behaviour.

It is downsides such as these which Klaus Schwab and Claude Smadja (1996) – two of the most prominent advocates of global trade and integration – had in mind when, at last year's Davos Forum, they referred to a 'mounting backlash against globalization', and a rising gap between those able to ride the wave of globalization because they are knowledge and communications-oriented, and those left behind. Jeremy Rifkin, in a fascinating monograph entitled *The End of Work* (Rifkin, 1995) has gone even further. He believes that the effects of the current generation of technological advances on the world's labour force may prove to be the Achilles heel of globalization.[16] Other commentators have gone further by asserting that, unless the less-desirable consequences of globalization are tackled and, at least, partially resolved, the utopian vision – and I paraphrase Aldous Huxley's words – of a 'brave new economic world' could quickly be turned into a cauldron of social unrest, political upheaval, cultural fragmentation and ideological conflict between nations, or even civilizations.[17]

Whether you are an optimist or pessimist on these matters, such a stark paradox, I believe, was much less in evidence at the turn of the last century. True, at that time there was much structural change, brought about, *inter alia*, by the advent of electricity, the telephone, the internal combustion engine and the introduction of the Fordist system of production. But, by and large, the pace and direction of economic growth in both the older and newer capitalist economies of the time was, in general, able to cope with the less-welcome consequences of the new technologies; the jobs created were generally more congenial than those which they replaced; while, for the most part, improvements in education and vocational training were able to keep pace with the needs of the marketplace. Moreover, most of the required social adjustments were contained within domestic economies; and it was not until after the First World War that FDI became a significant allocator of cross-border economic activity and, hence, jobs between countries.

At that time, too, there were far fewer non-economic claims on the resources of countries than there are today. Most social welfare programmes were in their infancy, and little attention was paid to environmental issues. In the main, the second industrial revolution of the late nineteenth century was accomplished with considerably more observable benefits and fewer observable costs than those resulting either from the emergence of the factory system of a century earlier, or (so it would appear) its successor a century later. Even the hierarchical system of managerial capitalism, although it had some adverse consequences on the entrepreneurship and fortunes of small family-owned enterprises, generally offered the ordinary worker more benefits and opportunities than it took away from him!

Again, the situation is totally different in the emerging global neighbourhood of the 1990s. This is apparent both at the level of the individual firm and that of the nation state. Almost daily, it seems, one reads about huge restructuring and relocation programmes of corporations, which frequently have traumatic effects on people's lives and livelihoods not just in one country, but in several. Often the slogan 'one man's job is another man's dole' is all too true. Often, too, the gains – as well as the costs – of McWorld are exploited by ethnic or religious fundamentalists to advance the course of Jihad.[18] In the short run (and in practice this can be quite long!) there are both losers and winners in the globalization process; and the very pace of economic change often requires major adjustments even in the lives of the winners. Over the last two decades, I would suggest, the international restructuring of economic activity has involved more people-adjustment, both within and between countries, than at any other time since the late eighteenth century.

At the level of the nation state, globalization is requiring one of basic tenets of comparative advantage – viz. the cross-border immobility of resources – to be questioned. Not only are many firm-specific assets mobile across national boundaries, but the demands being made by the owners of these assets on those which are spatially more sticky is changing. Thus, for example, in their choice of investment locations, both between and within countries, MNEs are being increasingly influenced by the presence of subnational agglomerative economies, and by the quality of human and physical infrastructure.[19] As it is, the latter type of assets and quality is strongly influenced by government policies. If these policies are perceived to be inappropriate, or less congenial in their effects than those offered by other governments, then those assets which have the opportunity to do so will move elsewhere.[20] In such an event, globalization may result in more – or more abrasive – economic disbenefits than benefits – certainly to the countries and to the immobile assets losing the economic activity. Equally, because of differences in age, structures, social policies and the competence of national administrations, the ability of countries to respond to the 'yang' of globalization will vary considerably.

How can one hope to reconcile the conflicting consequences of globalization – which, in the economic arena at least, are time-related and are mainly distributional? I believe the first essential thing is to recognize that, barring natural or man-made catastrophes or a major reconfiguration of social values, the globalization of economic activity is largely irreversible. This is because it is the result of technological advances which, themselves, cannot easily be reversed. However, the pace and form of globalization can be affected as can the recognition and response of governments to some of its more daunting challenges. And, it is the extent to which countries can successfully devise new ways to minimize these costs by effective 'voice' rather than 'exit' strategies which will determine the net benefits they derive from globalization. In the last few years, among the advanced nations, Japan and the US have done rather better than most European countries; and, in the developing world, China and Malaysia rather better than Brazil and India, in their structural adjustment programmes.

Since many of the less-welcome effects accompanying the advent of the global village are non-economic, it might be thought that the actions of MNEs can be of only limited relevance to governments. This would be incorrect, and for two reasons. The first is that the more socially-aware MNEs are demonstrating that there need be no real conflict between their economic aspirations and their social responsibilities. Nowhere is this more clearly seen than in the area of environmental standards. Far from being the main exporters of pollution – as was once thought – MNEs are among the trail-blazers of environmentally-friendly, yet competitive enhancing, innovations; and often set, rather than follow, the dictates of governments. Similarly, in their redeployment, retraining and pension schemes, the more progressive global companies, and those more responsive to the needs of their workforces, offer a microcosm of the type of policies which governments would do well to study. Secondly, because they span the globe, many MNEs provide a salutary reminder to national administrations that 'best-practice' techniques – particularly in minimizing the social hardships of structural change – are not always 'home-grown'; and there is much to learn from other cultures and institutional regimes.

I accept, of course, that by themselves corporations cannot – and indeed should not – be expected to resolve the challenges of globalization; although initiatives such as the Business Leaders Forum, set up by His Royal Highness the Prince of Wales in 1989 to consider the corporate response to the social, cultural and spiritual dimensions of globalization, are to be warmly commended. But the potential for dialogue and collaboration between the main instruments of globalization, and the stakeholders affected by it, remains largely untapped. In this connection I particularly welcome the recently published report by the Commission on Global Governance entitled *Our Global Neighbourhood* (1995). The Commission – the brain-child of ex-German Chancellor Willy Brandt – was set up in 1992 under the joint chairmanship of the (then) Prime Minister of Sweden, Ingvar Carlsson, and Shridath Ramphal, the ex-Secretary General of the Commonwealth; and comprised 28 very distinguished statesmen, businessmen, bankers and Presidents of international agencies throughout the world. In its 'call to action', the report makes many astute recommendations on matters ranging from global security, to managing economic interdependence and fostering a global civic ethic. It also urges the United Nations to convene a World Conference on Global Governance in 1998, to which (it suggests) should be invited not only the political leaders of the world, but those of 'the wider human constituency' who are 'infused with a sense of caring for others and a sense of responsibility to the global neighbourhood' (Commission on Global Governance, 1995). Such a gathering of men and women of goodwill would, indeed, be an expression of the 'yin' of international cooperation, which, I would argue, is needed to counterbalance the 'yang' of international competition.

CONCLUSIONS

To conclude: as we approach the twenty-first century, we do so with a mixture of optimism and pessimism, and of hope and trepidation. The future seems both more complex and more daunting than that faced by our forefathers a century ago. This, I have suggested, is for four reasons. The first is the increasing dichotomy between the territorial space open to individuals and corporations, and under the jurisdiction of governments. This is leading to a number of paradoxes and dilemmas – particularly as far as the intercountry distribution of the gains and losses of globalization are concerned. The second is the erosion of the boundaries of the leading institutions for organizing economic activities – and particularly those of firms, markets and governments. *Inter alia*, this is resulting in a more intricate and pluralistic network of interinstitutional arrangements, and to a new complementarity between the 'yin' or competition and the 'yang' of cooperation.

Third, improvements in standards of living – especially among wealthier nations – are increasingly taking the form of quality-of-life enhancing goods and services (for example, computer software, telecommunications, education, health care, environmental protection and the absence of crime, terrorism, and so on), the supply of which governments, by their actions or non-actions, strongly influence. The consequences of globalization are being increasingly evaluated by their effects on the availability, character and distribution of these 'public' products. Insofar as communication advances and the cross-border integration of economic activity are being accompanied by a renewal of national or subnational (for example, tribal) specific cultures and values, this is creating a range of interrelational tensions and dilemmas quite different in scale and effect from those arising from the second industrial revolution.

Fourth, while twentieth century hierarchical capitalism has generally been accompanied by an expansion in the economic role of national governments, twenty-first century alliance capitalism and the renaissance of the market economy seem likely to not only demand changes in the nature of that role, and an upgrading in the capabilities of public sector decision-takers; but to increase and deepen that of the tasks of both subnational and supranational authorities.

In seeking to reconcile the paradoxes of globalization, I have further suggested that the ways in which the more successful MNEs have adapted their organizational and economic strategies to the changes demanded of them by recent economic events bear close scrutiny by public authorities as they seek to reconfigure their own actions, particularly in respect of labour market flexibility. I have also suggested that, up to now, most of the attentions of scholars – and indeed of most governments – has been focused on the gains of globalization, and that in the future, at least as much attention needs to be paid to its downsides – both actual and perceived.

At the same time, it is important that governments do not attribute to globalization all the woes in the world – most of which I believe would have been a lot worse had the introduction of market-friendly economic policies not been implemented. Moreover, the cross-border activities of firms – noticeably via FDI and strategic alliances – may themselves assist national governments not only to upgrade the competitiveness of their own firms and indigenous resources, but to do so in ways which promote their longer-term economic and social goals. Of course, the strategies of MNEs, like those of governments, may be protective and result in a vicious circle of market–state interface, and the discouragement of these is as important as any competitive enhancing actions which both firms and governments might implement.

Looking further ahead into the twenty-first century, as the Yale historian Paul Kennedy did in a BBC television broadcast in 1996, one cannot but be sobered by one final paradox which, in many ways, overarches everything I have written up to now. That is, currently the wealthiest 12 per cent of the world's population owns or controls 85 per cent of the world's stock of created assets; while the rest, that is 88 per cent of the population, owns or controls only 15 per cent of these assets. Moreover, virtually all of the 50 per cent increase in the world's population over the next 30 to 35 years is likely to occur in the less wealthy parts of the world. Clearly, the geographical imbalance between the current technology revolution and the population revolution (to use Kennedy's terminology) is a potential social time-bomb. Whether or not the bomb is defused will, I suggest, largely rest on two factors. The first is the nature and pace of Indian and Chinese economic development, as, between them, these two super-giants are expected to account for between 25 per cent and 30 per cent of the world's population by 2025. The second is whether the peoples of the world – and their leaders – can summon up enough determination and emotional intelligence to reconcile the growing threat of ideological and class warfare which is epitomized by the Jihad vs McWorld syndrome. For I fear that unless this is done our global dream could so easily turn into a global nightmare!

As a University educator and researcher, I should like to make one final comment. The future shape of our planet is now being fashioned by the decisions being taken in the boardrooms of larger corporations, in the corridors and chambers of government departments, and around the conference tables of international agencies. Anything we, in the University community, can do to provide the decision-makers with information and objective analyses about the costs and benefits of globalization, and what is required to be done at various institutional and decision-taking levels, is surely to be applauded. Indeed, I believe it is our duty so to participate, and to influence those who guide our destinies and those of our children.

Notes

1. This is a revised and extended version of a chapter previously published in John H. Dunning, *Alliance Capitalism and Global Business* (London and New York: Routledge, 1996). Published with permission of Routledge.
2. Some economists, for example Carlota Perez (1983), would go as far as to argue that both the 1880s and the 1980s heralded in a new Kondratiev cycle of techno-economic and socio-institutional change.
3. Although, when combined with those of the first two decades of the 20th century, they did bring quite climaterical changes to some societies, such as Russia.
4. Eric Hobsbawm is a distinguished historian who has authored several books with titles depicting (what, to him, is) the key characteristic of the period he is writing about. Among these are *The Age of Revolution, 1789–1848; The Age of Capital, 1848–1875; The Age of Empire, 1875–1914* and *The Age of Extremes, 1914–1991* (1995).
5. Viz. *Jihad vs. McWorld* (Barber, 1995). Jihad refers to an ideology of parochial ethnicity, which is often portrayed as extreme ethnic or religious fundamentalism. McWorld is the ideology of the global corporation, which is primarily interested in economic gain and would like to ignore all national or political boundaries.
6. Put more accurately, 'perceived paradoxes', as we believe the paradoxes described are more 'imaginary' than they are 'real'.
7. And more than is commonly realized. For a contemporary account of the interventionist – albeit catalytic – role of the US government in the development of US industry and agriculture in the nineteenth century, see Kozul-Wright (1995).
8. See World Bank (1997).
9. The concept of core and complementary assets has been explored by several business scholars, but particularly by David Teece (1987).
10. These are our own estimates derived from data contained in the annual *World Investment Report* published by the United Nations Conference on Trade and Development (UNCTAD).
11. See also a perceptive article on a related theme by Richard Florida (1995).

12. The same might well be true of most Eastern economies, but here the func-
    tions of government were viewed in a very different light to those in the
    West.

13. An expression first coined at the time of the American Revolution to re-
    flect the extent to which firms and/or individuals could escape (through
    emigration) unacceptable taxes and other fiscal duties imposed by national
    governments.

14. As is reviewed, for example, in Dunning (1994) and Panic (1995).

15. As documented, for example, by Bartlett and Ghoshal (1993).

16. He points to similar, but less-dramatic, consequences (as they tended to be
    confined within national borders) of the technological advances, coupled
    with the mass advertising of the 1920s and 1930s, and migration of un-
    skilled jobs from the Northern to the Southern US in the 1950s.

17. See Barber *op. cit.* and Huntington (1993).

18. Barber (1995) gives some fascinating examples of how practical application
    of the two starkly opposing ideologies often aid and abet each other; and
    that neither is complete without the other. For example, he points out that
    modern transportation and communication technologies, and the export to
    Jihad ideologies and practices often lead to non-Jihad nations or regimes
    becoming more dependent on Jihad nations or regions for their economic
    well-being.

19. For a review of the literature, see Dunning (1993a), Braunerhjelm and
    Svensson (1995) and Mariotti and Piscitello (1995).

20. For an excellent review of the role of investment incentives offered by govern-
    ments on the location of mobile investment, see UNCTAD (1996).

Part One

Subsidiaries and their Strategies

Introduction

Fred Burton

The traditional academic approach to the multinational corporation (MNC), partly in reflection of the North American ethnocentricity of the principal researchers in the field, tended to regard its structure as being determined purely by the parent company, with power and strategic decision-making being completely centralized. Accordingly, during the 1960s and 1970s, most company-level research concentrated on the broad thrust of internationalization processes and associated corporate strategies and, less frequently, on issues involving the control and management of overseas subsidiaries by headquarters (for example, Alsegg, 1971). Any autonomy which a subsidiary had was viewed as having been granted by headquarters: a subsidiary, for example, was *permitted* independence in developing products (for example, White and Poynter, 1984). In this conception, a multinational firm was a clearly defined unit, with subsidiaries acting as the limbs merely obeying the head(quarters). There were, of course, exceptions. Aylmer (1970) had detected a tendency for MNCs to allow increasing market scope to their affiliates, and studies by Brandt and Hulbert (1976, 1977) examined aspects of communication and strategy-making between headquarters and subsidiaries.

MNCs have gradually consolidated their extended global networks and established affiliates have become more entrenched. As a subsidiary ages, local management's knowledge of the specific markets in which it operates is highly likely to surpass that of the parent company, causing an evolutionary process in which the subsidiary will gradually acquire increasing degrees of autonomy. Accordingly, it has become necessary for theories to develop to deal with this and to question former assumptions.

Some would argue that the real impetus to the study of subsidiaries came from a volume of papers edited by Otterbeck (1981). Two of these are of particular interest here. In an extensive study of 24 subsidiaries of six large Swedish MNCs, Hedlund (1981) suggested that the headquarters–subsidiary relationship was likely to be characterized by informal management processes dependent on the degree of autonomy at affiliate level. This early identification of autonomy as a key determinant of subsidiary strategy was supported by later studies of US MNCs by Garnier (1982) and Gates and Egelhoff (1986). The second consequential paper from the Otterbeck volume was a more conceptual piece by Bartlett (1981) based on a study of five American healthcare companies.

25

Bartlett emphasized the need for large international firms to develop management capabilities at both global and local levels. This was a forerunner to the rich seam of research into subsidiaries he and Ghoshal have conducted and the related work of Prahalad and Doz (1987).

White and Poynter (1984) produced a typology of subsidiary strategy, which injected two concepts to research in this field. First was the notion that neither strategy nor autonomy were necessarily under head-quarters' control, but rather could become affiliate-oriented through the bargaining responses of subsidiaries. Second was the notion that the behavioural characteristics of the subsidiary's management team may be the determinant of overall strategy involvement.

White and Poynter's work can be linked with two lines of subsidiary research that have recently emerged. Birkinshaw and Morrison (1995) have used a reduced form of the White and Poynter typology to adduce linkages between subsidiary type and performance. More recently, Birkinshaw (1996) has returned to these notions of subsidiary capability to explore how subsidiary mandates are gained and developed or some-times lost. Empirical scepticism by Taggart (1996) about such operational and structural approaches has led a return to the early work of Hedlund (1981) to produce a behavioural model of affiliate strategy based on autonomy and procedural justice as perceived at the subsidiary level (Taggart, 1997).

A review of these and other influential studies identify the MNC as a decentralized company of diversified, geographically scattered units working towards divergent and mutual goals in varied economic, social and cultural environments (Hedlund, 1986; Doz, 1986; Bartlett and Ghoshal, 1989; Forsgren, 1990; White and Poynter, 1990). The external networks in which the subsidiaries are embedded are often highly consequential for their evolution, prompting innovations which enable them to play a strategic role in the corporation as a whole (Ghoshal and Nohria, 1989; Bartlett and Ghoshal, 1990; Andersson and Pahlberg, 1997). The literature has emphasized the semi-autonomous state which subsidiaries can attain, but also increasing interdependencies: networks of capital, commodities and knowledge transactions across organizational borders, and such transfers are regarded as significant for competitive advantage (Herbert, 1984; Prahalad and Doz, 1987; Bartlett and Ghoshal, 1993; Papanastassiou and Pearce, 1996a).

The authors in Part One tackle various aspects of the autonomy of subsidiaries and the impact of their local experience and knowledge on the strategies of the MNC. In Chapter 3, James Taggart, a leading researcher in the field, compares the strategy of US manufacturing subsidiaries in the UK with European-owned counterparts. He employs a truncated White and Poynter model, supported by case studies, to test for the degree of autonomy subsidiaries have to pursue market scope and value-added scope. Taggart concludes that American subsidiaries have both higher market scope and higher value-added scope than their European counterparts, giving them a competitive edge in existing activities and in developing new products and markets.

In Chapter 4, Marina Papanastassiou and Robert Pearce discuss ways in which the operations of subsidiaries are technologically interdependent with elements of the host-country economy as well as with the rest of the group to which they belong. One facet of these operations involves transfers of knowledge (products, processes and techniques) to host-country suppliers. This can occur when subsidiaries are mandated to develop new goods, but especially when the subsidiary is pursuing high levels of efficiency in supplying established products. They discern that technological collaborations with host-country scientific institutions may be becoming more prominent, helping to regenerate the core technology of the MNC group.

Not only does the MNC contain a variety of perspectives within it, but the level of autonomy which subsidiaries can possess might allow them significant influence over the development of the group as a whole, whose evolution may reflect the interests of influential subsidiaries (Andersson and Pahlberg, 1997). Power and control are therefore no longer assumed to be solely linked to authority conferred by ownership (for example, Forsgren, 1990; Ghoshal and Bartlett, 1990). Rather, central management has been viewed as determining the MNC's development within the frame of its key subsidiaries' innovative achievements (Andersson and Forsgren, 1996; Birkinshaw, 1996; Taggart, 1997). In Chapter 5, Mo Yamin investigates one aspect of this concept of embeddedness, namely autonomous innovative activity by subsidiaries and the implications of such activity for the group as a whole, particularly the 'reverse' transfer of technology from subsidiary to parent.

In Chapter 6, Ram Mudambi discusses a novel aspect of the factors governing the choice of location for overseas subsidiaries. While it has been suggested that experience of a particular location in the form of duration of operations may be a motivating factor, the question of resolving such considerations with opposing portfolio risk considerations has not been addressed. The question is posed whether the longer the duration of operations in a particular location the more likely is the MNC to make further investment there after allowing for portfolio risk considerations. Location decisions in Mudambi's sample were found to be significantly duration-dependent.

Much of the international human resource management (HRM) literature has concerned itself with the expatriation and repatriation of international managers, their adjustment to foreign cultures and factors affecting their performance (Kamoche, 1997). In Chapter 7, Monir Tayeb, escapes from these confines to discuss overall HRM strategies, using case-study evidence to identify factors that have contributed to the successful implementation of HRM policies in a Scottish subsidiary of an American MNC. The research shows that even policies with a proven track record elsewhere need to be implemented with a sensitivity to local workforce traditions.

3 US MNC Subsidiaries in the UK: Characteristics and Strategic Role

James H. Taggart

INTRODUCTION

After the minor unpleasantries in the last part of the eighteenth century, the diplomatic and political relationship between the United States
and the United Kingdom has improved quite dramatically, more slowly
in the nineteenth century while the UK was still a great power, more
rapidly in the twentieth as the US has gradually emerged as the world's
only superpower. In the last 80 years they have been firm allies in two
world wars, they have a long record of mutual support in the United
Nations, they are key founder members and critical operational entities
within NATO, and – particularly since 1979 – the UK government has
willingly adopted the role as America's staunchest ally in world affairs.
Much of this may be explained by enlightened self-interest on both sides,
but common language, cultural heritage and values have also played a
part. Inevitably, a powerful commercial relationship has resulted between
the US and the UK. America has long been the British businessman's
prime target for exports, whilst the US has always been a principal source
target of foreign direct investment (FDI) in the UK economy. Thus, the
'special relationship' between the two states seems well-established in
many spheres of activity, and the purpose of this chapter is to evaluate
the last-mentioned aspect, the strategic role and characteristics of manufacturing subsidiaries of US-owned multinational corporations (MNCs)
located in the UK.

AMERICAN MNCs IN THE UK

During the early part of the nineteenth century, US firms were involved
in many foreign direct investments in Canada and South America, but
the MNC as we know it today had its origins in the manufacturing subsidiaries established by US companies in Europe from about 1850
onwards. Appropriately, the first such investment in Europe was Samuel

Colt's London factory, established in 1852 to manufacture the eponymous revolvers. In 1856, J. Ford and Company of New Jersey established a rubber production plant in Edinburgh, which subsequently metamorphosed into North British Rubber, then Uniroyal, and finally Englebert. Neither of these early investments remained long in American ownership, and the first long-term US manufacturing affiliate was probably the Singer factory that started production of sewing machines in Clydebank in 1867; it was a mainstay of the local economy until it closed in 1980, with a total employment loss of some 8000. Until 1945, the build-up of US investment in the UK was slow and steady, and included such firms as Heinz, the Ford Motor Company, General Motors (through the acquisition of Vauxhall), Goodyear, Firestone, Remington Rand, Hoover, Procter & Gamble, and Champion Spark Plugs (Hood and Young, 1982, pp. 4, 42).

Subsequently, the rate of American foreign direct investment increased substantially, initially in the South of England but spreading throughout mainland Britain, with a peak in Scotland between 1965 and 1975. By the mid-1980s, there were over 1400 US-owned manufacturing establishments in the UK employing nearly three-quarters of a million personnel. On both counts this comprised over 60 per cent of foreign production activity in Britain; indeed, in terms of net output the proportion was over two-thirds. However, following the UK's accession to the European Economic Community (EEC) in 1973, the rate of inward investment from this source increased rapidly, while new American investment slowed somewhat. Nevertheless, the US is still the largest foreign direct investor in the UK, a position that is likely to remain unchallenged for many years to come. The US roll-call in the UK now includes DEC, Hewlett Packard, Honeywell, IBM, Compaq, Gates, NCR, ITT, Motorola, Terex, Merck, Esso, Kodak and Texaco (Stopford and Turner, 1985, pp. 14–15).

Such inward investments have a negative side. There may be an adverse impact on the current account balance of payments due to payment of dividends, royalties, loan interest and management charges to the parent company. Transfer pricing policies also caused some problems here, particularly in the petroleum industry in the 1960s and 1970s, though much of the agitation seemed to emanate from trades unions pressing for profit-related pay increases for members. As regulation has tightened, and as UK corporate tax rates have come more into line with those of America, this problem has developed a much lower profile. MNCs may also be criticized in that they somewhat distort competition within a particular foreign market due to the greater economic power their subsidiaries may bring to bear as parts of very large enterprises. Many foreign affiliates, for example, will have access to headquarter skills and resources, where such knowledge and expertise is much more difficult to obtain for the indigenous company.

Finally, there has been comment, much of it politically biased and somewhat uninformed, about the negative impact of MNC affiliates on long-term levels of national sovereignty. Granted, there may be some effect brought about by variable levels of local autonomy granted to affiliate management teams, and there may also be some reasonable concerns about the cultural effects of corporate value systems imported from other cultures; however, in the case of the UK, the overall effect of these sovereignty issues palls into insignificance when compared to the degree of sovereignty willingly given up by the UK government to the EC as it moves towards economic and political union (Hood and Young, 1979, pp. 179–80).

Large-scale inward investment also has many positive features. For a new investment – acquisition or greenfield – there is an immediate boost to the UK capital account of the balance of payments, and the current account often benefits very substantially indeed through the long-term build-up of exports from MNC subsidiaries. Inwards-FDI benefits the national competitive situation by reducing concentration, diluting oligopolies, increasing product differentiation, introducing new technologies and skills, and widening the existing range of competitive methods. Overall, the judgement must be that foreign affiliates are a net benefit to the UK, and this is particularly so for the presence of US affiliates who bring with them so many of the positive attractions noted above. This would certainly seem to be the view of policy-makers, as the early successes in attracting inward investment to Scotland by the Scottish Development Agency has been followed up by the establishment of similar official bodies covering Wales, Northern Ireland and many of the regions of England.

SUBSIDIARY STRATEGY

Early attempts at evaluating the roles and strategies of MNC subsidiaries tended to be exploratory and conceptual (see for example, Perlmutter, 1969; Brandt and Hulbert, 1977). These were helpful in assessing some of the broad dimensions involved, and Perlmutter's ethnocentric-polycentric-regiocentric-geocentric (EPRG) profile has been particularly useful in linking corporate and subsidiary value systems to strategy orientation. He suggested that the ethnocentric type requires acceptance of home-country values and standards throughout the international network (implying centralized control); while in the polycentric firm, corporate headquarters accepts that local managers know what is best for each country/subsidiary. The regiocentric and geocentric types involve collaboration between affiliate and headquarters to establish broad, universal standards with an acceptable degree of local variation on the basis of which decisions may be taken.

Hedlund's (1981) empirical evaluation of MNC subsidiaries in Sweden established the central role of the degree of autonomy possessed by a subsidiary in determining its overall role or strategy; indirectly, this work also indicated the importance of linkages between (or integration of) subsidiaries within an international network. In discussing the importance of subsidiary autonomy, Hedlund was careful to indicate that intangible factors like management style and management discretion have an important role to play in the use to which subsidiary autonomy is put, especially where this impinges on the overall HQ/subsidiary relationship.

This, perhaps, is the linking concept with his later notion of the heterarchical MNC (Hedlund, 1986), which he sees as a very particular form of geocentricity. The heterarchy looks to its own global spread to develop competitive advantage, rather than depending on home-country attributes. It does not depend solely on headquarters, but has many centres of strategic advantage; these centres are of different kinds, including functionally-based centres. In many cases, subsidiary managers of such centres have a strategy role that encompasses not only their own affiliate, but the network as an entity. Normative control procedures are used, highlighting the importance of corporate culture, management ethos, management style and management values. This concept has had some empirical support (Hedlund and Rolander, 1990; Forsgren, Holm and Johanson, 1992), and a substantial literature is developing around the idea of such centres of excellence.

As noted above, Hedlund (1981) also emphasized the role of integration, related particularly to material flows to and from sister subsidiaries, and detected evidence of a trade-off with the affiliate's degree of autonomy. Prahalad and Doz (1987), among others, identified a further trade-off between integration and the degree of local responsiveness and developed a spectrum of strategies (locally responsive to global integration) that has strong conceptual linkages to a typology proposed by Bartlett and Ghoshal (1989).

Jarillo and Martinez (1990) proposed a model of subsidiary strategy using integration and localization (local responsiveness) as dimensions; their three-way taxonomy identified three strategy types – receptive, autonomous and active strategies. The first corresponds to a combination of high integration (I) and low responsiveness (R), a strategy likely to be used by subsidiaries of global firms operating within global industries. At the opposite end of this spectrum (low I–high R) we find the autonomous subsidiary, commonly found competing in multi-domestic industries. Finally, the active subsidiary (high I–high R) is characterized by many value-chain activities being carried out by the subsidiary; these activities are highly coordinated with parallel activities in sister subsidiaries, and the active strategy would be comfortably operated within Porter's

(1986) low configuration–high coordination corporate strategy. Recently, Taggart (1997) has identified a fourth classification in the low *I*–low *R* quadrant (quiescent subsidiary), which tends to be both younger and smaller than other types.

These two streams of research emanating from Hedlund's study are linked by the argument of Prahalad and Doz (1987) that local responsiveness requires subsidiary autonomy in terms of resource-based decisions. In many ways, the work of White and Poynter (1984) previewed this linkage. They defined three crucial strategic dimensions:

- *Product Scope*: the degree of freedom the subsidiary may exercise in product-line extensions and new product areas; affiliates with high product scope may have a product line virtually as wide as the parent's activity in the same industry.
- *Market Scope*: this refers to the geographical spread of markets served by the subsidiary; in some cases, an affiliate may be serving its own and the corporate parent's customers worldwide.
- *Value-added Scope*: the range of ways in which a subsidiary can add value to its output and/or final products through marketing, development and manufacturing activities; in some cases, the subsidiary's value-added scope may be almost as extensive as the parent company's, but is likely to be more limited in the general case.

The combination of these different dimensions led White and Poynter (1984) to identify four discrete subsidiary strategies for manufacturing firms, though a subsidiary with more than one major line of business may employ more than one of these (see Figure 3.1). In the miniature replica strategy, some of the parent company's lines or related products are manufactured for the local market by the affiliate, and the business operates as a small-scale replica of the parent. There may be an R&D unit, and its complexity will determine which of the three sub-types of miniature replica apply – adopter (no R&D), innovator (significant product-related R&D), and adapter (intermediate). The rationalized manufacturer type produces a set of components for a multi-country or global market because it can deliver, for example, lower labour costs or economies of scale. Since product scope and value-added scope are limited, the rationalized manufacturer's output may be further processed at other nodes of the international network. Marketing, R&D and new product decisions are usually made centrally by the parent.

The product specialist affiliate develops, manufactures and markets a limited product line, selling to multi-country or global markets. Included here are subsidiaries with a world or a regional product mandate (Rugman and Bennett, 1982; Birkinshaw and Morrison, 1995). The strategic independent subsidiary is autonomous in R&D, production and marketing;

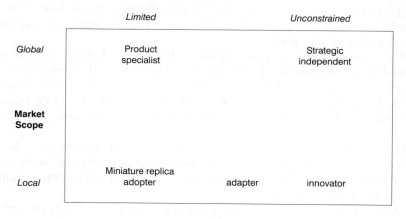

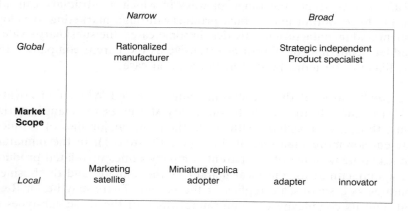

Figure 3.1 Types of subsidiary strategy

it is allowed virtually complete freedom in strategy-making, with the parent being close to a passive investor. In most cases, headquarters has only administrative and financial links to the true strategic independent. White and Poynter's research was carried out on MNC subsidiaries in Canada; further empirical support has come from a study of foreign manufacturing affiliates in Scotland (Young *et al.*, 1988).

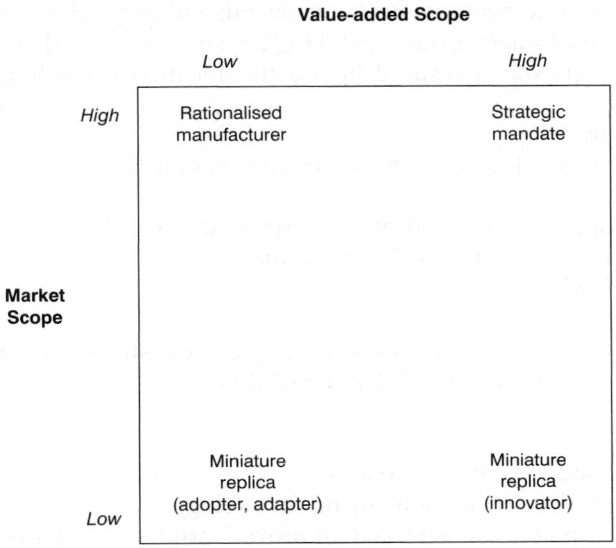

Value-added Scope

	Low	High
High	Rationalised manufacturer	Strategic mandate
Market Scope		
Low	Miniature replica (adopter, adapter)	Miniature replica (innovator)

Figure 3.2 Types of subsidiary strategy: reduced model

RESEARCH SURVEY

The strategy and characteristics of US-owned manufacturing subsidiaries located in the UK is identified by using their European-owned counterparts as a basis for comparison. A simplified version of White and Poynter's (1984) model of subsidiary strategy will be used for this purpose, as it has many links with other models described above. All of White and Poynter's subsidiary types are shown in the lower part of Figure 3.1, and a reduced version of this is shown in Figure 3.2. For ease of identification, the strategic independent and product specialist types shown in the high value-added scope – high market scope quadrant are referred to below as 'strategic mandate'.

A pre-tested research instrument was mailed to the Chief Executive Officer (CEO) of each of 400 subsidiaries drawn randomly from Jordan's listing of US and European-owned firms manufacturing in the UK. A total of 150 (37.5 per cent) complete replies were received, comprising 75 US subsidiaries and 75 that were European-owned. As the evolution of strategy over time was a particular focus of interest here, subsidiaries established less than five years were not used, leaving a total of 131 – 68 US subsidiaries and 63 European-owned. Chief executives were responsible for 71 (55 per cent) of the replies, other directors for 31 (24 per cent), and other executives for 29 (21 per cent). Twenty-seven (20.6

per cent) respondents were in the chemicals industry, 61 (46.6 per cent) in some form of engineering, and 43 (32.8 per cent) in other industries.

Market scope was measured by a 6-classification variable as follows:

1 = mainly UK
2 = UK plus selected countries in continental Europe
3 = Europe
4 = Europe plus selected other parts of the world
5 = worldwide with specific exclusions
6 = worldwide

Value-added scope was also measured by a 6-classification variable that focused on the subsidiary's R&D capability:

1 = no R&D
2 = customer technical services
3 = adaptation of manufacturing technology
4 = development of new and improved products and processes for UK/European markets
5 = development of new and improved products and processes for world markets
6 = generation of new technology for corporate parent

For the purposes of grouping the respondents, low market scope was taken as 1–3 on the preceding classification and high market scope as 4–6; low value-added scope was taken as 1–3 and high as 4–6. This gave four groups of subsidiaries, corresponding to the typology of Figure 3.2. A cluster analysis, using market and value-added scope as the input dimensions, gave a similar 4-cluster solution.

In order to evaluate the strategic characteristics of the four types of firm, a number of other structural and operating variables were also measured, and details of these are given in Table 3.1.

Finally, to allow an evaluation of strategy evolution, respondents were asked to indicate the position for 'five years ago', as well as the current situation for each variable on the research instrument. Respondents were requested to use their knowledge of corporate and subsidiary strategic plans as a basis for answering these questions. This is a technique used by Prahalad and Doz (1987) and Jarillo and Martinez (1990) which has given acceptable results, though the dangers of response error must be borne in mind when evaluating results.

Table 3.1 Variables used to differentiate subsidiary strategy

Variable		Measure
Structural		
AGE	Number of years since establishment in UK	Years
EMPL	Level of employment	Number of personnel
SALES	Gross sales revenues	$
XPORT	Exports as proportion of gross sales	Percentage
Coordination		
CTECH	Process technology transferred between subsidiaries	5-point Likert scale
CPROD	Linked product requirements between subsidiaries	5-point Likert scale
Integration		
IMANUF	Capacity decisions designed to provide multi-plant linkages	5-point Likert scale
IPROD	Product and quality specifications developed by HQ or subsidiary	5-point Likert scale
INPUT	Percentage of material inputs coming from other group plants	6 classifications
OUTPUT	Percentage of outputs going to other group plants for further processing	6 classifications

SURVEY RESULTS

US affiliates are very similar to European firms in age and employment levels; at $450 million they have, on average, much higher sales than European subsidiaries ($180 million), though the difference is not statistically significant due to high variances. US-affiliate exports, however, are very much higher at 46 per cent of sales, compared to only 21 per cent for European subsidiaries. The level of network coordination within which US firms operate seems to be substantially higher. In particular, they are much more likely to transfer process technology and production know-how to other group plants or subsidiaries than their European counterparts, and they are also much more responsive to the market needs of other group subsidiaries when developing new or improved products.

Though UK subsidiaries as a whole transfer little material outputs to other group plants for further processing and/or final assembly, US firms (6.6 per cent of outputs) are more integrated in this respect than European affiliates (3.8 per cent of outputs). This higher level of integration also shows in other areas: in US subsidiaries, capacity and manufacturing technology decisions by headquarters that involve the subsidiary are much more likely to be made with a view to providing multi-plant linkages and multi-plant sourcing than is the case for European affiliates; in developing product and quality specifications, European firms are more likely to do so with only their own markets in mind, whereas US subsidiaries are more network-oriented.

Table 3.2 shows the cross-tabulation of subsidiary strategy against home country; there is a clear relationship between the two dimensions (chi-square = 10.59, p = 0.01). Among US subsidiaries, there are fewer of both types of miniature replica than would be expected, and more of both rationalized manufacturers and strategic mandate subsidiaries.

Following Table 3.2, differences in the characteristics of US and European subsidiaries may now be evaluated at the level of subsidiary strategy. Among the miniature replica (adopter and adapter) types, US subsidiaries have a much higher export propensity (36 per cent against 8 per cent); they are much more likely to participate in technical transfer within their respective networks, and product and quality specifications are drawn up with the international network in mind whereas European subsidiaries tend to concentrate on their own market areas.

Miniature replica (innovator) types show no differences across country of origin. In line with the opening discussion, however, US rationalized manufacturers have been in operation for very much longer than their European counterparts (41 years against 18); they have less autonomy in financial matters; their R&D tends to be much more dispersed throughout their network than is the case for European subsidiaries, and they

Table 3.2 Analysis of strategy types by home country (number of subsidiaries)

Strategy	US-owned	European-owned	Total
Miniature replica (adopter, adapter)	10	15	25
Miniature replica (innovator)	10	26	36
Rationalized manufacturer	12	7	19
Strategic mandate	36	15	51
Total	68	63	131

are very significantly more network-oriented in matters of product and quality specifications than European firms.

US strategic mandate subsidiaries are characterized by a relative stability of technology and a high level of manufacturing sophistication relative to European firms. Their products are more mature, and production-technology improvements and cost-minimization are seen as important. Accordingly, they also develop and/or adapt a much lower proportion (just over 50 per cent) of their own product line than do European subsidiaries (over 90 per cent). Thus, we may conclude that US rationalized manufacturers are very well differentiated from the equivalent European type, miniature replicas (adopter and adapter) and strategic mandate subsidiaries are fairly well differentiated, and miniature replicas (innovator) types not at all.

STRATEGY EVOLUTION

Figure 3.3 shows the overall changes in subsidiary strategy over the past five years. The number of miniature replicas (adopter and adapter) has fallen from 34 to 24, while the innovator type has dropped from 45 to 37. The number of rationalized manufacturers has remained relatively stable (18 to 19), so the big increase has come in strategic mandate subsidiaries, increasing by 50 per cent to 51. Within this, there is a fair degree of strategy stability; 19 miniature replica (adopter and adapter) types out of 34 (56 per cent) have retained the same strategy, as have 29 (64 per cent) innovator types, 10 (56 per cent) rationalized manufacturers, and 31 (91 per cent) strategic mandate subsidiaries. The latter, therefore, is by far the most stable strategy configuration.

When these overall figures are broken down by country of origin, some rather interesting situations are highlighted. Among miniature replicas

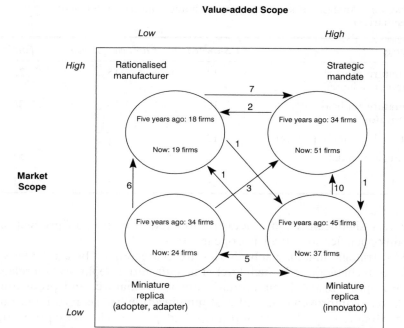

Figure 3.3   Strategy evolution

(adopter and adapter), 12 European and seven US affiliates maintained this strategy. One US firm became an innovator type, two became rationalized manufacturers, and three moved all the way to a strategic mandate posture. The corresponding figures for European subsidiaries were five, four and zero respectively. Of the innovator type, eight US and 21 European subsidiaries had a constant strategy. Two US affiliates dropped back to the adopter type (three European firms), one (zero) moved into the rationalized manufacturer sector, and eight (two) became fully-fledged strategic mandate affiliates.

Seven US rationalized manufacturers maintained that position, one dropped into the miniature replica (adopter and adapter) zone, none became innovator types, and five developed into strategic mandate subsidiaries; the corresponding movements for European affiliates involved three, zero, zero and two firms respectively. The strategic mandate sector is particularly interesting; 20 US and 11 European firms had a constant strategy over the five years, there were no instances of subsidiaries of either geographic origin falling into the miniature replica (adopter and adapter) sector, only one (US) became an innovator type, and only two (both US) dropped back to become rationalized manufacturers.

These strategy evaluations may be broadly summarized as follows. Virtually all of the subsidiaries in the strategic mandate sector have preserved this strategy, while this is true for just over half the firms in each of the other three quadrants. Three each of US and European affiliates moved from some other strategy into the miniature replica (adopter and adapter) position. Two US and five European firms moved into the innovator strategy. Thus, overall, the miniature replica half of the strategy space became more heavily populated by European firms over the five-year period. Five US and four European subsidiaries moved into the rationalized manufacture strategy space, while 16 US and only four European firms developed into strategic mandate subsidiaries. Thus, over the five years the high market-scope strategies became relatively more heavily populated with US subsidiaries, and this was also true of the high value-added scope strategies.

CASE EXAMPLES

The previous discussion has laid out the main characteristics of the four types of subsidiary strategy and how they apply to US firms manufacturing in the UK. In order to evaluate further these characteristics and link them to other important strategic parameters, four US affiliates in the UK are now examined in some detail. These were not part of the original sample, but were selected as being representative of the four strategic alternatives; they include Air Products (miniature replica, adopter type), W.L. Gore (miniature replica, innovator type), Motorola (rationalized manufacturer), and Hewlett Packard (strategic mandate). All of these firms have multiple operational units in the UK, so in each case attention is focused on just one of these.

Air Products

Air Products is almost the perfect archetype of the adopter type of miniature replica. It manufactures oxygen and a range of other gases, active and inert, for use in industry, health services and leisure. The firm was set up in the UK in the early 1960s to challenge (successfully in the long run) the virtual monopoly established by the British Oxygen Co. Ltd. It focuses strictly on the UK market, with other markets being serviced by other country-specific subsidiaries. Despite the technical nature of its product and production operations, the maturity of much of its product line means that R&D may be effectively centralized in the US; locally the emphasis is on process engineering, and there is no R&D facility.

The subsidiary is fairly compact in employment terms (less than 250 employees) and its product range is very similar – almost identical, in fact – to that of the parent corporation. Decisions about which parts of the UK are to be served by this subsidiary are usually taken by the parent, though after consultation with the subsidiary; decisions about the product line are taken solely by headquarters. There is some degree of material flows between subsidiaries; in the case of both material inputs from other subsidiaries and material outputs to them for further processing, this amounts to 5–10 per cent by volume. Conversely, well over three-quarters of material inputs are sourced within the local economy, and an even higher proportion of service inputs.

The technology intensity of the subsidiary tends to be increased mainly by the introduction of new products from the parent corporation, though corporate literature and technical conferences are also important. From the subsidiary's perspective, the main advantage of being part of an international network lies in the reputation of the parent corporation, though the parent's technical expertise is also an important factor. The subsidiary has no marketing department – this activity is carried out by regional headquarters. The parent corporation is clearly carrying out a country-centred strategy (Porter, 1986), and the affiliate's miniature replica (adopter) status has a number of similarities to the receptive subsidiary strategy (Jarillo and Martinez, 1990) described earlier.

W.L. Gore

W.L. Gore manufacturers a range of high-quality waterproof fabrics that are used extensively in premium-priced outdoor clothing. Its brand (Goretex) is possibly one of the most widely recognized and appreciated in this market sector. As with Air Products, the parent corporation of W.L. Gore has traditionally operated a country-centred corporate strategy, but there have been indicators that this is moving to what Porter describes as 'high foreign investment with extensive coordination among subsidiaries'. This coordination is currently moving to the European level and may, ultimately, be global; it is concerned mainly with 'soft' characteristics like customer and competition knowledge rather than with operational activities. Within this corporate strategy, the subsidiary operates happily and effectively as a miniature replica (innovator) type, and this is most unlikely to be affected by changes in strategic posture at corporate level.

The subsidiary currently confines its activities to the UK, though it is rapidly developing a high level of value-added scope. From a position a few years ago where its main focus was the adaptation of manufacturing technology, it is now producing new and improved product initiatives that the parent will be able to use internationally. Indeed, the rate of progress in this area has been so impressive that the subsidiary may be generating new fabric technology for the corporate parent in the not-too-distant future. Again, its product line has developed rapidly, and is now only slightly narrower than the parent's. The subsidiary employs just under 500 employees, though this is likely to rise over the next few years. Market area decisions are, of course, wholly at the discretion of corporate headquarters, though product-line decisions are largely made by the affiliate after consultation with headquarters. The local affiliate sends no material outputs to overseas subsidiaries for further processing, though it does receive about 15 per cent of material inputs from this source. No doubt this figure will reduce as the subsidiary's technological and production capabilities increase.

Material sourcing is, in fact, widespread with only some 30 per cent coming from the local economy. Service inputs, on the other hand, are sourced almost entirely within the UK. The subsidiary has a marketing department, established 28 years ago when the affiliate was set up. Its main advantage from being part of a multinational comes from the inward transfer of group technology, though parent expertise and reputation are also important. Technology transfer is mainly by means of new products implanted by headquarters together with the new equipment to produce them; technical conferences, however, are also an important source. Comparison with the Jarillo and Martinez typology would suggest that this miniature replica (innovator) profile of W.L. Gore's has strong linkages to the active subsidiary strategy described on the integration–responsiveness framework.

Motorola

Motorola is one of the world's leading electronics multinationals, and has key leadership positions in sectors like personal communications and semiconductors. It is one of the best-run MNCs, and has a deserved reputation for highly trained and well-motivated employees at all levels of the hierarchy. This UK subsidiary was established in 1992 specifically as a rationalized manufacturer, though there is some evidence that a strategy change is under way. Initially, it served the UK cellular telephone market, but quickly extended its interest to Europe, and it now has global marketing in its sights. Similarly, the R&D activity was initially very low, but the affiliate has ambitions to develop new and improved products for world markets. Thus, as described in a previous section, this subsidiary may be a classic case of a move from its current status of rationalized manufacturer to a strategic mandate profile.

The affiliate currently employs some 1500 employees, though this is likely to reach 2000 in the next five years as growth plans mature. As Motorola is a fairly diversified company, comparison of the subsidiary's product-line width is best made with the parent's appropriate international division, which carries a similar number of product lines. In matters of both markets served and product-line carried, the decisions rest primarily with the parent, though the subsidiary will be consulted before a final view is arrived at.

Material inputs from the UK economy are still under 50 per cent, but this should climb to 75 per cent by the end of the century. Virtually all service inputs are sourced within the UK. This is a very impressive performance by a relatively new manufacturing unit operating within a high technology global industry, and underlines the firm's objective of being a good corporate citizen in every sense. The subsidiary produces finished product only, and so sends none of its material outputs to sister subsidiaries for further processing. Due to the nature of the industry and product, however, about a sixth of material inputs come from other group subsidiaries, a proportion that is unlikely to change in the near future.

A very high proportion of electronics MNCs follow Porter's 'high foreign investment with extensive coordination' type of corporate strategy, and Motorola is no exception, with the coordination taking place at the global level and focusing mainly on aspects of knowledge (customer, competitor, technology) and skills (operational, training, education). Within this, the subsidiary's rationalized manufacturer strategy fits well, and the fit will be even better if the projected move to a strategic mandate posture takes place. Like W.L. Gore, the main advantage of being part of an MNC network lies in the value of inward technology transfer, followed by the highly-valued expertise of the parent corporation; the opportunities for achieving economies of scale, facilitated by the potential strategic mandate profile, is also helpful. Unlike W.L. Gore, the main means of transferring technology is seen to be technical conferences, which fits well with Motorola's pronounced people-orientation; introduction of parent-inspired products, together with the associated manufacturing processes, is also important. In terms of the Jarillo and Martinez typology, Motorola currently operates a receptive strategy within this UK subsidiary, but it may well become an active role in the future.

Hewlett Packard (HP)

Hewlett Packard is also a highly respected name in the global electronics industry. Its people-orientation credentials are attested by the well-known 'management by walking around' syndrome. This UK subsidiary was established in 1966 and now manufactures, designs and markets telecommunications, electronic measuring and test equipment. There has been a marketing department operating within and on behalf of the affiliate from the beginning. The subsidiary strategy is a classic case of the strategic mandate type; the subsidiary has served global markets for at least ten years, and over the same time period its high quality R&D

facility has been producing new and improved products for these same world markets. In addition, it carries a very wide product line indeed, indicating that it operates well beyond the 'world product mandate' (Rugman and Bennett, 1982) role that outside observers often ascribe to certain HP subsidiaries.

The unit employs in excess of 1000 staff, and this figure has been fairly stable for a number of years. Both market and product decisions are made largely by the affiliate, though headquarters will be consulted as a matter of course and/or courtesy. As it has some involvement in component and sub-assembly manufacture, there is a substantial flow of materials to and from other group subsidiaries. Some 10 per cent or so of output goes to sister subsidiaries for further processing, and in excess of a quarter of material inputs come from this source. Material inputs from the local economy, however, have climbed rapidly in recent years and are now over 50 per cent. HP operates the same generic corporate strategy as Motorola – high foreign investment with extensive global coordination; in this case, however, the coordination mechanisms also apply significantly to operational characteristics.

The subsidiary's strategic mandate posture is, perhaps, not altogether a comfortable fit with the corporate strategic direction, and this may account for some of the creative tension that HP sees as central to its approach to running a business. For this subsidiary, the most useful aspect of being part of a multinational is the access it affords to parent-group markets and customers worldwide; the parent's reputation and opportunities for inward transfer of technology are also helpful. Technology transfer is mainly carried out through the R&D unit, though technical licences and professional conferences also have a part to play. Classifying this subsidiary with respect to Jarillo and Martinez is more difficult; it may be that the parent would prefer to see a receptive strategy, while the affiliate's preference is for the active mode.

CONCLUSIONS

The purpose of this chapter was to evaluate the strategies of US MNCs in the United Kingdom and, indirectly, to assess the overall importance of such subsidiaries to the UK economy. Taking the last point first, it has to be said that all inward investment is, of course, highly welcome in an open economy like the UK's, and most multinationals, whatever their country of origin, bring added value of some kind. Despite, or maybe because of, their long period of establishment in the UK, American subsidiaries are still trail-blazers of establishment in many respects. In particular, this research suggests that they tend to have both higher market scope and higher value-added scope than their European counterparts. This may give them something of a competitive edge in maintaining existing markets and products, and in developing new ones. This marginal competitive advantage brings benefits to the UK economy in terms of overall technological trajectories, increased exports, and – not least – an important demonstration effect for indigenous UK firms.

While the integration–responsiveness framework and the coordination–configuration model were of some assistance in strategy-evaluation here, the simplified form of White and Poynter's model – based on market and value-added scope – was very helpful indeed in assessing and tracking the strategies of US affiliates in the UK, and in comparing them with a sub-sample of European-owned subsidiaries. Proportionally, there are more rationalized manufacturers and strategic mandate subsidiaries among the US firms, and these firms also showed the greatest propensity to develop into the strategic mandate sector and remain there once established. From the perspective of the local management team, this is likely to be the most fulfilling subsidiary role. From the perspective of UK policy-makers, this must be a welcome tendency in US subsidiaries, though the strategic evolution of European subsidiaries may engender less enthusiasm.

Perhaps the main message of this research for UK policy-makers is that old friends are maybe the best. Finally, from the perspective of US MNC parents, the important finding here is that the UK, America's oldest global partner in business, still provides an economic, industrial and management environment that encourages subsidiaries to be proactive and even aggressive, internally and externally, in maximizing the opportunities afforded by rapidly-changing national, regional and global markets.

4 Host-Country Technological and Scientific Collaborations of MNE Subsidiaries: Evidence from Operations in Europe

Marina Papanastassiou and Robert Pearce

INTRODUCTION

It has been argued (Papanastassiou and Pearce, 1996a, b; Pearce and Papanastassiou, 1996a) that the increasingly strategic positioning of some multinational enterprise (MNE) subsidiaries not only involves the creative *application* of current group technology but also the *development* of local technological competencies that complement those that are acquired intra-group. These subsidiaries then seek to build on locally-developed competencies in individualized ways. This chapter aims to evaluate two types of linkages that MNE subsidiaries may establish in their host economies to achieve these objectives. These links may both facilitate the effective local implementation and productive use of extant group technology, and also seek to enrich these knowledge capacities in ways that particularly reflect local competencies and traditions. The investigated linkages are, firstly, the implementation of arrangements with local suppliers that involve technology transfers; and, secondly, the establishment of collaborative agreements with local scientific institutions for the creation of new knowledge or improvements in the effective local application of existing technology.

The results reported here derive from a much larger study (Papanastassiou, 1995) of the strategic roles, and technological positioning, of MNE subsidiaries in Europe. The study analysed results of a postal questionnaire survey, which included replies from 145 subsidiaries located in the UK, Belgium, Greece and Portugal. The questionnaire was sent to 533 subsidiaries in 1992/93. Out of the 145 responses received, 99 were from subsidiaries in the UK, 20 in Belgium, 16 in Greece and 10 in Portugal (for more details see Papanastassiou, 1995, p. 10). The following two sections of this chapter deal with technology transfer to local suppliers of inputs and components. The first establishes the extent of these transfers, and the second establishes the nature of the content of such knowledge collaborations of MNEs with these local companies. The third section then looks at the creative cooperations of MNE subsidiaries with various types of local scientific institutions, seeking to discern how the relative prevalence of such links may reflect the strategic and technological positioning of the subsidiaries. The final section draws conclusions.

EXTENT OF TECHNOLOGICAL ADVICE TO SUPPLIERS

In the past, MNEs' subsidiaries offered a rather static and limited lump-sum deal to their host countries. This package crucially included employment opportunities for host-country nationals within the premises of the company (Hood, Young and Lal, 1994). However, as demand in the host countries expanded and supply was increasingly reshaped by adaptation to host-country characteristics, more dynamic local supplier linkages had to be pursued (Stewart, 1976). Local independent suppliers of intermediate or semi-final goods became a basic part of the production process and extended the scope of MNEs' operations in the host market by adding further local value to the subsidiaries' production (Pearce and Singh, 1992, p. 180).

The role of such suppliers has become very demanding, for, although they remain in the same location, they are often internationalizing indirectly and frequently supply inputs or goods that need further processing in MNE plants in other countries. Thereby, the multinationality of the product itself is increased. Similarly, indigenous suppliers can also become more dispersed domestically and even multinationally. When suppliers build their reputation and improve their expertise in the production of inputs, they may be able to expand their operations into other parts of their local economy through a network of distribution centres or through the establishment of additional production sites in areas where foreign direct investors operate. Also, they may achieve multinationality through trade, that is in countries where their clients operate and where the local suppliers lack the expertise these clients need. This can then expand even further to on-site production of inputs as part of a *keiretsu*-type of operation. This, of course, presupposes that this type of advance in inputs is able to follow the direction of certain production lines into more advanced trajectories.

Empirical Evidence

Firms in the sample declared that they more often had a 'regular' provision of technological advice to their local suppliers than 'rarely' or 'never'

Table 4.1 Frequency of provision of technological advice by MNE subsidiaries to local suppliers[1]

Industry	Frequency of provision (percentage)				
	Frequently	Sometimes	Rarely	Never	Total
Food and drink	44.4	22.2	33.3		100.0
Industrial and agricultural chemicals	25.5	55.0	10.0	10.0	100.0
Pharmaceuticals and consumer chemicals	35.7	57.1	7.1		100.0
Electronics and electrical appliances[2]	53.8	26.9	7.7	11.5	100.0
Mechanical engineering	45.5	36.4	9.1	9.1	100.0
Metal manufacture and products	33.3	50.0		16.7	100.0
Petroleum		75.0	25.0		100.0
Automobiles (incl. components)	50.0	33.3	8.3	8.3	100.0
Other manufacturing[3]	37.5	43.8	12.5	6.3	100.0
Total	39.8	41.5	11.0	7.6	100.0
Home country					
USA	33.3	47.4	14.0	5.3	100.0
Japan	42.9	42.9	9.5	4.8	100.0
Europe[4]	47.4	31.6	7.9	13.2	100.0
Total[5]	39.8	41.5	11.0	7.6	100.0
Host country					
UK	37.5	42.5	11.3	8.8	100.0
Other Europe[6]	44.7	39.5	10.5	5.3	100.0
Total	39.8	41.5	11.0	7.6	100.0

Notes:
[1] Respondents were asked 'if you have any local suppliers of components parts or other inputs do you provide them with technological advice (i) frequently, (ii) sometimes, (iii) rarely, (iv) never.'
[2] Includes computers and telecommunications.
[3] Includes building materials, instruments, rubber, miscellaneous.
[4] Covers subsidiaries of European MNEs in countries other than the home country.
[5] Includes subsidiaries of Canadian MNEs.
[6] Covers subsidiaries in Belgium, Greece and Portugal.

(see Table 4.1). This frequent knowledge-transfer connection between MNEs and local suppliers may have started as an effort to overcome the lack of experience on behalf of those suppliers, and resulted in a process of assurance of quality and cost-saving. Looking at industrial sectors that provided technological advice 'frequently' or 'sometimes', then pharmaceuticals is most committed to the provision of such advice and food and drink least so. In terms of explicitly providing such advice 'frequently', electronics and automobiles were strongest with 53.8 per cent and 50.0 per cent of respondents respectively. For the Japanese, such supplier-collaboration is part of what are now well-known behavioural practices. Thus, the Japanese are above average for both 'frequently' and 'sometimes', though Europeans are notably strongest (and US weakest) for 'frequently'. Overall, Japanese MNEs are thus most likely to provide advice. For European MNEs, this may suggest that for some (but not all) firms, there is an increasingly cohesive European supply strategy, with high-quality suppliers being sought throughout the region. The strong 'sometimes' response (47.4 per cent) of US firms may suggest that these may offer advice to suppliers when inadequate performance makes it necessary, but have a less systematic collaborative approach to suppliers than Japanese or some European firms.

Subsidiaries in 'other Europe' tend to cooperate more frequently with their suppliers than subsidiaries in the UK, probably due to a lack of expertise of the 'other Europe' suppliers which therefore require more regular contact. In Greece, in the main dynamic and exporting sectors, food and pharmaceuticals, subsidiaries have a very regular relationship with their suppliers, which also benefits the host-country industrial structure. It seems that once the suppliers are involved in more competitive exporting sectors, lack of experience on their behalf motivates the subsidiaries to stand by them and guide them. Where production is oriented to the local market this relationship seems to be more relaxed, perhaps because the local suppliers know their market (in some cases better than the MNE) and do not need so much control. Industries with low export ratios, like food and pharmaceuticals, provide technical advice to suppliers less systematically. Industries such as chemicals and automobiles, which have a high intermediate-product export ratio (Papanastassiou, 1995), regularly provide suppliers with technical advice. However, as already noted, there seems a more systematic relationship in the automobile industry as this industry faces the price and quality competition of Southeast Asian suppliers. Thus, the European suppliers must have more regular supervision in order to achieve the quality and cost standards of their competitors, and to convince the major automobile companies to maintain their operations on European soil.

TYPES OF ADVICE TO SUPPLIERS

Three types of advice to suppliers were specified in the survey. The first two of these were defined as (i) specification of component or input to be supplied, and (ii) details of the production process for the components or inputs to be supplied. The exchange of these types of information is often likely to occur simply because it is necessary to clarify an understanding of what is to be supplied and the ability of the supplier to produce it satisfactorily. However, it may be a far from routine operation, embracing a heterogeneous and complicated process and often embodying an element of forward planning (that is, shared creativity between the MNE subsidiary and the local supplier).

One possibility is that the subsidiary is involved in a more complicated value-chain and is not at the end of a vertically integrated system. To meet the detailed needs of its own customers, it may have little technological discretion and may need to dictate precise specifications and processes to its own local input suppliers. This imposes a degree of technological dependency on local suppliers. By contrast, where a subsidiary has responsibility for market development (that is, a mandated subsidiary with discretion over product creation and evolution), it may provide less-complete initial requirements to input suppliers, allowing them to use their expertise in a collaborative programme of component creation.

The third type of information transfer was defined as wider advice on industrial production processes. This indicates support information (quality control techniques, stock control, plant layout and other organizational practices) that is not specific to the particular input to be manufactured, but that generally seeks to improve the efficiency of output capacity. If these techniques and practices are distinctive to the MNE passing them on, this may suggest the will to build a more long-term relationship with the supplier.

All firms pay attention to the first two mentioned types of advice because these are directly associated with quality and cost-saving matters. Reputation in the present always builds up positively or negatively in the future. The role of suppliers can be very significant in the overall industrial performance of particular sectors. Once foreign firms seek the collaboration of local suppliers, those local suppliers are often the first local production agents to become, to some extent, integrated with the incoming MNEs. The ownership characteristics that urged MNEs to invest abroad (Hymer, 1976; Caves, 1982) are disseminated in part to these local firms. Thus, local suppliers can become scanners of the new directions of industrial activity. They can sense when the production of a local firm is outdated and when to innovate in a particular product line. If necessary, on the basis of the information gained through its relationship with the MNE, the local firm can choose to cease production of a line, or, in the extreme case, choose to diversify completely away from its current activities. The local firm responds to the imperatives to maintain or expand a particular product line in which it should already possess superior ownership assets than the MNE.

By contrast, the MNE can obtain relevant information about local production activities through the *'curriculum vitae'* of their suppliers, and then rationalize its production line, thus avoiding possible conflicts with the local environment or duplication of resources. Thus, initial contacts between MNE subsidiaries and local suppliers may provide the first signs of the nature of the long-term relationship (for example, routine cost-based or creative) that will emerge. The role of wider advice is more obvious in those sectors that hide a competive advantage, for example electronics in the case of the UK or food and pharmaceuticals in the case of Greece.

Empirical Evidence

Specification of components is shown in Table 4.2 to be the most popular form of advice in our sample (as would have been expected), in particular with electronics (an average response of 2.91), food and drink (3.00), mechanical engineering (2.89), automobiles (2.92) and metal manufacture (3.00). Details on the production process is the second favourite choice in food and drink, automobiles, pharmaceuticals and other manufacturing in particular. Although we would expect industrial chemicals to show a preference for this type of advice, we notice that this industry does not have a consistent preference as all the types of advice have average responses below the total average. On the other hand, automobile subsidiaries seem to provide all types of advice, and have relatively strong commitment to those that go beyond component specification.

Subsidiaries in 'other Europe' are more prone to providing details of the production process to their suppliers than UK subsidiaries, probably indicating a rationalized product (RP) subsidiary (Pearce, 1992; Pearce and Papanastassiou, 1996a) type of operations in these countries. Thus RP subsidiaries are themselves often technologically dependent and need to pass group technology on to their suppliers. If UK subsidiaries are more creative, they may take the abilities of likely suppliers into account when developing products, and thus have less need to transfer process knowledge to them. Also, wider advice is somewhat more popular in 'other Europe', perhaps because of the fact that newly-established subsidiaries seek to familiarize their suppliers with the wider production goals of their company. In this way they can create a climate of confidence and trust, and integrate suppliers efficiently with the group's targets, at the same time assuring quality in their production. Supplier linkages can thus be very important for the industrialization of the host country.

The prevalence of product specification as the dominant type of advice, rather than process or wider advice, may suggest that often (though not always) all that the MNE subsidiaries need to transfer are details about how the required input differs from those the supplier already produces.

Table 4.2 Types of advice provided to local suppliers

Industry	Types of advice (average response)[1]		
	Specification of component	Details of production process	Wider advice
Food and drink	3.00	2.63	2.00
Industrial and agricultural chemicals	2.84	1.47	1.44
Pharmaceuticals and consumer chemicals	2.83	2.25	1.67
Electronics and electrical appliances[2]	2.91	1.95	1.50
Mechanical engineering	2.89	1.67	1.50
Metal manufacture and products	3.00	1.75	1.67
Petroleum	2.75	1.75	1.00
Automobiles (incl. components)	2.92	2.27	1.90
Other manufacturing[3]	2.77	2.38	1.83
Total	2.88	2.02	1.63
Home country			
USA	2.83	2.12	1.67
Japan	2.94	2.06	1.59
Europe[4]	2.91	1.82	1.58
Total[5]	2.88	2.02	1.63
Host country			
UK	2.88	1.91	1.61
Other Europe[6]	2.88	2.26	1.67
Total	2.88	2.02	1.63

Notes:
Types of advice provided were (i) specification of component or input to be supplied; (ii) details of the production process for the component or inputs to be supplied; and (iii) wider advice on the industrial production process.
[1] Respondents were asked to grade each type of advice as important, relatively important, or not important. The average response was calculated by allocating a response of 'important' the value 3, 'relatively important' 2, and 'not important' 1.
[2] Includes computers and telecommunications.
[3] Includes building materials, instruments, rubber, miscellaneous.
[4] Covers subsidiaries of European MNEs in countries other than the home country.
[5] Includes subsidiaries of Canadian MNEs.
[6] Covers subsidiaries in Belgium, Greece and Portugal.

This may reflect the unique characteristics of the subsidiary's technology, so that any new knowledge gained by the component supplier may have little use outside of its relationship with the MNE subsidiary.

The role of R&D within subsidiaries can also affect the production of suppliers associated with the MNEs' operations by improving and enlarging the scope of their operations. The fact that industries like pharmaceuticals, industrial chemicals and electronics regularly provide advice to suppliers (in particular, the specification of components) and that they also often rely on imported technology which then needs to undergo extensive adaptation, shows another aspect of the globalization of technology on the one hand and the localization of the nature of the product, based on demand factors or supply requirements, on the other. Even a globalized product like Coca-Cola will have its distinct regional or national versions, which will reflect particular customer tastes and production processes. The participation of local suppliers in a product like Coca-Cola may involve metal providers supplying cans, and/or glass companies supplying bottles.

As already suggested, an important consideration here is how much the provision of advice by MNE subsidiaries to local suppliers results in 'spill-over' or 'external' benefits to the local economy via these suppliers. Thus, the local suppliers will usually be established component producers that supply intermediate goods to other local final-product-producing firms. If the knowledge transferred to them by MNE subsidiaries improves their wider efficiency (rather than just the efficiency with which they supply the MNE subsidiary), then they can improve their knowledge in the particular market and adjust quickly to new market-orientation requirements. Once suppliers experience collaboration with foreign companies, they also become accustomed to foreign production and management techniques. However, this widening of local suppliers' expertise may have negative effects on their association with old-established local firms. This might occur, for example, if local firms produce an older version of the same or similar products or when their orders do not justify the need for further cooperation (for example, when the foreign customer's business proves to be more demanding, dynamic, time-consuming or more profitable). If the local company's bonds with these suppliers are close and based on goodwill, however, then the supplier could transfer its new experience and thereby stimulate the local company to improve its production line. So, if a local economy is to benefit overall from such positive supplier 'spill-overs', then the decisive responsiveness of the rest of the local productive agents is required.

How are such spill-over benefits to occur from the three types of advice covered? In summary:

1. Specification of the component or input to the suppliers by the MNE subsidiary can provide limited benefits if the component is very specific to the needs of the MNE, and very different from the components

supplied to the local final-product firms. Positive spill-over effects will occur only if the argument in the previous paragraph is practised.

2. The same sort of perspectives may apply when the MNE subsidiary provides local component suppliers with details of the production process they should use to produce the new component/input that they have been commissioned to supply. The process knowledge may be totally specific to a particular component and have no applicability to the established processes of the suppliers. However, if some elements of the new production process *are* transferable to the processes already used to produce existing components for local firms, this may lower costs or improve reliability of supply, and thus improve the competitiveness of the local firms that use components of these suppliers.

3. The wider types of industrial knowledge relate to types of know-how or skills (including organizational or administrative practices) that are not specific to the supply of the particular component to the MNE subsidiary. This, then, for example, could involve particular industrial skills, or quality control procedures or ways of optimizing the local factory layout. If the MNE helps to improve general types of expertise like these, they should spread throughout the supplier's complete operations (providing they are applicable to the improvement of its existing activity), and this will increase the local supplier's contribution to the local industrial sector by improving its ability to supply this with inputs and components.

The most important spill-over for local industry occurs when one of its key, and often most immobile, elements – its suppliers – changes their mentality. Once suppliers become involved in internationalized operations and have a better understanding of different production systems, they learn to adapt to a more cosmopolitan environment and become more flexible, open and self-conscious in reacting to international changes.

The three types of advice to local suppliers were used as dependent variables in the regressions (see Table 4.3). The first set of independent variables in these regressions were dummies for industry (with 'other manufacturing' serving as the omitted industry dummy), for the UK as a host country (with 'other Europe' as the omitted dummy), and for the US and Japan as home countries of subsidiaries (with Europe as the omitted dummy). The next pair of independent variables provide quantitative measures of the subsidiary; these being SALES (annual turnover in $ millions as an indication of absolute size) and RELSIZE (the subsidiary's sales as a percentage of the total worldwide sales of its MNE – as an indicator of its relative importance in the group). These quantitative indicators of a subsidiary's importance may be related to its need or ability to develop technological links with local suppliers or scientific institutions (see Papanastassiou, 1995, pp. 129–33).

Table 4.3 Regressions with types of advice to local suppliers as dependent variables

	Component specifications	Production process for components	Wider advice
Intercept	2.0606***	1.7720**	2.8455***
	(5.61)	(2.21)	(2.92)
Mechanical engineering	0.2853	−0.4609	−1.1317
	(1.10)	(−0.90)	(−1.42)
Electronics and electrical appliances	0.2374	−0.6479*	−0.5940
	(1.38)	(−1.77)	(−1.35)
Food and drink	0.2862	0.0685	0.2014
	(1.57)	(0.18)	(0.67)
Automobiles	0.1614	−0.3527	−0.1478
	(1.02)	(−1.11)	(−0.38)
Industrial and agricultural chemicals	0.0028	−0.8120**	−0.4713
	(0.02)	(3.09)	(−1.51)
Pharmaceuticals and consumer chemicals	0.1656	−0.3635	−0.1991
	(0.99)	(−1.02)	(−0.45)
Metal manufacture and products	0.2113	−0.9714**	−0.6947
	(1.07)	(−2.18)	(−1.26)
Petroleum	0.2207	−0.9824**	−0.9731*
	(0.98)	(−2.15)	(−1.74)
UK	0.0220	−0.5187**	−0.0208
	(0.18)	(−2.01)	(−0.06)
USA	0.0019	0.2781	−0.0849
	(0.02)	(1.42)	(−0.34)
Japan	−0.0166	0.5594	−0.0655
	(−0.10)	(1.58)	(−0.16)
SALES	0.0001	−0.0001	−0.0002
	(0.27)	(−0.54)	(−0.66)
RELSIZE	−0.0012	−0.0019	0.0170**
	(−0.38)	(−0.29)	(2.02)
EXPRAT	0.0019	−0.0023	0.0001
	(1.10)	(−0.64)	(0.04)
INTRAEXP	−0.0016	−0.0010	−0.0018
	(−1.16)	(−0.40)	(−0.53)
INTEREXP	0.0009	0.0031	−0.0003
	(0.94)	(1.47)	(−0.16)
IMPTECH	0.1395*	0.1000	−0.1264
	(1.64)	(0.58)	(−0.60)
HOSTTECH	0.0438	0.0706	−0.1813
	(0.77)	(0.60)	(−1.30)
SUBRAD	0.1191**	0.2175*	−0.1086
	(2.04)	(1.82)	(−0.72)
R^2	0.2270	0.5164	0.2918
F	0.74	2.36***	0.91
n	68	62	62

Note:
*** significant at 1 per cent
** significant at 5 per cent
* significant at 10 per cent
Figures in brackets are t statistics.

Three aspects of a subsidiary's market-orientation are also included as independent variables, in the expectation that the nature of the strategic positioning reflected in them would suggest the need for input supply efficiency, or creative interdependency with local supplier companies, with this, in turn, indicating the likely nature of technology transfer. The first of these variables was the overall export-orientation of subsidiaries; that is, the proportion of total production exported, or export ratio – EXPRAT. Next, the importance of intra-group trade was included; that is, the proportion of a subsidiary's exports that go to other parts of the group – INTRAEXP. Finally, account was taken of the role of intermediate goods in a subsidiary's trade; that is, the proportion of a subsidiary's exports that are intermediate products – INTEREXP (see Papanastassiou, 1995, pp. 151–70).

The final group of three independent variables cover sources of technology used by the subsidiary. These are (i) 'imported technology from elsewhere in the MNE group' (IMPTECH), (ii) 'established host-country technology' (HOSTTECH), and (iii) 'results of R&D carried out by the subsidiary' (SUBRAD). The relative prevalence of these types of technology in a subsidiary's activity may determine the extent and nature of the associations which they need to establish with the local suppliers and/or scientific institutions (see Papanastassiou, 1995, pp. 180–3).

The first dependent variable, 'component specification', is expected to be positively related with EXPRAT, especially if the exports are existing goods which the MNE needs to continue to supply to markets that have established expectations with regard to quality. In line with this, another hypothesis is that IMPTECH will be positively related, as component suppliers will need to conform to predetermined MNE group specifications and standards. Where SUBRAD is a source of technology in the MNE subsidiary, its relationship with advice to component suppliers can be more unpredictable. If SUBRAD means that the subsidiary develops a new product, then it may still need to provide details of this to component suppliers (that is, a positive relationship will be observed). But, if the new product development is actually carried out in collaboration with the component suppliers, such a one-way transfer of specifications is not needed (that is, these will be an insignificant or negative relationship). Where HOSTTECH is a source of technology into subsidiaries, it is likely that the component suppliers will already be in tune with this knowledge, and are then less likely to need transfers from the MNE subsidiaries.

EXPRAT is positively related to this first dependent variable, 'component specification', but does not approach significance. Taken with its weak relationship with the two other dependent variables, this suggests that the market orientation of a subsidiary is generally not a strong determinant of its need to supply information/advice to its host-country suppliers. Positive relationships with component specification emerge for both IMPTECH and SUBRAD. The latter result clarifies the point that, when a MNE subsidiary embodies its own newly-created knowledge in a product, it still has a considerable priority to transfer a new component's input specifications to local suppliers, to whom this will represent an extension of their knowledge and scope.

The second dependent variable is 'specification of the production process to be used in making the components to be supplied'. In the dummy variables, electronics, industrial chemicals, metal manufacturing and petroleum were significantly negative, showing less need for process advice than the omitted sector. UK subsidiaries give less process advice to their suppliers than those in the 'other Europe' group, which could reflect the greater involvement of UK subsidiaries in the creation of new products, with the abilities of component suppliers taken into account in this process. Still, the fact that the subsidiaries in the 'other Europe' countries provide this type of advice implies that the local value-added has increased and that local suppliers are getting acquainted with MNE production, acquiring knowledge that did not exist for them previously. This reminds us of the different significance that the same activities take in different environments and circumstances. Here SUBRAD is again significantly positive, indicating once more that new research results are embodied in new products, with additional process advice then needing to be communicated to component suppliers involved in production of these goods.

The third dependent variable is 'wider advice on industrial processes'. The strong positive relationship with RELSIZE suggests that subsidiaries that are relatively strong in their group tend to establish strong and sustained bonds with, and commitment to, their local suppliers. This perhaps reflects the fact that their relatively independent position in their MNE group allows them to seek a long-term commitment with a network of collaborators.

SCIENTIFIC LINKS WITH LOCAL INSTITUTIONS

A clear theme of much recent analysis is that subsidiaries of MNEs play an interactive role in the creative activity of the overall group. Thus, a global-competitive MNE is likely to have a pervasive dominant technological trajectory (Pearce, 1995) which will influence the evolution of the operations of each of its subsidiaries (Jaffe, Trajtenberg and Henderson, 1993). However, visionary firms should not only rely on their own scientific expertise in the process of technology-making. The complexity of today's competitive environment requires much more flexibility in the organization of the group.

Thus, individual subsidiaries should scan the technological resources beyond the boundaries of their group in order to implement their responsibilities in a global-innovation strategy (Pearce and Papanastassiou, 1996a) as competitively as possible in their own market area. It is evident that these subsidiaries, alongside their integration into the wider operations of the MNE, will interact significantly with other elements of the scientific community in the host countries. As has been observed elsewhere (Papanastassiou, 1995, pp. 82–7), an effective interdependence between an MNE subsidiary's technological work and host-country institutions may have sustained benefits for both which go beyond the solution to short-term problems. Thus, where an MNE subsidiary moves its R&D role forward from adaptation of existing products to the more challenging role of product development, local scientific linkages and inputs should expand considerably. Therefore, local scientific inputs assist the subsidiary in undergoing a substantial creative transition (Papanastassiou and Pearce, 1994) in its capabilities and ambitions.

It is however also likely that in many cases the local scientific institutions involved may benefit considerably from such links in terms of substantial evolution of their own scope and capacities (Pearce, 1989). Work by Feldman (1994) shows how such links with universities not only expand the technological trajectories of firms, but also have positive spillover effects on the scientific community, and consequently on the industrial development of the country or region where this type of collaboration is performed.

Empirical Evidence

Firms were asked to evaluate their scientific links with four types of institutions: universities, independent research laboratories, industry research laboratories, and 'other firms' (Behrman and Fischer, 1980; Nelson, 1988; Westney, 1990; Howells 1990a; Pearce and Singh, 1992; Peters, 1994).

On average, scientific links (see Table 4.4) seem to be rather weak, indicating overall that either the host countries do not possess competent scientific resources (which contradicts previous findings), or firms' operations do not yet accommodate a deeper use of the local scientific ability (Osborn and Baughn, 1987; Howells 1990a,b; Häusler, Hahn and Lütz, 1994). Universities seem to be the favourite and most regular scientific partner, while 'other firms' follow. So, firms collaborate with those that better fit their needs, either in research or in development. Independent research laboratories are the least popular choice, probably because they can be of high cost and occasionally unreliable.

Therefore, although collaborations with local universities were quite widespread, with 59.3 per cent of respondents reporting that they had such links, they rarely seem to be particularly intensive, with only 14.4

Table 4.4 MNE subsidiaries' evaluation of their collaborative research with local institutions

Industry	Research collaboration (average response[1])			
	Universities	Independent research laboratories	Industry research laboratories	Other Firms
Food and drink	2.00	1.63	1.22	1.38
Industrial and agricultural chemicals	1.86	1.47	1.61	1.84
Pharmaceuticals and consumer chemicals	1.88	1.50	1.20	1.13
Electronics and electrical appliances[2]	1.44	1.05	1.21	1.48
Mechanical engineering	1.67	1.44	1.63	1.17
Metal manufacture and products	1.50	1.25	1.50	1.25
Petroleum	1.40	1.25	1.50	1.25
Automobiles (incl. components)	1.86	1.18	1.36	1.27
Other manufacturing[3]	1.93	1.90	1.69	1.62
Total	1.74	1.37	1.40	1.45
Home country				
USA	1.81	1.41	1.43	1.50
Japan	1.42	1.17	1.21	1.33
Europe[4]	1.73	1.42	1.44	1.39
Total[5]	1.74	1.37	1.40	1.45
Host country				
UK	1.69	1.34	1.40	1.54
Other Europe[6]	1.84	1.44	1.39	1.25
Total	1.74	1.37	1.40	1.45

Notes:
[1] Respondents were asked to evaluate each type of collaboration as 'extensive', 'moderate' or 'non-existent'. The average response was then calculated by allocating responses of 'extensive' the value of 3, 'moderate' the value of 2 and 'non-existent' the value of 1.
[2] Includes computers and telecommunications.
[3] Includes building materials, instruments, rubber, miscellaneous.
[4] Covers subsidiaries of European MNEs in countries other than the home country.
[5] Includes subsidiaries of Canadian MNEs.
[6] Covers subsidiaries in Belgium, Greece and Portugal.

per cent of respondents rating such collaborations as 'extensive'. In the case of collaborations with independent research laboratories, only 3.7 per cent of respondents reported that such links were 'extensive', whilst 66.7 per cent had established no such research connections. Only 3.7 per cent of respondents considered collaborations with industry laboratories to be 'extensive', and 63.9 per cent omitted them. Research collaborations with other firms were described as 'extensive' by only 6.8 per cent of respondents, and only a further 31.1 per cent implemented them to a more moderate degree (Chesnais, 1986; Harrigan, 1987; Von Hippel, 1987; Jorde and Teece, 1989; Hagedoorn and Schakenraad, 1991; Hagedoorn, 1993; Freeman and Hagedoorn, 1994).

We would expect that collaboration with other firms would be on basic research or, less likely, on development projects that will not result in competitive friction. Research in universities will be mainly basic. Independent research laboratories could do quality assessment or elements of basic research, and finally industry research laboratories would be expected to be closer to development than basic research.

Japanese companies are the least likely to have developed links with the local scientific community, while US firms have the strongest commitment to such collaborations.

Two alternative sets of regressions were run using the degree of collaboration with each of the four types of scientific institution as dependent variables. The first set of regressions used precisely the same set of independent variables as reported in Table 4.3 and described in the previous section. As an alternative, a second set of regressions replaced the sources of technology amongst the independent variables with indicators of the role played by an R&D laboratory in those cases where the subsidiary possessed one (see Papanastassiou and Pearce, 1996a, p. 213). This reflects the suggestion (Papanastassiou and Pearce, 1997a) that where collaborations with host-country scientific institutions occur, they are most likely to be articulated through an R&D unit of the MNE. Indeed, one reason why the results already reported here may understate the extent of these scientific collaborations is that some of them may be implemented through 'stand-alone' laboratories that are not part of production subsidiaries and, therefore, are not detected in this survey (Pearce and Singh, 1992; Papanastassiou and Pearce, 1997b).

The first of the three laboratory roles used as an independent variable (see Papanastassiou, 1995, pp. 177–80) was defined as 'adaptation of the product or production process' (ADAPT). The second then represents an increase in ambition in terms of support for producing operations, being defined as helping in the 'development of a new product' (DEVEL). The last laboratory role, however, turns the focus away from immediate production operations and instead emphasises 'provision of scientific knowledge to a broader research project organized by

Table 4.5 Regressions with links with host-country scientific institutions as dependent variables

	Universities	Independent research laboratories	Industry research laboratories	Other firms
Intercept	1.1075	1.3131	0.9772	2.9509***
	(1.46)	(1.62)	(1.55)	(3.98)
Mechanical engineering	0.6754	0.3985	0.3520	−0.3654
	(1.62)	(0.89)	(0.89)	(−0.52)
Electronics and electrical appliances	0.3130	−0.1851	−0.1554	−0.0780
	(0.87)	(−0.48)	(−0.51)	(−0.24)
Food and drink	0.4302	−0.1068	−0.5233	−0.1850
	(1.02)	(−0.25)	(−1.57)	(−0.51)
Automobiles	0.0804	−0.2277	0.0516	−0.6894**
	(0.20)	(−0.52)	(0.19)	(−2.21)
Industrial and agricultural chemicals	−0.3068	−0.4309	0.0927	0.2159
	(−1.06)	(−1.37)	(0.42)	(0.89)
Pharmaceuticals and consumer chemicals	0.1607	−0.4516	−0.3412	−0.4964
	(0.42)	(−1.15)	(−1.12)	(−1.44)
Metal manufacture and products	−1.0336*	0.1596	0.8370**	−0.3937
	(−1.92)	(0.27)	(2.10)	(−0.83)
Petroleum	−0.1022	−0.5580	−0.0550	−0.3342
	(−0.19)	(−0.86)	(−0.13)	(−0.74)
UK	0.1297	0.0574	−0.1241	−0.3174
	(0.54)	(0.23)	(−0.58)	(−1.24)
USA	−0.2765	−0.2930	0.0313	0.2712
	(−1.24)	(−1.17)	(0.18)	(1.28)
Japan	−0.5819	−0.6868	−0.1589	0.4622
	(−1.45)	(−1.53)	(−0.58)	(1.56)
SALES	0.0007***	0.0003	0.0005*	0.0002
	(3.00)	(1.21)	(1.97)	(0.88)
RELSIZE	−0.0208***	−0.0003	0.0012	−0.0133
	(−2.92)	(−0.04)	(0.18)	(−1.66)
EXPRAT	0.0024	−0.0064	−0.0036	−0.0045
	(0.68)	(−1.64)	(−1.26)	(−1.30)
INTRAEXP	−0.0073**	0.0020	0.0002	−0.0003
	(−2.17)	(0.55)	(0.08)	(−0.12)
INTEREXP	0.0039	0.0054*	0.0011	0.0003
	(1.39)	(1.90)	(0.54)	(0.15)
ADAPT	−0.0657	0.0995		
	(−0.46)	(0.63)		
DEVEL	0.2098	0.1318		
	(1.12)	(0.61)		
GROUPRAD	0.2331*	0.0069		
	(1.77)	(0.05)		
IMPTECH			0.0518	−0.4843***
			(0.37)	(−2.71)
HOSTTECH			0.0672	0.1236
			(0.67)	(1.08)
SUBRAD			0.2129**	−0.0711
			(2.06)	(−0.60)
R^2	0.5728	0.4127	0.3563	0.4643
F	2.28**	1.16	1.36	1.91**
n	55	54	70	65

Notes:
*** significant at 1 per cent
** significant at 5 per cent
* significant at 10 per cent
Figures in brackets are t statistics.

the MNE group' (GROUPRAD). Table 4.5 reproduces the regressions that provided the most relevant information about factors influencing the prevalence of the various scientific links.

The first dependent variable is 'links with universities'. We would expect a positive relationship with SALES, since larger subsidiaries will be able to finance this type of research, which, as we have already assumed, will be either basic or ambitious development. A positive relationship with RELSIZE would also be expected, as a subsidiary's position in the group is likely to determine its ability to get permission to pursue links that can support these types of R&D, and therefore its own independent position. We would expect a positive relationship with DEVEL and GROUPRAD because of the types of knowledge likely to be pursued through links with universities. Similarly, of the sources of technology used by subsidiaries, SUBRAD (its own R&D) is most likely to generate university links.

The results on industry composition showed that food and drink was positively signed (though not significant), which provides some evidence that this industry is more scientifically involved than it used to be, as consumer tastes and different kinds of regulations turn food research into a very sophisticated activity. Metal manufacturing is negatively signed, which implies that this sector has less need for university links than the omitted one. There is also a strong positive result with SALES, which implies that subsidiaries that want to undertake scientific cooperation with universities can do it as long as they have the resources to finance it themselves. RELSIZE, however, was strongly negative, contrary to what we would expect. This is, however, still in line with a previous argument (Papanastassiou, 1995) that relatively smaller subsidiaries seek scientific support from the host-country technological base in order to start the move towards technological independence as a basis for improving their position. Therefore, this negative result can now be seen as an extension of the view that relatively small subsidiaries have stronger university links, as they need access to reliable and experienced scientists that will enable them to overcome their problems and build a stronger individualized production base.

The positive relationship on SALES and the negative relationship on RELSIZE indicates that a subsidiary of a given absolute size (SALES) is more likely to have university links the larger its overall MNE group and therefore the smaller its own RELSIZE. Thus, the larger an MNE group worldwide, the more likely that a subsidiary of a particular size will feel vulnerable and pursue independence in this way, and/or the more likely the group will be prepared to allow subsidiaries to develop this type of research collaboration. In turn, it can then be said that such university links are more likely the larger is both the subsidiary itself and the MNE group of which it is part.

Also, INTRAEXP is negatively related with university links (significant at 5 per cent). This indicates that such collaborations are likely to emerge where products are developed that are basically focused on individual 'arm's-length' export markets of the subsidiaries in question, and that these subsidiaries are therefore more likely to have a world product mandate or regional product mandate rather than being rationalized product subsidiaries. Finally, GROUPRAD is positively significant at 10 per cent, which means that MNE laboratories and universities are cooperating on pre-competitive (basic) research, though (in the unreported, alternative equation) SUBRAD was not significant.

In addition, the two negative results for the USA and Japan, although not quite significant, again point out the differences between European subsidiaries and the other two groups. The local-market orientation of European subsidiaries (Papanastassiou, 1995) suggests it may be that the knowledge they seek from universities is not ultimately to support their own work, but to add to new research results available to the group (that is, paralleling the positive result for GROUPRAD).

In the second regression, the dependent variable is links with 'independent research laboratories'. Here, the only significant result is that of INTEREXP (positive at 10 per cent), which may mean that these laboratories are often employed to do a quality-assessment job, especially where the subsidiaries supply the intermediate products in 'arm's-length' markets and need quality reassurance to provide to such independent customers.

In the third regression, industry research laboratories were found to be positively related with metal manufacture, which probably reflects that this industry is more oriented to development or adaptation than other manufacturing. There is also a positive result with SALES, as large subsidiaries can choose their technological partners according to the objectives they have at the time. Another explanation is that, although sales tells us about the likely solvency of a subsidiary, it is relative size that informs us about the role it plays in the group. Therefore, a positive relationship between scientific links and sales not only tells us about the quality and range of research undertaken, but also indicates the fact that these subsidiaries have to finance their research individually (especially the more development-oriented work in these industry laboratories), and that resources from the group are not so readily available. The result for SUBRAD showed a strong positive relationship. This probably means that the results that are produced initially from the in-house laboratory (SUBRAD) are then put through a more stringent market-development test in the industry research laboratories, which have broader local experience of aspects of commercial application of technology.

In the final regression, where the dependent variable is 'collaborative R&D with other firms', we see that IMPTECH is negatively related, indicating that such collaboration is being promoted by more independent and technologically mature subsidiaries that can both narrow down their individual research aims and protect the wider group technology in such cooperation. However, the insignificance of SUBRAD suggests that subsidiaries that have this link are unlikely to be doing research themselves, but are still developing a move towards technological independence (IMPTECH is negative as seen, and HOSTECH is positive though not significant). Thus, this research link with local firms may be a quite high-risk strategy by subsidiaries lacking the size (SALES is insignificant) and group position (RELSIZE is almost significantly negative) to fund their own R&D in an attempt to break out of a vicious circle (a weak group situation, resulting in no R&D and an even more dependent group position). If strategic alliances belong in this category, it is obvious that the stronger technological parts of the group would participate in such alliances in order to be more successful.

CONCLUSIONS

This chapter has explored details of one aspect of the technological interdependency that help to define the strategic position of subsidiaries in the contemporary MNE. Overall, it may be suggested (Pearce and Papanastassiou, 1996b) that the role played by an individual subsidiary reflects the balance of its position in two technological communities or networks, that of its MNE-group and that of its host country. The more a subsidiary can individualize its technological competencies through strong collaborative arrangements in the local economy, the more it can assert a position of technological interdependency, rather than dependence, in the MNE group (Papanastassiou and Pearce, 1996b).

The first area of host-country technological cooperation investigated is that with local suppliers. One possibility is that MNE subsidiaries simply provide local input suppliers with precise details of the products (and/or their production processes) to be provided. This may reflect the subsidiary itself being in a technologically dependent position (within the MNE network), and thus needing inputs to precise quality standards in order to fulfil its own externally-determined position in group-level supply programmes. The evidence does suggest that where subsidiaries use established group technology, they do need to pass this type of information to their local input suppliers.

On the other hand, where MNE subsidiaries seek to achieve a more individualized and creative position in their group through product development, they are likely to involve local suppliers in this process in a more proactive way. Thus, subsidiaries that use their own in-house R&D as part of their own product development activity also pass details of the new products and processes to local suppliers, who are then likely to be creatively involved in the subsidiary's individualization efforts. This may give the local supplier the chance to assert a high-value-added position in the subsidiary's development that itself aims to achieve a strong and distinctive role in its group. In this regard, it is interesting to recall that the more significant a subsidiary is in its group, the more likely it is to provide wider types of advice (techniques and skills) to suppliers. This may achieve cohesion of key practices between the subsidiary and the supplier which enables them to share in mutually-supportive long-term progress, including collaborative creative activity.

A second type of host-country collaboration, through research association with local scientific institutions, does not yet seem to be decisively established as a dominant practice. Nevertheless, suggestions of its likely position in the technological progress of MNE subsidiaries, and also of their overall group, do seem to be emerging. Associations with universities are, so far, the most pervasive. Here, it is the generation of new knowledge as part of group-level programmes (of mainly pre-competitive work to regenerate the company's core technology) that emerges as the prevalent motive. However, use of these university collaborations to reinforce and individualize a subsidiary's own sources of competitiveness can also be observed. Thus, there is some suggestion that association with universities is also related to the presence in subsidiaries' laboratories of the provision of support for product development. Also, subsidiaries that rely extensively on their own R&D as a source of technology also involve themselves in collaborations with host-country industry laboratories, probably to help with the effective application of new knowledge to local commercial conditions.

The contribution of MNE subsidiaries to host countries is seen as potentially taking a variety of forms. If it is to be of a high-value-added nature, the subsidiary needs to embody locally-derived individualized competencies that integrate it proactively with the long-term development of the group, rather than subject it to dependence on creativity that is defined by skills and motivations that emerge elsewhere. The successful and beneficial interdependency with group-level technological progress can only be achieved through an equally committed and creative interdependence of subsidiaries with host-county suppliers and scientific institutions as analysed here.

5 An Evolutionary Analysis of Subsidiary Innovation and 'Reverse' Transfer in Multinational Companies

Mo Yamin

INTRODUCTION

This chapter is intended as a contribution to the understanding of the role of subsidiaries in the development of technological capability in the multinational enterprise (MNE). The analysis is evolutionary in that technological development and innovation are viewed as largely incremental and localized processes. From this position, it is argued that autonomous innovative activities by subsidiaries, even though of necessity largely oriented towards the domestic markets of particular host countries, nevertheless constitute major building blocks in the technological development of the MNE as a whole.

Independent innovative activity by subsidiaries generates a rather differentiated population of new products and processes within the MNE. From the perspective of the parent, it is important whether a subsidiary's innovative efforts have wider implications for the group, as this sort of cross-unit applicability provides a potential for significant economies of scope in product development for the MNE as a whole. In particular, one mechanism by which subsidiary-level innovative activities may be an input to the development of MNE-wide technological competence is through the transfer of innovation from a particular subsidiary to the parent itself. In evolutionary parlance, such 'reverse' transfer may represent a selection process through which some subsidiaries' innovations are 'elevated' to a higher corporate level. Although the parent entity is likely to be the main instigator or driver of reverse transfer, it is constrained by certain characteristics of the subsidiary that generates the innovation. In particular, it is argued that how the subsidiary is formed – whether through a 'greenfield' (or *de novo*) entry or through the acquisition of an existing entity in the host country – has significant implications both for a subsidiary's innovation activity and for the reverse transfer of any innovations generated by it.

The chapter is divided into five sections. The first eleborates on the importance of subsidiary innovations in MNEs. The second examines the formation of a subsidiary as an example of imperfect organizational replication, and suggests that the subsequent development of a subsidiary's capabilities reflects the dual influences of environmental adaptation and organizational path-dependency. The third section compares acquired and *de novo* subsidiaries from this perspective, and offers a number of propositons relating to subsidiary innovations and reverse transfer that seem to be implied by this comparison. The fourth section uses data relating to UK-owned affiliates in the US to test the resulting propositions. The final section highlights some implications of the findings.

SUBSIDIARY INNOVATIONS AND THE DEVELOPMENT OF TECHNOLOGICAL CAPABILITY IN MNEs

The evolutionary perspective views innovation as an incremental, cumulative and path-dependent process (Nelson and Winter, 1982; Pavitt, 1987). Technological change is seen as both organizationally and locationally differentiated. In recent years, a number of authors have applied this perspective to the analysis of the multinational corporation (Cantwell, 1989; Kogut and Zander, 1993; Cantwell, 1995). One contribution of the evolutionary perspective is to provide a coherent explanation of country variations in the extent and pattern of international involvement – that is, the relative importance of exports, licensing and foreign direct investment (FDI).

Extensive previous research has shown that the pattern of corporate internationalization is related to types of firm-specific assets or advantages. However, with the notable exception of Dunning's eclectic theory, little was offered to explain why such assets should vary systematically amongst firms of different nationalities. However, from an evolutionary standpoint such variation is almost inevitable. Two related points are stressed. First, firms follow a differentiated path to learning even when their fields of research are similar. Second, the nature of their tacit knowledge is path-dependent and, in particular, reflects their starting points in nationally differentiated types of expertise. For example, Italy has a surprisingly low share of world direct investment given the level of its wealth and general economic performance. One partial explanation for this may be that direct investment is impeded by the specific character of the innovation process in Italy. Thus, Kogut and Zander (1993, p. 626) point to the 'difficulty in transferring knowledge grounded in the close ties within industrial and regional networks'.

A similar sort of explanation may apply to the low (though rapidly rising) degree of internationalization amongst Japanese firms. For example,

Hedlund (1994), amongst others, argued that the organizational peculiarities of Japanese firms create a preference for exporting products rather than skills, and that they have resorted to FDI (as a vehicle for exporting skills) only when forced to do so by protectionist measures. The proposition suggested by Kogut and Zander that 'the characteristics of social knowledge, that is how it is known to groups of people, influences the ability to transfer technology and hence direct investment flows', implies that national specificities can help or hinder particular modes of internationalization.

The notion that technological and innovative capabilities of firms have a strong national 'imprint' suggests that the MNE cannot easily be treated as a single unit of analysis as, by definition, it straddles a number of distinct national domains of innovation and technological activity. Some authors have argued that for most MNEs the 'home'-country technology is dominant (Patel and Pavitt, 1991) and have thus downplayed the practical significance of subsidiary innovative activities. Such a view, however, runs counter to perhaps the strongest conclusion emerging from recent studies concerned with organizational issues within MNEs: that innovative capabilities are dispersed in such companies and that 'subsidiaries' are often in control of strategic assets.

Briefly, two main strands in this literature can be identified, both of which lend direct, or at least implicit, support to the notion of subsidiary innovative autonomy. Firstly, a number of studies have investigated the MNE as an evolving network (Ghoshal and Bartlett, 1990; De Meyer, 1992; Andersson and Forsgren, 1996; Andersson and Pahlberg, 1997). The common theme of these studies is that the large multinational firm is best viewed as a federative organization (rather than a unitary one), in which different units are embedded in a number of intersecting internal and external networks. Andersson and Pahlberg (1997) put particular emphasis on the concept of subsidiary embeddedness in external networks of customers, suppliers and other stakeholders, and on the importance of such embeddedness to subsidiary innovation. This adds confirmation to broader innovation studies that have demonstrated the importance of 'learning by interacting' (Von Hippel, 1988; Lundvall, 1988; Malerba, 1992). The main contribution of studies by Andersson and Pahlberg (1997) and Andersson and Forsgren (1996) is to point out that such embeddedness significantly reduces the parent's control over the subsidiary, while enhancing the ability of the subsidiaries to exert influence on the direction of the MNE's strategy.

The second strand of literature applies a resource-dependency framework to explore the evolution of different roles and strategies at the subsidiary level (for example, Birkinshaw and Morrison, 1995; Birkinshaw, 1996; Taggart, 1996, 1997). An important finding is that subsidiary roles should not be viewed as hierarchically 'assigned' from the centre. Rather, subsidiary roles are often asserted or earned through the entrepreneurial activities of the subsidiary itself. Thus, even in relatively weak or peripheral subsidiaries, significant and successful initiatives by the subsidiary may confront the headquarters with a *fait accompli* and compel it to acquiesce with changing subsidiary roles (Birkinshaw and Ridderstrale, 1996).

Overall, therefore, there is broad convergence towards regarding subsidiaries as centres of innovative activity within MNEs. There is also evidence that much of this innovative activity is oriented towards the economies of the host country of the subsidiary (Dunning and Nurala, 1994; Pearce, 1994; Papanastassiou and Pearce, 1996; and Ghoshal and Bartlett, 1988) *and* that top decision-makers in the MNE, to a degree, encourage such a local orientation on the part of subsidiaries. Thus, Leung and Tan (1993) report that most top decision-makers within MNEs agreed that 'the *primary* role of . . . overseas units is to find out and take advantage of opportunities within the countries in which they operate' (Table 1, p. 458, emphasis added).

On the other hand, the MNE is increasingly regarded as an institution for international technology-creation and innovation rather than primarily for the international diffusion or transfer of (home-country) technologies (Cantwell, 1995; Dunning, 1993). Is there a contradiction between international creation of technology and innovation at the level of the MNE on the one hand, and the localized orientation of innovative activities by subsidiaries on the other? Only if 'international technology development' is to be seen in terms of the MNE's headquarters creating a 'unique vision' (Pearce, 1994) and then 'assigning' roles and resources to subsidiaries in order to realise the vision.

However, this is *not* how international technology-creation typically comes about. As Pearce (1994) has pointed out, although the parent unit ultimately determines the overall direction or trajectory of the MNE's technological development, it can only do so within the context of 'independent evolutionary capacities and potential' of its major subsidiaries. Its role is mainly to 'juggle and balance separately determined capacities' (*ibid.*). It is the very diversity implied by 'separately determined capabilities' that creates a *potential* for significant scope-economies of learning and innovation at the level of the MNE as a whole. In its 'juggling and balancing' the MNE is, presumably, motivated primarily by maximizing the realization of this potential (Ghoshal and Bartlett, 1988; Bartlett and Ghoshal, 1990).

Thus, innovative activities of subsidiaries must be considered as a *main* building block for innovative performance for the MNE as a whole. In a related vein, Dunning (1993, 1996) has argued that the competitive advantage of MNEs are increasingly derived not only from the 'diamonds' of their home base (Porter, 1990), but also from the 'diamonds' of other countries, particularly those with which the home-country firms have the most dealings by way of trade, FDI and non-equity cooperative ventures (Dunning, 1996, p. 3). Such a view, indirectly, acknowledges the importance of subsidiaries' locally-oriented innovative activities. After all, the influences of 'foreign diamonds' are mostly felt by the subsidiaries rather than by the parent. The implication is, therefore, that whatever the precise mechanism by which MNEs' technological capabilities are internationalized, it must be a 'bottom-up' rather than a 'top-down' process.[1]

DIRECT FOREIGN INVESTMENT AS ORGANIZATIONAL REPLICATION: SUBSIDIARY ADAPTATION AND INNOVATION

As Nelson and Winter (1982, pp. 188–21) have pointed out, organizational growth can take the form of replication, whereby the organization enacts existing routines and standard operating procedures in a new productive entity. In particular, they note that

> the replication assumption in evolutionary models is intended primarily to reflect the advantages that favour a going concern to do more of the *same* as contrasted with the difficulties that it would encounter in doing something else. (p. 119, emphasis added)

Viewed from the perspective of the new entity, 'the existing routines serve as a template' for it to copy. It seems highly plausible to argue that the establishment of foreign subsidiaries is a similar process of replication to that suggested by Nelson and Winter (1982). Early empirical studies have noted the similarities between subsidiaries and headquarters and utilized terms such as the 'mirror effect' (Brooke and Remmers, 1978) and 'miniature replicas' (White and Poynter, 1984) to describe this similarity. Organizational affinity between the parent and the subsidiary is particularly helpful in the process of technology and knowledge transfer to the young subsidiary.

Although Nelson and Winter consider 'perfect' replication to be a theoretical possibility, they nevertheless view the 'feasibility of close (let alone perfect) replication as being quite problematic' (p. 118). Thus, replication is practically always partial. Organizational routines, it might be said, do not 'travel' very well. Significantly, Nelson and Winter note that routines 'have their clearest relevance at the establishment level' and that 'the memory of an organisation that comprises many *widely separated establishments* exists mainly in the establishments' (p. 97, emphasis added). The parallel between the parent and other units within an MNE is transparent.

The incomplete or imperfect nature of organizational replication from the parent to the subsidiary is in fact beneficial to the latter. Because subsidiaries typically inherit an incomplete 'template', they are forced to engage in a process of search for market and other knowledge about the local environment; knowledge which, due to its often tacit, localized and experiential nature, will not be transparent to the parent. Incomplete replication forces the subsidiary to become more self-reliant and more adaptable to the local environment. Interestingly, it has been suggested that Japanese FDI represents a higher degree of replication compared to Western FDI; the former often literally consists of 'transplants', that is, full-scale transfers of an identical copy from the Japanese to a foreign environment. There is little 'evocation of adaptation to the local circumstances that characterizes much of Western FDI' (Hedlund, 1994, p. 80).[2]

The need for adaptation to local circumstances is widely recognized, for example, in the marketing literature, but recently a number of contributions from the perspective of institutionalization theory (Westney, 1993; Rosenweig and Singh, 1991) have provided a deeper analytical base for adaptation. Institutionalization theory holds to the premise that organizations are affected by 'common understandings of what is appropriate and, fundamentally, meaningful behaviour' (Rosenweig and Singh, 1991, p. 342). As a result, organizational change is partly a function of efficiency-seeking, but it is also a product of *adaptation* to the institutional environment, defined as a 'set of highly established and culturally sanctioned action patterns and expectations'. Applied to the MNE, the implication is that to survive and prosper the subsidiaries of a multinational firm tend to 'take on the characteristics of other organizations in the local environment' and are under pressure to adapt their products to local preferences. More broadly, they also tend to reflect the 'values, norms and "locally accepted practices" of the societies in which they operate' (*ibid.*, p. 345).

Can we expect that isomorphic adaptation by the subsidiary evolves into innovative capabilities for the latter? There seem to be two schools of thought on this issue. On the one hand, isomorphic adaptation does entail the development of additional capabilities for the subsidiary; its product, process and administrative 'repertoires' are all likely to expand significantly. It may also establish new avenues for attracting additional resources as it becomes an 'insider' in various information, finance and science and technology-oriented networks. Hence, it becomes even less reliant on the rest of the MNE and more able to exert autonomy. As we have already seen, the network approach to subsidiary innovation has shown that relationships with external partners are particularly important in the technological development of the subsidiary.

On the other hand, it may be that the subsidiary's socialization and acculturation to the host environment, while enhancing its average performance, makes it less inclined or capable to act in 'deviant' ways that innovation may demand (March, 1991; Levinthal, 1991) This desire to adapt tends to increase the perceived risk associated with innovation since an innovation may cause 'isomorphic misalignment'. More generally, adaptive learning by the subsidiary may create a competency trap; as the organization becomes better at performing current activities, it becomes less inclined to experiment with new ones (Levinthal and March, 1993).

It seems reasonable to suggest, however, that, for foreign subsidiaries, the danger that isomorphic adaptation leads to inertia rather than to innovation is somewhat reduced. Like any other organization, the development of a subsidiary's capabilities is likely to be path-dependent. But a subsidiary's path-dependency reflects two, usually competing, pressures; on the one hand there is the pressure for local isomorphism, but on the other there is also a pressure for organizational consistency with the rest of the MNE (Rosenweig and Singh, 1991). This diversity of perspectives may thus cancel out inertial tendencies that may flow from local adaptation.

Emerging evidence indicates that the initial replicated or inherited organizational processes and technological capabilities have a remarkably durable influence on the subsequent development of the subsidiary. Because subsidiary capabilities grow incrementally, it takes a long time for the influence of initial capabilities inherited from the parent to disappear. As a result, as Pearce (1994) has pointed out, the key technology management skill for innovative subsidiaries is to:

> understand and implement its position within two distinct communities, with its independence perhaps deriving from its ability to benefit from a unique intermeshing of the potentials of these two sources of inputs. The first of these communities is the MNE itself, the second is the science base of the host country. (p. 2)

DIRECT FOREIGN INVESTMENT THROUGH ACQUISITION VERSUS *DE NOVO* ENTRY

We believe that the analysis of the previous section applies to all subsidiaries. In other words, all subsidiaries are faced simultaneously by pressures to adapt to their local environment and to the MNE of which they are a part. Clearly, however, the force of these competing pressures is weighted differently depending on whether the subsidiary is *de novo* or acquired.

To begin with, organizational replication is clearly a much more likely and natural process when a firm establishes a *de novo* or 'greenfield' subsidiary compared to when foreign market entry is through the acquisition of an already existing enterprise. However, organizational replication is not necessarily absent in such cases; depending on what form of integration the parent chooses for incorporating the acquired entity, different degrees of organizational replication are possible. Haspeslagh and Jemison (1991) have identified three common forms of post-acquisition integration: *preservation*, *symbiosis* and *absorption*. 'Preservation' integration occurs when the acquired company is treated as a stand-alone and autonomous organization with little attempt to impose the parent's organizational structures and management styles on the subsidiary. 'Absorption' integration, on the other hand, is where the parent attempts to impose its own organizational structure and management styles on the subsidiary. And in the case of 'symbiosis' integration, the aim is to achieve a balance between preserving the organizational characteristics of the acquired company while transferring strategic capabilities between the two organizations.

From the parent's point of view, particularly if the acquired subsidiary is in an important market and has significant innovative capability, symbiotic integration would seem to be preferred to either preservation or absorption. A policy of absorption integration, assuming that the MNE has the ability to implement it, would seem inappropriate. As Pisano (1991, p. 248) has argued, this type of acquisition is a 'dangerous policy' in that it is difficult to 'guarantee that the key asset of the [acquired] company, the people, will stay'. On the other hand, a policy of preservation integration would possibly forgo any opportunity for gaining economies of scope across the company as a whole.

The preferences of the MNE notwithstanding, it seems likely that the parent will find it more difficult to establish a smooth working relationship with an acquired subsidiary compared to a greenfield subsidiary. A number of studies have pointed out the difficulties involved in the incorporation of acquired companies into multinationals (Jemison and Sitkin, 1986; Rosenweig and Singh, 1991; Olie, 1994). These difficulties are likely to be magnified since, as Andersson and Forsgren (1996) have firmly illustrated, the possibilities of subsidiary control by headquarters are significantly circumscribed by the extent to which subsidiaries are embedded in local networks. An acquired subsidiary is, by definition, an ongoing concern that has established a number of linkages with businesses and other interaction partners in its domestic market. At the same time, it is not technologically dependent on the parent or sister organization to the same extent as a *de novo* subsidiary would be.

Its position in local networks and its relative technological independence from the parent make the acquired subsidiary well-equipped to resist pressures for consistency with the rest of the MNE group. Furthermore, the resulting conflict may obstruct the development of 'normative integration' as the coordination mechanism linking the subsidiary and the parent. Thus, an acquired subsidiary is more likely to become an 'autonomous baron' (Prahalad and Doz, 1987) or be very 'militant' (Taggart, 1997) compared to *de novo* subsidiaries.

Kogut (1990) has warned that innovative activities by the subsidiary may have negative consequences for the MNE as a whole:

> much like a Byzantine Empire, a multinational corporation may slowly deteriorate by the entropy stemming from the need of the country subsidiaries to adapt to, and draw resources from the local environment . . . The drawback is that local entrepreneurship not only deflects managerial attention from corporate-wide products, but also the evolution of country subsidiaries' capabilities will deter an internationally co-ordinated network. (p. 60)

This scenario, however, again assumes that forces for adaptation and isomorphism with the local environment are much stronger than the forces for consistency with the rest of the MNE. In other words, 'entropy' is only likely, if at all, with acquired subsidiaries.

Comparing greenfield and acquired subsidiaries with respect to innovations suggests that, other things being equal, the latter are more likely to be innovative. By definition, an acquired subsidiary has already obtained a degree of isomorphic adaptation to its environment, and is more likely to develop market-related innovative capabilities. A greenfield subsidiary on the other hand, as already noted, would need to first go through a process of isomorphic adaptation.

With regard to the reverse transfer of innovations, the perspectives of the parent organization and subsidiary are likely to be different. The forces behind product innovations are, in the main, of a local character. From the point of view of the subsidiary it is more important to nurture local relationships by tailoring innovation to customer needs than to produce less-customized, or more 'standardized' products that may also be of interest to other units within the MNE as a whole. The parent, on the other hand, is more likely to be interested in coordinating innovative efforts across subsidiaries to avoid unnecessary duplications. Thus, from the perspective of the parent, it is important whether any subsidiary's innovative efforts have a wider implication for the group as a whole. As Ghoshal and Bartlett (1988) argue, innovation diffusion from the subsidiary to the parent and sister-affiliates is highly valued by the parent, as it is the mechanism through which the MNE can realize the scope-economies of learning inherent in its geographically dispersed operations.

Given the more organic organizational linkages that exist between the parent and a *de novo* subsidiary, the clash of perspectives is less than would be the case if the subsidiary joined the group through acquisition.

A *de novo* subsidiary is likely to be more amenable to pressure from the centre. Furthermore, such a subsidiary may also have its own reason to follow a strategy of 'influence' – that is, a strategy that would give it the opportunity of affecting overall corporate policy. The 'influence' strategy would require that the subsidiary has resources that the rest of the corporate system needs or values, and therefore implies that the subsidiary may be more inclined to generate 'standard' products or services that other units of the corporate system may also be able to apply in their respective businesses (Andersson and Pahlberg, 1997). In fact, such an 'influence' strategy may be formalized in a 'product-mandate' that the subsidiary may acquire or further develop through its own efforts (Birkinshaw, 1996).

By contrast, an acquired subsidiary may be less inclined to follow an 'influence' strategy. Furthermore, given that its existing capabilities have largely grown in isolation from the parent or sister-affiliates, it may also be less *able* to follow such a strategy. Its preferred strategy may be to seek greater autonomy and to minimize control from the centre.

By way of summarizing the above discussion, we offer the following propositions relating to subsidiary innovations and their subsequent transfer to the parent company.

Proposition I: Greenfield subsidiaries are less likely to be innovative than acquired subsidiaries. However, innovations by greenfield subsidiaries are more likely to be transferred to the parent. In particular, greenfield subsidiaries are more likely to be assigned to, or develop (on their own initiative), product development roles for the MNE as a whole.

Proposition II: The age of the subsidiary (defined as the number of years since the subsidiary was either formed or acquired) is likely to be positively associated with the innovativeness of the subsidiary. In the case of newly-formed subsidiaries, this association is straightforward. In the case of acquired subsidiaries, this association may still hold. This is because its ability to link innovative opportunities in its external network with existing capabilities within the MNE is likely to increase with age.

It is likely that the need for adaptation is dependent on the type of activity undertaken by the subsidiary. In particular, it is reasonable to expect that service activities are subject to greater localization and adaptive demands.

Proposition III: Propositions I and II apply more strongly to service activities than they do to manufacturing activities.

THE DATA AND EMPIRICAL FINDINGS

Most of the data used in this study is based on the questionnaire responses from the chief executive officers of 101 UK firms with at least one US subsidiary.[3] The respondents were asked, amongst a range of other questions, to indicate:

1. how many innovations have *originated* with and have subsequently been *developed and introduced* in the USA by this subsidiary?[4]; and
2. how many of the innovations were subsequently transferred to the UK, or other parts of your organization outside the USA?

Of the 101 respondents, 33 indicated that the subsidiary undertook no innovations.[5] The remaining 68 indicated that the subsidiary had made at least one innovation, and of these 17 had not transferred any innovations to the UK, while the remaining 51 transferred at least one.[6] Respondents were also asked to indicate:

(a) whether the subsidiary was formed through acquisition or was a 'greenfield'?
(b) whether the main activity was manufacturing or services?
(c) the date when the subsidiary was formed or acquired;
(d) whether the subsidiary has a specialist role in product development within the company? (Likert-type scale 5 = strongly agree; 1 = strongly disagree);
(e) the number of foreign subsidiaries in the company.

Utilizing the above responses, we were able to investigate the following questions with respect to subsidiary innovation and reverse transfer:

The Influence of Entry Method on Subsidiary Innovation

As can be seen from Table 5.1, there is some support for the proposition that acquired subsidiaries are likely to be more innovative than greenfield subsidiaries, even though, in the sample, greenfields on average entered more-technology-intensive industries and hence faced a more favourable opportunity for creating innovations.

Significantly, the impact of acquisition is more pronounced for subsidiaries whose main activity was services rather than manufacturing. Overall, therefore, there is some indication that innovation by subsidiaries is related to their ability to adapt to isomorphic pulls from the local market. On the other hand, there is no indication that greenfield subsidiaries are more likely than acquired ones to adopt an 'influence' strategy, and to take on or accept product development mandates within the MNE.

Table 5.1   The influence of entry method on subsidiary innovation

Variable	Mean value for acquired subsidiaries	Mean value for 'greenfield' subsidiaries	Significance of t-value
R&D intensity of US industry the subsidiary entered*	3.9	4.9	5 per cent
Number of subsidiary innovations – in manufacturing	11.8	8.2	not significant
Number of subsidiary innovations – in services	7.5	1.4	4 per cent
Product development role: Likert score	2.9	2.6	not significant

Note: *R&D intensities for US industries are reported in Dunning (1993, Table 11.5).

The Influence of Age on Subsidiary Innovations

Age remains consistently a positive and significant variable in all the equations where the number of *service* innovations is the dependent variable. The 'best' equation, in terms of the overall significance of the equation, is shown in Table 5.2.

On the other hand, age is *never* a significant variable for the equations in which the number of manufacturing innovations is the dependent variable. The 'best' equation is shown in Table 5.3 (note that R&D and product role are not defined for services).

Once again, isomorphic adaptation has more relevance for service activities than for manufacturing activities. The key influence on subsidiary innovation in manufacturing industries is the existence of a product development role. Thus, it would appear that subsidiary innovation in manufacturing subsidiaries takes place in the context of interdependence between the parent and the subsidiary. Even though, as already noted, product mandates are often gained and developed through subsidiary initiatives (Birkinshaw, 1996), they are based on capabilities that are in part inherited from the parent and developed through the subsidiary's interaction with the MNE as a whole (Pearce, 1994).

The number of subsidiaries is a highly significant variable in *both* of the above equations. Although this variable was not explicitly considered in our discussion, its influence is certainly consistent with our line of argument. Basically, the number of subsidiaries captures two interrelated influences.[7] First, the number of subsidiaries captures the 'maturity' of the MNE. It is reasonable to expect that MNEs with a large number

Table 5.2 Equation 1

Dependent variable	AGE	SUBS	Constant	R^2	Adjusted R^2	F stat
INVOSERV	0.340 (2.491)	0.457 (3.282)	−2.710 (−0.817)	0.621	0.587	18.058

Note: The dependent variable is INVOSERV: the number of service innovations. Independent variables are AGE: the length of time since subsidiary was formed or acquired; and SUBS: the number of foreign subsidiaries in the company. The figures in brackets are t-statistics.

Table 5.3 Equation 2

Dependent variable	SUBS	PDROLE	Constant	R^2	Adjusted R^2	F stat
MFCINVO	0.173 (2.760)	4.120 (1.953)	−5.872 (−0.793)	0.228	0.190	6.045

Note: The dependent variable is MFCINVO: the number of manufacturing innovations. Independent variables are SUBS: the number of foreign subsidiaries in the company; and PDROLE: the product development role.
The figures in brackets are t-statistics.

of foreign subsidiaries are more likely to have developed control and coordination systems that rely more on 'normative integration' than on bureaucratic control (Birkinshaw and Morrison, 1995). Secondly, the larger the number of subsidiaries, the easier it may be for a particular subsidiary to assert a degree of autonomy from the parent. Further, the larger the number of subsidiaries, the more thinly 'control-resources' are likely to be spread, and the greater the opportunity cost of concentrating such resources on one subsidiary. Both factors indicate that the degree of multinationality is associated with the degree of autonomy that the subsidiary can enjoy. As a number of scholars have noted (for example, Ghoshal and Bartlett, 1988) subsidiary autonomy does encourage innovation.

What Factors Explain the Absence of Reverse Transfer of Innovations?

We asked respondents where none of the subsidiary's innovations had been transferred to rate the possible reasons shown in Table 5.4 (5 = very important, 1 = not important).

Table 5.4 seems to indicate that the main reason for lack of transfer was the perceived suitability of the innovations to the UK market, rather

Table 5.4   Reasons for non-transfer of subsidiary innovations

Reason for lack of innovation transfer	No. of respondents rating reason as 'very' important
Because, typically, there was no market for the innovation(s) in the UK	11
Because, typically, the introduction of the innovation(s) was not considered commercially attractive for our organization	7
Because of the high degree of organizational complexity involved in such a transfer	1

than organizational complexity involved in any possible transfer.[8] In this respect, it is again noteworthy that the non-transfer ratio (the percentage of innovations that were not transferred) is much higher for service activities compared with manufacturing ones and, in fact, very few service innovations were transferred.

Logit analysis tends to show a somewhat similar situation. In a logit equation, the dependent variable takes binary values. In the present context, the dependent variable takes the value of 1 if any transfers took place and 0 if there were no transfers. The 'best' logit equation, judged by the significance of the chi-squared statistics, involves two variables: product role and entry method. This equation is shown in Table 5.5.

The negative sign of DUMENTRY (which is significant at 3 per cent) indicates that innovations produced by greenfield subsidiaries are more likely to be transferred than innovations produced by acquired subsidiaries. The strong positive impact of PDROLE is logical because the transfer of innovations to the parent is what a specialist product development role is designed to achieve.

IMPLICATIONS FOR FURTHER RESEARCH

As demonstrated, innovation within MNE subsidiaries is an evolutionary process significantly affected by the organizational history and origin of the subsidiary. The study has also revealed strong indications that subsidiary innovations develop incrementally in a continual process of adaptive change by the subsidiary. In particular, service-industry innovations have been shown to be particularly sensitive to the isomorphic pulls from the immediate market environment and, consequently, such innovations appear to be largely non-transferable to other units within the MNE.

All previous studies concerned with the internationalization of tech-

Table 5.5 Equation 3

Dependent variable	PDROLE	DUMENTRY	Constant	Chi-square
BRI	0.955	−2.632	0.464	15.407
	(7.312)	(4.830)	(0.138)	

Note: The dependent variable is BRI: a dichotomous variable taking the value 1 (innovation transferred) or 0 (innovation not transferred). Independent variables are PDROLE: the product development role; and DUMENTRY: a dichotomous variable taking the value 0 (greenfield entry) or 1 (entry by acquisition).
Figures in brackets are Wald statistics.

nological development within the MNE have ignored service activities. This is because these studies have used mainly patent data or R&D expenditures in measuring innovative activity or output. The clear implication for future research is that much greater attention needs to be paid to the service industries in studying innovations within the MNE.

Secondly, our analysis has suggested that international expansion by acquisition may have somewhat dysfunctional consequences for the technological development of the MNE as a whole. This issue also clearly merits further research.

Notes

1. This view of technological development within the MNE is a parallel to new conceptualizations that suggest organizations need to be developed and managed on a principle of '*proliferation and subsequent aggregation* of small independent entrepreneurial units from the bottom up rather than one of *division and devolution* from the top down' (Bartlett and Ghoshal, 1993 emphasis added; see also Hedlund 1994 for a distinction between combination vs division as organizational principles).
2. There is some evidence that Japanese subsidiaries in the UK are significantly less innovative compared to US and European subsidiaries (Pearce, 1994). De Meyer (1993) has suggested that recent growth of foreign R&D by Japanese MNEs may be largely motivated as an antidote to the high degree of organizational replication that has characterized internationalization of Japanese companies. Thus, he notes that Japanese companies have used internationalization of R&D in order to counteract the internal isomorphism which exists in Japanese companies.
3. All UK companies with at least one US subsidiary were sent a questionnaire in June 1995. A full description of the sample and the questionnaire is available as an appendix from the author.
4. The intent of the question is thus to isolate technology 'creation' from mere 'adoption' (see Ghoshal and Bartlett, 1988). Additionally, the focus of the question is on *product* rather than process innovations.
5. If firms had more than one US subsidiary, respondents were asked to provide information on the largest subsidiary.

6. Only two subsidiary innovations were transferred to units outside the UK.
7. It is noteworthy that the number of subsidiaries is not a proxy for size of the MNE. When direct measures of size (sales or total employees) were entered in the above equation, they had a negative and marginally significant influence, but the number of subsidiaries remained highly significant.
8. A number of respondents who had not transferred subsidiary innovations refused to answer this question. A few respondents indicated 'other' reasons, such as legal restrictions in the case of defence-related innovations.

6 On the Duration Dependence of MNE Investment[1]

Ram Mudambi

INTRODUCTION

A number of theoretical studies have investigated factors underlying the location of foreign direct investment (FDI) by multinational enterprises (MNEs) from several perspectives (de Meza, 1979; Buckley and Casson, 1981; Eaton and Grossman, 1986; Dunning, 1988; Collie, 1992; Mudambi, 1995a). The factors underlying the location decision include market size and growth; trade policy, including tariff and non-tariff barriers; exchange rate dynamics; tax considerations; and costs such as the relative cost of borrowing, transport costs and labour costs. The importance of most of these factors has been confirmed in empirical work (Scaperlanda, 1967; Gilman, 1981; Lunn, 1983; Culem, 1988; Ray, 1989; Caves, 1990; Stevens, 1993; Mudambi, 1995b). Dunning (1993) and Caves (1996) provide good surveys of this work.

In the literature, investment location is typically investigated within a partial equilibrium framework under the umbrella of Dunning's (1977) ownership–location–internalization (OLI) paradigm. However, even such partial equilibrium analysis must take into account historically-determined constraints. Typically, the existing location profile of the MNE's operations will be an important factor. This profile will provide important advantages to locating additional investment within known environments, particularly when investment decisions need to be based on short implementation periods (Vismer, 1994). Known environments provide important tangible and intangible advantages (Gresser and Gaskell, 1993; Porcano, 1993).

The measurement of these benefits is a difficult task. However, nearly all such benefits can be traced, directly or indirectly, to experience (Davidson, 1980; Benito and Gripsrud, 1992). It may be argued that experience is a summary measure of the intangible benefits of a known environment. This 'experience' theory implies that a firm with a greater experience of a particular location is more likely to invest there than a firm with less experience.

Portfolio considerations would appear to argue against this theory.

Given that each location represents a given risk structure, increasing investment within a given set of locations increases the firm's overall risk exposure. From the MNEs' perspective, multiple locations can be viewed as an additional avenue of diversification. Bowman (1980) showed that firms with high returns can have low risk. Subsequent contributions to the literature (for example, Bettis and Hall, 1982; Bettis and Mahajan, 1985; Madura, 1992) indicate that this result can be explained by examining the firms' patterns of locational diversification. There is a large literature asserting that the internationalization of business activity can be explained as a portfolio decision by MNEs (Rugman, 1976, 1979; Thompson, 1985; Kim, Hwang and Burgers, 1993).

The experience and portfolio theories seem to offer conflicting predictions regarding the location of additional investment by MNEs. This chapter attempts to reconcile these two theories. It suggests that MNE investment flows are the sum of two independent components, which may be termed systematic and unsystematic. The systematic component is determined by factors comparable across different locations (portfolio factors), whereas the unsystematic component is determined by factors unique to a given location (experience factors). This reconciliation is tested using a cross-sectional data set of MNEs operating in the UK. The empirical results provide strong support for the proposed reconciliation.

These results are of considerable importance to policy-makers in government in general, and to inward investment agencies (IIAs) in particular. They suggest that a successful investment-attraction strategy should incorporate, to the extent possible, both portfolio and experience considerations. In other words, in addition to working on deficiencies in portfolio factors (for example, shortfalls of skilled labour and a poor infrastructure) relative to its effective competitors (see, for example, Kotler, Haider and Rein, 1993), IIAs should spend time nurturing MNEs which have existing investments in the area. This is because experience considerations suggest that they are the firms with the highest probabilities of making new investments in the area.

The results also provide the basis to conjecture that portfolio and experience considerations function independently in determining MNE investment patterns. Portfolio consideration would appear to determine the primary investment pattern, while experience would seem to influence incremental changes. This conjecture must necessarily be tentative, as it is based on the study of MNE investment in a single country. Extension of this methodology to a multi-country data-set would be a useful avenue for further research.

RESEARCH QUESTIONS AND DATA

The basic question concerns the effect of the duration of local activity on the volume of investment. The answer to this question has important implications for IIAs in a world where competition for FDI is becoming increasingly intense. If MNE investment volume is duration-dependent, IIAs would do well to spend more of their resources on maintaining the goodwill of firms which are long-established in their jurisdictions. In contrast, if investment volume is not duration-dependent, location marketers may prefer continually to seek to attract new firms.

Data Collection

Data was obtained in two stages. In the first stage, a list of MNE engineering and engineering-related operations in the West Midlands region of Britain was compiled from business directories. The region was chosen because it has been Britain's most successful region for attracting inward investment, with more than 900 companies investing over £3 billion and employing over 100 000 workers (Griffiths, 1993). After telephone confirmations, a final list of 224 companies with personal contact names was assembled for the purpose of a directed mail survey.

Overall, 85 responses were received to the mail survey (37.9 per cent). Of these, four were found to be national firms mistakenly identified as MNEs and seven were unusable for various other reasons, leaving 74 (33.0 per cent) valid responses for evaluation. The response rate is well within the range expected for an unsolicited mail survey. The survey collected information on MNE investment flows into the UK, the rate of return on corporate liquid funds, and measures of corporate risk.

In the second stage, several international statistics were computed for the host countries of the MNEs in the sample. These statistics were obtained from *International Financial Statistics* published by the International Monetary Fund. In addition, country risk indices were drawn from the capital markets publication *Euromoney*.

Survey responses were cross-checked against company annual reports where possible. A high degree of correspondence between published data and survey responses was found, lending support to the veracity of the survey responses.

The variables assembled for use in this study are described below. The dependent variable is:

INV94 = MNE investment flows into the UK in 1994 (£ million).

The explanatory variables measuring location-specific portfolio factors for the MNE are:

RINF   = Relative inflation rate, home country/host country (UK); average, 1991–94.

ΔEXRT   = Change in exchange rate, 1993–94.

RISK   = Variance of corporate rate of return on capital, 1986–94.

RORFF   = Rate of return on corporate liquid funds (free cash flows as defined by Jensen, 1988), used as a proxy for the opportunity cost of investment funds.

The variables describing firm-specific characteristics are:

EMPL   = Employment in the UK subsidiary

SALES   = Sales of the UK subsidiary (£ million).

DT   = Duration of operations in the UK (years).

GOVTAID   = Government investment supports received by the UK subsidiary (ordinal scale, 1 to 7).

WEXPORT   = Exports as a percentage of the UK subsidiary turnover.

GSALES   = Global sales of the MNE (£ million).

RLOCRSK   = Relative location risk (Home country/host country (UK); *Euromoney* index).

METHODOLOGY

Since the objective is to test investment volume for duration-dependence after accounting for portfolio considerations, it is necessary to purge the investment volume data of the influences of portfolio variables. This is done using ordinary least squares (OLS) regression analysis. This procedure divides the dependent variable into two *additively independent* components, as the OLS residuals have the property of being independent of the regressors.

If, as we suggest, portfolio and experience considerations work concurrently and additively in determining the volume of MNE investment, then two sets of results must be obtained. First, the investment equation must be able to explain a significant portion of the investment volume. Second, the residuals from the regression procedure (which represent the experience component of investment volume) must exhibit duration-dependence; that is, firms with longer tenure should be more likely to invest than firms with shorter tenure.

The first set of results is obtained using regression analysis. Obtaining the second set of results is more involved. Firms which have undertaken experience-induced investment must be identified, and this is done by applying outlier analysis to the residuals from the regression analysis. (The effects of duration are likely to be highly non-linear and so cannot be tested by simply inserting tenure into the investment equation.) Once these firms have been identified, their investment flows must be tested for duration-dependence.

The first part of the analysis, using the OLS estimating methodology, is fairly standard. The base-line estimated equation is:

$$INV94 = f[\text{Portfolio factors}] + v_i \qquad (6.1)$$
$$= f[\text{RINF, }\Delta\text{EXRT, RISK, RORFF}] + v_i$$

While the estimation of equation (6.1) is standard, the residuals utilized in the outlier analysis were generated in a non-standard manner. Since it was necessary to ensure that each firm's investment was explained on the basis of market information external to the firm, the residuals were generated and standardized through repeated re-estimation, using the method suggested by Belsley, Kuh and Welsh (1980). The resulting standardized residuals are called BKW residuals and denoted by u_I.

These residuals are used to identify firms that exhibit outlying investment flows. The distribution of u_I is standard normal (with a mean of zero and a variance of unity). All firms with $u_I \geq 1$ are defined to be positive outliers, while all firms with $u_I \leq 1$ are defined to be negative outliers. It is claimed that positive outlier firms have significant 'experience-generated' investment flows, or investment flows in excess of the level that can be explained by purely portfolio considerations. Similarly, negative outlier firms have smaller investment flows than would be expected on the basis of portfolio considerations.

The duration analysis using outliers concentrates attention only on those firms which have significant positive experience-generated investment flows, and contrasts them with the firms with the weakest experience-generated flows. While this testing procedure has great power due to the clear distinction between the two groups of firms, it necessarily requires the elimination of a large number of degrees of freedom. The cost of the testing procedure's power is paid in terms of a lower statistical significance of the results. In addition, a question mark hangs over the nature of the experience-generated investment flows of firms that are neither positive nor negative outliers.

In an attempt to deal with these issues, the characteristics of *all* firms are related to the BKW residuals. This creates a secondary test of the relationship between experience-generated investment flows and tenure.

The theoretical position propounded in this chapter can be examined by assessing three testable hypotheses:

Hypothesis (a): the duration of operations of positive outlier firms is longer than that of negative outlier firms;
Hypothesis (b): the significant experience-generated investment flows of positive outlier firms are dependent on the duration of operations;

Hypothesis (c): the experience-generated investment flows of *all* firms are related to the duration of operations.

Hypotheses (*b*) and (*c*) are successively stronger statements concerning the duration-dependence of MNE investment flows.

Testing for Duration Effects

The second part of the analysis is concerned with testing these three hypotheses. Hypothesis (*a*) is tested using a simple two-sample difference-of-means test. Hypothesis (*b*) is tested using two innovative duration-dependence tests developed by Mudambi and Taylor (1995). Hypothesis (*c*) is tested using principal component factor analysis.

The tests used in assessing hypothesis (*b*) are non-parametric; parametric tests would be inappropriate since the underlying data-generating process under the alternative hypothesis of duration-dependence is unknown. In the case of duration-independence, the data must follow a constant probability process; that is, the probability of investment in any period must remain the same regardless of the length of tenure. This process generates a geometric distribution of investment outcomes.

It is necessary to explain the *order of duration-dependence* in the context of MNE investment. All the component parts of an investment project are rarely implemented within one year. Once a location decision has been made, the associated investment flows usually occur over several years. The span over which the investment flows engendered by a single decision are completed is defined to be the order of duration-dependence. Once begun, investment cannot be terminated before this minimum period has elapsed.

The duration-dependence tests are sensitive to the order of minimum duration. The actual order is likely to vary from industry to industry, which is why the survey was limited to firms in a single industry group. Opinions about this minimum order were sought from survey respondents. The duration-dependence tests are performed for several different orders, chosen on the basis of the responses to the survey.

In order to formulate the tests, it is convenient to transform the data to order zero. Thus, if X denotes the duration of operations and t denotes the order of minimum duration, then $y = (X - t)$ represents duration transformed to order zero. The duration tests may now be applied to the transformed data. The first test is a zero-plim test and generates a test statistic denoted by Z_1. The second test is a method-of-moments test and generates a test statistic denoted by Z_2. The specification of both test statistics is presented in the Appendix.

Table 6.1 MNE Investment Estimation

Regressor	Base-line regression results		
	Coefficient	*'t' statistic[1]*	*p value*
OLS			
Constant	130.25	**9.742**	0.0000
RORFF	119.24	1.065	0.2907
RISK	−4.9303	**19.047**	0.0000
RINF	0.005398	0.062	0.9504
ΔEXRT	−52.468	**4.156**	0.0001
Diagnostics	*Value*		
R^2(adj)	0.5826		
ANOVA: $F(4,69)$	13.0678		
Log-likelihood	−262.3394		
$(S_u)^2$	113.4819		
Amemiya PC	2121.5877		
Breusch–Pagan $\chi^2(7)$;[2]	2.6356;		
p value	(0.3795)		

Notes:
Regressand: INV94 = 1994 MNE investment flows into the UK (£ million).
[1] $t(62)_{0.95}$ (crit) = 1.999. *t*-statistics significant at the 95% level are displayed in bold type.
[2] The Breusch–Pagan (1979) test for heteroscedasticity.

ESTIMATION AND RESULTS

The quantitative analysis proceeded in four steps. The first step consisted of regression analysis to estimate the base-line equation and assess the fit provided by portfolio considerations. The second step consisted of performing the outlier analysis on the residuals from the first step. In the third step, the non-parametric duration tests are applied to the firms identified in the second step. Finally, in the fourth step, factor analysis was used to assess the investment residuals from the first step.

Regression Analysis

The results of the base-line regression are presented in Table 6.1. Heteroscedasticity in the error term is a particular fear, since the firms differ considerably in size. This is an issue of great importance in the context of this study, since the error terms are to be used in subsequent outlier and factor analysis. Therefore, the Breusch–Pagan (1979) test was performed on the error terms from the base-line regression. As can be seen, this test is passed comfortably, leading to the conclusion that heteroscedasticity is not present.

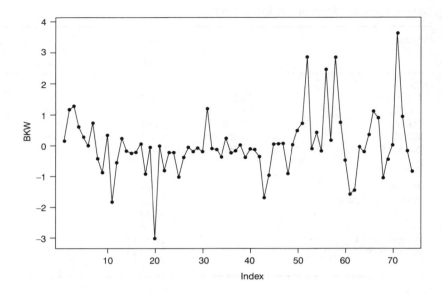

Figure 6.1   BKW residuals from the investment equation

The fit of equation (6.1) is found to be very good, with an adjusted R^2 value of almost 60 per cent. In addition, the F statistic from the analysis of variance is extremely high. Tests of regressor parsimony using the Amemiya Prediction Criterion indicate that the inclusion of all regressors is justified. However, only company-specific risk at the location (RISK) and the exchange rate (ΔDEXRT) appear to be statistically significant in determining the flow of MNE investment. The effect of RISK is negative. This is as expected, since as this risk rises, *ceteris paribus* the location appears less attractive. The effect of the exchange rate on investment flows is negative. This is also expected, since as the local currency appreciates, investment flows decline. Similar results are reported by Stevens (1993).

It would have been expected that relative inflation (RINF), would appear significantly. Examining the data more closely, it is found that for the period considered, 1991–94, the inflation rates in the home countries of many of the major MNEs in the sample were comparable with the UK rate. Thus, the variance of RINF is very low, leading to a very high variance in its regression coefficient and an insignificant 't' statistic. The sign of the estimate itself is positive as would be expected. Finally, the rate of return on the firm's free cash flows (RORFF) does not appear to be significant. It would be expected that the opportunity cost of investment funds would appear negatively in the investment equation. It may be conjectured that the proxy used does not adequately capture this opportunity cost.

Outlier Analysis

The plot of the BKW residuals is presented in Figure 6.1. These residuals are standardized, and vary between a maximum of 3.27 to a minimum of -2.12. A total of 18 positive outlier firms are identified ($u_I \geq 1$), with a mean duration of operations in the UK of 17.89 years. Similarly, 14 negative outlier firms are identified ($u_I \leq 1$), with a mean tenure of 4.21 years. A two-sample difference-in-means test yields a 't' statistic of 12.38, registering strong evidence in favour of hypothesis (a) that the mean tenure for the positive outlier group is longer than that for the negative outlier group.

Tests of Duration Dependence

It is now possible to apply the two duration tests to the outlier firms. The shortest observed tenure for firms in the positive outlier group is seven years, suggesting a minimum order of duration-dependence of less than or equal to six years for this group. The shortest observed tenure for firms in the negative outlier group is zero (a newly-established subsidiary), suggesting that the order of minimum duration is zero for this group of firms.

The computed values of the statistics Z_1 and Z_2 for the appropriate orders of minimum duration are presented in Table 6.2, together with the value of the estimated probability parameter $p°$. Values are computed for the positive outlier group up to an order of minimum duration of 6, while for the negative outlier group, values are only computed for a minimum order of zero.

While both Z_1 and Z_2 have standard normal distributions for large samples, the observed sample sizes are small enough to raise some concern about the use of asymptotic critical values. In an attempt to establish the results beyond any reasonable doubt, the finite sample distributions of Z_1 and Z_2 were simulated in order to obtain exact sampling critical values.[2] Experimental values of 't', the order of minimum duration, were chosen to correspond to those cases where the conclusions based on the asymptotic critical values were most questionable. For the positive outlier group, this occurred for 't'= 4, 5 and 6. For the negative outlier group, 't' was set at zero.

The results of the simulation exercise are presented in Table 6.3. Critical values of 1 per cent, 5 per cent and 10 per cent are presented, together with the observed values of the statistics Z_1 and Z_2. In the positive outlier group, for minimum durations up to five years, duration-independence

Table 6.2 Calculated values for duration-test statistics at various orders of minimum duration

Order	p°	Z_1	Z_2
Positive outliers ($n = 18$)			
0	0.05294	5.62450	5.89140
1	0.05590	5.07296	5.33979
2	0.05921	4.52138	4.78821
3	0.06294	3.96980	4.23663
4	0.06716	3.41821	3.68505
5	0.07200	2.86663	3.13347
6	0.07759	2.31505	2.58189
Negative outliers ($n = 14$)			
0	0.17722	0.88579	1.35109

Table 6.3 Finite sample critical values for Z_1 and Z_2 (based on 10 000 replications)

Statistic	Order	Lower			Upper			Observed
		1%	*5%*	*10%*	*10%*	*5%*	*1%*	*value*
Positive outliers ($n = 15$)								
Z_1	4	−1.433	−0.998	−0.732	1.483	1.869	2.788	3.4182*
	5	−1.439	−1.001	−0.741	1.485	1.877	2.794	2.8666*
	6	−1.446	−1.009	−0.752	1.490	1.904	2.802	2.3150^
Z_2	4	−1.376	−0.946	−0.678	1.517	1.938	2.871	3.6850*
	5	−1.384	−0.951	−0.686	1.541	1.965	2.883	3.1335*
	6	−1.397	−0.958	−0.701	1.587	2.005	2.901	2.5819^
Negative outliers ($n = 17$)								
Z_1	0	−1.004	−0.716	−0.545	1.794	2.389	4.186	0.8858
Z_2	0	−0.949	−0.661	−0.481	1.917	2.560	4.409	1.3511
Asymptotic value		−2.327	−1.645	−1.281	1.281	1.645	2.327	

Notes: Observed values that cause a rejection of the null hypothesis at the 1% level have been marked with *. Observed values that cause a rejection of the null hypothesis at the 5% level are marked with ^.

can be safely rejected. The results from both the test statistics Z_1 and Z_2 are in agreement.[3] For the firms identified as having investment flows which are positive outliers relative to portfolio considerations, these flows appear to be duration-dependent. Thus, the evidence favours hypothesis (*b*).

For the negative outlier group, again both the test statistics Z_1 and Z_2 are in agreement. Both support the conclusion that duration-independence

Table 6.4 Firm characteristics: factor loadings and communalities (varimax rotation)

| Variable | Factor loadings | | | | Communality |
	Factor 1 Local dependence	Factor 2 Experience	Factor 3 External dependence	Factor 4 Location risk	
GOVTAID	**0.890**	−0.186	0.066	−0.054	0.833
EMPL	**0.900**	−0.060	0.086	0.189	0.857
U_I	0.311	**−0.838**	−0.136	0.056	0.821
DT	−0.016	**−0.896**	0.094	0.085	0.819
WEXPORT	0.272	0.117	**0.711**	0.037	0.595
SALES	−0.088	−0.090	**0.848**	−0.035	0.737
RLOCRSK	−0.036	0.047	0.150	**0.848**	0.746
GSALES	0.167	−0.203	−0.177	**0.696**	0.585
Eigenvalue	2.2927	1.4382	1.1542	1.1093	–
Variance	1.8104	1.6097	1.3182	1.2563	5.9946
% variance	0.226	0.201	0.165	0.157	0.749

Note:
Loadings of variables associated with particular factors are shown in bold.

cannot be rejected. Thus, for the firms which are identified as having negative or zero experience-generated investment flows, these flows appear to be duration-independent.

Factor Analysis

While the above duration tests are based on a subset of the entire dataset, the cost due to the loss of degrees of freedom is light, since the results emerge as highly statistically significant. However, a supporting test, using the experience-generated investment flows of *all* firms can provide evidence with regard to the stronger hypothesis (*c*).

The results of the principal component factor analysis are presented in Table 6.4. The latent root criterion was used to determine the number of factors extracted. The rationale is that the variation in each variable is unity after the variable has been standardized. Thus, each factor should account for the variation in at least one variable if the factor is to be considered useful from a data summarization perspective (Churchill, 1995). There were four factors with eigenvalues greater than unity (see Table 6.4). The eigenvalue of the fifth factor was 0.8045. Thus, four factors were extracted. Over 80 per cent of the variation of most individual variables is captured. The two lowest communalities are observed for the share of exports and global sales, and even in these cases almost 60 per cent of the variation is captured. Thus, factor analysis provides a strong basis upon which to assess hypotheses.

The first factor may be termed *'local dependence'*. Both the importance of government assistance (GOVTAID) and subsidiary employment (EMPL) load heavily on this factor. The second factor may be termed *'experience'*. Both experience-generated investment flows (u_1) and duration of UK operations (DT) load heavily on this factor. This provides evidence that the experience-generated investment flows of all firms are related to the duration of operations, supporting hypothesis (*c*).

The third factor may be called *'external dependence'*. The sales of the UK subsidiary (SALES) and the share of exports in these sales (WEXPORT) both load on this factor. This seems to indicate that larger subsidiaries are more export-orientated. Finally, the fourth factor may be termed *'location risk'*. Both the relative country risk of the UK (RLOCRSK) and the global sales of the MNE (GSALES) load heavily on this factor, suggesting that larger MNES may be more sensitive to country risk indices.

CONCLUDING REMARKS

Our principal objective has been to explore the question of duration-dependence with respect to MNE investment flows. While experience in a particular location has been specified as a factor motivating investment flows, portfolio considerations militate against this. It is suggested that portfolio and experience considerations may work in tandem to determine actual investment flows. Thus, if total investment flows are divided into portfolio-generated and experience-generated components, the latter can be tested for duration-dependence.

Using regression analysis, total investment flows are split into portfolio and experience-generated components. The experience-based components are tested using two approaches. First, outlier analysis is used to identify firms with significantly high experience-generated investment flows and then non-parametric duration tests are applied to these firms. Second, factor analysis is applied to a set of firm characteristics including experience-based investment flows. In all cases, the tests yield results which support duration-dependence.

In other words, firms whose investment is significantly *above* that predicted by portfolio considerations, are firms whose probability of investment rises as their tenure in the location (the UK) increases. In contrast, it is found that firms whose investment flows are significantly *below* that predicted by portfolio considerations are firms whose probability of investment is unaffected by the length of their tenure in the location. Further, it is found that the experience-generated investment flows of *all* firms is related to tenure in the location.

The basic implication of this analysis is that both portfolio and experience considerations are important in determining MNE investment flows. Thus, neither one set of factors can explain MNE investment in the absence of the other. In particular, a firm considering *de novo* investment at a particular location on the basis of portfolio advantages is not more likely to invest than a firm which has a pre-existing presence at the location. Location-marketers structuring investment incentives would do well to segment their target firms on the basis of portfolio considerations and then concentrate their efforts on those which have the longest running local operations.

Practically, this means that duration is an important factor in the targeting strategies of the IIAs. In other words, duration should be incorporated into an overall targeting framework, such as that suggested by Young, Hood and Wilson (1994). Within their framework, the critical role of duration implies that the monitoring and aftercare of MNE investors is extremely important. The results in this chapter suggest that IIAs such as the Northern Development Company, which have set up units dedicated to liaising with existing MNE investors, are making good use of their resources.

Notes

1. The author would like to thank Neil Hood, participants of the 1996 World AIB Conference in Banff, Canada and at the UK AIB Conference in Leeds as well as seminar participants at Case Western Reserve, Purdue, Cornell and Maryland for helpful comments on earlier drafts of this study.
2. The simulations were performed on a Sun Sparcstation machine using LIMDEP 7.0, with the observed sample sizes of 18 (for the positive outliers) and 14 (for the negative outliers).
3. In fact, even in heavy engineering firms, the horizon for investment decisions rarely exceeds three years (Vismer, 1994).

Appendix

The Zero-plim Test: Under the null hypothesis of duration-independence, y is distributed according to the geometric distribution and

$$\text{plim } [(\bar{y}/S_y) - 1] = 0 \tag{A1}$$

where $\bar{y}$ is the mean of the transformed investment duration and S_y is the standard error. A test statistic may be developed based on this relationship between the mean and variance of the geometric distribution. The zero-plim test statistic is defined as

$$Z_1 = T^{1/2} [(\bar{y} / S_y) - 1] \tag{A2}$$

It is possible to claim, using the Central Limit Theorem, that the distribution of Z_1 converges to the standard normal as sample size increases. Moreover, since the distribution of y under the null hypothesis is known, it is possible to simulate finite sample critical values, even for relatively small samples.

The Method-of-Moments Test: An analogous test can be constructed using the method-of-moments. Define 'p' to be the probability that experience-generated investment flows occur in any year. Noting that $\bar{y}$ and S_y are consistent estimators for their respective population parameters, it can be shown that

$$p^\circ = \frac{[-1 + (1 + 4S_y^2)^{1/2}]}{2 S_y^2} \tag{A3}$$

converges in probability to p under the null hypothesis of duration-independence. Conditionally on S_y, the test statistic

$$Z_2 = \frac{[\bar{y} - (1/p^\circ - 1)]}{S_y/T^{1/2}} \tag{A4}$$

is approximately standard normal for samples large enough to invoke the Central Limit Theorem. Again, it is possible to simulate finite sample critical values for relatively small samples.

7 Culture and HRM Strategies: The Case of an American Subsidiary in Scotland

Monir Tayeb

INTRODUCTION

One of the major areas of study to have stimulated lively debate among analysts of the management of multinational companies is parent–subsidiary relations in general, and human resource management in particular. The study reported here is an attempt to contribute to this debate.

The chapter is divided into three sections; the concept of human resource management (HRM) and its strategic role in organizations; a brief review of the literature on HRM and parent–subsidiary problems; and a presentation and analysis of the findings of a study of HRM policies and practices in a UK subsidiary of an American multinational corporation.

HUMAN RESOURCE MANAGEMENT

The origins of HRM in modern organizations can be traced to personnel management functions, such as the recruitment, training and remuneration of employees, usually performed by the personnel department. The literature from the early 1970s documents the emergence of HRM and the relative decline of personnel management, and describes changes in the boundaries, substance and objectives of the personnel function. HRM is characterized by commitment, consensualism and communitarianism, and high trust and self-control (Gardner and Palmer, 1992), an ideological and philosophical underpinning which is absent from personnel management (Storey, 1989). In addition, there is an emphasis on integrating human resource planning with the strategy of the organization, a radical departure from the earlier 'maintenance' model, characterized by Burack and Smith (1982) as 'Taylorism, control, efficiency, low cost and the containment of conflict'.

The traditional personnel management function, in contrast to HRM, lacks strategic relevance and is locked in to a mainly administrative-type role (Rowland and Summers, 1981). Legge (1989), for instance, argues that HRM is distinctive from personnel management in at least three ways. First, whereas personnel management focuses on the management and control of subordinates, HRM concentrates on the management team. Second, line managers play a key role in HRM in coordinating resources towards achieving profit, which is not the case under personnel management. Finally, the management of organizational culture is an important aspect of HRM, which plays no role in personnel management. Thus, Legge argues that HRM has more centrally-strategic tasks than personnel management. Similarly, other researchers (Poole, 1990; Blyton and Turnbull, 1992; Storey, 1992) regard the linking of human resource practices to the strategic aims of the business to be the core feature that distinguishes HRM from personnel management.

According to Wilhelm (1990, p. 30), this strategic approach requires that the HRM function should translate corporate strategy into a human resource strategy; that is: design or re-design the organizational structure to serve the strategy; recruit and select employees to fit both the strategy and the desired organizational culture; implement motivation and reward systems that energize the workforce; adopt benefits that complement strategy; introduce employee development and career management programmes; and guide and support line management to accomplish desired organizational change.

PARENT–SUBSIDIARY RELATIONS

Relationships between a parent company and its subsidiaries are inherently prone to tension and conflicts, which arise mainly from a need to maintain the integrity of the company as a coherent, coordinated entity, while allowing for subsidiaries to respond to their differentiated environments (Laurent, 1986; Bartlett and Ghoshal, 1989; Ghoshal and Bartlett, 1992; Schuler, Dowling and De Cieri, 1993).

The concepts of differentiation and integration, originally a focus of debate among sociologists, were first discussed within the context of management and organization studies by Lawrence and Lorsch (1967). They argued that for an organization to perform effectively in diverse environments, it must be both appropriately differentiated and adequately integrated in order that the separate units and departments are coordinated and work towards a common goal. In the context of international business, their model has been used to explain the dynamics of managing organizations operating across borders.

Doz (1976) described the need for differentiation in political terms, emphasizing the tension that exists between the 'economic imperative' (large-scale efficient facilities) and the 'political imperative' (local content laws, local production requirements). Prahalad (1976) developed a typology of multinational companies which stressed 'the need for managerial interdependence' (integration) versus the 'need for managerial diversity' (local responsiveness), so highlighting the need for differentiation on a geographical basis. To maintain an equilibrium between these two conflicting forces, Prahalad and Doz (1987) suggested a multifocal solution where the focus of decision-making shifts between the international and the local depending on the problem under consideration. They argue that the mindset of managers should have a global framework, balancing the needs between local responsiveness and a global vision of the firm. However, the appropriate mix of differentiation and integration may vary from company to company depending on the form and extent of their internationalization, their industry, the markets they serve, and the kind of employees they have (Tayeb, 1996).

Given these perspectives, the question of how foreign subsidiaries manage their human resources could be approached from at least three angles. First, there are the parent company's overall HRM policies. Multinational firms have three broad subsidiary management options at their disposal (Perlmutter, 1969): they can choose to implement similar HRM policies and practices to those customary in the home country and ignore local conditions entirely (an ethnocentric policy); largely follow the practices prevalent in individual host countries (a polycentric policy); or they can devise and implement a universal company-wide policy, fostered by their organizational culture and philosophy (a global policy).

Specific characteristics in the countries in which subsidiaries are located, however, might interfere with a straightforward choice of options and force multinationals to opt for a 'hybrid' strategy. In one study of Japanese multinational companies, for example, differences were found in the degree and nature of home-grown practices that were introduced into their US manufacturing and service subsidiaries (Beechler and Yang, 1994). Another factor which might complicate HRM policy choices is the manner in which subsidiaries are set up. It is easier, for example, to impose home-grown policies on a greenfield subsidiary than on one which has been acquired through acquisition or merger (Tayeb, 1994).

A relevant point to make here is that there is a qualitative distinction between HRM *policies* and HRM *practices* (Schuler *et al.*, 1993) . Whereas multinational firms might find it feasible to have company-wide philosophies and policies of a global or ethnocentric nature, they might find it necessary to be responsive to local conditions when it comes to HRM practices and, therefore, to adopt polycentric practices. The guiding principle in such cases is to keep the company as a whole intact and integrated, while at the same time allowing for a measure of differentiation when needed or desirable (Prahalad and Doz, 1987; Welch, 1994).

There is also the question of the cross-cultural transfer of HRM policies and practices. Whatever HRM strategies multinational firms adopt, they are bound to confront culturally-rooted 'gaps' which are likely to exist between the policies perceived, from a distance, as desirable by home-country managers, and what host-country managers are able to implement successfully.

This question has for three decades or so been the central point of a lively debate among academics, and a focus of interest among managers. Some authors have emphasized the universality of organizations and similarities between them (for example, Kerr *et al.*, 1952; Cole, 1973; Hickson *et al.*, 1974; Form, 1979; Negandhi, 1979, 1985), and some others the cultural uniqueness of organizations (for example, Crozier, 1964; Meyer and Rowan, 1977; Hofstede, 1980; Lincoln, Hanada and Olson, 1981; Laurent, 1983). There are those who argue that technology carries its own imperatives: for an assembly-line automobile technology to be utilized properly a certain organizational design and management style must be adopted. An electronics company, on the other hand, would find a different design more appropriate; and so on.

As Tayeb (1988) argues, however, the various sides of the debate are not mutually exclusive; rather, they complement one another. That is, certain aspects of organizations are more likely to be universal, such as shopfloor layout (influenced in part by technological requirements) and hierarchical structure and division of functions, whereas some areas are more culture-specific, such as human resource management. Moreover, the fact is that organizations and their employees do not live in a vacuum, separated from their societal surroundings. National culture, as a set of values, attitudes and behaviours, includes elements which are relevant to work and organization. These are carried into the workplace as part of the employees' cultural baggage. Work-related values and attitudes, such as power distance, tolerance for ambiguity, honesty, pursuance of group or individual goals, work ethic and entrepreneurial spirit, form part of the cultural identity of a nation (Hofstede, 1980; Tayeb, 1988), and although employees may be required to perform certain *practices* at work, they cannot be deprived of their *values* (Hofstede, Neuijen and Ohavy, 1990).

National culture apart, there are other societal factors, such as government policies, industrial relations' rules and regulations, the power of pressure groups, and membership of regional and global agreements and institutions, all of which have a direct or indirect bearing on an organization's HRM policies (Tayeb, 1996).

There remains the organizational culture of a subsidiary, which plays its own part in shaping the character of HRM strategies employed by its management. Compared to a newly-founded subsidiary, an older well-established subsidiary is more likely to have developed its own way of life, which may at times be resistant to ideas imposed on it from the parent company.

These arguments and debates informed the framework of the study, whose findings are discussed below.

THE STUDY

The study was carried out in a Scottish manufacturing subsidiary (here referred to as NCR Dundee) of NCR Inc., an American multinational corporation whose headquarters are located in Dayton, Ohio.

The main objectives of the research were to explore:

- The extent to which the American firm had implanted its home-grown policies and practices in Scotland as a matter of corporation-wide strategy.
- The extent to which local social, political and economic conditions had imposed constraints, and/or created opportunities, which could have modified the parent company's approach to HRM in Scotland.
- The extent to which there were differences between HRM 'policies' and 'practices'.
- Those aspects of HRM which could be said to be easily transferable across the two cultures, and those which would presuppose certain culture-specific conditions for their successful implementation in the subsidiary.

Using semi-structured interviews, information was collected on the following HRM functions: the strategic role of HRM; recruitment; employee training and development; compensation, benefits and pensions; industrial relations; teamwork; flexible working patterns; and quality control.

Altogether, 13 employees participated in the interview programme. Their position in the subsidiary ranged from the chief executive and senior directors and managers, down to middle managers, a union convenor and an assembly worker. The interviews, which lasted between 45 and 90 minutes, were tape-recorded and subsequently transcribed. Relevant company documents and literature were also consulted.

FINDINGS

The Strategic Role of HRM

HRM in NCR Dundee is much more than run-of-the-mill personnel management; it is an integral part of the company's overall strategic plans and the responsibility of a senior director. In many respects, therefore, the subsidiary follows the parent company's overall HRM policies, although there are various areas where compliance is less stringent than others, and local conditions and traditions are allowed to modify the parent's policies in favour of practices which are more suitable to the day-to-day running of the subsidiary. A local manager also has the freedom to do some things differently because this is considered to be better for business, whether in the USA or in the UK.

In the early 1980s, for instance, NCR Dundee introduced a non-redundancy policy which aimed to minimize the risk of people losing their jobs and thus to create a feeling of security of employment. The subsidiary, believing this would result in better employee performance, applied the policy rigidly throughout the 1980s. This was in a sharp contrast to the 'hire and fire' policy pursued by the headquarters at Dayton for most of the same period.

Recruitment

Recruitment policy is fairly centralized. In recent years, the parent company has controlled the pace of local recruitment, mainly because of financial problems within the group. For instance, NCR Dundee would not be exempt from a corporate-wide freeze on hiring from outside, whatever the business outlook of the subsidiary.

The subsidiary incorporates its recruitment plan into its overall annual business plan, subject to unforeseen changes in business conditions. Even so, in a particular year the subsidiary might be prevailed upon by headquarters to keep the number of new recruits down. The actual recruitment process is implemented in Dundee without interference, except for very senior jobs, once headquarters has approved overall targets. Recruitment procedures are worked out locally and depend very much on the particular job. The practical means of selection, such as interviews, tests, assessment centres and so on, are more or less like those employed in Dayton, or indeed anywhere else in the world for that matter.

The subsidiary tends to fill the majority of vacant positions by giving permanent status to temporary employees or by taking on former employees. Because of a persistently high level of unemployment in Dundee, there is always an ample stock of people seeking employment with the subsidiary, including many who have worked for it before, or who are 'temps' seeking full-time positions.

Employee Training and Development

NCR Dundee's training and development programme, headed by a senior manager, is one of the central planks of its HRM policy and plays a significant part in overall company policy. Programmes are closely linked to the skill requirements the subsidiary requires to compete successfully in international markets. Extensive links are maintained with Scottish universities and colleges for training and recruitment purposes. The manager dedicated to this works with other managers and teams within the organization to identify training needs and to ensure that these needs are met. Training activities are evaluated for their worth and effectiveness to ensure that they are appropriate for, and relevant to, the subsidiary's needs.

The training programme takes several forms, depending on the circumstances. For instance, new graduate recruits would join a group and go through an induction process of understanding the different parts of the company and its products and markets. At meetings to appraise the nature of the business overall, they would also get the opportunity to meet with new graduates from other functions. All graduates go through much the same training and are encouraged to spend time together as a group. In addition, there are outdoor development-type activities that focus on teamwork, decision-making and problem-solving in a group environment. They then receive on-the-job training in their specialist areas but are brought together for short induction sessions at which senior managers talk about other functional areas.

As for employees already with NCR Dundee, there is an education-for-all policy which broadly states that any employee wishing to take a course of study leading to a nationally-recognized qualification will be supported. The only other criterion is that the course must link in some way to the business, but not necessarily to the employee's current job. The subsidiary also uses other forms of training activities, such as secondments and projects at Dayton or elsewhere.

In general, every employee, on average, gets ten days of training annually, which could be both inside and outside the company. However, some people, for example in software development, will probably receive more training than the average and others less so. Also, training days per particular employee can vary greatly around the average from year to year, such differentiation arising from the nature of the work. If there is felt to be a particular need to train a group of people or just one person, it will always be done.

Although there is a corporate programme which NCR Dundee follows, almost all the education and training policies and specific programmes implemented in the subsidiary are defined there. For example, concerning the company's relationships with universities, the subsidiary puts the programmes together jointly with the universities, to which headquarters has no input at all. The whole process, the identification of training needs, assessment of their relevance to business objectives, the kind of training and development to be provided and the individuals or institutions which the company would want to use, are all determined locally.

Compensation, Benefits and Pensions

Pay and benefits' policies mostly follow those of the parent, but there are also instances where these policies are translated into practices and procedures in a manner specific to NCR Dundee. For example, with regard to salaries and bonuses the parent company has market surveys conducted in all the countries in which it has subsidiaries to find out the local pay levels of their main competitor for similar jobs. Each subsidiary then sets its pay lines around the median of that competitor. NCR Dundee, which is a manufacturing plant, views this policy as being more appropriate for marketing and sales personnel. For their workforce, they focus instead on internal operational results, which are considered more suitable as a basis for pay awards in manufacturing.

The subsidiary's policy on pensions is also slightly different from that of headquarters. In the US, for social, cultural and historical reasons, pensions are generally frozen in time. That is to say, individuals do not have a right to a pension increase and the company has no legal obligation to offer one. As a common practice, however, there may be an increase every decade or so. In the UK, in contrast, there is a general principle and practice of annual increases in pensions. NCR Dundee has always taken the view that the local practice, in principle, should be to provide guaranteed increases on an annual basis, but headquarters is uncomfortable about this because it does not reflect corporate policy. Thus, the subsidiary has had to modify its local policy in that there are no guarantees of an increase, but the subsidiary can provide one at its discretion. In practice, rather than increase pensions annually, they are staggered from between 12 to 15 months – a compromise that takes account of corporate policy and local practice.

Industrial Relations

Traditionally, the City of Dundee has had a heavily unionized workforce, a tradition that also exists in NCR Dundee, in which around 1200 employees, represented by one of three unions, are currently unionized. The current trend among many companies, especially NCR Dundee's competitors, is to have single union representation, even to de-recognize trade unions in their organizations. The Dundee subsidiary has not gone along with this trend because of the strong local union tradition and heritage.

A policy inside the subsidiary since the early 1980s has been to emphasize and build trust between unions and management. Judging by the attitudes of the employees expressed in the interviews and the impressions gained of the subsidiary's organizational culture, the company has succeeded in doing so. For example, the personal style of the management, which is reflected in a 'walk about' and 'open door' management culture, has created an atmosphere in which people at all levels talk and listen to each other face-to-face about issues which concern them.

Concurrently, the management in conjunction with the unions have also made a conscious effort to break down traditional barriers between manual workers and staff, which had in part been a result of differentiated treatment of the two groups, especially with regard to working conditions. For instance, formerly, a clerk off sick for two or three days would get full pay, but a manual worker in the same circumstances would receive social security payment. This sort of differentiation, along with the traditional staff–manual worker dichotomy, has now disappeared.

The management maintains effective and informative communication with employees through meetings, conferences and internal-circuit television. The information given to employees is wide-ranging, such as proposals to set up a new plant overseas, new models to be produced, assembly workers' workload, and visitors to the company. On their part, the workforce, both unionized and non-unionized sections, has contributed greatly to the good relationship between management and employees. Employees have learned to adapt to the changes that management, in response to competitive pressures, has had to introduce to working patterns and other organizational aspects. Through consultation processes and meetings, employees have come to recognize the benefits that such changes might bring to them. As a result, the infamous 'them and us' attitude which characterizes industrial relations in many British companies does not exist in NCR Dundee.

Teamwork

Most employees at various levels work in groups and work teams. As we saw above, both new recruits and the established workforce undergo training in teamwork skills. The cooperative character of industrial relations and the culture of the company also foster a team approach to work. The desirability of work teams is not perceived as a fashionable Japanese-style fad or an imposition by the parent, but as a response to the need to function more effectively.

Teamwork appears to have helped bring people from different levels and statuses work together. In the past, if there were work teams they tended to be comprised of people who were working at the same level. But now members of a team are there not necessarily because of their status or which department they come from, but because of what they can bring to the group and the experience that they possess, especially skills which are particularly suited to the task at hand.

Alongside selling new ideas such as teamwork to the workforce through consultation and involvement, managers began to implement the new style in other, selective, areas. For instance, a new software section was manned by a young team. Although software development has been going on in the subsidiary for some time, old traditions have not constrained the implementation of a teamwork approach. By focusing on the software business, an artificial wall was created which made successful teaming possible. When the team achieved its objectives it was disbanded and absorbed into a bigger unit.

One way to foster a team approach is to link incentives and rewards to the collective performance of teams. Although the merits of this policy are recognized in the subsidiary, in practice it has not been easy to implement. The subsidiary's appraisal system assesses a person's individual and collective roles, but nobody is assessed solely on the basis of a team role or a team's success. Rather, no more than half of an individual's assessments are based on team performance because there is strong cultural resistance to go beyond this. The introduction of a solely team-assessment procedure would have a negative effect, in the short term at least. The subsidiary is working its way towards increasing the assessment ratio in favour of the employees' team effort or the success of a team project, but it is unlikely to ever be 100 per cent because there are always individual activities that a person has to perform that are independent of team activities.

Teamwork is not as pervasive in the company as senior managers would prefer, but they are all working towards this end. One reason for underachievement in this regard stems from a legacy of history; that is, the subsidiary started out as a severely hierarchically-oriented manufacturing firm. Another reason for a lingering residual resistance to teamwork lies in past confrontational industrial relations practices which used to characterize the company, and which took a great deal of effort to change. Nevertheless, the commitment to teamwork certainly goes well beyond lip service and company slogans.

Flexible Working Patterns

In the past, in NCR Dundee, as in many other companies, there was a rigid hierarchical structure within which a small number of senior people, managers and technologists took most of the managerial decisions. Also, there was a high ratio of semi-skilled and unskilled people, both in offices and in manual jobs. This situation has now changed. Most employees are now skilled, education-based workers, whether in offices or on the shopfloor. Employees regularly operate computers on the shopfloor, attend more meetings, and push for consultative, team decisions rather than authoritative instructions handed down from a supervisor. The roles of managers and supervisors are changing to those of supportive team leaders. Job flexibility, part of this new working pattern and more effective than traditional patterns, ties in more closely with the education and training programmes of the company.

As with teamwork, job flexibility is seen not so much as a policy imported from Japan or imposed by headquarters, but as an essential tool, developed locally, to improve employee productivity and the subsidiary's ability to respond quickly and effectively to market conditions. A vigorous training programme and other organizational devices, such as teamwork, link with job flexibility to ensure the latter's successful implementation.

Quality Control

Skills in quality control are new requirements for all NCR employees, in Dundee and elsewhere in the company. Moreover, quality is built in at every stage of the manufacturing process. In the distant past, in the Dundee subsidiary, assembly workers and inspectors were almost equal in number. Now employees are responsible for their own quality control, subject only to a final check – an arrangement which has had a major impact on the elimination of waste and a reduction in rejects.

The subsidiary has experimented with various quality initiatives over the years, including quality circles, which have had only limited success. More recently, quality troubleshooting, particularly in the production area, has been through teams assigned the responsibility for the root-cause analysis of problems arising in different areas. Managers emphasised that these teams, though not quality circles, function just as quality circles do in other companies.

DISCUSSION AND CONCLUSIONS

The findings of the study merit appraisal from different angles; parent–subsidiary relationships, the transfer of HRM policies cross-culturally, distinctions between HRM policy and practice, and major factors which influence or shape the Scottish subsidiary's HRM strategies.

The relationships between Dundee NCR and its parent company are characterized by a complex process of give and take. In clashes between parent and subsidiary, the subsidiary has often been able to assert its identity and character. Sometimes it has rejected policies issued from the centre; sometimes it has implemented them with some flexibility; sometimes it has argued with headquarters and has won its consent for more freedom of action than headquarters had initially been prepared to concede. In areas such as recruitment, training, pay, benefits and pensions, the subsidiary has deferred to the parent company's overall policies and principles, but has adopted locally-acceptable practices and availed itself of local opportunities in ways that were thought appropriate and beneficial.

Regarding the transfer of HRM polices from other cultures, some practices imported from headquarters and Japan, such as quality circles, have been modified to suit local conditions. The company has shifted away from the traditional separation of production and quality inspection to a process of production with built-in quality control. Teamwork and flexible working practices have been introduced in conjunction with extensive employee training and education programmes and open communication. The close-knit company culture, which fosters a feeling of belonging, has contributed to the process of change.

With respect to industrial relations, the management and unions have cooperated to eliminate some of the causes of employee grievances which were entrenched in the company. Various rules and regulations which discriminated against blue-collar workers *vis-à-vis* staff and other white-collar employees have been removed. Open communication, information-sharing and dialogue have increased understanding between managers and workers. Teamwork and training have helped workers to acquire useful skills and have a say in the decisions affecting their jobs.

On the whole, a clear distinction between policies and practices can be discerned both with regard to what the parent company has succeeded in imposing on its Scottish subsidiary and those which the latter has attempted to import from elsewhere. Many policies have been accepted only as general guidelines, and have been converted to practices that are compatible with the way in which the Scottish company functions and manages its affairs.

The Scottish subsidiary's HRM strategies are influenced and determined by a mix of internal and external factors, including the socio-cultural characteristics of the location in which it is situated, its organizational culture, business and technological imperatives, and the parent company's HRM strategies.

Location

Scotland in general, and Dundee in particular, has a long history of strong unionism through which employees have traditionally voiced their views. For example, an American car manufacturer dropped its plans to set up a plant in Scotland because it could not get the local workforce to agree to de-unionize. Moreover, industrial relations in Scotland, as elsewhere in the United Kingdom, is characterized by a 'them and us' attitude. The closure of a subsidiary of another multinational company located in Dundee, following intractable disputes, provides a sad example of how things might go badly wrong because of entrenched attitudes.

Industrial relations apart, the Scots are a people with a distinctive cultural heritage, characterized by, among others, individualism yet caring for the community, austerity, hard work, integrity and honesty. More-over, they are proud of their 'Scottishness' and seek to emphasize this *vis-à-vis* other nations, especially their English neighbour. NCR Dundee managers, themselves Scots, are well aware of this, and have devised their HRM policies and practices to be compatible with the culture of the country and to avoid conflict. To this end, they have sometimes changed or even ignored some of the parent company's policies, which has paid off in terms of employee satisfaction and commitment and the overall performance of the company.

Organizational Culture

The company enjoys a strong organizational culture which has evolved over a period of half a century. Following a change of leadership in the early 1980s, managers and employees alike have undergone an extra-ordinary shared experience of turning an ailing subsidiary into a competitive world class organization. Alike, they are proud of the concessions they have had to make to achieve this. Interwoven in this organizational cul-ture is a leadership and HRM style which glues the various parts of the company into a coherent entity. This entity, although it is capable of absorbing change and accommodating new ways of doing things, resists overt imposition and interference from outside, be it a management fad or a directive from on high.

Business and Technology Imperatives

NCR Dundee is a high-tech company at the forefront of innovation and invention in its line of business, especially automatic teller machines. It also pursues strong competitive strategies to maintain its global lead in certain areas and to catch up and overtake its competitors in others. HRM policies are fully sensitized to hard-nosed business strategies. Education and training programmes, team work and job flexibility are examples of various HRM tools that the subsidiary has successfully employed in support of its overall plans and strategies. The subsidiary's organizational culture has allowed changes to be introduced and imple-mented, not through coercion, but through open and frank communication and information processes. Moreover, managers have been able to dem-onstrate a correspondence between the company's fortunes and those of its employees, and thereby to secure their cooperation and commitment.

The Parent Company

As a subsidiary, NCR Dundee cannot go it alone, and its policies, in-cluding HRM, are those of the parent company's to a large extent. The exceptions are in no way detrimental to the overall interests of the

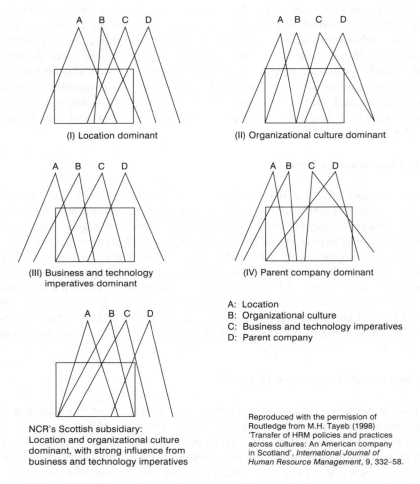

(I) Location dominant

(II) Organizational culture dominant

(III) Business and technology imperatives dominant

(IV) Parent company dominant

A: Location
B: Organizational culture
C: Business and technology imperatives
D: Parent company

NCR's Scottish subsidiary:
Location and organizational culture dominant, with strong influence from business and technology imperatives

Reproduced with the permission of Routledge from M.H. Tayeb (1998) 'Transfer of HRM policies and practices across cultures: An American company in Scotland', *International Journal of Human Resource Management*, 9, 332–58.

Figure 7.1 A dynamic model of foreign subsidiaries' HRM

company. In sum, NCR Dundee is a successful example of a balance between differentiation and integration, sought after by so many multi-national firms with subsidiaries around the world. However, some of the parent company's HRM policies have been interpreted in a locally acceptable manner and translated into practices which work better hundreds of miles away from where they originated. This local interpretation has been one of the major reasons why successful differentiation and integration processes have gone hand-in-hand in NCR Dundee.

The findings of the study show clearly that the management of the workforce in a foreign subsidiary is a complex affair. The choice between one of three major options, polycentric, ethnocentric or global policies, advocated by many scholars, is too simplistic a model for understanding what actually goes on in a subsidiary and between it and its parent organization. Moreover, the amount of influence that each of the four factors identified above can exert on a company's HRM is argued here to be a dynamic one. The configuration of these influences could change over time and space. In other words, HRM needs to be viewed as an ever-evolving series of policies and events.

Figure 7.1 represents a dynamic model showing four hypothetical subsidiaries in each of which one of the above-mentioned clusters of factors dominates. The figure incorporates a model constructed on the basis of the study reported here. In short, in NCR Dundee there is considerable emphasis on both organizational culture and locational factors (factors A and B), and their constant interaction with business and technology factors. The parent company, factor D, appears in the model but its influence is rather circumscribed.

Note

This chapter draws in part on the following article: Tayeb, M. (1998) 'Transfer of HRM policies and practices across cultures: an American company in Scotland', *International Journal of Human Resource Management*, 9, 2, pp. 332–58.

Part Two

Entry Strategies

Introduction

Adam Cross

It is axiomatic to state that, if cross-border business is to be conducted by any means other than just trade, then an entry mode of some description will necessarily be involved. The selection and management of a foreign market servicing strategy therefore remains a cornerstone of international business, both as an academic discipline and as an activity (Contractor, 1997). The second section of the book is concerned with this important aspect of the organization of international business.

Two thematic approaches to the investigation of entry strategy can be discerned in the literature. The first addresses the subject in terms of the firm's *choice* between discrete entry mode alternatives. Typically, this is articulated as a choice between two or more of the following options: exporting, market-based technology transfers under contractual agreements (such as licensing, franchising and management contracts) and intra-firm transactions. Transactions internal to the firm arise in the context of foreign direct investment (FDI), for example, equity joint ventures and wholly-owned operations. This approach has driven much international business theorizing over the past thirty years, particularly that pioneered by Hymer (1960) on the *raison d'être* and growth of the multinational enterprise (MNE).

In the 1970s and 1980s, several threads in the theory emerged, each with a different emphasis. Buckley and Casson (1976) applied the concept of internalization to show how the substitution of imperfect external markets (for licensing) by more perfect internal markets (within the firm) for the exchange of intermediate goods and services led to FDI. Others identified and trod what has become that 'most travelled boulevard' (Caves, 1998, p. 29) of transaction cost analysis (for example, Anderson and Gatignon, 1986; Hennart, 1989). This stream of research focused on the costs associated with searching for, negotiating with and monitoring independent foreign parties to a contract relative to the costs of corporate governance. Dunning (1993a) synthesized these threads in his eclectic paradigm. This viewed the entry decision as depending upon the interaction of ownership advantages (needed by the MNE to out-compete indigenous local firms and offset the additional cost of non-domestic production), location advantages (to prompt international production rather than exporting to foreign markets) and internalization advantages (to preclude the sale of property rights to foreign parties under contract).

Contractor (1990) also attempted to integrate the various threads in the theory, but introduced into his model as well the revenue, profit and risk implications that arise across the range of ownership possibilities. A number of empirical studies (for example, Gatignon and Anderson, 1988; Anderson and Coughlan, 1987; Erramilli, 1990; Agarwal and Ramaswami, 1992) confirmed much of this theorizing, although, as evidenced by later work, several deficiencies in the theory still prevailed.

Later theoretical refinements have incorporated a number of advancements. For example, the corporate strategy dimension has been added. This acknowledges that entry-mode choice must be considered in relation to the overall strategic posture of the firm (Hill, Hwang and Kim, 1990; Kim and Hwang, 1992). The temporal dimension has also been added, with analyses of the timing of the switch between entry modes in terms of fixed and variable costs (Buckley and Casson, 1981) and of evolving firm experience (Johanson and Wiedersheim-Paul, 1975; Johanson and Vahlne, 1977; Erramilli, 1991). Latterly, the theory within this first thematic approach to entry modes has expanded to explain the proliferation of international strategic alliances (Contractor and Lorange, 1988). It also now incorporates variables such as the nationality of the entrant (Erramilli, 1996) already familiar from earlier mainstream research on country-specific propensities to engage in FDI (Clegg, 1987). At the leading edge of theoretical research, rigorous economic modelling seeks to predict entry-choice in the face of changing market size and environmental volatility (Buckley and Casson, 1996).

Two chapters in this section adopt the theoretic standpoint of this first thematic approach. In Chapter 8, Mark Casson and Nigel Wadeson use meta-rationality to re-evaluate, if not debunk, the Williamsonian concept of bounded rationality in conventional organization theory. Bounded rationality, they assert, is merely a rational response to information costs. A thorough and discursive analysis of three components of information costs – observation costs, communication costs and memory costs – provides insight into the origins of procedures and routines in the firm and how these are planned and memorized. Implications for internal and external communication and organizational learning are also raised. In highlighting the importance of information costs in the analysis of the organizational structure – and management style – of the international firm, the authors argue for the supremacy of hierarchy; that is, equity-based as opposed to contract-based forms of organization. For them, the question is not so much whether hierarchy is appropriate, but what form works best under what circumstances. They reason that firms in less-volatile environments should adopt autocratic management styles whereas firms in more volatile environments would benefit from a consultative managerial approach.

The unambiguous support for the hierarchical organization of market entry is also argued by Peter Fu in his study, in Chapter 9, of a particular type of MNE – the international bank. Transaction costs analysis reveals how, by integrating forward across borders, the internalization of markets for intermediate inputs (that is, information) in the banking industry economizes on the transaction costs that arise between ultimate lenders and borrowers due to information asymmetry.

The second thematic approach to the investigation of entry modes examines the characteristics, *modi operandi* and determinants of the success of particular entry methods in isolation to alternatives. This approach has rich antecedents in the literature, both as prescriptive guides for managers (for example, Brooke and Buckley, 1988; Brooke and Skilbeck, 1994) and as empirical works (surveyed, for example, by Young, Hamill, Wheeler and Davies, 1989). The next three chapters in this section fall in this category.

In Chapter 10, Keith Glaister continues his insightful work on equity joint ventures (EJVs) by investigating two important aspects of EJV formation; the strategic motives that firms have for entering into an EJV, and the criteria they use to select a suitable EJV partner. The research focuses on EJVs between UK firms and partners from other industrialized countries, posing the question of whether UK firms place a similar importance on a number of identified strategic motives and selection criteria as do their foreign partners. The study concludes that the UK and foreign firms in the sample have fundamentally the same motives for entering the venture, which relate primarily to facilitating foreign market access. Strong support is also found for the role of trust, or mutual forbearance, in selecting a suitable EJV partner. However, variation is found in the task-related selection criteria employed, with firms seeking from their foreign partners those key inputs which they lack themselves.

In their review of the literature on EJVs in Chapter 11, Margreet Boersma and Pervez Ghauri catalogue the diversity of measures employed by researchers to assess the performance of EJVs and illustrate the methodological limitations of using a single performance measure. They argue for a consistent approach to the investigation of EJVs. In support, they present and discuss the operation of a five-fold classification scheme of EJV performance indicators. This is complemented by a similar categorization of factors which, they suggest, contribute to the success or otherwise of EJVs. Throughout, the authors stress the importance in understanding the changing behaviour of the partners in an EJV – and its concomitant performance – over time.

In contrast to the other chapters in this section, in Chapter 12, Keith Brouthers, Lance Eliot Brouthers and Wilfred Sleeman argue against the presumption of the ubiquitous optimality of equity-based foreign operations. They propose that firms which service a significant number

of their foreign markets by contract-based means can nevertheless develop
the internal mechanisms and external relations to allow them to be, at
the same time, both globally-integrated and locally-responsive. Using case-
study evidence, they demonstrate how a major international franchising
firm has the organizational capacity to achieve this and compete successfully in a turbulent global environment in order to become a truly
transnational corporation.

8 Bounded Rationality, Meta-Rationality and the Theory of International Business

Mark Casson and Nigel Wadeson

INTRODUCTION

The concept of bounded rationality is often applied to international business behaviour (see for example Kogut and Zander, 1993). It is a key element in Williamson's (1975) version of transaction cost theory, and underpins Hedlund's (1993) arguments in favour of the 'heterarchy' – otherwise known as the 'network firm'. There is, however, no consensus over what exactly 'bounded rationality' signifies. The term itself is a curious one. It indicates what it is not – namely full or substantive rationality – but not exactly what it is. There are a number of different views. As a result, a casual reference to bounded rationality is ambiguous, since it is not clear to which particular interpretation of bounded rationality it refers.

The object of this chapter is to clarify the concept of bounded rationality by reinterpreting it in terms of information costs. This introduces much-needed rigour and precision into the analysis of the organization of multinational firms. Many effects imputed to bounded rationality can be explained more simply in terms of a rational response to information costs.

According to Simon (1947, 1982, 1992), bounded rationality involves the use of satisficing routines. The concept of satisficing indicates, firstly, that decision-making involves a search for solutions, and secondly, that the search is likely to terminate before the ideal solution has been found. The chosen solution is merely satisfactory – it is not necessarily the fully optimal one. The concept of routine indicates that satisficing problem-solvers tend to follow the same search procedure time after time. The behavioural perspective favoured by Simon suggests that these routines are programmed into people. They are not the product of individual choice. The routines may be either innate – being biologically programmed – or socially acquired – for example, by a programmed propensity to imitate other people's behaviour.

119

While Simon argues that bounded rationality is necessary to explain administrative behaviour within a firm, Williamson (1975) emphasizes that bounded rationality has implications for the nature of the firm itself. In Williamson's theory, bounded rationality has one major task. It explains why complex contingent contracts cannot be written, and hence why labour must be hired to work under the management of a firm. The same idea can also be used to explain the integration of successive stages of production.

Prior to Williamson, Cyert and March (1963) developed a behavioural theory of the firm in which they specified algorithms that managers could use to set prices, output and inventory levels. These specifications were essentially *ad hoc*, however. They were not so much an explanation of what managers did, as a description of what they did in a typical firm. The theoretical content was restricted to abstracting from minor details of the administrative process.

The behavioural approach, in its simplest form, suggests that managers cannot modify their patterns of behaviour when circumstances change. Yet, there is plenty of evidence to suggest that such modifications do occur. These modifications are not arbitrary – the direction of change is dictated by the need for efficient adaptation. A successful firm selects whichever routine is most efficient under the prevailing circumstances. Indeed, Baumol and Quandt (1964) demonstrated that successful routines can be reinterpreted as rational rules once the appropriate managerial costs of decision-making are taken into account. This is a point to which we return below.

Nelson and Winter (1982) revitalized the behavioural approach by allowing for greater flexibility in organizational behaviour. They also widened the scope of the theory to incorporate rivalry between firms. However, the degree of flexibility permitted to the firm within their theory is still relatively small. Moreover, key elements of the theory remain *ad hoc*. Nelson and Winter argue that much of the intangible knowledge-base of the firm is comprized of routines. These routines are tacit: they are not sufficiently codifiable to be bought or sold through licensing agreements. Managers are so thoroughly bounded in their rationality that they can only memorize these routines by carrying them out; and they habitually repeat a routine so long as it performs reasonably well. The routine with which a firm commences is arbitrary. Managers learn from their mistakes, but only in a myopic way: the unexpected failure of a routine stimulates a search for another routine that is as good as the original routine used to be. This search is modelled as a behavioural satisficing process. The incremental effects of learning gradually adjust a firm towards an optimum, without it ever actually getting there.

Firms that learn most effectively tend to increase in size at the expense of others, as following each shock to the industry they tend to

increase their market share. One consequence of this is that the industry as a whole tends to converge upon a rational pattern of routine
behaviour. Despite the emphasis on bounded rationality in individual
firms, therefore, the evolutionary process that selects in favour of the
most rational firms means that, in any case, rationality reasserts itself at
the industry level. This shows that even in a theory that is meant to be
critical of orthodox rationality, the tendency to rational behaviour proves
to be quite robust, because it is underpinned by evolutionary selection
mechanisms.

BOUNDED RATIONALITY – AN EMPTY BOX?

Bounded rationality is appealing because it seems to explain in a single
stroke all the quirks of behaviour that we observe in other people. But
this explanation is an illusion. Bounded rationality is certainly *consistent*
with such behaviour, but only because it is consistent with just about
any type of behaviour. Unless it is coupled with other assumptions, it
actually predicts nothing, since it rules nothing out. Predictions can be
obtained by postulating arbitrary behavioural rules, but modern writers
on international business are reluctant to do this, because, as indicated
above, these behavioural rules are too inflexible to form the basis of an
acceptable theory.

Another approach, based on the concept of artificial intelligence, is
to model people as computers or as users of genetic algorithms (Moss
and Rae, 1992). The difficulty here is that the theory is so complicated
that definite results are hard to obtain without recourse to simulation.
Furthermore, the kind of results that are generated are only of limited
help in developing a theory of the firm.

Behaviourism and artificial intelligence are not the only way of obtaining predictive power. For example, if bounded rationality were taken
to imply that all behaviour was irrational, then it would at least predict
that nothing explicable in rational terms would ever occur. But writers
on bounded rationality usually leave open the possibility that behaviour
may sometimes be rational too. They know that the predictions of total
irrationality are false. As a consequence, many modern writers invoke
bounded rationality without recourse to either behaviourism or artificial
intelligence. The main consequence is to make the use of substantive
rationality within the theory optional. Thus, a scholar who invokes bounded
rationality for one purpose may invoke substantive rationality for some
other purpose. For example, Williamson (1985) explains the authority
relation created by the contract of employment in terms of bounded
rationality, but then analyses managerial choice between alternative contractual arrangements as a substantively rational one.

Bounded rationality is often commended as an assumption that is obviously more realistic than substantive rationality. This point fails to address the question of what makes a good theory, however. A good theory is easy to understand: there is a logical transparency to the way it works. This logical transparency is needed because, just as the bounded rationality postulate suggests, people have difficulty understanding theoretical constructs and putting them to proper use. From this perspective, logical transparency is necessary in theories constructed for use by boundedly rational people, because it makes the theories easy to understand. The assumption of rational action provides just the kind of logical transparency that is required in a good theory. It is necessary to assume that people behave *as if* they were rational simply because we know that we would otherwise have difficulty in understanding their behaviour. A rigorous theorist needs to assume rationality because students of the theory cannot cope with the complexity that an alternative approach would involve. The paradox of rationality is that it has to be assumed because we know that it isn't true. More precisely, rationality has to be assumed of the agents in the model because it isn't true of those who study the model. If the rationality postulate is rejected, then some other equally simple postulate must be put in its place. So far, a satisfactory alternative has not been found.

Logical transparency is also important in revealing inconsistencies and contradictions in the construction of a theory. Scholars of any persuasion are unfortunately prone to logical error in the construction of their theories because, being boundedly rational, they share in human fallibility. The fallible individuals who invoke the rationality postulate are easily found out when they make a mistake, because the symptoms of the problem are so clear, and this obliges them to correct the fault. But those who refuse to invoke the rationality principle, or any equivalent postulate, may escape detection because of lack of clarity in what they write. Bad theorists dislike the rationality postulate, because they know that if they used it they would be quickly found out. They take refuge in postulating bounded rationality instead.

There is certainly a lot of bad theory to be found in international business. Contemporary organizational theories of international business are particularly prone to logical flaws because of their heavy dependence on the bounded rationality postulate. Modern writers exploit the freedom to switch between rationality and irrationality in order to construct theories that have no internal logical consistency at all. An example drawn from the literature on globalization will illustrate the point.

Following Bartlett and Ghoshal (1987) there has been an increasing flow of visionary papers purporting to demonstrate the benefits of flexible organizational structures in meeting global competition (Hedlund and Ridderstrale, 1992). There is no sign of this flow abating (see, for example,

Hamel and Prahalad, 1996). But none of the writers who set out these ideas invoke an explicit assumption, such as rational action, which would guarantee the internal logical consistency of their analysis. Instead they use the concept of bounded rationality to disguise the fact that their underlying assumptions about human behaviour are changing as their argument develops. No coherent view of human behaviour emerges from their work because the discipline imposed by the rationality postulate is missing in each case.

The problem of maintaining intellectual standards in international business theory is particularly regrettable when the foundations for a more rigorous approach have already been laid. Egelhoff (1991) has shown how multinational organizations can be analyzed coherently from an information-processing perspective. This more rigorous approach recognizes the obvious benefits of the hierarchical organizational form (Casson, 1994). It is no accident that the hierarchical principle dominates so much of organizational life. The essence of organization is a division of labour in information processing, with senior managers synthesizing information channelled to them from junior managers. This arrangement allows the junior managers – functional specialists and managers with local knowledge – to specialize in collecting information from the specific sources that they know best. It permits the senior managers, who have more general knowledge and wider vision, to specialize in synthesizing information from these diverse sources in order to take decisions. These decisions are then communicated back to junior managers for implementation.

Issuing instructions from headquarters is a parsimonious way of sharing a synthesis of information within the organization. This approach is perfectly consistent with arguing that hierarchy should take a flexible form. Indeed, it is a direct implication of the theory that the form that a hierarchy takes must adapt to the changing pattern of volatility in the environment (Casson, 1995, Chapter 4). But this is far removed from suggesting that hierarchies themselves should be replaced by some totally different form.

RATIONALITY – WHAT EXACTLY DOES IT MEAN?

Distinguishing the rational from the irrational is not, in fact, so simple as it may seem. To properly define what is meant by bounded rationality it is necessary first to know precisely what rationality means, in that different definitions of rationality have different implications for the concept of bounded rationality (Elster, 1986; Hargreaves Heap, 1989).

In economic theory the most useful interpretation of rationality is an instrumental one (Blaug, 1992). Rationality is a feature of the choice of the means by which a given end is to be achieved; it is not a property of the end itself. A successful business executive who makes a large anonymous donation to charity is not behaving irrationally, even though a selfish and materialistic person might perceive it this way. It is not irrational to be altruistic. The executive may be fully aware that their disposable income will be reduced by this action. The most likely explanation is that the executive has a conscience which is eased by the donation; a rational altruist will increase the magnitude of the donation to the point where the marginal emotional benefit from a further increase in the amount donated is just equal to the material sacrifice involved.

When ends are given, it is not possible to say that one end is more rational than another. The only sense in which ends are rational is that preferences must be transitive – consistency requires that if strategy A is preferred to strategy B, and B is preferred to C, then A is preferred to C.

It may, however, be possible to persuade people that some ends are more *reasonable* than others. Thus, a Kantian philosopher may persuade a young vandal that damaging public property is unreasonable because if everyone did the same then it would be self-defeating. There would be no undamaged property left to vandalize, while the cumulative effect of the damage would make everyone worse off. This argument does not show that vandalism is irrational, for the vandal may be someone who derives so much satisfaction from it that it pays them to run greater risks than other people in order to carry it out. It is more of an attempt to influence preferences, so that the vandal associates guilt with acts of vandalism, and therefore finds that such acts no longer make him feel better off.

This manner of treating ends can, if handled wrongly, trivialize the principle of rational action, since it can be used to 'rationalize' any action in terms of unusual ends. Restrictions need to be imposed on ends if instrumental rationality is to have predictive implications. An obvious restriction is that 'more is always better' so far as ordinary goods are concerned. Tastes may be constrained to be convex, implying that people prefer variety to monotony in the range of goods that they consume. The idea that ends are fixed is also important. It is this assumption that is used in economics to predict that decision-makers will substitute against means that have become relatively scarce. If ends are allowed to change, then their laws of change must be fully specified, so that the effects of these changes can be accounted for before the effects of changes in means are considered as well.

Different views of instrumental rationality also prevail. A very narrow view is that a rational decision is based on full information, but this is a very strict criterion which is hardly ever satisfied in practice. For this reason, it is the definition favoured by those who wish to argue that bounded rationality is ubiquitous. In terms of constructing an alternative model of human behaviour, however, this approach does not get us very far.

A broader and more helpful view of rationality is that it involves making the best possible use of available information. In this view, the decision-maker acts under uncertainty, but responds to uncertainty in a particular way. Missing information is replaced by subjective beliefs, and these beliefs are expressed as probabilistic statements. This approach is fairly common in modern neoclassical microeconomic theory (Lippman and McCall, 1979). It is nevertheless controversial. There are those who claim, on the basis of experimental evidence, that people cannot think logically about probabilities. Against this, it is argued that such evidence is generated by placing people in contrived and unfamiliar situations, and that in situations with which they are familiar people behave as though their logic were sound.

A refinement of this broader view allows people to decide how much information they will collect before they make their decision (Marschak and Radner, 1972). Decision-making then becomes a two-stage process. In the first stage, the decision-maker decides what information to collect, and in the second stage he decides how to act on the basis of what he found out. The logic of the process requires the rational decision-maker to consider at the outset how he would behave in each case according to what he has found out. Each possible item of information needs to be considered, and its implications for the ensuing decision worked out. If the information would make no difference to the decision, whatever it turned out to be, then there is no point in collecting it. To know which particular discovery would make a difference, the decision-maker must know to begin with what his decision would be in the absence of any information. This decision reflects his subjective probabilities. Having decided what the consequences of various items of information would be if he had them, the decision-maker then decides which items are worth collecting and which are not.

While this refinement may seem a little complicated, it has one very significant implication, which alone indicates that the approach is very useful. It shows that a rational decision-maker will normally gather information as a sequential process. Indeed, provided there are no physical economies in observing several things at once, it is impossible to improve upon a sequential information-gathering approach with a simultaneous one. The advantage of the sequential approach lies in the option it provides – the option not to continue further searching if it seems unnecessary in the light of what has already been found out.

The optimal procedure is always to gather one particular item of information first, and then to gather a second item depending upon what the first turns out to be. The first item may well be decisive, in the sense that further investigation is unnecessary because it is already obvious what decision to take. If the first decision is not decisive then the second may well be, and so on. In a typical case, the decision-maker goes on to collect several items of information, but not all of them. He stops before collecting all of them because the cost of collecting and processing the next item of information is less than the benefit it is expected to confer. The benefit conferred by reducing the risk of a mistaken decision is more than outweighed by the cost of the additional information. The implications of this result are examined in detail in later sections of this chapter.

META-RATIONALITY

The remainder of this chapter is concerned with developing the implications of rational behaviour in situations where information is costly to process. It is assumed that a rational agent, in deciding how he will take his or her decision, takes full account of the information costs they face, which is known as *meta-rational* behaviour. The simplest example might be a decision-maker who is uncertain about a single parameter in the environment, and who decides whether to observe the value of this parameter before taking the decision. A more sophisticated example might be a decision-maker who faces several uncertainties, and decides to investigate them in turn, in a specific order, using a rule which prescribes how to proceed at each step according to what the information discovered at the previous steps turns out to be.

Meta-rationality also applies to decisions jointly taken by the members of a group. The obvious reason for joint decision-making is that it allows people to specialize in different aspects of decision-making according to their personal comparative advantage. Economic decisions are typically taken in a complex environment where a variety of factors need to be investigated, and where information on these different factors is likely to be dispersed. The dispersion may be geographical – for example, when different sources of information are located in different countries – or by product – when specialists in different markets have to be consulted. Finally, information may be dispersed by functional area; it is quite common, for example, for a synthesis of production information and sales information to be used to plan the next period's output of a product.

The division of labour is not the only reason for using joint decisions. Joint decision-making can reduce the incidence of errors by allowing people to act as checks and balances against each other (Sah and Stiglitz, 1986). It can also improve the implementation of a decision; people who have participated in a decision are more likely to feel a share of the responsibility for it, and so work harder to make it a success. Greater efficiency in the implementation of collective decisions is one of the advantages of the democratic political process, and also of adopting a consultative style of corporate management.

In a centralized group a single individual – the leader – will normally take responsibility for deciding upon the division of labour in decision-making. The leader will choose a set of individual procedures that harmonize with each other, and determine which person should have responsibility for implementing each procedure. The group therefore operates as an organization, its structure geared to the implementation of a particular set of administrative routines. Meta-rationality implies that the structure is optimized by the leader, and that the routines constitute an efficient response to the costs and benefits of information.

In a decentralized group, the division of labour will normally be set by negotiation, which can complicate the analysis quite considerably. Fortunately, decentralization is often a partial process. Instead of everyone negotiating for themselves, everyone belongs to one of a small number of subsidiary organizations. These, together with their inter-organizational links, constitute the organization of the group; the leader of each subsidiary organization negotiates on behalf of its members. Thus, in an example, all the individuals belong to one of two firms. One firm buys a product from the other. The leaders of the two firms negotiate over who investigates what, and who takes responsibility for communicating which information to the other. Each leader decides upon the internal routines that are appropriate to carry out the investigations that his firm has to make.

An obvious objection to meta-rationality is that a decision-maker who selects a procedure, or set of procedures, has to know what the costs of information are. If he does not know the costs, then he cannot do his calculations. He could find out what the costs are by investigation, but then the question would arise as to whether this investigation was itself worth carrying out. The decision-maker would then embark upon an infinite regress, in which every decision would require the cost of information to be known, and where, in order to decide whether this cost was worth discovering, the cost of finding out this cost would need to be discovered as well.

Although this problem may seem insuperable, it is not in fact so serious as it first appears. To begin with, the theory does not in fact require that the cost of information be known, but only that subjective probabilities of the cost should be available. If the decision-maker is risk-neutral, then the missing value of information cost can simply be replaced in the calculations by its expected value. In this case, the solution of the problem is no more complicated with uncertainty than it is without. If the decision-maker is risk-averse, then additional calculations need to be carried out, but there is no reason in principle why these cannot be performed (though see below). Indeed, provided that subjective probabilities can always be invoked, there is no type of uncertainty that the model cannot address. It is therefore possible to pursue the regress as far as required. Of course, there comes a point where the model has to be closed by stopping further regress, but this feature is not unique to the model. Indeed, it is a feature of every formal model that it needs to be closed in such a way. There is, therefore, no better model available on this score – the only alternative is no model at all.

Several components of information cost can be distinguished. These include:

- *observation costs* incurred in direct measurements of the firm's environment;
- *communication costs* of transmitting information between one location and another, and between one person and another;
- *memory costs* of holding information in store for us on a future occasion;
- *deposit and retrieval costs* of putting information into store and getting it out again; and
- *calculation costs* associated with processing information using logical or mathematical operations in order to arrive at decisions, and in order to make it easier to store and to share.

It is possible to devise other ways of classifying information costs, but these are the most useful for present purposes. The importance of the first three cost components is fairly obvious. The fourth component – deposit and retrieval costs – is often quite substantial because of the need to use a filing system to locate the information in the store. The final component – calculation cost – is important not just in terms of economic incentives, but in terms of the entire philosophy of rational action.

The focus of this chapter is on the first three components. Deposit and retrieval costs, and calculation costs, raise quite sophisticated issues which have been discussed in detail elsewhere (Casson and Wadeson, 1996, 1998).

PROCEDURES AND ROUTINES

Meta-rationality is particularly useful in explaining the origins of procedures and routines. It has already been emphasized that optimal information strategies are sequential, which this means that they have an obvious procedural quality to them. In general, they specify that a certain type of information should be collected first, and that further action should be taken depending on what this information turns out to be.

Many of the situations faced by a typical decision-maker are similar to one another, in the sense that the value of the resources committed, the risks attributable to ignorance, and the cost of gathering information are roughly the same in each case. This is certainly the case within the typical firm which confronts the same set of markets in each successive period. Under these conditions, an optimal procedure for one decision is an optimal procedure for every similar decision too. Thus, the same procedure will be applied in each successive case. This procedure identifies the transitory factors in the recurrent situations, and indicates how to respond to the various sets of transitory events that may occur. The optimal procedure forms the basis of a procedural routine.

The significance of this result is most clearly seen when there are set-up costs in devising the optimal procedure. One important cause of set-up costs is that there are certain persistent factors in the environment which dictate what particular form the response to transitory factors should take. These persistent factors are costly to investigate. Once they have been investigated, the chosen procedure can be repeated successfully so long as these factors remain unchanged. The fixed cost of collecting this information on the persistent factors can therefore be spread over all subsequent applications of the procedure.

Suppose, for example, that every period the demand for a product undergoes a transitory change on account of fashion. The procedure dictates how output should respond to this change. It dictates, for example, that the state of fashion should be observed, and output adjusted in some prescribed way. The way that output is adjusted depends upon a persistent factor in the situation. Suppose that, following a transitory shock, demand tends to revert towards some long-run norm. The level of this norm is a persistent factor which governs the rational response to a transitory shock. Suppose, furthermore, that this norm is governed by the availability of substitutes for the product, and that the number of substitutes is not known at the outset. The set-up cost of the rule therefore includes the cost of investigating the number of substitutes. Once this investigation has been made, the information so obtained is encoded in the procedure that is to be applied on all subsequent occasions. Thus, the cost of devising the strategy is spread over numerous decisions.

Meta-rationality therefore predicts that where a decision-maker faces a succession of similar and uncertain situations, behaviour will be governed by the routine application of a particular procedure. This shows that the use of procedures does not have to be explained as a consequence of programmed behaviour, nor as a consequence of some all-pervading bounded rationality. It is a direct consequence of meta-rational behaviour in a particular type of environment. In this environment, intermittent disturbances create temporary problems within a basically stable system. From this perspective, the firm is a functionally specialized organization dedicated to the formulation and implementation of a particular type of decision process based upon procedural routines.

MEMORY

Repeated application of a procedure requires that the procedure be memorized. If memory costs are high, then it may be cheaper to investigate the persistent factors all over again each period, rather than to remember the procedure. In general, the decision-maker faces a trade-off between memorizing a procedure and 'reinventing' it each time it is required (Casson, 1995, chapter 6).

Memory costs generally depend upon the complexity of the procedure. Complexity in turn depends on a number of factors: in particular, on the number of different combinations of circumstances that can be identified by the information collected, and the number of different strategies that are conditional on this information. The ease with which the conditions can be formalized is also important. If the procedure is complex and difficult to formalize then memory costs are high, remembering the procedure is discouraged, and repeated improvization of the procedure is preferred instead.

To reinvent a procedure, the persistent factors in the environment must be observed again. Memorizing a procedure involves observing the persistent factors only once. Use of memory therefore spreads the costs of observing the persistent factors over repeated uses of the procedure in a way which improvization does not. The less frequently the procedure is required, the more difficult it is to spread the memory costs. A procedure is therefore more likely to be memorized the more frequently it is used. The higher the cost of observing these persistent factors, the greater the advantage of memorizing the procedure in order to spread the cost.

Much recent research on organizational behaviour is preoccupied with the idea that procedures are memorized inside people's heads, rather than recorded in a written form. It is said that all the managers within an organization rely upon essentially the same procedures, and they socialize with each other in order to reinforce their memories of these procedures. This is linked with the view that problems of any given type are liable to occur almost anywhere within an organization: procedures are not specific to particular functional or geographical areas but are common to all the areas in which the firm is involved. Those who regularly use a given procedure should therefore share their knowledge with those who only need to use it on an intermittent basis.

These procedures are said to constitute the organizational culture of the firm, and they are crucial to the firm's success. When the persistent factors in the firm's environment change, these procedures need to change as well; but these procedures may be deeply embedded in managerial psychology, and legitimated by the past successes that are widely imputed to them. Under these conditions, the prime requirement for effective leadership of the firm is 'change management' – to legitimate changes in the key routines without damaging the social cohesion of the management team.

While there is a good deal of insight in this view, there is a danger that by placing exclusive emphasis on the social aspects of management, some of the impersonal aspects are overlooked. In many technologically progressive industries, scientific competence in the application of formal procedures in functionally specialized areas remains crucial to the firm's success. For example, the ability to decide intelligently how much information is required to resolve a technical issue in product development governs the speed with which the firm can innovate in order to 'stay ahead' of the competition. Similarly, in mature industries facing intense price competition, the control of cost through highly formal accounting procedures is crucial to competitive success. Scientific and accounting procedures of this kind are usually implemented by technical experts who do not need to socialize extensively with other managers in order to do their job. Moreover, the procedures they employ can be formalized sufficiently for subordinates to be given a rule book to allow them to play their part in carrying out the procedures. Organizational memory is localized in functional areas, and not distributed evenly throughout the firm. Moreover, a good deal of it is not locked away inside people's heads, but is recorded in writing to facilitate dissemination within the relevant functional group.

The same point may be made about the localization of organizational memory within multinational firms. While local memories may be socially embedded in the managerial teams of individual national subsidiaries, the case for teams from different subsidiaries to share their memories is often weak. The more specific the marketing and production requirements in each country, the less is to be gained by sharing organizational memories on a companywide basis.

INTERNAL COMMUNICATION

Communication costs are of two main kinds. There are geographical costs of transmitting information over distance, and there are costs of interpersonal transfer of information. The geographical costs reflect such factors as higher telephone charges for long distance calls, and higher postal charges for international mail. The costs of interpersonal communication include the costs of encoding messages in a manner that is intelligible and unambiguous to the people to whom they are addressed.

Recent literature on international business emphasizes the tacit nature of much of the information communicated within the firm, and argues that such communication is possible only because of the shared values and beliefs created by the corporate culture. This is equivalent to the proposition that costs of communication are much lower within firms than they are between firms.

However, this proposition sits uneasily with the growing evidence for strong interorganizational links between independent firms (Ebers, 1997). A closer examination of the issue suggests that many firms rely upon professional cultures to mediate relationships between managers. Thus, a high-technology manufacturing firm may rely upon the culture of the engineering profession; a financial conglomerate may rely upon the culture of the accounting profession, and so on. It makes economic sense for firms to 'free ride' wherever possible on other institutions which build up understanding and trust between the managers they employ. This strategy also affords the flexibility to build interorganizational links with other firms that employ people from the same professional group.

The problem with the conventional approach to tacit information is two-fold: firstly, it assumes that tacitness, and not transactions cost, is the dominant factor dictating the boundaries of the firm. Secondly, it plays down the influence of tacitness on the internal organization of the firm. While tacitness is of limited significance for the boundaries of the firm, it is of considerable significance for organizational structure and management style. By mistakenly emphasizing the former effect, the latter effect has been overlooked.

The high communication costs associated with tacit information tend to impair the managerial division within the firm. The more tacit the information, the more difficulty managers have understanding one another. If people cannot understand what other people say, then there is little point in basing their decisions on what other people try to tell them. If a chief executive cannot understand what his subordinates tell him, then he will manage in a highly autocratic style. The only information that he will use in arriving at a decision is information that he has collected himself. This may be adequate if the firm depends upon just a few key sources of information – for example, a small number of business publications to which the chief executive subscribes. It may also be adequate if the sources of volatility in the firm's environment are few, so that it is easy for one person to monitor them all (see Lawrence and Lorsch, 1967, p. 117). But, if information sources are dispersed, and there are many different kinds of volatility to contend with, then an autocratic management style is likely to result in seriously mistaken decisions.

An autocratic style normally implies a highly-centralized organizational structure, but this is not invariably so. It is possible for a firm to operate as a federation of autocrats, who bargain with each other on behalf of the groups they each control. Each senior manager collects his own information locally and acts upon it without consulting his subordinates. He bargains with other senior managers on an individual basis if he needs resources from them. Communication is confined to giving orders within each group, and quoting prices to other groups. This model is most appropriate where activities are loosely coupled – for example, where the firm is exploiting different local brands in different national markets, when the strategies pursued in one national market have few knock-on effects so far as other markets are concerned. It is, however, inappropriate where the firm's activities in different locations are tightly coupled – for example, where production in different countries involves different stages of a vertically-integrated process, or where different national sales subsidiaries are responsible for maintaining the reputation of the same global brand.

Explicit information affords lower communication costs and therefore permits a more consultative management style. The consequent pooling of information from diverse sources generally results in a better decision. It may also help to sustain higher levels of innovation. Much of the information contributed by a manager to a consultation process involves updating other managers on how circumstances have changed in his own particular field. Through the consultation process, therefore, managers as a group come to appreciate the full extent of all the changes they confront, and to appreciate the collective need to respond. By contrast, an autocratic style of management tends to suppress information on change, and therefore allows outdated strategies to be sustained.

Low communication costs not only improve the static efficiency of the firm, therefore; they also boost dynamic efficiency by encouraging consultation which promotes regular change. This is one reason why an evolving business environment, in which persistent factors change from time to time, tends to favour a consultative management style. The faster the pace of evolution, the greater the need for consultation, and the greater the incentive for the firm to invest in lowering communication costs.

This result links back to the earlier discussion of corporate culture. It shows that the advantages of reducing communication costs are particularly great in situations of rapid change. In so far as a homogenizing corporate culture reduces communication costs, it increases managers' appreciation of the scope of change, and builds consensus on the need for innovation. Volatile environments, therefore, favour investing in corporate culture in order to reduce communication costs, as an instrument for promoting innovation.

EXTERNAL COMMUNICATION

External communication costs are a neglected topic in the modern theory of the firm. This is most surprising, given the great importance attached to the marketing function in modern consumer societies. It is also surprising in the light of the growth of interfirm linkage relationships noted above.

External communication costs are fundamental to marketing strategy. It is by communication with customers that the nature of the product is explained to them. More importantly, it is by listening to its customers that the firm discovers the kinds of improvement in the product that its customers would most like to see. Effective marketing therefore requires a two-way flow of information, in which customers are not confined to receiving advertising messages from the firm, but get an opportunity to express their preferences for different products as well. These preferences relate not merely to existing products – which customers can easily signal through their purchasing decisions – but to products which do not yet exist.

The idea that firms need to engage in dialogue with their customers is an attractive one. There is a problem, however. If customers were to share all their information with the firms, then they would almost certainly express preferences for certain types of product which it is quite impossible to produce. This is because customers can visualize what their ideal product is like, but lack the technical knowledge to assess whether it is feasible or not. Likewise, if firms were to share all their knowledge of the production possibilities with their customers, they would almost certainly describe many kinds of product which are irrelevant to customers' needs.

What is required is a system by which customers and producers can select information that is relevant for each other (Casson and Wadeson, 1997). This selection needs to be informed by a message previously received from the other party. The object of this message is not to convey a lot of information in itself, but rather to indicate what kind of information it is desired to receive. In other words, the opening message may simply be a question. The answer sought is not necessarily a comprehensive one, it is one that is just sufficient to determine the follow-up question that needs to be asked. After a number of questions and answers, the crucial information begins to be exchanged. This is information which has been selected, by the preceding conversation, from all the information that might conceivably have been communicated for its pertinence to the problem. It may, for example, relate to which variant of the product a customer would choose from two highly-desirable variants, both of which are feasible for the firm to produce.

By structuring questions and answers in different ways, the exchange of the crucial information is arrived at in varying numbers of steps. The most efficient dialogue is that which achieves an exchange of pertinent and decisive information in the minimum number of steps. The exchange of this pertinent and decisive information is what brings the communication process to a close, since it establishes which amongst a small number of highly-desirable and technically-feasible variants is closest to what the customer really wants.

Of course, the most efficient form of dialogue depends upon what the optimal variant of the product really is. Since this is not known in advance, the dialogue is chosen using subjective probabilities of what the best solution may turn out to be. In terms of the meta-rational approach, the producer and the customer agree to maximize the joint benefit from their conversation. They agree on the subjective probabilities to be used in the calculation of the optimal conversation, and then optimize the structure of the conversation and proceed to share their information in the agreed way.

There are a number of different dimensions of a conversation that need to be optimized. One is the subject to which the questions are addressed. The producer and the customer must agree on which aspects of the product design are to be considered. The sequencing of the conversation needs to be decided too – should the customer ask the first question, or should the producer initiate the process instead? Should the conversation be terminated if it does not seem to be getting far, in terms of matching product design to customer needs, and if so how quickly should it be abandoned?

If a producer is trying to improve a mass-produced branded product, then he will naturally consult with a very large number of customers before he makes any change. These customers will be chosen as a representative sample of the wider population of customers with whom he deals. The conversation will normally be implemented through market research, which implies that the protocol governing the conversation will be fairly rigid. The producer will take the initiative in approaching the customer, and only after the customer has answered a few questions will the producer begin to divulge information of his own, such as what kinds of new variants he considers that it may be feasible to produce. The customer may be offered prototypes of these products to examine, and in some cases may even be able to try them out. The results of the market research are then fed back into the product development programme. When the prototypes have been modified the process may iterate.

The opposite extreme to mass production is where each unit of output is customized to a particular buyer's requirements. This is often the case with intermediate products, and in particular with capital equipment. A producer of durable capital goods may liaise individually with each customer over the design of the good. This resembles the kind of one-to-one conversation which is common in normal social intercourse. The customer may begin by indicating, in general terms, the kind of performance requirements he has in mind. The producer then sketches out a couple of designs, and the customer indicates which is the most preferred. He may also indicate that either will do and that the cheapest is preferred, or that neither will do and that a new set of designs should be submitted instead. Compared to mass production, the dialogue is more likely to begin with the customer, rather than with the producer. The customer's requirements are likely to be stricter, with less scope for substitution between different product characteristics. The process is also more likely to terminate with no feasible solution to the customer's problem being found.

The meta-rational approach to external communication therefore predicts that the protocols governing the interfirm marketing of intermediate products will differ significantly from those that apply to the marketing of consumer products. Although this result is already familiar from the industrial marketing literature, the meta-rational approach affords a rigorous explanation of the result in terms of efficient communication. It also provides a means of extending the analysis to deal with differences in the marketing of various types of intermediate product, and of various types of consumer product too.

It is important to emphasize that although these dialogues take place across the boundaries of the firm, the question of how the dialogue is constructed is logically distinct from the more familiar issue of where the boundaries of the firm are drawn. Though distinct, the issues are, however, related, as might be expected. The connection is stronger, the greater the degree of distrust. Each party incurs costs in terms of the time tied up in the process of conversation. At each stage of the conversation, one party may learn more useful things from the other party than the other party learns from them. At various points where the process may be terminated without success, one party may have sunk far greater costs in the conversation than the other.

When each party is suspicious of the other, each party will wish to minimize their own contribution to the conversation. They will try to persuade the other party to divulge information which is useful to them for other purposes, whilst minimizing the amount of such information they divulge themselves. The producer will be reluctant to go to the expense of constructing prototypes in case the customer should reject them on quite trivial grounds. A devious customer may claim that a prototype is unsuitable for his purposes when it really is quite suitable, in the hope of acquiring the prototype for a heavily discounted price. In general, when each firm reduces its commitment to the communication process, misunderstandings are likely to become more frequent and the efficiency of the outcome is reduced.

When the gains from collaboration between the firms are high, but the level of trust is very low, it may therefore be advantageous for the firms to integrate. By pooling the financial interests of the firms, neither any longer stands to gain from economizing on communication cost at the expense of the other. Communication becomes much richer, and it is much more likely that an appropriate product is supplied for a reasonable cost. It is, therefore, because of distrust, and the need to control its consequences, that the location of the boundaries of the firm and the pattern of communication across these boundaries are linked.

RATIONAL LEARNING

Meta-rationality also provides a means of tackling the difficult issue of what is meant by rational learning. Learning is a key theme of the recent literature on organizational change (see for example Nohria and Ghoshal, 1994). Learning is clearly connected with bounded rationality in the sense that bounded rationality defines the initial conditions in which learning takes place. A fully-informed individual would have nothing to learn. Once again, however, there is a tendency in the recent literature to discuss the issue in a superficial way. The meta-rational approach provides greater analytical rigour, and as a result it becomes possible to derive a connected set of hypotheses concerning when and where learning will occur, and how it will actually take place.

Rational learning may be said to involve the updating of subjective probabilities in the light of new information. Bayes' Rule provides the logical framework in which this is done. The decision-maker begins at the outset with a set of alternative hypotheses, but is unsure which of them is true. These hypotheses typically relate to the unknown value of a key parameter, such as the rate of growth of the market, or the price-elasticity of demand.

The implementation of Bayes' Rule is not a simple matter, though (Kirman and Salmon, 1995); non-linearities make it computationally complex. It is much easier to update probabilities using simple procedures that approximate to the non-linear relations implied by Bayes' Rule. The use of these alternatives may be rational when the costs of calculation are particularly high. A rational individual can compare alternative learning strategies, and select the one that is most suitable for their purposes.

A common objection to arguments of this type is that the kind of uncertainty that learning has to contend with is too radical to permit the apparatus of rational choice to be used. Subjective probabilities cannot be formed, it is said, and the underlying model into which they are supposed to be inserted is not known either. People may know that they are uncertain, but not what they are uncertain about.

A person confronted with radical uncertainty of this kind can still pursue a strategy of trial and error, however. It is still possible to 'play around' with something and to remember which experiment produced the best result so far. The crucial questions in experiments of this kind are two-fold. The first is to decide in what order to try out the various possibilities. The second is to decide when to stop experimenting and to stick with the best strategy discovered up to that time.

The interesting thing is that these are essentially the same problems that were discussed earlier, but in a different guise. Both sets of issues concern the optimization of a search strategy. The difference between them lies in the nature of the information collected, and the use to which it is put. In the first case, the information concerns some aspect of the firm's environment, and it is inserted into a model of the firm's environment that the decision-maker is using to guide his decision. In the second case, the information relates to the performance achieved by a trial action of a given type. This is not inserted into a model of the firm's environment because such a model does not exist in this case. It is put into a model of the learning process instead. This model estimates, in the light of past experience, how much further improvement may be possible in the light of further experiment. Information on the latest trial informs the judgement on whether further improvement is likely if another trial were to be made.

It could, of course, be asserted that because of the radical nature of the uncertainty, it is impossible to apply any model of the learning process in this way. The alternative view is that the order in which the experiments are undertaken is arbitrary, and so is the time at which the experiments stop. But this negative view ignores the possibility that a decision-maker, confronted over time with a succession of radically un-certain situations, can experiment with different experimental procedures. If these radically uncertain situations have certain elements in common, then the adequacy of the solution obtained by a given learning proce-dure in any given case can be taken as an indicator of the probable efficiency of the procedure in other cases. Given a sufficient number of radically uncertain situations with which to experiment, therefore, the decision-maker will tend to converge, by pragmatic adjustment, upon an efficient learning procedure. This efficient learning procedure is the one that trades off correctly the expected gain from fewer mistaken decisions in the future against the expected cost of experimental failure today.

The analysis of learning by experiment indicates that the accumula-tion of experience is the key to successful decision-making. Those who have encountered similar cases of radical uncertainty before can form a better judgement about what learning procedure works best than can those who have not. Even those with no experience of their own, how-ever, can attempt to free-ride on the experiences of others, copying what they do. Even if other people's learning procedures cannot be directly observed, the speed of learning achieved by the most successful people acts as a benchmark against which a person's own performance may be judged. The discrepancy between current performance and benchmark performance indicates the scope for improvement in learning procedures that could be achieved by further experiments.

It follows that even under conditions of radical uncertainty, useful predictions about behaviour can be derived from the rationality postulate. Rational action is a principle whose scope is not confined to well-specified situations. The application is certainly easier when situations are well-specified, but the principle is not so fragile that it disintegrates when confronted with loosely-specified problems instead.

SUMMARY AND CONCLUSIONS

The essence of meta-rationality is that the decision-maker calculates in advance of any decision how they will respond to various components of information cost. Five main components of information have been identified, and three have been discussed in detail. From a meta-rational perspective, the most straightforward type of information cost is observation cost. Meta-rational analysis of observation cost illustrates very simply the costs and benefits of dispelling uncertainty in decision-making. Memory costs are a little more difficult, and to analyse them it is necessary to adopt a dynamic, or intertemporal, perspective. Memory allows the set-up costs of gathering information on persistent factors to be spread over all subsequent decisions where information on these factors is required. The meta-rational perspective on memory explains why routine procedures are memorized in order to deal with repetitive situations in which the same persistent factors apply.

Communication costs add a further dimension to the analysis. Unlike observation and memory costs, it impossible to analyse communication costs fully without allowing for the fact that more than one person is normally involved. Communication costs are incurred both within and between organizations. The easiest to analyse are those within an organization, and in this context an employer seeks to optimize the internal division of labour in information-handling by structuring information flow between his employees. This optimization process is easiest to see in the planning of routine procedures. It is the optimization of the implementation of routines that governs the organizational structure and management style of the firm.

Communication between organizations is most readily handled by assuming that the organizations seek to maximize their joint rewards. Again, it is most useful to situate the analysis in terms of the planning of routines, or protocols, which structure communication between the organizations on a regular basis. Meta-rational structuring of communication between two organizations is exemplified by the arrangements used for collaborative design between an assembler and a subcontractor.

Meta-rational theory places many of the insights of conventional organization theory on a more rigorous footing. An important consequence of this greater rigour, however, is that it highlights the contingent nature of many of the conclusions which have previously been advanced in an unqualified way. In other respects, meta-rational theory undermines some of the claims to be found in the recent literature. It shows, for example, that the hierarchical form of organization has many inherent advantages. It suggests that the key issue in organizational design for international business is not so much whether hierarchy is appropriate, as what form of hierarchy works best under what conditions. Firms in a stable and sheltered environment may operate most effectively under a fairly autocratic style of management. But the greater the number and diversity of shocks, and the greater the need for innovation, the more appropriate is a consultative management style instead. Meta-rational theory has the power to predict exactly what form such consultation will take. It can predict the decision procedures used within the firm, and the way in which different parts of each procedure are allocated to different people. As such, it goes into much further detail than the more visionary discussion of organization that is characteristic of recent international business literature.

Note

The idea for this chapter stemmed from a discussion with the late Gunnar Hedlund at the Conference on Perspectives in International Business, at Columbia, South Carolina, and from a subsequent conversation with Oliver Williamson at the European International Business Association Annual Conference at Reading (both in 1992). Although this chapter is somewhat critical of certain aspects of these authors' work, the usual *caveat* applies: the criticism is directed at the most eminent and persuasive expositors of the alternative point of view. A preliminary version of this chapter was delivered at the Academy of International Business (UK Chapter) Annual Conference at Leeds, April 1997, and a revised version at the Conference in honour of Brian Loasby held at Stirling, August 1997. The authors are grateful to the organizers and to the discussants for their comments.

9 Internalization and Multinational Banking

Peter Chi Ming Fu

INTRODUCTION

Most advocates of internationalization theory, such as Buckley and Casson (1976), Dunning (1981), Hennart (1982) and Rugman (1981), have contended that firms will have no economic reason to participate in international production if there are no benefits for them to internalize markets where there are imperfections. Market imperfections are derived from two basic sources. The monopolistic-advantages approach put forth by Hymer (1976), Kindleberger (1969) and Caves (1971) emphasizes 'structural' imperfections of the monopolistic type which result from product differentiation, marketing skills, special access to inputs and proprietary technology, economies of scale and scope, and government intervention. On the other hand, the internalization approach postulated by McManus (1972), Buckley and Casson (1976) and Hennart (1982) focuses on the 'natural' imperfections derived from the concept of transaction costs. Dahlman (1979, p. 148) crystallized the concept of transaction costs by describing them as 'search and information costs, bargaining and decision costs, policing and enforcement costs' (quoted from Coase, 1988, p. 6).

According to Casson (1989, p. 1), a multinational bank (MNB) is an enterprise that owns and controls banking activities in more than one country. The concept of transaction costs in explaining multinational banking is particularly appropriate because banks' businesses involve currency which has evolved in order to reduce transaction costs. Internalizationists view the multinational enterprise (MNE) as a special case of a multi-plant firm in which the plants happen to be located in different countries. In the internalization approach, a profit-maximizing firm will carry out value-adding activities within the firm when the benefits of doing so are greater than those of purchasing the intermediate product/service from an 'arm's-length' partner in the market. In other words, firms and markets are viable means of organizing economic activity. What distinguishes the two is the way that the activities of economic agents are organized and directed. In markets, economic agents

141

are autonomous and prices convey the information they require in order to make optimum joint decisions. In firms, information for decision-making is channelled by employees to managers who coordinate organizational activities and issue instructions for execution.

In a perfectly functioning market, where there are large numbers of economic agents (buyers and sellers), when each of them is perfectly honest and has complete information, and where there are no externalities,[1] market prices can costlessly perform the tasks of organizing economic activities, such as informing, rewarding and eliminating bargaining. In this case, the costs of market transactions are zero, and there is no economic basis for the existence of the firm. In reality, markets are imperfect and transaction costs are always positive. Sellers and buyers spend significant amounts of time and effort to disseminate and collect information, and to bargain and negotiate deals or contracts. In addition, enforcement and policing costs are also high – products are weighted and graded, and consumer councils, police and courts are established to ensure contracts are fulfilled and deals are fair. Due to these market imperfections, firms are created to replace markets in organizing economic activities.

Firms, however, may not replace all kinds of markets because, on the one hand, some markets are quite efficient and transaction costs are fairly low (for example, the foreign exchange markets of international financial centres), while, on the other, firms' hierarchies incur organization costs in performing their functions (for example, resources used to monitor the performance of employees and to administer and negotiate their wages). The firm will take over when the organization costs of certain economic activity carried out within a hierarchy are lower than its transaction costs through a market. In other words, the firm internalizes the market for such activities when the latter fails to perform, or performs poorly, its resources-allocating function.

This chapter attempts to identify the sources of market imperfections for banking activities in order to assess the bank's incentives to internalize markets across national borders. The following section reviews the process of financial intermediation and explores the reason why financial intermediaries come into existence. The third section identifies the principle functions of a bank and analyses their interdependence. The fourth section examines the nature of banking services and their role in the multinational bank's decision to internalize non-domestic activities. The final section compares retail banking and wholesale banking in terms of location of facilities and discusses the alternatives to multinational wholesale banks.

THE PROCESS OF FINANCIAL INTERMEDIATION

Financial intermediaries (FIs) are firms which produce financial services. The essential function of an FI is to channel funds from the surplus units (the ultimate lenders) to the deficit units (the ultimate borrowers). The result of this fund-channelling function is the speeding up of the capital formation process of an economy. Capital formation occurs when an economy's capital goods or productive capacity increases. It requires the surplus units to postpone their current consumption so that resources are directed to the purchases of capital goods. By postponing current consumption, the surplus units can make use of their surplus purchasing power to purchase a variety of financial assets, which are claims on the issuers for a future stream of payments.

When the financial assets are issued by non-financial units or corporations (such as, for example, IBM and BT), they are called primary securities, which are in the form of debt and equity instruments such as commercial papers, bonds and company shares. Proceeds of the issues are used to purchase capital goods (real assets) for the production of goods and services. When the financial assets are issued by financial intermediaries, such as banks, they are called secondary securities, which are normally in the form of certificates of deposits, demand deposits, pensions and shares of various types of fund. Proceeds of the issues form the pool of loanable and investment funds, which are redirected to the deficit units or ultimate borrowers through lending and purchase of debt and equity instruments issued by them. This is known as the asset transformation process.

Intermediary services can be classified into two basic kinds: the distribution function and the asset transformation function.[2] The direct and indirect fund-transfer process is shown in Figure 9.1. Direct financing, as in the case of barter exchanges, will only take place when a condition is met: double coincidence of financial needs. The specifications of financial needs for borrower and lender includes the amount of fund, interest rate, maturity, repayment schedule, acceptable security and risk. Direct financing is inefficient because often the search or transaction costs (the time and money spent) involved in finding and negotiating with potential counter-parties are high.[3] Differences in preferences between borrower and lender have to be overcome when designing a financial contract. Borrowers may wish to borrow for longer terms than lenders are willing to lend because the borrower knows more about the investment he makes with the fund and is more certain about the repayment. On the other hand, Diamond (1991) contends that an entrepreneur who knows that his project is profitable will finance it with short-term debt, with the intention of refinancing it later on when new information arrives, whereas an entrepreneur who knows that his project is unprofitable

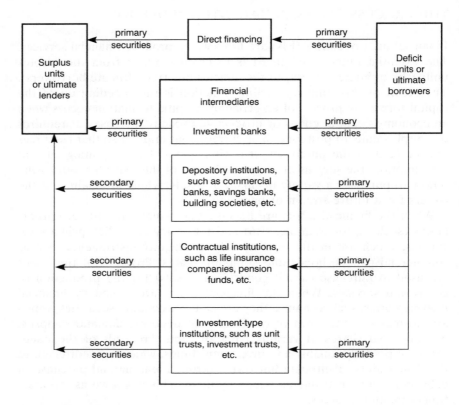

Figure 9.1 The direct and indirect fund-transfer process

will use long-term debt. The reason for this is that the 'high-quality' entrepreneur is prepared to bear the risk that the new information about the project's profitability will be adverse, while the 'low-quality' entrepreneur is not prepared to bear this risk (Hart, 1995, p. 118).

Asymmetric information forms a major source of market imperfection in direct financing. According to Mattesini (1993, pp. 73–82), the study of the problem of asymmetric information has stimulated a new line of research that aims to understand: why intermediaries exist; why they differ from other types of firms; and what the effects are of financial intermediation on the rest of the economy. Mattesini also notes that there are two lines of research in the study of financial intermediation. The first contends that FIs (and particularly banks) arise in order to satisfy a demand for insurance against an uncertain demand for liquidity in a situation characterized by informational problems. Suppose that investing in illiquid assets is more profitable than investing in liquid assets, but there are costs of being illiquid: investors will try to obtain insurance against the state of being illiquid. However, in reality investors' contingencies are private information, and consequently there is no public information on which the payment to an insurance pool can be based. The insurance contract therefore cannot be designed and implemented. By offering demand deposits, banks are able to rely on the 'the law of large numbers' and can obtain such insurance and satisfy the demand for liquidity. Although some individual depositors may withdraw their deposits, others will add theirs at the same time, and banks can rely on a considerable degree of stability in their deposit-base as a whole. They can then invest a proportion of their deposits for long-term loans from which the return is more than enough to secure interest payments to the depositors.

The second line of research identified by Mattesini (1993) focuses on the role of FIs in minimizing the costs imposed by asymmetric information on the economy. Lewis and Davis (1987, p. 25) summarize information difficulties in making a financial contract as: (i) the *ex-ante* problem of imperfect information, where lenders are unable to accurately assess the future prospects of a borrower; (ii) the *ex-post* problem of monitoring the actions of the borrower for consistency with the terms of the contract, and ensuring that any failure to meet the delivery promise is for genuine reasons; and (iii) the need for much information to devise a solution should the borrower be unable to meet their commitment. In this instance, FIs which specialize in the acquisition of information arise to minimize the cost of information.

An investment bank that underwrites the primary issues of borrowers, and repackages and redistributes them to lenders or investors,[4] may help in matching the funding requirements of a borrower to the needs of lenders. The investment bank is specialized in advising, administrating and market-making for primary securities. It is an information centre where information on lenders' asset preferences and borrowers' financing needs are collected and exchanged. This *distribution* function of the investment bank helps to reduce search costs. In addition, by pooling information of various borrowers and lenders, the investment bank can increase the opportunity of diversification (and hence reduce the risk) for both sides of the funding process.

Borrowers can issue different and specialized types of securities to meet a wider range of preferences of individual lenders. An international investment bank may also broaden the base of supply of funds for the borrower by promoting and distributing the issues abroad. However, the distribution function may sometimes leave unresolved some of the difficulties associated with the double coincidence of financial needs. For borrowers of smaller size, particularly those whose debt instruments are not traded in the secondary market (for example, the non-listed private company), maturity of the contract and their creditworthiness become serious impediments for potential lenders to enter the market.

To overcome the difficulties of double coincidence of financial needs, FIs very often engage themselves in *transforming* the primary securities into secondary securities. Consequently, the FIs are liable to claims from the lenders. Secondary securities, such as demand deposits, time deposits and pension fund shares, are particularly attractive to small lenders (or savers in this case) because of their higher liquidity, the greater choice of maturity and size of transaction, and lower risk. FIs are regarded as more reliable than commercial firms for savers to invest their money in because they are normally under tighter scrutiny by government.[5] The role of government as lender-of-last-resort and the existence of deposit insurance schemes often enhance savers' confidence in deposit-taking institutions. In addition, by pooling the resources of many smaller savers, FIs are more capable of diversifying their asset portfolios.

On the other hand, borrowers also find the function of financial assets transformation of benefit because, with such functions, FIs can offer borrowers the financial contracts that meet their needs in terms of amount, maturity, repayment schedule, security requirement, and so on. FIs are able to do this because borrowers are more willing to provide private and specific information to them than to the lender's public. Moreover, FIs are specialized in credit evaluation, enforcing loan compliance, and rescheduling loan contracts in case of liquidity problems for individual borrowers. In conclusion, the asset-transformation function of FIs can help ultimate lenders and borrowers to reduce transaction costs so that the risk-adjusted return to lenders is raised, and the cost of borrowing for borrowers is reduced.

MAJOR FUNCTIONS OF BANKS AND THEIR INTERDEPENDENCE

As discussed above, FIs perform the function of intermediation by making financial contracts with lenders and borrowers who find it too costly to search, negotiate and monitor each other on their own. Among different types of FIs, banks provide an additional function which is fundamental to the growth of an economy – money transmission which facilitates the transfer of means of payments within and outside a country. In many countries, traditionally only banks have been permitted by law to offer chequing accounts or other similar paper-based payments services (for example, the Giro system), although other non-bank depository institutions (such as building societies in the UK) can now offer cheque-writing facilities by means of cooperative ventures. On the other hand, substitutes of paper-based payments services like the electronic funds transfer systems, credit cards, and autopayment systems are becoming increasingly more popular in many countries. In spite of this blurred distinction between bank and non-bank FIs, the functions of providing payments or transaction services, safekeeping of deposits, and lending are generally regarded as the three primary banking functions which correspond with the three basic financial needs of individuals and businesses: transactions facilities, wealth accumulation and financial security (Lewis and Davis, 1987, p. 192).

The phenomenon of banks combining money transmission with financial intermediation functions can be understood by looking at the historical development of banks in developed countries; that is, the evolution of private banks from money changers and goldsmiths who accepted deposits of coins and bullion for safekeeping and issued receipts which were later circulated freely as a means of transacting business. The integration of payment and financial intermediation functions by a bank provides advantages to both customers and the bank itself. To the customers, this integration allows them to conduct 'one-stop shopping' and thus gain in terms of convenience and lessened travelling costs (Lewis and Davis, 1987, p. 173).[6] To the bank, this integration is equivalent to an internalization of the market for payment services. Economies of joint production (for example, bank offices can be shared by the collection and processing of deposits and cheques) is an obvious advantage. In addition, risk for both customers and banks will be lower through integration (as compared to the case where cheque collection and processing are performed by an agent which is completely independent of the bank) because the extra layer of short-term credit is avoided.

The ongoing banker–customer relationship generates competitive advantages for banks over other types of FIs. Lewis and Davis (1987, pp. 61–2) identify two aspects of informational advantages associated with the relationship. Firstly, by being the main banker of a customer who routes most of his transactions (including both the payments and receipts items) through his current or chequing account, the bank can obtain specialized information about the customer's fund flow. Secondly, if a potential borrower is also a depositor or holder of other financial assets issued by the bank, the bank can keep a record of such deposit or investment history. Coupled with the many opportunities of informal contacts with customers, the customer's transactions and deposits records enable the bank to build up a profile of a customer's creditworthiness.[7]

However, the basic problem of the transfer of information or knowledge is information asymmetry. The market for information is imperfect due to high transactions costs (Buckley and Casson, 1976; Casson, 1979; Rugman, 1981; Hennart, 1982; Teece, 1983). In these circumstances, the bank can capitalize on its informational advantages by undertaking lending based upon its specialized information on customers. In other words, the bank *integrates forward* to the market-making of lending to final users or ultimate borrowers (through the same branch office which take deposits), instead of lending to an independent firm which specializes in lending, such as finance houses. Sometimes, a bank with idle funds will place call or short-term deposits at the interbank money market looking for another FI to borrow. This is done normally only in a situation when the bank needs to maintain its liquidity position but does not want to forgo interest, as in the case of holding cash.

In addition to the three key functions – payment facility, deposit safe-keeping and lending, banks provide other functions as well. Among others, the conventional ones are: providing trust services to individuals and business firms, financing international trade, acting as a safe repository for securities and other valuables, and offering financial planning services to personal and corporate clients (Graddy and Spencer, 1990, p. 33). In the next section, the nature of banking services will be explored and the implications this raises for the incentives of a multinational bank to internalize functions across national boundaries will be analysed.

NATURE OF BANKING SERVICES AND INTERNALIZATION

Moutinho (1991, pp. 141–9) describes the characteristics of services as the four I's, namely:

  (i) intangibility (services do not consist of physical attributes which can be held, touched or seen before the purchase decision);
 (ii) inconsistency (the quality of service varies because people who provide them have different capabilities and vary in their job performance from day to day);
(iii) inseparability (services are supplied and consumed simultaneously, and the consumer cannot be separated from the deliverer or the setting in which the service occurs); and
(iv) inventory (services cannot be stored).

The inventory cost of a service is the cost of reimbursing the person used to provide it. As Buckley, Pass and Prescott (1992, p. 40) note, few services display all these feature, although most exhibit more than one. Due to the heterogeneous nature of the service industry, it would be virtually impossible to identify a list of characteristics applicable to all sectors. With illustrations on how different service industries vary in number and in degree of these characteristics,[8] Boddewyn, Halbrich and Perry (1984, pp. 29–33) contend that to determine which industries belong to the service sector, it is necessary to define the distinguishing characteristics of a service enterprise. A service enterprise is defined as one that meets at least one of the following two criteria: product intangibility and/or the dependence of the product's production on the consumer or user input, in the form of the consumer's person or possessions. According to these criteria, banking is a service industry (although it often produces tangible outputs for the customer, such as a bank statement or a loan document) since customer input is a critical element in the process of production of banking services.

In the banking industry, the production, delivery and consumption of services often come together. The personnel and customers of banks have to maintain close contact in order to complete a sale satisfactorily. Information and feedback from bank customers are often a critical part of the production input (for example, when investment consultants and insurance agents discuss matters with customers in order to design for them a tailor-made financial package). Although banking services often do not require the high level of contact required in personal services (such as hairdressing), direct contact with actual and potential customers is essential. Personal contact facilitates non-verbal communication from which 'qualitative' information can be received so that production of banking services can be adjusted and better delivered. Within the banking industry, different types of services may require different degrees of personal contact between the service renders and customers. For example, deposit and financial advising services require higher personal contact as compared to trade financing. Production of the latter involves processing of standardized documents (such as letters of credit, bills of exchange, commercial invoices, bills of lading, and so on) for which communication between the importer's and exporter's banks and other parties can be carried out without the presence of the customers.

Turning now to the international context, Boddewyn, *et al.* (1984, pp. 4–5) classify international services into three types: (i) a foreign-tradeable service which is separable from the production process itself and is transportable across national boundaries (for example, financial loans made across borders); (ii) a location-bound service which is tied to the service-production location, is not capable of foreign trade, and thus requires a foreign presence (for example, hotel accommodation); and (iii) a combination service whose production process is segmented into two parts – one that is location-bound and another that produces a foreign-tradeable product (for example, remote computer data-processing).[9] Adopting this taxonomy of international services, trade financing is a combination service. The foreign-tradeable product in this case includes the information that can be transmitted by telecommunications and the documents that can be sent by post.

Casson (1990, pp. 15–17) identifies two seemingly contradictory propositions for banking services. The first is that, because banks are part of the service sector and services are not readily tradeable, banks must be located where the customer resides. The second is that banking services are tradeable, because they involve information that can be transmitted by telecommunications and documents that can be sent by post. Indeed, because tariffs are difficult to levy on transmissions and documents, trade in banking may potentially be freer than in most manufacturing industries. In the banking industry, deposit services seem to support the first proposition, whereas trade financing and investment banking support the second. But, even in the case of banking services which are tradeable (for example, global investment funds and financial loans made across national borders), foreign direct investment (FDI), in the form of a branch or agency,[10] is still the dominant foreign market-servicing mode for MNBs, unless this is restricted by host-country legislation (as was the case in, for example, Australia and Canada in the early 1980s, see Pecchioli, 1983, pp. 70–4).

The dominance of equity-based overseas operations of MNBs can be explored in two ways. Firstly, financial deregulation in developed countries has blurred the distinction between bank and non-bank FIs through the relaxation of restrictions on the activities of the former, and allowing the latter access to banking markets. The consequence is the emergence of universal or full-service banks whose activities have expanded into the domain of investment banks, securities firms and insurance companies. A full-service bank, as compared to a conventional bank, has to market both banking and non-banking products. It may still be the producer of banking products such as deposits and loans, but for non-banking products it may simply act as a sales outlet for products, such as unit trusts and insurance products, produced by an affiliated or independent non-bank FI. Economies of scope (for example, when a bank teller is also an insurance agent) and the benefit of 'one-stop shopping' for customers are two key drivers in the development of full-service banking. When an MNB decides to enter a new market abroad, it often aims to be a full-service bank in the host country, although initially its main target businesses are often trade banking and project financing. As discussed below, for the operation of a full-service bank in a foreign market, the branch is the most appropriate form.

The key incentive to internalize markets for intermediate services through forward vertical integration in the banking industry has already been highlighted above. In particular, knowledge of customers obtained through an ongoing bank-customer relationship can hardly be exploited through the market system due to information asymmetry and the public-good characteristic of knowledge. By internalizing the market for knowledge, the saving of transaction costs often outweighs the incremental costs of organizing additional transactions within the firm where the constraints of market prices are replaced by management control. It is generally recognized that members of a firm have less incentive to inflict external costs or to withhold external benefits on each other, while their income is no longer directly determined by their own efforts and by their ability to change the terms of trade in their favour (Hennart, 1982, 1991).

However, at the final stage of a production process, the internaliza-tion of markets for final users is not an option. A feasible solution for the bank is to adopt promotion devices that secure some control over purchasing behaviour of customers (Clegg, 1993, p. 89). Promotion for banks normally takes the form of institutional advertising aimed at building up a corporate image or reputation rather than product advertising. Product differentiation for conventional or near-homogeneous banking products, like deposits and loans, is difficult to achieve through advertising. For sophisticated and idiosyncratic banking products like swap arrangements and financial advisory services, advertising is effective in building up awareness, but it is not an effective means of helping target customers comprehend the product and prompt them into action. This is better performed by personal selling.

The importance of building up reputation rests on the profound level of buyer uncertainty over quality. This is particularly pertinent in ser-vices due to their characteristics of intangibility and inconsistency. According to Cowdell and Farrance (1993, p. 280), there are five key aspects to the perceived quality of banking services:

1. tangible assets (for example, physical facilities, equipment, appear-ance of personnel and decoration of bank);
2. reliability (the ability to perform the promised service dependably and accurately);
3. responsiveness (the willingness to help customers and provide prompt service);
4. assurance (the knowledge and courtesy of employees and their ability to inspire trust and confidence); and
5. empathy (the caring and individualized attention the bank provides its customers).

To improve its performance in these five areas, a bank has to ensure that appropriate investments have been made in physical facilities and human resources management for all of its sales outlets and customer contact points (in corporate banking, the contact function quite often rests on the shoulder of a customer service officer). The importance of quality assurance highlights the need for a bank to seek control over its human assets, especially when entering non-domestic markets. Similarly, investment in non-human assets is also a critical element in securing competitive advantage for a bank.

Coase (1937, reprinted in 1988) argues that the distinguishing feature of the employer-employee relationship is that an employer can instruct an employee what to do, whereas an independent contractor must bribe another independent contractor to accomplish this. But, why should an employee pay attention to an instruction while the independent contractor does not? Hart (1995, pp. 57–9) provides an answer based on the control of non-human assets. He argues that when a relationship breaks down in the case of a firm, the employer retains all the firm's non-human assets. However, when a relationship breaks down in a market-based transaction, each independent contractor walks away with a proportion of the non-human assets involved. Non-human assets (such as the licence of operation, reputation, distribution network, files containing important information about a bank's operations and its customers) are critical for an individual to be productive in the banking industry. A bank's need for control over such non-human assets, which leads to the securing of control over human assets, provides a key incentive to internalize when expanding in local and, more especially, overseas markets.

MULTINATIONAL RETAIL BANKING VS WHOLESALE BANKING

The tradeability of various banking services and the location patterns of various types of customers affect the internalization decisions of a multinational bank. Grubel (1977) classified MNBs into three types: retail banks, wholesale banks and service banks. Retail banks provide deposit-taking, lending, financing and related banking services to individuals and small firms. Wholesale banks provide these same services to large corporations, governments, other banks and financial institutions. Service banks provide advice, information, fund transfer and other financial services to travellers and home-country expatriates, and to foreign subsidiaries of firms whose headquarters are located in the parent bank's home country.

Under this classification, retail banking requires a more intensive distribution network as compared to wholesale banking and service banking. For retail banking, the core businesses are location-bound deposits and loans. Convenience is still the paramount criterion for retail banking customers when choosing their banks. Although communication technology, such as electronic payment systems and telephone banking, has reduced the need to establish branches in traditional shopping centres and suburbs, competition among retail banks will mean that branches in commercial and business districts will be needed to gain new customers and to retain existing customers.

For wholesale banking, customers are large corporations and wealthy individuals or families. Large corporations are normally clustered and located in commercial centres or industrial districts from which they enjoy economies of agglomeration. Wealthy individuals are targets of private banks and they are normally served by individual banking officers who are stationed at offices in major cities and contact their customers by personal visits and by telephone. Service banking arises as a consequence of a customer-following strategy. Customers who travel or work overseas expect to access banking services from their own banks in major tourist spots or commercial cities. The overseas subsidiaries of multinational enterprises normally have offices in national or regional financial centres. Thus, service banking and wholesale banking can be operated through banking offices located in strategic districts of host countries.

Lewis and Davis (1987, pp. 94–101) suggest that, in terms of the role of producing liquidity services for non-bank customers, retail and wholesale banking are similar activities – both of them undertake maturity transformation. However, they differ in the manner in which liquidity creation occurs. Lewis and Davis argue that retail banks provide for their own safety by using the 'law of large numbers' to determine the size of reserves needed to insure against the risks of withdrawal and to determine the amount of equity capital needed to insure against default of loans. Wholesale banks, however, cannot operate so readily on the same stochastic principle; their customers are smaller in number, while the transaction amount is higher in value. If the 'law of large numbers' approach of liquidity protection were to be applied to a wholesale bank, the bank would have to be very large in size, possibly exceeding the point where the internal organization costs associated with an additional transaction is greater than the corresponding market transaction costs. How can smaller wholesale banks operate without the protection of the stochastic principles of the retail banks? The integration of retail and wholesale businesses under one bank may increase the level of protection but the risk of default of large loans remains detrimental. Matching of maturities may reduce liquidity risk but will impact negatively upon the bank's profitability.

Wholesale banks solve this problem by adopting the coinsurance and reinsurance practices of the insurance industry. They rely on securitization, loan syndication and the interbank market (Lewis and Davis, 1977, pp. 103–12). Securitization refers either to financial disintermediation (a switch of the assets transformation function to a purely distributive function), or to the process of bundling and repackaging of illiquid assets like mortgage loans into marketable securities. For a wholesale bank, securitization normally refers to the latter. Purchasers of these loan-backed securities receive interest and principal payments. The securities issuing banks earn fee income for administering the loans while increasing their funds through the sale. The banks can make use of the increased funds to satisfy the growing loan demand of borrowers. Through securitization, the banks can further exploit their 'know-how' in originating and monitoring loans, and in the issuing and marketing of financial instruments. This is equivalent to the marketization of loan assets without necessarily sharing much of the information of individual customers and knowledge of loan management to other banks and non-bank investors. Syndicates enable banks to spread loan risks by reducing exposure to single borrowers and allowing them to lend to a larger number of firms of different industries. This is equivalent to a joint venture company set up by pooling capital from different banks to finance a large loan, and can be compared to a coinsurance arrangement in the insurance industry.

Interbank markets assist banks in liability and asset management. When a large deposit is split and lent out to non-bank customers and other banks through the interbank market, it is like a reinsurance arrangement. Withdrawal of the large deposit can be met in part by the bank drawing upon its 'contracts' with the other banks (Lewis and Davis, 1987, p. 109). When a large, medium-term loan to a non-bank customer is funded by interbank borrowed short-term funds instead of by very short-term demand deposits from non-bank customers, a wholesale bank can share the burden of maturity transformation with other banks.

Securitization, syndicates and interbank markets provide mechanisms for wholesale banks to share the maturity transformation and liquidity creation process. In general, they rely more on the market system and collective arrangements. The transaction costs of international financial markets and of cooperation among multinational banks have been reduced due to the progress of communication technology, deregulation, and the unification of banking regulations of different nations (for example, the 'Basle Agreement') – all of which have facilitated the global integration of financial markets. They are alternatives to multinational wholesale banks when the incremental organization costs (and the risks) of internalizing an activity exceed the corresponding transaction costs through the market or through collective arrangements.

CONCLUSION

This chapter shows that the transaction cost approach can be used to successfully explain the existence of banks, and the incentives for international banks to internalize the market of intermediate inputs (that is, information) when they integrate payment, deposit and lending services. We have also explored the implications of the nature of banking services and the importance of quality assurance on the choice of branch or other equity-based organization forms permitted by host-country regulations when entering foreign markets. The chapter has traced the sources of natural market imperfections in the banking industry and demonstrates how banks can internalize non-pecuniary externalities. Internalization theory treats the multinational bank as a special case of a multi-office firm whose offices are located in different countries. It is suggested that different banking services may require various degrees of personal contact and customer inputs in the production process. A full-service bank compared to a specialized bank tends to adopt a high-control organizational form such as branch and subsidiary. Finally, the analysis of wholesale banks' participation in loan syndication, securitization and the interbank market sheds light on how multinational banks will find a balance between internalization, collective arrangements and market transactions in an ever-changing global environment.

Notes

1. An externality is defined as the effect of one person's decision on someone who is not a party to that decision (Coase, 1988, p. 24).
2. Both of them are regarded as financial intermediary services in the broad sense. In a narrower perspective, financial intermediation refers only to the asset transformation process.
3. The counterparty is either a lender or a borrower, although, in practice, it is often the borrower who pays the search costs or the management and issuance fees when an investment bank is appointed.
4. The redistribution of primary securities from ultimate borrowers to ultimate lenders by an investment bank does not involve any change of nature of the securities. It does not create any new financial assets, nor does it alter the form of the contracts. In other words, the investment bank performs purely a distributive function.
5. Banking regulations in many countries specify the maximum ratio of loans to individual borrowers (or group of related companies) to the bank's total deposits.
6. The recipient of a cheque can receive the payment to him by depositing the cheque in his bank or encashing it from the paying bank. When doing the former, he can consume other financial services from his bank at the same time. A bank often provides loans to borrowers by crediting their current or chequing accounts at the bank.
7. This spill-over benefit is one of the reasons why banks make great efforts to cross-sell different bank services to their customers. Other incentives for cross-selling include economies of joint production (for example, one bank statement that lists all types of transactions) and the higher potential for customer-retention since the customer's switching cost will be higher if he maintains multi-accounts with a bank.
8. For example, a management consultant's report is tangible and storable and yet management consultation is a service. Film-processing and off-site equipment repair are considered services for which production and consumption is separated. Consumer participation also varies within the same industry or within the same firm (for example, a full-service restaurant versus a fast-food chain store in the restaurant business, or a human teller versus an electronic teller in a bank).
9. In many instances, the foreign tradeable product is an intermediate product in semi-processed form.
10. Both branches and agencies are legal entities owned by the parent bank. Contrasted with a branch, an agency is not permitted to take deposits.

10 Strategic Motives and Selection Criteria in International Joint Ventures: Perspectives of UK Firms and Foreign Firms

Keith W. Glaister

INTRODUCTION

International joint ventures have become a crucial part of the strategy of many firms (Harrigan, 1985, 1988; Bleeke and Ernst, 1993), with an increase over the past two decades in the incidence of joint venture formation between firms from developed market economies (Anderson, 1990; Hergert and Morris, 1988). Firms have increasingly adopted joint ventures as a purposeful strategic response to changing market conditions, often forming them with their direct competitors, and this trend is likely to persist (Badaracco, 1991; Yoshino and Rangan, 1995). A number of underlying reasons have been advanced for the growth of joint venture formation in recent years with the increased globalization of markets, higher levels of technological, market and capital risk, and the high investment costs of alternative forms of firm growth being highlighted (see Goold, Campbell and Alexander, 1994, Appendix D for a summary). A number of theoretical perspectives have been developed for joint venture formation, the most prominent being those based on the transaction cost approach (Hennart, 1988, 1991; Beamish and Banks, 1987; Buckley and Casson, 1988), organizational learning (Kogut, 1988; Hamel, 1991; Mody, 1993) and resource dependency (Pfeffer and Nowak, 1976).

It has been demonstrated that UK firms have increasingly participated in international joint venture formation with partners from Western Europe, the USA and Japan (Glaister and Buckley, 1994). Also, the strategic motives for joint venture formation and issues in partner selection in international joint ventures have been analysed from the perspective of UK partners (Glaister and Buckley, 1996, 1997). However, to date no studies have examined the perception of foreign partners in joint ventures with UK firms regarding strategic motives and partner selection. This chapter adds to the joint venture literature by presenting new findings on strategic motives and partner selection criteria in international joint venture activity by examining differences between UK firms and foreign firms in UK international joint ventures.

In this chapter international equity joint ventures are considered. Equity joint ventures (EJVs) are created when two or more partners join forces to create a newly incorporated company in which each has an equity share, and each thereby expects an appropriate allocation of dividend as compensation, representation on the venture's board of directors, and active participation in the decision-making activities of the venture (Harrigan, 1985; Geringer, 1991). A joint venture is international in dimension if at least one partner has its headquarters outside the venture's country of operation, or if the joint venture has a significant level of operation in more than one country (Geringer and Hebert, 1989).

The purpose of this chapter is twofold. First, it identifies differences in relative importance of the strategic motives for international joint venture formation between a sample of UK firms which have established joint ventures with partners from either Western Europe, the USA or Japan, and foreign firms from Western Europe, the USA and Japan which have established joint ventures with UK partners. Secondly, the study considers differences in the relative importance of a set of selection criteria between this sample of UK firms and foreign firms.

The chapter is set out as follows: the next section briefly discusses the literature relating to strategic motives for joint venture formation and partner selection, and puts forward the hypotheses of the study. The third section outlines the research methods of the study and sample characteristics. Results and discussion are presented in the fourth section, followed by a summary and conclusions together with recommendations for further investigation.

LITERATURE REVIEW AND HYPOTHESES

The Strategic Motivation for Joint Venture Formation

A number of authors have provided several reasons for joint venture formation from a strategic perspective (for example Mariti and Smiley, 1983; Harrigan, 1985; Porter and Fuller, 1986; Contractor and Lorange, 1988). Several of the identified motives are the same while some of the motives overlap. Hagedoorn (1993, p. 372), for instance, in reviewing the literature relating to motives for interfirm technology cooperation, identifies three groups of motives in this context: motives related to the sharing and further advancement of research and the restricted diffusion of some basic scientific and/or technological knowledge between partners; motives related to concrete innovative projects in a joint activity (for example, to capture the partner's tacit knowledge of technology); and motives related to market access and the search for new business opportunities.

While there are a wide range of feasible motives for joint venture formation, the main elements of the strategic motives identified in the literature are: risk-sharing, product rationalization and economies of scale, transfer of complementary technology/exchange of patents, sharing competition, conforming to host-government policy, facilitating international expansion and vertical linkages. Each of these strategic motives is now considered briefly.

Risk Sharing
Joint ventures are seen as an attractive mechanism for hedging risk because neither partner bears the full risk and cost of the joint venture activity. More broadly, Contractor and Lorange (1988) have identified the ways in which joint ventures can reduce a partner's risk. These include spreading the risk of a large project over more than one firm; enabling product diversification and thus reducing market risks associated with being reliant on only one product; enabling faster market entry and quicker establishment of a presence in the market, which in turn allows a more rapid pay-back of investment; and cost-subaddivity (when the cost of the partnership is less than the cost of investment undertaken by each firm alone). A joint venture can lower, therefore, the total investment cost of a particular project or the assets at risk, by combining expertise and slack facilities in the parent firms.

Product Rationalization and Economies of Scale
Where production is characterized by economics of scale and 'learning by doing', firms may attempt to reduce costs by expanding output to achieve these benefits. Joint ventures allow firms in the same industry to rationalize production, thus reducing costs through economies of scale and 'learning by doing', while avoiding the uncertainties and difficulties of full-scale merger (Mariti and Smiley, 1983).

Joint ventures also reduce costs by using the comparative advantage of each partner. For example, where components are made by both partners in different locations and with unequal costs, production can be transferred to the lower cost location (that is, the location which has the greatest comparative advantage) thus lowering sourcing costs. The larger volume produced in the more advantageous location also provides further reductions in average unit costs by realizing economies of large-scale production (Contractor and Lorange, 1988).

Transfer of Complementary Technology/Exchange of Patents
Joint ventures provide strategic benefits from the exploitation of synergies, and technology or other skills-transfer (Harrigan, 1985). However, a joint

venture must be more than a simple interfirm transfer of technology, it must involve a longer-term relationship. In general, joint ventures may be used to bring together complementary skills and talents which cover different aspects of the know-how needed in high technology industries (Contractor and Lorange, 1988). Significant innovations are likely to result from the fusing of these complementary skills, a result which is unlikely to be achieved by one firm acting alone.

A further advantage of exchanging patents is that faster entry into a market may be possible if the testing and certification completed by one partner are accepted by the other partner's territories. An important consideration with respect to patents is that they also often allow the right to a territory, to the extent that the marketing or territorial rights is the dominant strategic issue behind the formation of a joint venture (Contractor and Lorange, 1988).

Shaping Competition
Joint ventures can influence who a firm competes with and the basis of competition. They may be used, therefore, as a defensive ploy to reduce competition, for example by coopting potential or existing competition into a joint venture. Alternatively, a joint venture may be used as an offensive strategy, for example by linking with a rival in order to put pressure on the profits and market share of a common competitor (Contractor and Lorange, 1988).

Conforming to Host Government Policy
One of the oldest rationales for joint ventures has been building links with local companies in order to accommodate host government policy. Many governments in developing countries and the former Soviet bloc insist that access to the local market can occur only if the foreign company works in cooperation with a local partner (Beamish, 1988). These protectionist policies are not confined, however, to developing countries or to former planned economies. Japan has had what in effect is a policy of exclusion, which has been a major contributory factor in many US and European firms using joint ventures as the most practical way of selling products in the Japanese market (Contractor and Lorange, 1988). Host government pressure to form joint ventures also applies in particular industries. Firms in the defence industry, telecommunications and parts of the financial services industry are often obliged by host government requirements, intended to safeguard particular sectors of the economy, to establish links with local firms (Mariti and Smiley, 1983).

Facilitating International Expansion
It is necessary to distinguish between the role of joint ventures in establishing corporate linkages as opposed to their role in corporate entry strategies (Young *et al.*, 1989, p. 19). Firms faced with foreign market

entry have a wide array of entry modes to choose from (Root, 1987). Hill, Hwang and Kim, (1990, p. 118) note that most of the international business literature focuses on three distinct modes of entry into a foreign market: licensing or franchising, entering into a joint venture or setting up a wholly-owned subsidiary. Each entry mode has different implications for the degree of control (that is, authority over operational and strategic decision-making) that the parent firm can exercise over the foreign operations; resource commitment (that is, dedicated assets that cannot be redeployed to alternative uses without cost) to the foreign operation; and the risk of dissemination (that is, the risk that firm-specific advantages in know-how will be expropriated by a licensing or joint venture partner) that the firm must bear to expand into the foreign country. Hill *et al.* (1990) argue that, for a given context of strategic, environmental and transaction-specific variables, identifying the optimal entry mode is a complex and difficult task.

Despite the problems associated with identifying the optimal entry mode, joint ventures may play an important role in facilitating foreign market entry. A firm may, for example, have the production capability but lack knowledge of foreign markets for which it depends on its partners. Contractor and Lorange (1988, p. 15) argue that, in general, it is an expensive, difficult and time-consuming task to establish a global organization and a significant international competitive presence. In this respect, a joint venture offers considerable time savings (Contractor and Lorange, 1988).

While this argument is usually applied to firms undertaking international expansion for the first time, in principle it may also apply more generally to firms with international experience. The move to new foreign markets and the development of either a multi-domestic or a global strategy can be facilitated by joint venture formation even for firms with considerable overseas experience. Also, the speed of internationalization may be critical, given the benefits that may accrue to early entrants such as the ability to command premium prices and the possibility of gaining significant market share (Gannon, 1993). The speed of market entry may therefore be an important determinant of the choice of entry mode. Speed of entry must be balanced, however, against the associated costs and risk.

Vertical Linkages
Strategic joint ventures can create competitive strengths such as vertical linkages (Harrigan, 1985). Contractor and Lorange (1988) argue that joint ventures can be a form of vertical quasi-integration with each partner contributing one or more different elements in the production and distribution chain.

In an empirical study of UK partner firms using a subset of the data reported here, Glaister and Buckley (1996) identified the main strategic motives for joint venture formation by UK partner firms as being intrinsically linked to the market and geographical expansion of the firm. They point out that the transition from an overall theoretical perspective to the firm's strategic motives is not a straightforward one, as the theoretical approaches do not map directly on to the strategic motives. This is partly because the motives implied are not pure or perfectly distinct and also because theory-builders are mainly concerned with issues other than the firm's motivation.

Nevertheless, Glaister and Buckley conclude that the main strategic motives identified in their study are underpinned by the theories of strategic positioning and organizational learning. A weakness of the Glaister and Buckley (1996) study is that they reported data only from UK firms. This chapter builds on the findings of Glaister and Buckley (1996) by considering motives for joint venture formation from the perspectives of both UK and foreign firms.

Partner Selection Criteria

The importance of selecting the 'right' partner to the success of the joint venture has been suggested by a number of authors (Berg, Duncan and Freedman, 1982; Killing, 1983; Harrigan, 1985; Beamish, 1987). Harrigan (1985) stresses that joint ventures are more likely to succeed when partners possess complementary missions, resource capabilities, managerial capabilities and other attributes that create a strategic fit in which the bargaining power of the venture partners is evenly matched. Despite this emphasis on the importance of recognizing respective partner-needs and of matching with the appropriate partner, there is a paucity of literature that specifically addresses the issue of partner-selection in joint venture formation, and particularly in the instance of joint ventures established between firms from developed market economies. A notable exception is Geringer (1988, 1991), who examined data from US-based organizations.

Geringer (1988) has suggested a two-fold typology of categories of selection criteria which is based on the distinction between 'task-related' and 'partner-related' criteria. The former are associated with the operational skills and resources that a venture requires for its competitive success. Thus, task-related criteria refer to those variables that are intimately related to the viability of a proposed venture's operations, irrespective of whether the chosen investment mode involves multiple partners. Geringer provides examples of task-related criteria such as patents or technical know-how, financial resources, experienced managerial personnel, and access to marketing and distribution systems. In contrast, partner-related criteria refer to those variables that become relevant only if the chosen investment mode involves the presence of multiple partners.

Geringer cites examples such as the national or corporate culture of a partner, compatibility or trust between the partners' management teams, the degree of favourable past association between the partners, and the size or corporate structure of a partner.

In an empirical study of UK partner firms using a subset of the data reported here, Glaister and Buckley (1997) identified the main task-related and partner-related selection criteria identified by UK partner firms in equity joint ventures. The highest ranked task-related selection criteria were 'access to knowledge of local market', 'access to distribution channels', 'access to links with major buyers' and 'access to knowledge of local culture'. The highest ranked partner-related selection criteria were 'trust between the top management teams', 'relatedness of partner's business' and 'reputation'. As with the study on strategic motives, a weakness of the Glaister and Buckley (1997) study is that they reported data only from UK firms. Again, this study seeks to build on the findings of Glaister and Buckley (1997) by considering task-related and partner-related selection criteria for joint venture formation from the perspectives of both UK firms and foreign firms. It should be stressed that the main aim of this study is to explore similarities and differences between UK and foreign firm responses to the issues of strategic motivation for joint venture formation and task-related and partner-related selection criteria.

Hypotheses

The purpose of this study is to compare firm responses to the underlying strategic motives and selection criteria employed in a set of international joint ventures. In comparing the motives for international joint venture formation between UK firms and foreign firms, it is plausible that the motives driving joint venture formation will differ fundamentally between UK firms seeking joint ventures with foreign firms, and foreign firms seeking joint ventures with UK firms. For instance, for a UK firm there may be a strategic motive of entry to a new market underpinning the rationale for the venture, while for the foreign firm there may be a defensive motive of linking up with a competitor in order to put increased pressure on a common third rival.

Conversely, it is also possible to argue that both UK firms and foreign firms may have fundamentally the same objectives for joint venture formation, which is reflected in a common set of strategic motives. Therefore, there is, *a priori*, no clear logic for arguing that the dominant motives for international joint venture formation on the part of UK firms will be either the same as, or different to, the dominant motives for joint venture formation on the part of foreign firms. In order to empirically investigate this issue, the null hypothesis of no difference in the relative importance of strategic motives is adopted, as reflected in the first hypothesis:

Hypothesis 1: The relative importance of strategic motives for international joint venture formation will not vary between UK firms and foreign firms.

As noted, task-related selection criteria are associated with the operational skills and resources that a venture requires for its competitive success (Geringer, 1988). Clearly, if one firm has the necessary skills and resources to undertake the venture, then there will be no need to form a joint venture and obviously no need to link up with a partner firm. The venture only becomes necessary when certain essential skills and resources are absent from the first firm but can be gained through the formation of a joint venture with a second firm (Badaracco, 1991; Hamel, 1991). This, of course, necessitates the first firm providing a set of skills and resources which are key to the success of the venture but are absent from the second firm. Complementary sets of resources and skills are therefore required from each partner. This directly implies that the important task-related selection criteria will differ between partners, as reflected in the second hypothesis:

Hypothesis 2: The relative importance of an identified task-related selection criterion will vary between UK and foreign firms.

Partner-related selection criteria refer to those variables that become relevant only if the chosen investment mode involves the presence of multiple partners. As such, there may be a significant degree of overlap in the partner-related selection criteria of partners to a joint venture. While 'opposites may attract' in respect of task-related selection criteria, to the extent that compatible partners must be found it is likely that managements will seek similar partner traits. It is expected, therefore, that similarities of view with respect to partner-related selection criteria will prevail. This is reflected in the third hypothesis:

Hypothesis 3: The relative importance of an identified partner-related selection criterion will not vary between UK and foreign firms.

RESEARCH METHODS AND SAMPLE CHARACTERISTICS

A database of joint venture (JV) formation was derived from joint ventures reported in the *Financial Times* by UK firms with Western European, United States and Japanese partners over the period 1980 to 1989. In order to obtain the requisite level of detail on strategic motivation and selection criteria, a pre-tested postal questionnaire was administered.

Table 10.1   Strategic motivation for alliance formation

(*Motives listed by order of appearance on the questionnaire*)
1. Spreading risk of a large project over more than one firm
2. Sharing R&D costs
3. Enabling faster payback on the investment
4. Economies of scale: joint operations lower costs
5. Production transferred to lowest cost location
6. Enabling product diversification
7. Enabling faster entry to the market
8. To facilitate international expansion
9. To concentrate on higher margin business
10. To gain presence in new markets
11. To maintain position in existing markets
12. Exchange of complementary technology
13. Exchange of patents or territories
14. JV formed with existing or potential competitor to reduce competition
15. JV formed to more effectively compete against a common competitor
16. To conform to foreign government policy

From the prior literature and discussion based on semi-structured inter-views with eight representative managers of UK parent firms, a list of 16 strategic motives, 12 task-related selection criteria and 12 partner-related selection criteria were derived. The questions relating to strategic motives, task-related and partner-related selection criteria were *ex post* measures of managers' perceptions of the relative value of the variables at the time of JV formation. With respect to task-related criteria, for example, respondents were asked 'How important was the formation of the joint venture in allowing access to inputs that *your company* did not have?' Responses were assessed using a three-point scale: 1 = 'of no importance', 2 = 'of some importance', 3 = 'of major importance'. The 16 strategic motives, the 12 task-related selection criteria and the 12 partner-related selection criteria in the order they appeared on the ques-tionnaire are shown in Tables 10.1 and 10.2 respectively.

For UK firms, telephone contact was made with each UK parent that had a joint venture with a Western European, US or Japanese partner, to ascertain the name and position of the most appropriate manager to whom the questionnaire was to be personally addressed. To provide motivation and accurate responses, respondents were guaranteed anonymity and were promised a summary of the research findings. A questionnaire was sent to 203 separate UK partner firms just before the end of 1992. For the UK firms, after one reminder 94 questionnaires were returned, a response rate of 46.3 per cent. Of these, 29 were non-equity joint ventures and so were excluded from this study. The number of UK par-ent firms in the sample is 65. Of these, 37 had partners from Western Europe (57 per cent), 14 (21.5 per cent) had partners from the USA,

Table 10.2 Selection criteria for alliance formation

(*Criteria listed by order of appearance on the questionnaire*)

Task-related selection criteria
1. Access to materials/natural resources
2. Access to technology
3. Access to labour
4. Access to capital
5. Access to distribution channels
6. Access to the product itself
7. Access to knowledge of production processes
8. Access to regulatory permits
9. Access to local brand names
10. Access to links with major buyers
11. Access to knowledge of local market
12. Access to knowledge of local culture

Partner-related selection criteria
1. Degree of favourable past association between the partners
2. Trust between the top management teams
3. The partner company's size
4. Financial status/financial resources of the partner
5. Partner's ability to negotiate with foreign government
6. Experience in technology applications
7. Reputation
8. International experience
9. Management in depth
10. Established marketing and distribution system
11. Complementarity of partner's resource contribution
12. Relatedness of partner's business

and 14 (21.5 per cent) from Japan. A total of 38 (58.5 per cent) joint ventures were in the manufacturing sector with 27 (41.5 per cent) in the tertiary sector. In total, 21 (32.3 per cent) of the ventures had been terminated, and 44 (67.7 per cent) were still active at the time of data collection.

With the foreign partner firms, it was often difficult to identify the location of the foreign partners. Also, in the case of Western Europe, in order to encourage response the decision was taken to concentrate on the major partners that were located in France, Germany and Italy (Glaister and Buckley, 1994) and to translate the questionnaire into the respective languages, which thereby excluded the other Western European partners. A total of 180 French, German, Italian, United States and Japanese partner firms were contacted at the beginning of 1993. Respondents were guaranteed anonymity and were promised a summary of the research findings. A total of 34 questionnaires were returned, a response rate of 19 per cent.[1] Of these, 12 were non-equity joint ventures and hence were excluded from this study. The number of foreign partner

Table 10.3   Strategic motives for joint venture formation: UK and foreign firms

Strategic motive	UK firms (n =65)			Foreign Firms (n =22)			
	Rank	Mean	SD	Rank	Mean	SD	t-value
To gain presence in new markets	1	2.48	.69	2	2.31	.78	.90
Enabling faster entry to the market	2	2.44	.77	1	2.46	.80	−.04
To facilitate international expansion	3	2.32	.88	3	2.00	.82	1.44
To compete against a common competitor	4	1.79	.76	6	1.72	.88	.29
To maintain position in existing markets	5	1.72	.78	8=	1.59	.80	.68
Exchange of complementary technology	6	1.64	.72	4	1.90	.92	−1.38
Enabling product diversification	7	1.63	.72	5	1.77	.87	−.76
Economies of scale	8	1.60	.70	10=	1.55	.80	.30
To concentrate on higher margin business	9	1.52	.66	8=	1.59	.80	−.39
Enabling faster payback on the investment	10	1.51	.71	12	1.41	.73	.56
Spreading risk of large project	11	1.46	.69	7	1.68	.78	1.26
Sharing R&D costs	12	1.43	.64	10=	1.55	.80	−.68
To reduce competition	13	1.36	.65	13=	1.36	.66	.03
Produce at lowest cost location	14	1.34	.59	13=	1.36	.66	−.17
Exchange of patents or territories	15	1.26	.48	16	1.18	.50	.67
Conform to foreign government policy	16	1.15	.44	15	1.27	.46	−1.08

Note:
The mean is the average on a scale of 1 (= of no importance) to 3 (= of major importance).

firms in the sample is 22. Unfortunately, this did not provide a sample of 22 joint ventures with matching partners because for many JVs only one partner responded to the questionnaire. The total number of joint ventures where both partners responded was 11 (that is, a total of 22 partner responses).

Hence, this study concerns UK firms in partnership with foreign firms and foreign firms in partnership with UK firms, but in only 11 cases do the partners match. A sample of 11 is clearly too small to sustain a statistical analysis, and so the discussion is couched in terms of UK firms and foreign firms. Of the foreign partners, nine (40.9 per cent) were from Western Europe, seven (31.8 per cent) were from Japan, and six from the USA (27.3 per cent). A total of 13 (59.1 per cent) of the joint ventures were in the manufacturing sector and nine (40.9 per cent) were in the service sector. A total of nine (40.9 per cent) of the ventures had been terminated and 13 (59.1 per cent) were still in operation at the time of data collection.

RESULTS AND DISCUSSION

Strategic Motives

There is a good deal of support for Hypothesis 1. Table 10.3 shows that, although there is a slight difference in rank order, the first three ranked strategic motives for joint venture formation coincide for both groups of firms. These strategic motives were 'to gain presence in new markets', 'enabling faster entry to the market' and 'to facilitate international expansion'. For the majority of the other strategic motives, there is also a relatively close match in terms of rank order for both groups of firms. The only notable exception is the strategic motive of 'spreading risk of large project', which is ranked 11 for UK firms but seventh for foreign firms. The *t*-tests indicate that there are no significant differences in the mean values of the importance of the strategic motives.

Factor Analysis of Strategic Motives
As noted previously, there is a potential conceptual overlap between the identified strategic motives. An attempt was made, therefore, to identify a smaller number of distinct, non-overlapping strategic motives for the sample data by means of exploratory factor analysis in order to uncover any dimensions or structure underlying the data. The two subsets of UK firms and foreign firms were combined for the purposes of factor analysis. The factor analysis produced six underlying factors which appear to make good conceptual sense and which explain a total of 66 per cent of the observed variance, as shown in Table 10.4.

Hypothesis 1 was again considered in terms of differences in means of the factors of strategic motives, as shown in Table 10.5. Again, there is a good deal of support for Hypothesis 1, with none of the factors being significantly different between the UK and foreign firms.

The findings of this study clearly indicate that the strategic motives for joint venture formation are to a high degree consistent between UK firms and foreign firms. The discussion leading up to Hypothesis 1 indicated that the expected degree of conformity of strategic motive between these groups of firms was not unambiguous – it may be argued that for some sets of firms the motives will coincide while for others the motives may not be the same. Support for the hypothesis is, however, consistent with the logic that the fundamental motives for the formation of joint ventures will be shared by UK firms in partnership with foreign firms, and foreign firms in partnership with UK firms.

Task-related Selection Criteria

There is moderate support for Hypothesis 2. Table 10.6 shows that for the UK firms the highest ranked task-related selection criteria in terms of importance are 'access to knowledge of local market', 'access to distribution channels' and 'access to links with major buyers'. In contrast, the highest ranked task-related selection criteria for foreign firms are 'access to technology', 'access to the product' and 'access to knowledge of production processes'. The *t*-tests indicate that there are significant

Table 10.4 Factors of strategic motives for joint venture formation: UK and foreign firms

Factor	Factor loads	Eigenvalue	Per cent variance explained	Cumulative per cent
Factor 1		2.751	17.2	17.2
Enabling faster entry to the market	.755			
To gain presence in new markets	.735			
Produce at lowest cost location	−.607			
Factor 2		2.513	15.7	32.9
Economies of scale	.870			
To concentrate on higher margin business	.776			
Enabling faster payback on the investment	.535			
Factor 3		1.687	10.5	43.4
Exchange of complementary technology	.883			
Sharing R&D costs	.761			
Exchange of patents or territories	.532			
Factor 4		1.407	8.8	52.2
To reduce competition	.779			
To compete against a common competitor	.637			
To maintain position in existing markets	.545			
Factor 5		1.152	7.2	59.4
Conform to foreign government policy	.795			
To facilitate international expansion	.556			
Factor 6		1.054	6.6	66.0
Spreading risk of large project	.849			
Enabling product diversification	−.437			

Notes:
K-M-O measure of sampling adequacy = .57963.
Bartlett test of sphericity = 309.836; $p < 0.0000$.
Principal components factor analysis with varimax rotation.

differences between UK and foreign firms in the mean values of the first two ranked task-related selection criteria for UK firms; that is, 'access to knowledge of local market' ($p < 0.05$), and 'access to distribution channels' ($p < 0.1$).

The degree of support for Hypothesis 2 is encouraging. The logic of joint venture formation in terms of accessing partner resources and competencies is well-supported in the literature (see, for example, Kogut, 1988; Hamel, 1991; Badaracco, 1991). The results of this study provide support for the view that there will be variation in the nature of inputs that each partner finds necessary to access in order to ensure the success of the venture. Even though each set of firms apparently has broadly similar motives for joint venture formation, each sub-set of firms has identified different key inputs that it is necessary to obtain given these motives.

Table 10.5 Tests of differences in means for factors of strategic motives for joint venture formation

| | UK firms (n=65) | | Foreign firms (n=22) | | |
Strategic motive	Mean	SD	Mean	SD	t-value
Factor 1 Enabling faster entry to the market To gain presence in new markets Produce at lowest cost location	.023	.96	−.066	1.14	.36
Factor 2 Economies of scale To concentrate on higher margin business Enabling faster payback on the investment	.009	.98	−.028	1.09	.15
Factor 3 Exchange of complementary technology Sharing R&D costs Exchange of patents or territories	−.072	.94	.211	1.15	−1.15
Factor 4 To reduce competition To compete against a common competitor To maintain position in existing markets	.068	.96	−.201	1.12	1.09
Factor 5 Conform to foreign government policy To facilitate international expansion	.02	.97	−.06	1.11	.34
Factor 6 Spreading risk of large project Enabling product diversification	−.034	.98	.100	1.09	−.54

Partner-related Selection Criteria

There is some support for Hypothesis 3. Table 10.7 shows that the partner-related selection criterion of 'trust between the top management teams' is the first-ranked criterion for both the UK and the foreign firms. While there is a slight difference in rank order, the five top-ranked partner-related selection criteria for UK firms are the same for foreign firms with the exception of 'relatedness of partner's business', which, while ranked second for UK firms, is ranked sixth equal for foreign firms. Only three of the partner-related selection criteria display significant differences in means: 'relatedness of partner's business' ($p < 0.05$), 'established marketing and distribution system' ($p < 0.1$) and 'management in depth' ($p < 0.1$).

That trust is found to be important for both sets of firms is not surprising. This finding provides a degree of empirical support for the contention of Buckley and Casson (1988) that the basis of the relationship between the partners involved in a joint venture must be 'mutual forbearance', or, in other words, the absence of cheating between partners. Crucial to this, and to the success of the venture, is the degree of

Table 10.6   Task-related selection criteria: UK and foreign firms

	UK firms (n =65)			Foreign firms (n =22)			
Access to	*Rank*	*Mean*	*SD*	*Rank*	*Mean*	*SD*	*t-value*
Knowledge of local market	1	2.14	.85	5=	1.67	.91	2.18**
Distribution channels	2	2.06	.85	5=	1.67	.86	1.85*
Links with major buyers	3	1.89	.89	7	1.57	.81	1.47
Knowledge of local culture	4	1.88	.89	4	1.71	.90	.72
Technology	5	1.74	.85	1	1.95	.92	−.98
The product	6	1.69	.79	2	1.90	.94	−1.02
Knowledge of production processes	7	1.56	.75	3	1.81	.93	−1.16
Capital	8	1.51	.71	8=	1.47	.75	.17
Regulatory permits	9	1.44	.66	10=	1.19	.60	1.57
Labour	10	1.35	.57	8=	1.47	.68	−.81
Local brand names	11	1.31	.56	12	1.14	.48	1.22
Materials/natural resources	12	1.16	.49	10=	1.19	.51	−.17

Notes:
The mean is the average on a scale of 1 (= of no importance) to 3 (= of major importance).
** $p < 0.05$; * $p < 0.10$.

Table 10.7   Partner-related selection criteria: UK and foreign firms

	UK firms (n =65)			Foreign firms (n =22)			
Criteria	*Rank*	*Mean*	*SD*	*Rank*	*Mean*	*SD*	*t-value*
Trust between the top management teams	1	2.56	.56	1	2.67	.48	−.83
Relatedness of partner's business	2	2.45	.61	6=	2.05	.74	2.46**
Reputation	3	2.40	.63	3	2.19	.75	1.26
Financial status/resources of partner	4	2.11	.62	2	2.23	.70	−.82
Complementarity of partner's resource contribution	5	2.09	.72	4	2.14	.85	−.27
Established marketing and distribution system	6	2.01	.86	10=	1.67	.73	1.68*
Partner company's size	7	1.95	.67	5	2.09	.77	−.81
International experience	8	1.84	.76	9	1.91	.77	−.31
Experience in technology applications	9	1.79	.80	6=	2.05	.92	−1.26
Management in depth	10=	1.74	.69	6=	2.05	.81	−1.71*
Degree of favourable past association	10=	1.74	.76	10=	1.67	.73	.38
Partner's ability to negotiate with foreign government	12	1.43	.68	12	1.47	.75	−.26

Notes:
The mean is the average on a scale of 1 (= of no importance) to 3 (= of major importance).
* $p < 0.10$; ** $p < 0.05$.

trust between the management teams of the partner firms. More broadly, from a transaction-cost perspective it is recognized that partner-selection involves issues of trust and opportunism (or, in the terminology of Williamson (1975, p. 26) 'self-interest seeking with guile').

It is apparent that both for UK firms and for foreign firms the means for the task-related criteria are much lower than the means for partner-related selection criteria. This indicates that there is greater consensus amongst the firms in the sample on the relative importance of partner-related selection criteria than task-related selection criteria. This finding is to be expected. The relative importance of a particular task-related selection criterion will tend to be specific to the successful operation of the joint venture. Therefore, the criteria looked for in a potential partner, in terms of resources and skills in order to accomplish the task of the venture, will be predicated on the nature of the venture itself, and this may vary considerably between joint ventures.

In contrast, particular partner-related selection criteria will tend to be more general in nature, in the sense that the characteristics of a suitable partner will be more universal and will be associated far less with the specific activities of the joint venture than will task-related selection criteria. The relative importance of any one task-related criterion would then be dissipated across a number of joint ventures with different sets of task-related requirements – hence producing relatively low mean scores for the importance of the criterion.

Conversely, a partner-related criterion, being independent of the specific tasks of the joint venture, may be considered important across a range of joint venture purposes. This may account for the relatively high mean scores for the importance of partner-related selection criteria. In summary, the main point to emphasize is that task-related selection criteria are specific to particular joint ventures while partner-related selection criteria are more general in nature.

Factors of Selection Criteria
While there is a clear theoretical distinction between task-related and partner-related selection criteria, in practice it may be difficult to sustain this difference, and the selection criteria identified for this study may represent a number of overlapping perspectives. Given the potential for overlapping perspectives, an attempt was made to identify a smaller number of distinct, non-overlapping selection criteria for the sample data by means of exploratory factor analysis. The two subsets of UK firms and foreign firms were combined for this purpose.

The factor analysis produced eight underlying factors which make good conceptual sense and explained a total of 68.1 per cent of the observed variance. Table 10.8 shows that six of the eight factors are made up of combinations of both task-related and partner-related selection criteria, confirming the anticipated problem of overlapping perspectives. Of the two remaining factors both are composed of criteria that are identified as partner-related.

In order to further test for differences in selection-criteria between

Table 10.8 Factors of selection criteria for joint venture formation: UK and foreign firms

Factors	Factor loands	Eigenvalue	Per cent variance explained	Cumulative per cent
Factor 1		4.128	17.2	17.2
(P) Experience in technology applications	.891			
(A) Access to technology	.862			
(A) Access to knowledge of production processes	.708			
(A) Access to distribution channels	−.494			
Factor 2		3.600	15.0	32.2
(P) Partner's ability to negotiate with foreign government	.798			
(A) Access to knowledge of local culture	.736			
(A) Access to knowledge of local market	.629			
(A) Access to regulatory permits	.555			
Factor 3		1.817	7.6	39.8
(P) Financial status/resources of partner	.811			
(P) Partner company's size	.746			
(A) Access to capital	.612			
Factor 4		1.681	7.0	46.8
(A) Access to links with major buyers	.737			
(A) Access to local brand names	.624			
(P) Reputation	.490			
Factor 5		1.515	6.3	53.1
(P) International experience	.732			
(P) Management in depth	.716			
(A) Access to the product itself	.546			
Factor 6		1.319	5.5	58.6
(A) Access to labour	.722			
(A) Access to materials/natural resources	.638			
(P) Relatedness of partner's business	.524			
Factor 7		1.168	4.9	63.5
(P) Complementarity of partner's resource contribution	.838			
(P) Established marketing and distribution system	.616			
Factor 8		1.124	4.7	68.1
(P) Degree of favourable past association	.794			
(P) Trust between the top management teams	.673			

Notes:
K-M-O measure of sampling adequacy = .64332.
Bartlett test of sphericity = 731.105; $p < 0.0000$.
Principal components factor analysis with varimax rotation.
(A) = Task-related selection criterion.
(P) = Partner-related selection criterion.

UK and foreign firms, the hypothesis of no difference in selection criteria was considered in terms of differences in means of the factors of selection criteria, as shown in Table 10.9. There is a good deal of support for this hypothesis with only one of the means of the factors of selection criteria (Factor 4, $p < 0.05$) being significantly different between UK and foreign firms. In terms of a parsimonious set of selection criteria, therefore, for this sample there appears to be very little difference in the relative importance of selection criteria.

CONCLUSIONS

This study considers differences in the relative importance of the strategic motives for international joint venture formation, and task-related and partner-related selection criteria, for a sample of UK firms with partners from advanced industrial economies, and foreign firms from advanced industrial economies with partners from the UK. The main motives for joint venture formation are found to be similar for both UK and foreign firms, and are concerned with attaining relative competitive positions in either new or existing markets.

The study finds that the relative importance of the strategic motives for joint venture formation do not vary between UK and foreign firms. The task-related and partner-related selection criteria for the sample are also identified. The study provides some support for the view that the relative importance of task-related selection criteria will vary between UK firms and foreign firms, but that the relative importance of partner-related selection criteria will not vary between UK and foreign firms. Taken as a parsimonious set of criteria, however, in general the study finds no difference in the relative importance of the selection criteria between UK firms and foreign parent firms.

This is the first study to examine strategic motives and selection criteria from the perspective of foreign partners in UK equity joint ventures, and to compare the relative importance of motives and selection criteria with UK firms. As such, this contribution builds on prior studies which have examined these dimensions of joint venture activity.

A shortcoming of this study is the relatively few joint ventures in the sample that are represented by two parents. While our findings allow general statements to be made concerning the perspectives of UK firms and foreign firms in international joint ventures, the strength of these statements are weakened by the lack of correspondence between firms in the sample as far as joint venture units are concerned. In this sense, the findings of the study should be considered exploratory.

Further research is clearly required in the areas of strategic motivation and selection criteria with matched pairs of joint venture partners.

Table 10.9 Tests of differences in means for selection criteria for joint venture formation

	UK firms (n=65)		Foreign firms (n=22)		
	Mean	SD	Mean	SD	t-value
Factor 1 (P) Experience in technology applications (A) Access to technology (A) Access to knowledge of production processes (A) Access to distribution channels	−.070	.98	.226	1.06	−1.16
Factor 2 (P) Partner's ability to negotiate with foreign government (A) Access to knowledge of local culture (A) Access to knowledge of local market (A) Access to regulatory permits	.013	.98	−.042	1.10	.22
Factor 3 (P) Financial status / resources of partner (P) Partner company's size (A) Access to capital	.013	.94	−.043	1.20	.22
Factor 4 (A) Access to links with major buyers (A) Access to local brand names (P) Reputation	.150	.99	−.487	.89	2.57**
Factor 5 (P) International experience (P) Management in depth (A) Access to the product itself	−.086	.89	.280	1.27	−1.44
Factor 6 (A) Access to labour (A) Access to materials/natural resources (P) Relatedness of partner's business	.050	.90	−.162	1.28	.83
Factor 7 (P) Complementarity of partner's resource contribution (P) Established marketing and distribution system	.003	1.01	−.009	1.00	.05
Factor 8 (P) Degree of favourable past association (P) Trust between the top management teams	−.029	1.05	.094	.84	−.48

Notes:
** $p < 0.05$.
(A) = Task-related selection criterion.
(P) = Partner-related selection criterion.

The comparison and contrast between partners when investigating the core dimensions of a joint venture will obviously provide a richer data set, directly promoting greater academic understanding and ultimately informing practising managers to enable them to better intervene in the joint venture management process.

Note

1. While it would have been preferable to telephone the foreign firms and make contact with the appropriate person to whom the questionnaire would be personally addressed, this was not feasible with most of the foreign partners. In consequence, the foreign partner questionnaire was mailed to a named senior executive without making prior contact. Also, it was not possible to pre-pay the return postage for the foreign partner questionnaires. The questionnaire was sent in English to the Japanese partners as it was not feasible to translate the questionnaire into Japanese. For some fairly standard reasons associated with the postal questionnaire method of obtaining data, it is not surprising that the foreign partner response rate is somewhat lower than that expected in a study of this nature (Dillman, 1978; Dillman *et al.*, 1984). However, examination of non-respondents with respondents did not indicate any potential bias in the responding firms. Finally, it may be noted that the total response rate for the pooled sample is 33.4 per cent, yielding 87 usable questionnaires.

11 A Qualitative Meta-Analysis of Performance Measures and Factors Affecting International Joint Venture Performance

Margreet Boersma and Pervez Ghauri

A great deal of research has been undertaken to identify the factors affecting the success, failure, performance and stability of international equity joint ventures (EJVs) (see, for example, Beamish and Killing, 1996 for a review). Most of these studies, however, are static in nature. Although some scholars advocate a more dynamic approach to EJV research (for example, Parkhe, 1993; Stafford, 1995), to date only limited work has been done in this direction (Ring and van de Ven, 1994; Madhok, 1995a; Spekman *et al.*, 1996; Ariño and de la Torre, 1996).

Consequently, there is a need for research that has a temporal dimension to provide a greater insight into the complexities of managing an EJV as it evolves through time. Existing studies, however, do provide a useful foundation for developing such a dynamic framework for the investigation of EJVs. Complementary longitudinal research would focus, for example, on the factors that positively or negatively influence EJV performance, investigate how these factors change over time, and identify what the causes of these changes are.

Gaining insight into the factors affecting EJV performance, however, is problematic. This is because, amongst other reasons, the literature on this subject has until recently been rather fragmented (Parkhe, 1993). The use of different performance measures and the many variables put forward as affecting performance have not yielded a significantly greater understanding of EJV performance. The aim of this chapter, therefore, is to provide a structured overview of the literature on EJVs and to present a comprehensive review of performance indicators and factors affecting EJV performance. In so doing, this review seeks to advance the development of EJV theory (Parkhe, 1993) by concluding a period of static research and creating the basis for a longitudinal approach to the investigation of EJVs.

The term contractual joint venture refers to all contractual relationships between companies. These may be, for example, licenses, supply agreements or technical assistance contracts (Hennart, 1988). An *equity* joint venture, the focus of this chapter, goes one step further. Equity joint ventures are cooperative relationships between at least two firms who each contribute resources to a newly-formed, legally independent and jointly-owned subsidiary (Hennart, 1988). Thus, instead of merely concluding a contract, a shared subsidiary is created that gives shape to the cooperation. EJVs are an important form of cooperation, because, as the EJV is part of the hierarchical structure of both parent companies, the joint venture agreement aligns the incentives of the parties involved to a much greater degree than do contractual agreements (Glaister and Buckley, 1997; Hennart, 1988).

As the existing literature on EJV performance is fragmented, our review was obtained by analysing existing literature on international joint ventures in a qualitative manner (Hunter and Schmidt, 1990). The following steps were taken to achieve this. First, we gathered from the literature labels and definitions of performance. We then looked for commonalities between these definitions and ordered them in such a way that they referred to the same meaning. Finally, we assigned names to these joint definitions.

In this chapter, we begin by reviewing the different constructs and definitions of EJV performance employed in major contributions to the academic literature. We then examine the labels that authors have used to determine the performance of EJVs and discuss how these labels have been defined. We go on to provide an overview of the variables affecting these different performance indicators, and present a framework that introduces a dynamic component to the investigation of EJV performance. We then draw conclusions and suggest avenues for further research.

INTERNATIONAL JOINT VENTURE PERFORMANCE: A REVIEW

Performance Indicators

Only a few authors have attempted to devise an appropriate measure of EJV performance (Anderson, 1990; Geringer and Hebert, 1991). However, for several reasons these studies do not adequately address the task of presenting an accurate measure of EJV performance. The literature on EJV performance is weakened on three accounts. Firstly, some authors use the same constructs, but define them differently. Consider, for example, the notion of EJV 'success'. Geringer and Hebert (1991), Blodgett (1992) and Barkema *et al.* (1997) took the length of time the joint venture persisted as a measure of its 'success', while others, such as Beamish (1988), Lee and Beamish (1995), Madhok (1995a, b) and Hamill and Hunt (1993) employed instead a managerial perception of success. Thus, although both groups of researchers state that they investigated 'success', they use different definitions of what constitutes success.

Secondly, some authors use different constructs that, on deeper analysis, have the same definition. For example, whereas Beamish and Banks (1987) define 'performance' as managerial satisfaction, Inkpen and Birkinshaw (1994) give managerial satisfaction the name 'satisfaction'. Thirdly, some authors use an indicator for measuring a latent variable (for example, using longevity as an indicator for the latent variable 'success'), whereas others use the latent variable itself. More examples of such inconsistencies can be found in Table 11.1, which summarizes the literature on EJV performance.

Table 11.1 illustrates that, although some commonality is evident, several concepts are used in the literature to measure the performance of an EJV. This suggests that performance is seen by scholars as an overlapping concept; that is, a latent variable that encompasses several indicators. In the following discussion we classify these indicators into five groups, each referring to the latent variable 'performance'. It may be helpful to keep in mind that the labels we introduce have been deduced from earlier literature, and have been worded in such a way that, in our view, best reflect the definitions we found. Through this, however, a duplication may arise between the wording used and the concepts introduced.

We label the first indicator of performance as 'longevity'. Longevity is a combination of the constructs of 'continuity', 'evolution/dissolution', 'longevity', 'failure and the potential for failure', and some of the definitions of 'success'. Each of these variables is linked to the duration of the EJV. Researchers have quantified these variables using perceptual data on the expected duration of the EJV (obtained, for example, from the managers of the EJV or parent firms), or by using hard data such as the length of time that the EJV has been operational.

The second indicator of performance, we propose, is the 'quality of the working relationship' between the partner firms in the EJV. This indicator encompasses the constructs of 'trust', 'harmony', 'morale' (Anderson, 1990) and 'cooperativeness' (Deutsch, 1973). Of course, only perceptual data can be used to quantify these indicators. Such inter-partner relations may be treated as a *long-term* performance measure (Anderson, 1990).

We compile the third indicator of performance from the constructs of 'performance', and from part of the definitions of 'satisfaction' and 'success'. The commonality between these indicators is that they each infer something about the business performance of the EJV *itself*, as perceived by the partner firms or derived from hard data. Examples of such hard

Table 11.1 Performance measures used in EJV literature

Performance indicator	Operationalization used	Authors
Continuity	• Degree of partner firm's expectation of continued cooperation in the future	Madhok (1995 a, b); Shamdasani and Sheth (1995)
Effectiveness	• Meeting initial objectives • Perceived performance rating by EJV management • Overall effectiveness of EJV • Achievement of goals as specified in the documents of incorporation	Lyles and Baird (1994); Zeira, Newburry and Yeheskel (1995)
Evolution/dissolution	• Continuance and ending of the cooperative relationship	Ring and van de Ven (1994)
Longevity	• Numbers of years the EJV has persisted	Barkema, Shenkar, Vermeulen and Bell (1997); Parkhe (1991).
Failure	• Foreign general managers' view about terminating the EJV • Age and duration of the EJV	Pan, Vanhonacker and Pitts (1995); Park and Russo (1996).
Financial performance	• Managers' overall satisfaction with the EJV • Return on investment, return on assets, domestic sales growth, export growth of the EJV • Managers' perception of profitability, pay-back period, customer service and market share of EJV	Beamish and Banks (1987); Geringer and Herbert (1989); Lee and Beamish (1995); Luo (1995)
Satisfaction	• Foreign partner's satisfaction with the EJV • Meeting of objectives • The degree of partners' overall evaluation of the EJV relationship	Inkpen and Birkinshaw (1994); Shamdasani and Sheth (1995)
Stability	• Unplanned equity changes or major reorganization of the EJV • Increase in ownership for the party which contributes technology • Revision of contract • Buy-out of one partner by the other • Selling to an outsider • Change in ownership • Liquidation of EJV or major changes in equity	Beamish and Inkpen (1995); Blodgett (1992); Franko (1971); Gomes-Casseres (1987); Madhok (1995a, b); Stopford and Wells (1972)
Success	• Managerial assessment of success (satisfaction of both sides regarding performance) • Long-term viability • Satisfaction and dyadic sales • Endurance	Beamish (1988); Beamish and Banks (1987); Hamill and Hunt (1993); Lane and Beamish (1990); Madhok (1995a, b); Mohr and Spekman (1994); Spekman *et al.* (1996)
Trust	• Belief that partner will act sincerely in future dealings • The desire to work hard in the future to establish a close relationship • Reliance on the partner in future dealings • Expectation of a good future relationship with partner • Belief that the future behaviour of the partner will be consistent with past behaviour	Sullivan *et al.* (1995); Buckley and Casson (1988)

data might include financial indicators, such as profitability or return on investment, as well as data on technology transfer flows and the productivity of human resources. As our latent variable is already labelled 'performance', we call this third indicator of performance 'EJV achievement', thereby distinguishing it from our latent variable.

Our fourth indicator of performance is 'effectiveness'. This consists of two constructs, namely 'effectiveness' and 'satisfaction'. This indicator is often operationalized by measuring the partners' perception of whether or not their goals for entering the EJV have been achieved. The advantage of using this indicator is that the performance measure is coupled to goals specific to a particular joint venture. It therefore bypasses the problems inherent in using hard data as a measure of EJV performance. For example, profitability may not accurately quantify EJV success since firms are often motivated to enter into joint venture agreements for other reasons, such as learning about the customs of other countries (Anderson, 1990) rather than to generate short-term profit. When such knowledge of a country is obtained, a joint venture may be considered effective by one or more of the parent firms, and thus have a high performance measure, even though it may not have been profitable.

The final indicator we incorporate is the often-used measure of 'stability'. Most authors operationalize stability as a change in equity shares. However, Blodgett (1992) also uses as an indicator a change in contract but without a necessary change in equity. Note that we include the case of a total buy-out of one partner by the other in our first indicator, 'longevity'.

These five indicators, namely 'longevity', 'quality of the working relationship', 'EJV achievement', 'effectiveness' and 'stability', each highlight a different but important element of EJV performance. However, we recognize that there is some overlap between these indicators. For example, consider the instance when the goal of one partner in a joint venture is to make a profit, and profit is generated in accordance with these expectations. This performance would register on both our indicators 'effectiveness' and 'EJV achievement'.

Another overlap may be found between 'longevity' and 'quality of the relationship'. For example, when a manager's perception of trust is negative, that manager may also have a negative perception regarding the length of time the joint venture will endure. However, it is apparent that EJV performance is actually multidimensional. Consequently, in order to obtain a true understanding of JV performance, researchers must incorporate each of the five indicators outlined above. As we illustrate in the following section, merely using one of the five indicators we describe could fail to capture the precise circumstances of a particular EJV, and therefore inaccurately portray its overall performance.

DRAWBACKS TO USING A SINGLE PERFORMANCE MEASURE

There are a number of reasons why using a single performance measure may fail to accurately reflect the performance of a particular EJV. Let us consider each of our five indicators in turn. Firstly, using only the indicator 'longevity' creates difficulties when comparing an EJV that was created say 20 years ago with one created five years ago. With only information on the age of the venture, it is not possible to state that the former business is out-performing the latter, merely that it has existed for 15 years longer (Lyles and Baird, 1994). Furthermore, considering longevity alone ignores issues such as profitability, trust and the nature of the relationship between the partner firms (Geringer and Hebert, 1989, 1991; Anderson, 1990; Beamish and Inkpen, 1995). Indeed, the strong performance of an EJV may encourage one parent firm to buy out the other, leading to the demise of the venture. Such a joint venture would score low if performance were measured by longevity alone. Finally, some authors (for example, Buckley and Casson, 1988) argue that longevity may even be a sign of failure. This would be the case, for example, when a joint venture or alliance has been set up to achieve a given, but as yet unattained, objective (such as acquiring new technology and new products or meeting a market-share target).

Using only the quality of the working relationship as a measure of EJV success, however, is also problematic. For example, an EJV may underperform in generating profit or meeting predetermined objectives, even though a harmonious working relationship exists between the partners of an EJV, with good personal relationships and levels of trust between managers from parent firms. Such underperformance may result in the dissolution of the EJV, irrespective of the nature of the working relationship between the partner firms.

The disadvantage of using the third indicator, 'EJV achievement' as the sole indicator of performance is the short-term orientation of this measure. It is perfectly possible for the future prospects of the EJV to be favourable, even if its managers currently do not perceive the EJV as performing satisfactorily (for example, because profitability or productivity is low). Issues regarding the future prospects for the EJV are often not taken into account by scholars when using profit figures (Anderson, 1990), or when asking managers about their perception of performance. However, it is possible to argue that managers will, consciously or subconsciously, incorporate an anticipated perspective in their judgement of the likely future success of the EJV. Furthermore, profit measures will not suffice when profit maximization is not a principal goal of the EJV. This might be the case, for example, when the EJV is established to conduct research and development or other activities which might impact upon profitability only in the medium to long term.

Stability may also be an inadequate sole indicator of EJV perform-ance. For example, a change in equity may very well be viewed as fair by both partners to the EJV, irrespective of profitability, trust or what-ever. Moreover, a difference of opinion exists in any case about whether stability is indicative of EJV success. Whereas Beamish and Inkpen (1995) regard instability as one factor in the performance equation, Blodgett (1992, p. 481) argues that instability says nothing about performance. Indeed, Gomes-Casseres (1987, p. 97) asserts:

> when changes in equity result from adaptations to changes in envi-ronmental conditions, which sometimes resulted from actions of the joint ventures themselves, instability may be seen as a sign of success, not failure.

Finally, employing the last indicator, 'effectiveness', as a sole measure of performance becomes problematic when considering EJVs that have only recently been established since, in such instances, any initial long-term objectives are unlikely to have been met. Furthermore, the achievement of goals may mean that one or more of the partners in-volved may no longer wish to participate in the future development of the EJV. This behaviour may therefore imply future dissolution of the EJV instead of continuity. Consequently, 'effectiveness' only informs something about the past as opposed to the future.

Figure 11.1 summarizes this discussion. In this figure, the arrows illustrate the interconnected relationship between the five indicators of perform-ance. For example, it is likely that the longer the EJV has been in operation ('longevity'), the greater the probability that a good working relation-ship will have been developed between the partner firms and that respective managers will be more trusting and open with each other.

Similarly, effectiveness may influence stability. For example, the goal of one partner may be to gradually acquire the share of the other. This was, for instance, the case between Philips and Whirlpool. For market-ing purposes, both partners decided to have a joint venture as an intermediate organizational form. In time, Whirlpool's share of equity gradually increased, finally resulting in a total buy-out of Philips. Hence, the goal of Whirlpool (to acquire the white goods business of Philips) influenced the stability of the joint venture between the two firms.

FACTORS INFLUENCING EJV PERFORMANCE

Having proposed a classification of several performance indicators found in the literature, and considered issues regarding the operationalization

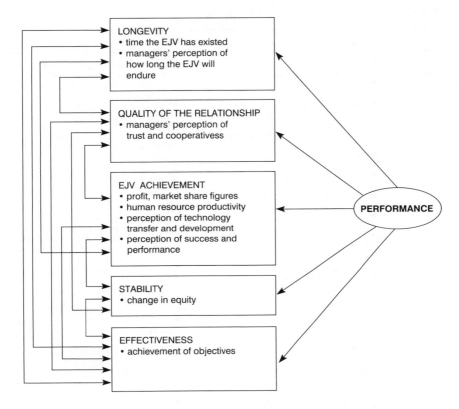

Figure 11.1 A conceptual analytic model of the performance measurement of EJVs

of these indicators, we now turn to the second part of our study, which is to categorize the factors suggested in the literature as determining EJV performance. This categorization is based upon models developed by Ariño and de la Torre (1996), Parkhe (1993) and Ring and van de Ven (1994). The categories we have identified are: 'partner characteristics', 'strategies of the partners', 'need of resources', 'structure of the EJV', 'behaviour of the parties', 'trust between the parties', 'dependence', 'environment of the EJV' and 'evaluation'. In addition, we divide the determinant factors into those that have, it is suggested, a positive influence and those that have a negative influence upon the performance of EJVs (see Table 11.2)

The first category, 'partner characteristics', consists mainly of factors derived from the firm characteristics of each partner, such as industry, culture, size and learning capability. In general, differences in culture between the partners (mostly on a country level) are observed to have a

Table 11.2   Factors influencing EJV performance

	Positive influence	Negative influence
Partner characteristic	• Competence of alliance partner (Shamdasani and Sheth, 1995) • Dissimilarity of parent industries (Zeira *et al.*, 1995) • Experience with domestic joint ventures (Barkema *et al.*, 1997) • Experience with international wholly-owned subsidiaries (Barkema *et al.*, 1997) • Growth in experience fit between partners (Gomes-Casseres, 1987) • Longer-term perspective (Madhok, 1995b) • Parental differences in Hofstede's masculinity index (Zeira *et al.*, 1995) • Politically strong and well-connected Chinese partners (Pan *et al.*, 1995) • Presence of other concurrent EJV between the partners (Park and Russo, 1996) • Prior interaction (Madhok, 1995b) • Support from top management (Spekman *et al.*, 1996)	• Concerns about legal and regulatory environment (Pan *et al.*, 1995) • Concerns about sourcing (Pan *et al.*, 1995) • Conflicts between role and interpersonal behaviour (Ring and van de Ven, 1994) • Corporate culture differences (Parkhe, 1991) • Cultural distance (Barkema *et al.* 1997) • Cultural diversity between the partners (Beamish and Inkpen, 1996) • Differences in partner firms' national context (Parkhe, 1991) • Direct competition between the partners (Park and Russo, 1996) • Diversity in the sponsoring firms' operating characteristics (Parkhe, 1991) • Growth in parent firm's international network (Gomes-Casseres, 1987) • Knowledge acquisition (Beamish and Inkpen, 1996) • Partner's acquisition of new capabilities (Gomes-Casseres, 1987) • Size differentials (Madhok, 1995b) • Societal culture differences (Parkhe, 1991)
Partner strategy	• EJV tied to strategic intent of firm (Spekman *et al.*, 1996) • Partner/s follow(s) a product diversification strategy (Franko, 1971) • Shared vision between partners on EJV direction (Spekman *et al.*, 1996) • Strategic compatibility [complementary goals, similar orientations] (Shamdasani and Sheth, 1995) • Strategic fit between partners (Hamill and Hunt, 1993)	• Change in strategy (Franko, 1971) • Divergence in strategic directions (Parkhe, 1991) • MNE follows a product concentration strategy (Franko, 1971) • Change in structure along geographical area lines by one of the partners (Stopford and Wells, 1972)
Need of resources	• Extent of desired partner need (Lee and Beamish, 1990) • Long-term and/or need mutual need (Lane and Beamish, 1990; Beamish, 1988; Madhok, 1995b) • Perception of long-term mutual need (Beamish and Banks, 1987) • Recognition of local partner needs (Lane and Beamish, 1990)	
Structure	• Number of partners in the joint venture (Park and Russo, 1996) • Careful planning-out of contract (Madhok, 1995b) • Contracts require binding arbitration instead of conferral when a Japanese has to cooperate with an American (Sullivan *et al.*, 1981) • Control-parent strategy fit (Geringer and Herbert, 1989)	• Adaptive structure (Luo, 1995) • Foreign partner control (Beamish, 1988) • Renegotiations of contracts before (Blodgett, 1991) • Unequal equity shares (Blodgett, 1991)

	Positive influence	Negative influence
	• Foreign partner control (Killing, 1983) • Local control (Lee and Beamish, 1990) • Minority or equal share of ownership for foreign partner (Lane and Beamish, 1990) • Shared or local management control (Beamish and Banks 1987) • Size of EJV (Lyles and Baird, 1994)	
Behaviour	*EJV* • Advertising (Lyles and Baird, 1994) • Application of HRM practices of the host culture (Zeira *et al.*, 1995) • Cultivation of good relationships with authorities and partners (Hamill and Hunt, 1993) • Employee advantages (Luo, 1995) • Operation according to clearly stated objectives (Zeira *et al.*, 1995) • Pricing (Lyles and Baird, 1994) • Product quality (Lyles and Baird, 1994) • R&D intensity (Lyles and Baird, 1994) • Sales force expenditure (Lyles and Baird, 1994) • Strong alliance managers (Spekman *et al.*, 1996) *Interaction* • Communication quality (Mohr and Spekman, 1994) • Cooperation (Inkpen and Birkinshaw, 1994) • Frank and immediate communication (Madhok, 1995b) • Frequent interaction (Madhok, 1995b) • Joint problem-solving (Mohr and Spekman, 1994) • Openness (Inkpen and Birkinshaw, 1994) *For one partner* • American partner requests mutual conferral to resolve disputes rather than binding arbitration (Sullivan *et al.*, 1981) • Assistance from the foreign parent (Luo, 1995) • Cooperative attitude of both partners (Lane and Beamish, 1990) • Domestic parent influence (Luo, 1995) • Participation (Mohr and Spekman, 1994)	• Avoidance of conflict (Franko, 1971) • Centralization (Franko, 1971) • Cost-cutting (Franko, 1971) • Escalating commitments to failing transactions (Ring and Van de Ven, 1994) • Excessive legal structuring and monitoring (Ring and Van de Ven, 1994) • Severe resolution techniques (Mohr and Spekman, 1994) • Smoothing over problems (Mohr and Spekman, 1994) • Standardization of marketing function (Franko, 1971)
Trust	• Commitment (Beamish, 1988; Beamish and Banks, 1987; Mohr and Spekman, 1994; Shamdasani and Sheth, 1995) • Commitment to international business and to working in difficult conditions (Lane and Beamish, 1990) • Commitment towards the EJV (Lane and Beamish, 1990) • Coordination (Mohr and Spekman, 1994) • Interpersonal ties which transcend the requirements of the business (Spekman *et al.*, 1996)	• Conditions for violation of trust (Ring and Van de Ven, 1994)

continued on page 186

Table 11.2   continued

	Positive influence	Negative influence
	• Personal bonds (Ring and Van de Ven, 1994) • Trust (Madhok, 1995b; Mohr and Spekman, 1994; Ring and Van de Ven, 1994) • Trust embodying a structural part (complementary of resources) and social glue (Madhok, 1995a)	
Dependence	• Non-abuse of power (Hamill and Hunt, 1993)	• EJV dependence on parent company resources (Zeira *et al.*, 1995)
Environment	• Restrictive investment policy of host country (Blodgett, 1991)	• Host government policy (Gomes-Casseres, 1987)
EJV evaluation	• Basis of fair exchange (Lane and Beamish, 1990) • Minority parent satisfaction with equity distribution (Zeira *et al.*, 1995) • Perception of equity and efficiency (Ring and van de Ven, 1994) • Satisfaction (Shamdasani and Sheth, 1995)	

negative influence on EJV performance. However, when a culture is divided into the several dimensions of Hofstede (1980), differences in 'masculinity' between the parent firms can positively affect EJV performance. As Zeira, Newburry and Yeheskel (1995, p. 15) state:

> one partner should be aggressive [masculine] and competitive and implement personnel policies... However, the other partner should be more yielding and more emotional, emphasizing the importance of co-operation, teamwork, job security, pleasant human interaction and avoidance of job stress.

Differences in industry are also seen to have a similar effect. This is because direct competition may lead to conflict as both partners seek to increase their share of the same or similar markets. Learning also exerts an influence when partner firms are in the same industry. For example, Park and Russo (1996, p. 878) state that 'learning is cumulative, and learning performance is greatest when the object of learning is related to what is already known'.

Learning from the partner via a joint venture is thus more likely to happen when both partners are active in the same industry. Furthermore, and from a similar perspective, learning may negatively influence joint venture performance, particularly in respect to 'stability' and 'longevity', when the internalization of the resources of one partner renders the other partner obsolete (Hamel, 1991). On the other hand, it is evident that learning may have a positive influence on joint venture performance when one or more of the partners has learned from its previous joint ventures; has previously operated in a foreign country by means of a wholly-owned subsidiary, or when the partners have had prior interaction.

The second category of factors influencing EJV performance focuses specifically on the strategies of both partners; in particular, the strategies which prompted the initial search for a partner. Examples include product-diversification and market-development strategies (or entering new markets with existing products). The strategies of both partners may differ but should be complementary in order for the EJV to be viable. A subsequent change in the initial strategies of one or both partners may result in less need for the EJV and, therefore, to dissolution.

However, other effects of incongruous strategies may be possible. For instance, a change of strategy may affect the relationship between the partners. A partner may alter its strategy such that this no longer conforms to the goals of the joint venture. This may negatively impact upon the amount of effort and support it directs towards the joint venture, which, in turn, may influence the other partner's perception of 'cooperativeness'. It is evident, therefore, that a long-term strategic fit between the partners should positively influence EJV performance.

A third category proposed is 'need for resources'. Joint ventures are created if one partner needs a resource that the other partner holds (Pfeffer and Nowak, 1976). Mutual need forms the *raison d'etre* for the joint venture (Parkhe, 1991).

The fourth category we propose is 'structure'. This refers to all formal agreements that the partners have entered into, as well as the design characteristics of the EJV. This category includes the nature of the contract, the formal division of control, the share of equity between the partners and the design characteristics of the EJV (such as the capitalization of the venture and the number of partners present). Contrary to expectation, Park and Russo (1996) found a positive and unexplained relationship between the number of partners and the performance of the joint venture. Similarly, Lyles and Baird (1994) report in their study of Hungarian joint ventures the surprising result that an adaptive structure (that is, a structure that allows changes in its rules and strategies in order to be flexible and creative) negatively affected joint venture effectiveness. One reason they give is that adaptive structures may be considered as informal and creative arrangements that may be threatening to the local partner firms in their study, which were former centrally-planned institutions that relied heavily on written communication, form-filling and formal procedures.

Findings on control are also contradictory. For example, although Beamish and Banks (1987) and Lane and Beamish (1990) found that shared or local management control systems produced enhanced EJV performance, Killing (1983) reported that dominant partner control ventures were more successful.

The fifth category of factors influencing EJV performance is the 'behaviour of the parties'. This category encompasses all of the actions carried out by one or both partners, or by the management of the joint venture. A bundle of factors can be identified, which we divide into factors specific to the joint venture, factors specific to the interaction between the parties and factors specific to one partner alone. Studies indicate that conflicts appear to have a negative influence on EJV performance. However, with techniques such as joint problem-solving, conflicts may not necessarily be destabilizing to the joint venture, but may instead lead to resolutions that are beneficial to all parties involved. Harsh words and domination may only lead to less satisfaction on the part of one of the partners (Mohr and Spekman, 1994). It is likely that, through frequent and open interaction in which frank and immediate communication takes place, performance of a joint venture will improve.

'Trust' has been cited as a factor reducing transactions costs and facilitating open and honest interaction (Buckley and Casson, 1988). Whereas trust comes about through cooperative behaviour, trust also encourages board members to support the business relationship when there are opposing interests among these members (Boersma and Ghauri, 1997). Following Sako (1992), trust can be divided into promissory-based trust, competence-based trust, and goodwill-based trust. Goodwill-based trust is defined as 'mutual expectations of open commitment to each other' (Sako, 1992, p. 38), where commitment in this sense refers to the willingness to do more than is formally expected (which conforms to the operationalization of commitment used by Beamish, 1988).

'Dependence' is another category of factors influencing joint venture performance. Dependence comes about through needing the resources held by another firm, but distinguishes itself from the category 'need for resources' described above in that this need, we suggest, does not lead to dependence directly. Rather, we refer to the category 'dependence' as occurring when the resources needed are only available (or best available) at one particular company. On starting a new joint venture, firms attempt to manage this dependence relationship (Pfeffer and Nowak, 1976). Power is closely connected with dependence, as the power of one party resides implicitly in the subordination of the other (Ghauri, 1983). In the case of an imbalance in dependence, it is probable that the non-abuse of power will positively affect joint venture performance.

Just as a firm's normal profits are partly dependent on the environment in which it acts, the environment too plays an important role in the performance of a joint venture. Examples of environmental influences include a devaluation of foreign currency that may affect transferred profits, a shortage of raw materials reflected in the purchase price or a decrease in demand through the introduction of an alternative good. Each of these changes in the environment will negatively influence the profitability, and, therefore, EJV achievement. Governments, too, may have influence, since in some countries joint ventures are subject to specific regulations drawn up by government. For example, for many years foreign companies were not allowed to have a majority share of equity in Russian EJVs (Boersma, 1995).

The last category, 'evaluation', embraces the partners' satisfaction regarding joint venture performance, based upon both equity and efficiency (Ring and van de Ven, 1994). Although efficiency has been the major criterion underlying the assessment of EJV performance, fair dealing is seen as an equally important criterion. For example, Ring and van de Ven (1994, p. 93) assume:

> The parties to a co-operative interorganisational relationship are motivated to seek both equity and efficiency outcomes because of a desire to preserve a reputation of fair dealing that will enable them to continue to exchange transaction-specific investments under conditions of high uncertainty.

Evaluation, based on both equity and efficiency, is an important factor to include in our model because both perspectives will influence managers' perceived outcome of the joint venture relationship. For instance, different viewpoints about fairness may influence how managers perceive the quality of the relationship or whether profits are divided equitably.

TOWARDS A DYNAMIC FRAMEWORK FOR ANALYSING JOINT VENTURE PERFORMANCE

As we have seen, until recently joint venture research has been fragmented and static in nature. In this chapter, we synthesize the findings of several major contributions to the literature on joint venture performance. These studies have been analysed qualitatively to identify five different performance measures and nine categories of factors considered to most influence joint venture success. We suggest that these classifications may serve as a basis for future research into joint venture development (Parkhe, 1993; Stafford, 1995).

We begin this process by incorporating a dynamic element into our study. We suggest that integrating three paradigms, namely the resource-based view of the firm (Penrose, 1959; Wernerfelt, 1984; Hamel, 1991), the transaction-costs approach (Williamson, 1975, 1985; Hennart, 1988; Kogut, 1988) and an economic sociology approach (Granovetter, 1985; Madhok, 1995b), will facilitate our understanding of the behaviour of

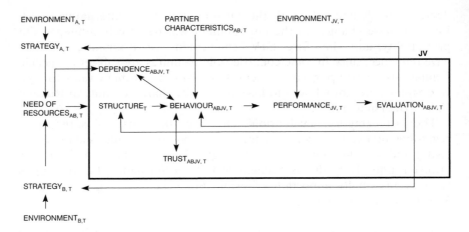

Figure 11.2   A conceptual model for studying the evolution of EJV performance

Note: ABJV,T: partner A, partner B, management of the joint venture (JV) in period T.

Source: Based on Ariño and de la Torre (1996), Parkhe (1993), Ring and van de Ven (1994).

the parties within an EJV and its subsequent performance through time. This integration is also proposed by de Jong (1998). We present such a model in Figure 11.2.

This model proposes that a firm's strategy leads to a need for resources, and from a resource-based perspective, a firm is viewed as a unique bundle of resources. When implementing its strategies, the firm may sometimes lack certain necessary resources. For example, when a firm seeks to expand beyond its national borders it may lack the experience of operating internationally or of operating in a particular foreign country. The accumulation of such knowledge is possible, but this is often a gradual and time-consuming process. In addition, the firm may lack the time (for example, when seeking first mover advantage), financial resources or willingness (because of turbulence in the local environment) to invest in these extra capabilities. In such cases, cooperation or merger with another party that possesses the unique bundle of resources that the firm itself lacks may be an appropriate option (Kogut, 1988).

Hence, the resource-based view seems of particular relevance in explaining why firms enter an alliance such as an EJV instead of developing the resources themselves. Furthermore, this view also helps to explain why EJVs may be dissolved at a certain time. Dissolution may occur, for example, when one of the partners has obtained the resources of the other partner, or when one partner has altered its strategy and no longer requires the resources for which the EJV was established.

The resource-based approach, however, only explains *why* firms start to cooperate, and not why they opt for a certain mode or structure such as an EJV. Transaction-costs economics (TCE) may be of help here. In general, TCE considers why firms choose between external market transactions and transactions within firms (often referred to as hierarchies). An EJV may be viewed as an intermediate or hybrid form of organization, although this organizational form is closer to hierarchy than the market (unlike non-equity joint ventures which are closer to market-based arrangements, Powell, 1990). Hennart (1988) and Kogut (1988) have used TCE to explain why some firms choose an equity joint venture while others favour a contractual, non-equity joint venture (including license agreements, distribution and supply agreements and other kinds of contracts). The basic question from a TCE perspective is why is hierarchical control chosen over transactions through spot markets or contracts? To answer this, the standard reasoning of TCE asserts that when the production costs of producing a resource internally are less than the transaction costs of obtaining that resource via the market, a hierarchy or, in this case, an EJV is selected. Conversely, the resource will be obtained through the market when internal production cost exceeds external procurement (or, more precisely, when the marginal cost of internal supply exceeds the price of buying-in the resource from the external market). Another argument for internalizing a resource instead of transferring it via the market involves the 'tacitness' of the resource. As Teece (1981, p. 90) suggests:

> this intangible know-how typically needs ongoing, future cooperation from the seller to obtain the full benefit of the know-how purchased, since all of the learning and experience of the developer of know-how cannot be captured in the codified descriptions, drawings, and data that are amenable to physical transfer.

The tacit part of the technology is more efficiently transferred if the transferor and the recipient are linked through common ownership (Hennart, 1988).

The chosen structure (that is, the extent of hierarchy and the nature of formal agreements made), together with partner characteristics and two social factors, namely dependence and trust, in time lead to certain behaviours on the part of both partner firms and the management team of the EJV (Zand, 1972). The economic sociology (ES) approach allows us to incorporate 'social embeddedness' of economic relationships (Granovetter, 1985) and trust (Madhok, 1995b) into our framework. The ES approach attempts to explain economic action and behaviour from a sociological perspective (Granovetter and Swedberg, 1992). By including the social aspect of human actors, latitude is created for explaining economic human behaviour from different angles. Whereas, from an economic perspective, mankind is motivated to exchange resources purely and solely for the purpose of material gain, sociologists consider several other drivers such as approval, status, power and sociability (Granovetter and Swedberg, 1992, p. 7), or, in other words, personal gain and emotional satisfaction (Blau, 1968). In addition, the social perspective gives leeway to trust, a concept non-existent in an economic perspective.

The behaviour (that, from an economic sociology perspective is not only driven by material gain) of the parties involved leads to a certain performance on the part of the EJV, which in time is evaluated in terms of efficiency and equity (Ring and van de Ven, 1994). Furthermore, equity may be seen as a concept from economic sociology. Evaluation may take place jointly or individually, and, of course, may be both negative and positive. When the evaluation is negative (for example, when one or more of the parties is dissatisfied with the performance of the EJV), several outcomes are possible.

Firstly, one or both of the partners may decide to change their strategy and exit the EJV. Secondly, both partners may decide to change the structure of the EJV. Thirdly, one or both partners, or the management team of the EJV, may decide to modify their behaviour. On the other hand, if the evaluation is positive, the partners and the management of the EJV may decide to maintain the status quo, but they may also change their behaviour to improve performance. Trust and dependence between the parties involved may also alter as a result of a change in their behaviour.

CONCLUSIONS AND FUTURE RESEARCH

Having reviewed the literature and developed a conceptual model, we believe that we are close to a composite measure of EJV performance. We do, however, accept that we cannot claim to have developed a universal model. Our conceptual model (as illustrated in Figure 11.1) provides a good synthesis of existing literature on factors influencing EJV performance, which we categorize under the headings 'longevity', 'quality of the relationship', 'EJV achievment', 'stability' and 'effectiveness'. By applying three theoretical paradigms, namely the resource-based view of the firm, transaction-costs economics and economic sociology to our discussion of the factors influencing EJV performance, we have developed a framework intended to form the basis of a longitudinal study of EJV performance (see Figure 11.2).

We believe that this model is now ready for empirical testing, and what is required is a measurement instrument for each variable. A quantitative analysis is recommended, preferably using LISREL, a method that allows for a joint estimation of both the measurement model (the indicators that measure the same latent variable) as well as the testing model (the relationship between the dependent and independent latent variables). This approach is recommended because it helps in testing very complex causal relationships, that is, relationships between variables that lack a one-to-one relationship.

12 A Proposed Solution to the Transnational Structure Paradox

Keith D. Brouthers, Lance Eliot Brouthers and Wilfred Sleeman

INTRODUCTION

The last decade has shown a dramatic shift towards transnational environments (Bartlett and Ghoshal, 1987). Both traditional multinational and classic global industries have increasingly been transformed into transnational industries. Multinational corporations (MNCs) were established to respond to the differing needs of various foreign locations. However, by so doing these MNCs developed country-specific strategies and even country-specific products, and little integration existed between individual subsidiaries of the traditional MNC.

More recently, global corporations have been expanding by providing a standardized set of goods and services to all foreign and domestic locations. Through this standardization, global corporations expect to achieve improved economies of scale for their production, marketing and R&D facilities. However, this global approach cannot respond to individual or regional differences in consumer tastes and needs. The international environment has created a need for transnational corporations (TNCs) that can respond simultaneously to the twin pressures of global integration (the traditional domain of global corporations) and local responsiveness (the domain of traditional MNCs) (Bartlett, 1986; Ghoshal and Nohria, 1993). Firms, however, are still struggling with a structural response to these twin environmental demands. Existing divisional (whether product or area) and matrix forms have shown an extraordinary inability to cope with transnational pressures: both forms have failed as the right form for the transnational organization:

> [Ford, IBM, Digital Equipment, and Texas Instruments] saw their increasingly important international operations become slow-moving – and at times redundant – clones of corporate headquarters. Little communication or coordination took place among regions. Worse, country organizations sometimes spent more energy competing with

each other than they did fighting with rival companies. In the late 1980s, many multinationals *thought* the answer to such provincialism was the matrix structure. (*Business Week*, 1994, p. 47, emphasis added)

However, the matrix structure did not solve this problem:

[Matrix] is precisely the kind of structure that companies such as Digital Equipment, Citibank, and Westinghouse all tried and then abandoned after just a few years of frustrating experimentation. (Ghoshal and Bartlett, 1995).

As described by Doz and Prahalad (1991), the reason that matrix and divisional forms failed lies in the heterogeneity and multidimensionality of firms operating in a transnational environment. The paradox of having to address both heterogeneity and multidimensionality in the same organizational form has created a situation in which existing models of organizational structure are of little value. Thus, what is needed is a new paradigm (Doz and Prahalad, 1991).

Doz and Prahalad (1991) have provided part of the solution to the transnational (TNC) structural paradox by defining seven demands that a transnational structure must fulfil. In this chapter, we describe a new structural solution to transnational conditions, based on these seven demands. The new organizational form draws heavily on concepts put forward by other scholars, which form part of the structural solution proposed to fill the gap that opened after the failure of divisional and matrix structures. The model in this chapter uses concepts offered by Miles and Snow (1984) on vertical disaggregation, and by Ghoshal and Bartlett (1990) for establishing a networked structure. In addition, we incorporate the advice of Hedlund (1994), who describes the *N*-form (which is based on managing knowledge-creation and transfer), and Bartlett and Ghoshal (1993, 1995), who focus on the managerial processes that make a structure work. Finally, the new model described in this paper integrates the concept of organizational 'tapping' proposed by Sölvell and Zander (1995). Combining the concepts described by these scholars, we have identified an organizational structure that meets all seven TNC demands, and has been successfully implemented by a number of leading transnational organizations.

The chapter proceeds as follows. First, we discuss the twin concepts of multidimensionality and heterogeneity which create an organizational paradox for TNCs. Second, we develop a propositional framework using the seven criteria for successfully structuring a TNC, as set out by Doz and Prahalad (1991). After that, we present a case example of a firm that has created a successful organizational structure that meets all seven TNC demands. Finally, we discuss this organizational form and its implications for other TNCs.

MULTIDIMENSIONALITY, HETEROGENEITY AND ORGANIZATIONAL STRUCTURE

Doz and Prahalad suggest that a new structural approach is needed for TNCs because TNCs must meet 'the combined consequences of multidimensionality and heterogeneity' (1991, p. 146). They argue that multidimensionality and heterogeneity are the two factors that distinguish TNCs from simpler organizational forms, which are monodimensional and homogeneous.

Multidimensionality refers to the principles on which an organizational form is structured. An organization can be structured according to geographical markets, products or activities in the value-chain. In simpler organizational settings, such as international and multinational environments, the firm is structured along one of these dimensions. TNCs, however, are much more complex; they need to balance market-level demands for local responsiveness with corporate-level demands for efficiency. In such operating environments, the views of different managers from different dimensions have to be integrated into the decision-making process. The TNC organization has to simultaneously address the concerns of product managers, country managers and functional managers. Thus, a TNC organization must provide for multidimensional managerial inputs.

At the same time, TNCs must manage organizational heterogeneity. Heterogeneity refers to 'a differentiated approach to businesses, countries and functions' (Doz and Prahalad, 1991, p. 146). In a TNC, management processes have to take into account the different settings in which subsidiaries operate. The major factor in which a particular market can differ from another is the level of competitive intensity (Porter, 1980). Porter (1980) captures the intensity of competition with his 'five forces' model, in which he argues that competition in a certain market depends upon the collective effect of the forces from industry competitors, potential entrants, substitutes, suppliers and buyers. Porter and others (Chandler, 1962; Miles and Snow, 1984; Ghoshal and Nohria, 1989, 1993; Ansoff and Sullivan, 1993) argue that, to maximize performance, organizational structure has to be matched (or aligned) with the specific environmental demands. Since each subsidiary of a TNC may function in a very different environment, each subsidiary has to adjust its structure to match the unique environment, resulting in a unique organizational approach for each subsidiary.

The combined consequences of multidimensionality and heterogeneity lead Doz and Prahalad (1991) to suggest that TNCs need to meet seven demands. Three of these are related to the multidimensional forces that confront TNCs: *structural indeterminacy*, *latent linkages* and *networked organization with fuzzy boundaries*. Three other TNC demands are related to the heterogeneity of TNCs: *internal differentiation*, *integrative optimi-*

zation and *information intensity*. The remaining TNC criterion, *learning and continuity*, is a result of the combined effect of multidimensionality and heterogeneity. Faced with the twin forces of multidimensionality and heterogeneity, the structural solutions of TNCs are more complex than previously conceived solutions have allowed. In the following section we discuss each of the seven demands and propose their relationship with the new TNC structure.

PROPOSITIONAL FRAMEWORK

Networked Organization with Fuzzy Boundaries

Ghoshal and Bartlett (1990) argue that there are a number of problems with applying intra-organizational theories to TNCs. First, subsidiaries in large dispersed organizations, such as TNCs, need to control the linkages with important actors in the local environment. This calls for explicitly incorporating linkages with external entities into the management task. Subsidiaries must form an external network with the environment. Second, although local environments are unique (that is, each location has some unique characteristics), interlinkages may occur because of common demands or common suppliers.

In such cases, relationships between subsidiaries may be appropriate. This calls for applying an internal network view of the relationships between individual subsidiaries. Thirdly, the headquarters/subsidiary relationship must be focused on the need to strategically coordinate the activities of the subsidiaries within the internal network. Since each subsidiary has a considerable amount of local autonomy, coordination prevents subsidiary units from 'wandering off' strategically, and helps to identify common strategies for interlinked local contexts.

The linkage between hierarchical power and ownership needs to be 'particularly weak in the case of [T]NCs because of the large physical and cultural distances between the owned and owning units' (Ghoshal and Bartlett, 1990, p. 607). Each subsidiary acts in a unique environment with a unique set of suppliers, competitors, buyers and regulatory agencies. To be locally responsive in such environments, headquarters have to encourage units to incorporate linkages with the external entities into the management task and to give subsidiary managers a considerable amount of local autonomy. This will encourage units to build and maintain external relationships.

The combination of a subsidiary's external entities is called an 'organization set' (Aldrich and Whetten, 1981). Nohria and Venkatraman (1987) point out that in *intra*-organizational theory there is a need to make a clear distinction between the organization and its environment.

The environment, in such cases, is nothing more than an exogenous entity that is the source of all kinds of uncertainties. The TNC, however, considers the environment an endogenous entity and incorporates the environment into its management task to form an external network. This results in a better understanding of the different organization sets. TNC subsidiaries need to form unique external sets and therefore need to be more independent because of differing local contexts; thus, hierarchy is not a good solution. Subsidiaries need to be viewed as (partly) independent, vertically-disaggregated units. Here, again, an *inter*-organizational relationship perspective is more appropriate.

All the organization sets of the subsidiaries together form the structured context of the firm (Homans, 1974). Ghoshal and Bartlett

> visualize this context as an external network consisting of all the organizations such as customers, suppliers, regulators, and competitors with which the different units of the [TNC] must interact. (1990, p. 604)

Although each TNC subsidiary context is unique, it may be connected with other subsidiary organization sets. For example, a supplier for unit A can also be a supplier for unit B. Or unit A may be competing with unit X from transnational T, while unit B has a competitor Y which also is a subsidiary of T. Therefore, corporate managers need to encourage linkages across organization sets, stressing the need for coordination of activities of subsidiaries, which will increase global efficiency. Prahalad and Doz (1987) refer to this as the 'global strategic coordination' of activities across countries. Units should be considered part of an internal network of relationships with other units and headquarters. To achieve this global strategic coordination, TNCs would benefit from taking a networked organizational focus with fuzzy boundaries in order to include linkages with entities outside the firm, as well as coordinating linkages within the firm.

> *Proposition 1*: A TNC organization will utilize both internal and external networks.

Learning and Continuity

The network point of view paves the way for introducing concepts to meet the learning and continuity demand. Learning is the result of the combined effects of entrepreneurial processes in the front-line (Bartlett and Ghoshal, 1993), and the 'tapping' (that is, sharing of information and experiences) of organization sets around the firm (Sölvell and Zander, 1995). The entrepreneurial process will create new knowledge (for example, products, technologies, markets and processes). To prevent this new knowledge from being locked up in a single unit, the firm should institute practices to share this knowledge with all units around the world. Learning thus stresses the need for new interaction patterns between organizational units in response to environmental stimuli. Those interaction patterns, however, have to be repeated to ensure organizational continuity (Doz and Prahalad, 1991).

To institutionalize the mindset in which units are encouraged to pursue opportunities in their environment, the firm should focus on the entrepreneurial process (Bartlett and Ghoshal, 1993). This process is driven by front-line managers. Their role as entrepreneur and performance driver makes them responsible for creating and pursuing opportunities. Although the entrepreneurial process is the main responsibility of front-line managers, middle and top management also have their tasks in the process. They should encourage front-line managers by focusing on tasks that support the entrepreneurial process. Middle management has to review, develop and support initiative. Top management has to establish strategic mission and performance standards to create a framework for entrepreneurial decision-making that supports overall firm-strategy. Through focusing on the entrepreneurial process, the firm unleashes creativity and makes use of the different organization sets of the firm that may require different innovative responses (Doz and Prahalad, 1991).

The organization sets in which units operate are also called dynamic industrial environments (Porter, 1990). The linkages between the local unit and its environment create a continuous information flow. Sölvell and Zander (1995) suggest that firms should gain access to these dynamic industrial environments through a process they call 'tapping'. Through tapping, the firm can locate advanced knowledge created in one subsidiary and transfer that knowledge to other subsidiaries. Without continuously tapping the subsidiaries, knowledge could be locked up inside single units and thus prevent organizational learning. Tapping results in small improvements to products and processes on an ongoing basis, and this, in turn, results in continual upgrading of the competitive advantage.

To ensure continuity and intra-firm learning, middle management has to focus on the integration process (Bartlett and Ghoshal, 1993), the aim of which is to link the skills, resources and knowledge developed in different units. Through this integration process, beneficial interaction patterns between units can be repeated, resulting in continuity of those patterns at a low cost (Doz and Prahalad, 1991). The organizational network thus has to allow the invention and selection of new interaction patterns in response to the environment (learning), and at the same time has to allow for those patterns to be retained and repeated (continuity). The combination of entrepreneurial integration and tapping processes makes this possible.

Proposition 2: TNCs will utilize mechanisms to coordinate intra-firm learning through the encouragement of entrepreneurship and intra-firm knowledge transfer.

Internal Differentiation

TNCs are heterogeneous organizations with their subsidiaries embedded in very different environmental settings. Because of this, TNCs need their management processes 'to differentiate between various countries, products, and functions' (Doz and Prahalad 1991, p. 147). This differentiation will lead to an internal structure with a variety of headquarters/subsidiary relationships.

The difference between the local contexts of subsidiaries has implications for the localization versus globalization dilemma. Some products may have a global appeal, while others need local adaptation. This dilemma also applies to functions/processes within an organization (Yip, 1994). Yip (1994) suggests that firms assign different 'location strategies' to different functions. With the help of his study, some generalizations about the location of activities can be made in the case of TNCs. For example, purchasing and production should be centralized to achieve efficiency. Centralization of production, in the TNC, embodies the production of a standardized core product, which has to allow for minor modifications that could be made on a country-by-country basis. Marketing functions can be globalized in the case of products with a global appeal, but should be localized whenever the context stresses the need for localization. The activities latest in the value-chain (for example, selling, distribution and service) should be localized to be responsive to local markets.

To ensure that differentiation in the internal structure does not lead to a different strategy for each subsidiary, the different headquarters/subsidiary relationships need to be structured with integrative mechanisms that strategically coordinate activities across countries. Ghoshal and Nohria (1989, 1993) argue that a firm can use three sorts of integrative mechanisms; centralization, formalization and socialization.

Centralization refers to the direct interference of headquarters in subsidiary decision-making; formalization refers to the use of systematic rules and procedures; and, socialization means the use of consensus and shared values (or organizational culture) as the basis of decision-making. A mixture of these three mechanisms can be used in TNCs to reach the appropriate level of local autonomy with assurance of strategic coordination.

Proposition 3: A TNC will utilize both formalized and socialized methods of coordinating subsidiary activities to assure a strategic focus.

Structural Indeterminacy

The structural indeterminacy demand of Doz and Prahalad (1991) gives two principles with which a TNC should conform. First, the firm should use radical decentralization to achieve responsiveness to differing local demands. Second, TNCs should assign different location strategies to different organizational functions to achieve efficiency.

Instead of using decentralization to give units autonomy, TNCs should use the concept of 'radical decentralization' (Taylor, 1991) to ensure local responsiveness. Radical decentralization goes a step beyond decentralization and is a difference of kind rather than of degree. Decentralization implies the allocation of resources and delegation of responsibilities to the subsidiary level, whereas radical decentralization is based on the concept of self-contained and manageable units. In a decentralized organization, resources are allocated to units by headquarters: in a radical decentralized firm, subsidiaries have their own resources. The concept closely relates to the entrepreneurial process (Bartlett and Ghoshal, 1993) and vertical disaggregation. The TNC can be conceptualized as a network of vertically-disaggregated entrepreneurial units pursuing opportunities with the aid of their own resources. Radical decentralization, therefore, leads to a whole new perspective of the firm. Consider the following passage by Bartlett and Ghoshal:

> The new organizational model . . . is based on an assumption that the organization needs to be developed and managed on a principle of *proliferation and subsequent aggregation* of small independent entrepreneurial units from the bottom up, rather than one of *division and devolution* of resources and responsibilities from the top. (1993, p. 42 emphasis added)

Adopting this view of the organization should lead the TNC away from simple hierarchical concepts.

TNCs cannot structure solely for efficiency as in the global product firm, or solely for responsiveness as in the multinational firm. Rather, TNCs have to do both. A TNC can achieve some level of global efficiency by differentiating between different products and functions, standardizing some and localizing others. Combining radical decentralization (for responsiveness) with assigning different location strategies to different functions (for efficiency) creates a multidimensional organization in which the demands of different management groups can be balanced.

Proposition 4a: TNC subsidiary managers should 'own' their own resources and be encouraged to pursue entrepreneurial objectives; and

Proposition 4b: Some TNC functions will be centralized while others will be localized.

Integrative Optimization

In TNCs, different viewpoints exist because of the differences in the perceived need for standardization or localization:

> headquarters executives' priorities for integration need to be actively managed and balanced with subsidiary managers' concerns for responsiveness. (Doz and Prahalad, 1984, p. 58)

The integrative mechanisms that are used to shape the headquarters/subsidiary relationships should also be used to reach decision trade-offs between the concerns for efficiency and responsiveness. Instead of intervening directly in the decision-making process (centralization), top management should put into place a broad framework in which decisions are made according to overall firm strategy:

> [I]n large complex firms ... top management should devote more attention to how decisions are made than to what decisions are actually made in the various businesses and countries in which the firm operates. Top management works on designing and implementing a 'structural context' (Bower 1970) which, in turn, provides a framework for individual decisions that is consistent with the strategic direction in which top management wants to see the firm move. (Doz and Prahalad, 1984, p. 60)

This framework should consist of rules and procedures, and means a role for top management that is different from the classic role of control (Bartlett and Ghoshal, 1993). To stimulate front-line initiative and sharing of information, top management should decrease the level of control and direct interference. Instead, they should focus on broad strategic objectives that guide managers through decision-making processes. Focusing on broad strategic objectives and corporate purpose, called the renewal process (Bartlett and Ghoshal, 1993), will lead to a cultural change within the firm. Instead of trying to implement the strategy laid down by top managers, front-line managers are strengthened in their efforts to renew the organizational strategy within the boundaries of the corporate purpose. Corporate purpose and broad strategic objectives will serve as the broader framework in which to apply management tools (Doz and Prahalad, 1984; Simons, 1994) that facilitate decision-making in those situations when there are multiple priorities expressed by different manager groups.

Proposition 5: Top managers of TNCs will supply overall strategic objectives to guide lower-level managers in their decision-making processes.

Information Intensity

TNC managers use the integration process (Bartlett and Ghoshal, 1993) to create information intensity within the TNC. Information intensity refers to a high level of information-sharing within the organization. Doz and Prahalad (1991) argue that managing information has to be a central task of TNC management because information both creates an implicit structure and can be the source of new competitive advantage.

Because TNC units operate in different organization sets, it is not possible to create uniform headquarters/subsidiary relationships to apply to all units in the same way. The lack of a unified structural solution for all subsidiaries creates the need to focus on information and control issues that shape different relationships. Thus, information flows define the relationships between the different layers in the organization.

This emphasis on information makes it possible to shift and mobilize resources for the purpose of pursuing opportunities that may arise in any of the organization sets. In this way, the organization is even capable of responding to short-lived opportunities, which is the key to gaining new competitive advantage (Doz and Prahalad, 1991).

In order to facilitate the information-flow process, a specific culture needs to be put in place to support the sharing of information. Although the organization consists of disaggregated units, the members have to have a sense of contributing to the entire firm. Norms, such as cooperation and individual action for the common good, must be deeply rooted in the organizational culture. The shaping of this culture is the task of top management:

> Corporate leaders must create a sense of community and help employees identify with the larger organization in a way that transcends personal interests and particular responsibilities. (Ghoshal and Bartlett, 1995, p. 92)

This new organizational culture creates the basis on which middle managers can perform their role as capability integrators and horizontal information brokers.

Proposition 6: TNCs will create organizational cultures in which information and resource-sharing are more important than parochial concerns.

Latent Linkages

Latent linkages are those linkages that cannot be institutionalized beforehand, but have to emerge whenever the need for them arises (Doz and Prahalad, 1991). The reasons for latency stem from the size of the TNC on the one hand, and the different organization sets on the other.

Linkages between units can be institutionalized in the case of small firms or those firms that operate in a limited geographical region. The TNC, however, typically acts in many countries around the globe with hundreds of business units. Linking each unit to every other would be impossible because of the simple fact that there would be an almost infinite number of linkages, and it would be too costly to maintain the links between all organizational units. For efficiency reasons, it would be much more desirable if appropriate linkages could appear whenever they are needed. As discussed in the learning and continuity section, efficiency can be improved further if the firm 'remembers' the useful linkages, so that they can be repeated at low cost.

The different organization sets are the source of an unpredictable number of opportunities and problems. Problems and opportunities could create the need for linkages between one or more sub-units to carry out a specific task, but, because managers do not know which problems or opportunities will occur, they cannot predict which linkages are going to be useful in the future. Again, it would be far more beneficial to let the network itself work out the appropriate linkages at any given point in time.

The process of emerging linkages is made possible by the culture of shared values and the integration process driven by middle managers. The culture of shared values increases the sense of community and, therefore, the level of cooperation between organizational units. As a result, the process of forming latent linkages is a decentralized self-structuring process that takes place in the decentralized network without frequent interference of top management.

Proposition 7: TNC management will encourage linkages between subsidiary units on an informal as well as a formal basis. Linkages may be changed as the demands of the market dictate.

CASE STUDY: McDONALD'S CORPORATION

There are a number of modern corporations operating in the transnational environment. According to Ghoshal and Nohria (1993), companies such as Digital Equipment, Volvo and Kodak are examples of such firms. To explore the propositions outlined above, we decided to follow a focused case method, in which one firm is examined in depth. The McDonald's Corporation (henceforth McDonald's) was selected for the case, since it was willing to participate and met the criterion of being a transnational corporation facing multiple environments with conflicting local and global demands. In addition, since McDonald's has been successful in most of its international operations, as well as domestically, it provides a strong example of successful organizational structuring (*Fortune*, 1994).

In 1984, only 20 per cent of McDonald's stores (units) were located outside the US, but by 1994 foreign based units represented 36 per cent of the total. In 1984, McDonald's had 1709 foreign stores (units) and operated in only 35 foreign countries; by 1994 those figures had grown dramatically to 5461 units in 78 foreign countries (McDonald's *Annual Report*, 1994). Total worldwide sales increased from about $9500 million in 1984 to over $25 000 million in 1994. In 1994, of the total of 15 205 units worldwide (that is, both domestic and non-domestic units), 10 458 were operated by franchisees, 3083 were company-owned and operated, and 1664 were operated by affiliates (McDonald's *Annual Report*, 1994). According to *Fortune Magazine* (1994), foreign units now generate 45 per cent of the total operating income of McDonald's.

Several case research methods were used to obtain information for this analysis. First, a personal interview was conducted with the senior manager of communications with McDonald's Europe. This interview was recorded for future reference and notes were taken by the researchers. Second, publications created by or concerning McDonald's were examined. Third, the McDonald's representative was available for further questions during the analysis phase, to clear up any uncertainty.

In the following sections we examine how the organizational structure of McDonald's has addressed each of the seven demands (as propositions) outlined above. For each of the seven propositions, we describe the solution devised by McDonald's and how the firm actualized this solution.

Networked Organization with Fuzzy Boundaries

McDonald's uses both internal and external networks, which are dubbed 'The McDonald's System'.[1] The company's internal networks encompass the relationships between the Home Office (headquarters), regional offices (regional offices set up franchised units in a specific geographical area and can be wholly-owned, partially owned, or licensed by McDonald's), and units (which can be franchised units run by franchisees or wholly-owned units that are employee-managed by McDonald's). The company's external networks include customers and suppliers. McDonald's incorporates all these relationships into the management task. The suppliers are independent entities, but many have open-book relationships with

McDonald's in which McDonald's determines their profit levels. Some suppliers have McDonald's as their only customer, yet no supplier has a contract (*Fortune*, 1994).

Strategic coordination is reached by communication between multiple layers in the organization. In the US, for example, McDonald's has divided the country into 40 regions. The owner-operators in a region choose one representative for the company's National Operators Advisory Board. In this Board, owner-operators exchange ideas and knowledge; they discuss their ideas with middle managers and try to devise integrating strategies (a similar system of regional boards are used internationally). In a related way, groups of owner-operators in a number of regions around the world (including Germany, France, the US and the UK) have formed a cross-national construction team to standardize restaurant design, because of similar customer expectations in these countries (McDonald's *Annual Report*, 1994). Thus, it appears that the organizational structure of McDonald's utilizes both internal and external networks and conforms to proposition 1.

Learning and Continuity

To encourage innovation and change, McDonald's has 'a system that is based on entrepreneurship and independent thinking'.[2] By focusing on the entrepreneurial process, McDonald's encourages franchisees (individual unit-level owner/managers) to search for opportunities in their local markets. For instance, the world famous food products Big Mac, Egg McMuffin and Filet-O-Fish were all developed from the ideas of individual franchisees (*Fortune*, 1994). Products developed by a single franchisee are made useful to the entire organization by constantly tapping the local organization sets and integrating the knowledge created there.[3] All the McDonald's restaurants around the globe form a huge source of new ideas, products and processes.

By focusing on tapping and integrating knowledge, skills and expertise, products developed in one region can become global winners. The food product Filet-O-Fish, for example, was developed in Pittsburgh, Pennsylvania. One of McDonald's franchisees noticed that on Fridays the Catholic community would not come into the restaurant because they were not allowed to eat meat on religious grounds. The franchisee therefore developed a fish sandwich, and now McDonald's serves this product around the world (*Fortune*, 1994). In this particular example, the local context combined with the entrepreneurial process allowed the franchisee to develop a local product. Tapping and integrating this knowledge allowed McDonald's to identify the local product and build it into a global winner.

As proposition 2 suggests, a TNC will utilize mechanisms to coordinate learning through the encouragement of entrepreneurship and intra-firm knowledge-transfer. McDonald's appears to have instituted a number of important learning mechanisms that support both entrepreneurship and intra-organizational knowledge transfer, and it therefore appears that McDonald's meets the second criteria of being a TNC.

Internal Differentiation

McDonald's addresses the issue of internal differentiation using both formalization and socialization systems, as suggested by proposition 3. McDonald's recognizes the different local contexts between countries by adjusting the franchise mode. In markets that resemble the US, wholly-owned subsidiaries are established. In the US and Europe the same type of franchising is used, where in each host country a wholly-owned subsidiary operates company-owned units and also licenses out to franchisees. This form of franchising is called subsidiary international franchising (Burton and Cross, 1993).

When markets are different from the US or are more complex and turbulent, McDonald's uses local people to help them understand the market and to be as responsive as possible. For example, in Asian markets McDonald's prefers joint-venture international franchising, through which the company can use the partner's contacts and local expertise. Also, McDonald's lets such partners negotiate with cumbersome entities such as the local and national government (Burton and Cross, 1993). In other – more exotic – countries, Africa and the Middle East for example, McDonald's uses master international franchising, where the risk is reduced by not putting equity capital into local operations; instead, McDonald's takes an option to buy in later (Burton and Cross, 1993).

Through training, managers are socialized in a set of shared values, goals and beliefs that shape their behaviour. All managers of McDonald's have either worked in a McDonald's restaurant or gone through training that showed them what working in one of the restaurants involves. As one of the interviewees commented:

> training is huge. We believe training is more than just how to prepare products in the restaurant. It is management, it is how to treat your employees, it is how to work together.[4]

Through training, everyone in the McDonald's corporation knows that they are working for a firm that encourages initiative, shares ideas and encourages people to work together. All layers in the organization undergo training sessions. The Hamburger University and the Center for Corporate Training and Education are McDonald's 'in-house' training facilities, initially established to service the US market. Managers and employees from all over the world are now trained through these two internal organizations. While the Hamburger University trains restaurant staff in operational excellence, the Center for Corporate Training and Education trains corporate staff in problem-solving tools, process re-engineering concepts, benchmarking techniques, and effective management practices (*Fortune*, 1994).

Structural Undeterminacy

McDonald's states that 'we are very decentralized',[5] but what the franchise structure actually uses is radical decentralization. At McDonald's, entrepreneurs join the organization at the bottom ('McDonald's is growing from the customer up'[6]). Franchisees do, however, have to have a considerable amount of money to join the organization. The entrepreneur will start with his or her own resources, and develop (or grow) their own resources in the future. The task of middle and top management is to aggregate these entrepreneurial units into the firm. Thus, as part of the McDonald's structure, resources are owned and controlled at the local individual unit level, while their efficient global coordination is what creates the added value for the individual unit entrepreneurs.

McDonald's is structured for responsiveness through radical decentralization. A difference in local markets implies differentiation in products. Some products are global and can be marketed globally (such as the food product Big Mac), while other products can only be sold in a local market (for example, blackcurrant drinks in Poland and teriyaki burgers in Japan) (*Fortune*, 1994):

> Every country operates autonomously with the responsibility of coordinating globally through the head office . . . we recognize the importance to standardize, but also the importance to localize. It is a constant balance.[7]

As the concept of radical decentralization allows for responsiveness, the organization also has to structure for efficiency. By assigning different location strategies to different functions, McDonald's can achieve a high level of efficiency. The owner-operators perform certain activities in the value-added chain, while other activities are performed more centrally. Production and procurement, for example, are highly centralized to keep the production costs and procurement costs as low as possible. The expensive computers and kitchen equipment that are used in McDonald's restaurants are bought on a global basis to create a cost advantage for franchisees, who are competing with local competitors. Furthermore, the various units of McDonald's identify common marketing programmes that can be executed simultaneously across regions to enhance efficiency (*Fortune*, 1994).

Radical decentralization appears to have allowed McDonald's to achieve both propositions 4a and 4b. Franchise owners own their own resources and are encouraged to pursue entrepreneurial objectives. In fact, in many instances these individual entrepreneurial objectives have lead to the development of globally-successful food products and organizational processes within McDonald's. In addition, the company has achieved centralization of some organizational processes while decentralizing many others, offering the individual unit managers a real voice in the way they operate their own units.

Integrative Optimization

At McDonald's, a system known as the 'Alignment Strategy' is used as a framework for unit-level decision-making and allows McDonald's to ful-fil the TNC role outlined in proposition 5. The purpose of the 'Alignment Strategy' is 'to define organizational roles and responsibilities, build effective leadership, and achieve a sharing of goals throughout the global McDonald's system' (McDonald's *Annual Report*, 1994). Another pro-cess that McDonald's uses to keep subsidiary strategy in line with corporate strategy is the 'Quality Management Program', which defines the phi-losophies, processes and behaviour that focus the entire McDonald's system on quality (McDonald's *Annual Report*, 1994). At McDonald's quality means the customer's complete satisfaction. Meeting customer's require-ments is a good example of a shared value throughout the McDonald's system used to resolve differences between local customer desires and global organizational efficiency.

The potential conflict between the perceived need for standardization (global efficiency) or localization (meeting local requirements) leads back to the foundation of the firm; the customer. 'The customer wins out. It is generally the local customer perspective that wins, because we con-stantly have to remember who drives our business'.[8] The first element of conflict-resolution (resolving the conflict between local customer desires – or localization – and global efficiency – or standardization) at McDonald's is talking face-to-face. The organization has structurally built in mecha-nisms for regular two-way dialogue between management and franchisees. A good example is the National Operators Advisory Board. Representa-tives meet here as a group with management and together they make decisions to resolve these 'standardization versus localization' conflicts:

Those meetings are not preprogrammed. People get together and exchange ideas and those talks are quite spirited. But they ultimately try to reach consensus because what is good for the customer, is good for the franchisees, and is generally good for McDonald's as a whole.[9]

Middle management is well-placed to make decisions and is responsible for the integration process:

> Probably the biggest job that our management has is listening. It is listening at all different levels. Listening to our franchisees, corporate employees, suppliers, and restaurant employees, and obviously, listening to our customers. And then helping make judgements based on all of that input. Management has to have an awareness of what is going on in all of these decentralized locations and make sure that everybody is communicating and doing things in a way that is cohesive and consistent.[10]

Information Intensity

Information intensity involves sharing information and knowledge. To achieve this, an organizational culture that puts shared values above individual desires is imperative. Cooperation and individual action for the good of the organization are key concepts in such a culture. How serious they are at McDonald's about creating this culture is made clear by:

> Internal communications for McDonald's are a huge priority and the company encourages communication at any level. Everyone from our top management, Chairman on down, is open to getting a telephone call or visit from a franchisee or supplier or another employee about an issue. Virtually all kinds of communication the company generates and uses to keep a regular flow of information going.[11]

McDonald's encourages the exchange of ideas generated anywhere in the firm. In the US, the National Operators Advisory Board provides a national forum for the exchange of ideas. Regional franchisee advisory boards and local franchisee cooperatives (consisting of groups of owner-operators) also provide valuable interaction. Internationally, McDonald's has followed the US pattern of creating and using regional advisory boards to effectuate information flows within the organization.

Clearly, McDonald's has created an organizational structure and culture in which the sharing of information and resources between units is considered an imperative by management. Thus, we suggest that the organizational structure of McDonald's conforms to the demands of information intensity and supports proposition 6.

Latent Linkages

Because it is impossible and undesirable to create linkages between all units beforehand, McDonald's has formed a culture of shared decision-making in which linkages can emerge whenever needed. Franchisees stay in touch via cooperatives and the National Operators Advisory Board and may decide at any point in time to link up to carry out some task. Within the broad strategic framework, this can lead to the forming of temporary cross-national and cross-functional teams to pursue new business opportunities. For example, in Brazil a cross-functional team of equipment managers, project managers, lawyers and suppliers created low-cost kiosks in shopping malls, and in the US a similar effort came up with creating alliances on new locations such as gas stations (McDonald's *Annual Report*, 1994).

Latent linkages are utilized throughout McDonald's global network of subsidiaries. Individual units are encouraged to join together on an 'as needed' basis, to resolve problems or explore new opportunities which may benefit customers on a local, regional or global basis. Once the task has been accomplished, these linkages can be easily dissolved and new linkages formed between operating units when and where needed. Thus, in McDonald's, latent linkages improve communication but also improve efficiency because of their temporary nature. The organizational culture of McDonald's therefore confirms our proposition 7 in that its management evidently encourages informal as well as formal linkages between units, which are modified as the demands of the market dictate.

CONCLUSION

In this chapter, we set out to identify a solution to the transnational organizational paradox. Because TNCs are faced with the challenges of managing multidimensionality and heterogeneity, traditional organizational structures have become a barrier to growth, and a new organizational structure is required (*Business Week*, 1994; Ghoshal and Bartlett, 1995). Based on the seven demands of a TNC organization as described by Doz and Prahalad (1991), we developed propositions that could be compared against proposed and existing organizational structures. After examining numerous structures, one appeared to meet all seven demands. That structure is currently used by a number of TNC organizations, including McDonald's Corporation. To test our propositions, an in-depth interview and literature review were undertaken to investigate McDonald's Corporation.

We found that McDonald's uses both internal and external networks through 'The McDonald's System'. Second, we found that McDonald's uses a radical decentralized system based upon entrepreneurship and independent thinking. The organization taps its worldwide subsidiaries for new products and processes, and transfers this knowledge throughout the firm using National and Regional Operators Boards and local cooperatives. Third, McDonald's uses different kinds of franchising owner-ship structures and socializes employees and managers in a common set of values and beliefs, through training in Hamburger University and the Center for Corporate Training and Education. Fourth, franchisees own their own resources that they bring when joining the firm. Efficiency is achieved by centralizing some of the production and procurement ac-tivities while still allowing for adaptation of other functions to meet local demands. Fifth, McDonald's uses its 'Alignment Strategy' to supply lower-level managers with a decision-making framework that leads to a common strategic direction. Sixth, through the National Operators Advisory Boards, Regional Advisory Boards, and local cooperatives, a culture is main-tained in which information and resource-sharing are important. Finally, McDonald's encourages a high level of information sharing by allowing the formation of cross-national and cross-functional teams.

This study of McDonald's shows that this organization utilizes all the different concepts responsible for meeting the demands placed on the TNC organization. Thus, it may be that the new transnational structure already exists and functions. It is possible that, because this structure is currently called franchising, many researchers and managers have ig-nored the structure when considering TNC options. General business reports tend to throw a disapproving light on firms that use franchising. However, the structure identified in this paper is capable of incorporat-ing all types of relationships in the management task. Franchising, licensing, joint-ventures and wholly-owned subsidiaries can all be integrated into one organizational structure that provides both the efficiency of global structures and the local responsiveness of multinational forms. Further research should be undertaken to examine in more detail how the franchising structure solves these paradoxical demands.

Notes

1. This information was obtained during a personal interview with M.F. Oakley, the Senior Manager of Communication at the headquarters of McDonald's Europe, Edgware Road, London, UK, in 1996.
2. *Op. cit.*
3. *Op. cit.*
4. *Op. cit.*
5. *Op. cit.*
6. *Op. cit.*
7. *Op. cit.*
8. *Op. cit.*
9. *Op. cit.*
10. *Op. cit.*
11. *Op. cit.*

Part Three

Emerging Markets

Introduction
Malcolm Chapman

This section of the book concerns, very broadly, emerging markets and the cultural and comparative organizational aspects of international business that arise within them. The study of such aspects of international business has become, over the last decade or so, a part of the mainstream of academic research activity in this area. This does not mean, unfortunately, that we have come very close to definitive theories or conclusions. It does mean, however, that many interesting areas of argument have been opened up, some at least of which have been tested and teased by research, and by the changing fortunes of the companies and countries under discussion.

We have come a long way, in business research and business education. The MBA, as established and institutionalized in the United States, was in the first place focused on domestic concerns. 'International business', in the early North American formulations, had a tendency to mean 'business conducted outside the USA by US companies'. US business had emerged strengthened rather than damaged from the war, and had entered a long period of effortless superiority. It is small wonder that theory and research in international business developed, in this period, a marked North American flavour. We might consider, for example, the work of Vernon (1966), on international product life-cycle theory; of Aharoni (1966), on behavioural contingency theories of market entry; and of Knickerbocker (1973), on 'follow my leader' investment activity. These were theories developed by North American researchers, and based upon the activities and experience of US companies outside the USA. They were theories which were, in an important sense, culturally innocent. They had behind them an economic theory and a behavioural psychology which were perceived (without reflection or examination) to be universal. Vernon's theory contained, to be sure, an explicit theory of cultural difference, but it was a cultural difference based in greater or lesser development, such that obsolete US products could be marketed outside the US because outside the US countries were less-developed; but they were perforce developing, and what they were developing into was something modern, and that meant something like the USA. One can still find strong, if often implicit, echoes of this form of thinking in US management and business literature. There have been, of course, early and major contributions by British scholars; Dunning was a very early pioneer (1958), and has been at the centre of intellectual development in this area ever since; and Buckley and Casson made an early and seminal contribution (1976).

The reemergence of European business activity in international business in the postwar period reoriented the focus of attention somewhat. European scholars came to prominence in the field. The European nations were perhaps sufficiently familiar to the USA that their reemergence caused no undue surprise or concern. It was, indeed, only the successful realization of the Marshall Plan. Theories of market expansion and entry that had worked for the USA could reasonably be assumed to work for Europe as well. Economics is economics; rationality is rationality. This was particularly true since the European nation which was most significantly involved in foreign investment was the UK, with its obvious historical and cultural links to the USA, and its shared institutional heritage.

It was the reemergence of Japan which really concentrated minds on the subject of cultural difference and business, in the most general sense. The result was a rather agitated concern with Japan and its business ways. Japan was visibly, disturbingly successful. Japan also, however, was different. It seemed to play by different rules, or even to play a different game. Japanese companies and banks were not like US companies and banks. Japanese corporate ambitions and investment decisions were differently structured, with different imperatives. Japanese work practices, hierarchies and career paths were different too. So what were they like? And could and should they be imitated? A large literature resulted (see, for a summary of some major aspects, Smith and Misumi, 1994).

It was the phenomenon of Japan that made cultural issues in business into an urgent practical concern. There is, however, a range of other problems which have been addressed within these terms. Among them are: the economic emergence of two waves of East and South-east Asian countries (variously labelled 'tigers' and 'dragons'), constituting what came to be called the 'Asian miracle'; the transition from socialism throughout the ex-Soviet bloc; the case of China, and its relationship to Hong Kong and to capitalism; the enduring comparative failure of Latin America; the enduring problems of sub-Saharan Africa; the evolving relationship of Islam, in all its varieties, to modern capitalism; the recent economic crisis in Asia; the nature and success of 'European' capitalism as against 'Anglo-Saxon' capitalism; the East/West orientation of Australasia; and so on. Each of these themes, and all the others unmentioned, has a large and contentious literature surrounding it.

The first chapter in this section, by Hugo Radice, looks at 'globalization' and the convergence of national business systems. Globalization, as a phenomenon and a concept, has been much invoked in recent years. Some deplore it; some strive towards it. Radice takes a calculated look at the various things that might be meant by globalization, and also looks at its implications for the enduring coexistence of different national business systems. On the face of it, the increased contact between different business systems that globalization brings about might seem inevitably to lead to some kind of convergence. Radice shows, however, that this assumption is by no means unproblematic, that there are counter-trends, and that in any case the problem can be answered differently at various different levels. The relative success and desirability of an 'Anglo-American' versus a 'German' or 'Japanese' model is immediately at issue here. As we have noted, the early North American assumption was that in order to become modern, the world would be obliged to become like the United States. This naive ethnocentricity receded in the 1970s, and it came to be widely accepted that the 'German' or the 'Japanese' model was in many ways the better recipe for success; there has been abundant publication and analysis attempting to establish this. Radice quotes one of his sources, from 1996, to the effect that convergence will 'have to be . . . on European and east Asian rather than Anglo-American terms'. Only two years later, and the picture has changed again. The practitioners of European and East Asian business, and the national business systems that they inhabit, in Germany, Japan, South Korea, are queuing up to convert themselves and their businesses into something Anglo-American in style (particularly if this can be painlessly achieved, which in most cases it probably cannot). The same oppositions are still invoked, but in the aftermath of the Asian crisis, the East Asian model is blamed for the crisis where it was previously praised for the success. Japan is widely committed to the view that its system has now 'failed'. Major German businesses force through 'Anglo-American'-style reforms. This is a tale told on a switchback, and pronouncements that sound wise one year can sound foolish the next.

The following chapter, by Sharpley, Buck, Filatotchev and Wright, concerns employee ownership and employment in Russian privatized firms. The concerns derive from two sources – one, the issue of incentives, and of agency and transaction costs, within the firm; and two, the particular case of newly-privatized firms in the chaotic commercial and legal environment of modern Russia. The Russian corporate world is not an easy environment to research, and Sharpley and his co-authors offer a rare empirically-based insight into this shadowy world. It is perhaps not unexpected, but nevertheless gratifying, that the theories and principles of ownership and incentives do lead to some hypotheses about Russian corporate life which can be empirically confirmed.

The chapter by Choi, Lee and Millar relates closely, and in different ways, to the two previous chapters. Choi and his co-authors look at enforcement costs and cooperative strategy in emerging business systems. We have already seen that a distinction has been drawn between

the 'Japanese' and the 'Anglo-American' style of business. Choi *et al.*
paraphrase this distinction as one between 'trust'-based systems, and
'market'-based systems. They give an extensive discussion of the need to
extend the transaction-cost literature to encompass issues of enforcement, and illustrate this through a contrast of the different modalities
of enforcement which are needed and required in 'trust' and 'market'-
based systems. They then ask, however, how enforcement can be achieved
in societies which lack a stable business environment, and where neither
trust nor market can be relied upon. The transition economies are in
just such a position, although how grave the problem is varies greatly
between the transition economies (contrast, for example, Poland and
Belarus, neighbours in geography, but far apart in the integrity and
reliability of the business environment). The recent political and economic crisis in Russia (with the collapse of the rouble in August 1998)
has shown how quite unpredictable and lawless the business environment in Russia can be. Choi *et al.* suggest that one rational and effective
response to this problem is to engage in counter-trade, at the same time
as exchanging hostages. The idea links interestingly back to Radice's
chapter on different national business systems, to Sharpley *et al.*'s chapter
on life inside the Russian business organization, and to Schoenberg's
discussion of the cultural mediation of intercorporate cooperation.

Coyne's chapter concerns an attempt to 'segment the market' of companies engaging in foreign direct investment (FDI). The producers here
are the countries which attempt to attract FDI, and which compete with
one another through packages of incentives, concessions and policies.
Coyne shows that this market is indeed one which can be segmented,
and that this can be achieved according to the different strategic ambitions that lie behind corporate FDI. The other chapters in this section,
while diverse in subject, are closely linked by many interconnecting themes.
The link between them and Coyne's chapter is less clear, since Coyne's
is more nearly linked to the strategy literature. As such, Coyne's chapter
can of course be left to speak for itself. Nevertheless, there are two
features of Coyne's work which make its inclusion here rather than elsewhere appropriate. The first is that he makes extensive background use
of the assumptions of transaction-cost economics. It has been argued
elsewhere that transaction-cost economics is one route through which
an interest in cultural variation can be smuggled into economics (on the
assumption, often borne out, that economics as a discipline is relatively
resistant to accepting the importance of cultural analysis). Transaction-
cost analysis has, indeed, been used as an area where the very different
subjects of economics and social anthropology might meet and talk to
one another (see Buckley and Chapman, 1997). In an address to a business studies conference in May 1998 I attempted to summarize the
possibilities by saying that 'any culture can be perceived as a particular

configuration of transaction costs', and the formulation was well received. It is clear from the other chapters in this section that the transaction-cost paradigm is meeting issues related to cultural difference in many different ways, and in this Coyne's chapter is true to the trend. Coyne's work is also relevant here in that FDI into different countries, and the different ways in which countries attract and deal with such FDI, are part of the very raw material out of which national business systems are constructed, and through which differences between national systems are tested and negotiated.

Schoenberg's paper focuses on a particular area of cultural difficulty in international business – the binational joint venture and merger. If cultural differences in business practice are important, then we would expect them to be thrown into sharp relief within such binational business activity, and, as Schoenberg shows, this expectation is to some extent realized. The picture, however, is once again far from simple, and the different effects of organizational and of national culture prove themselves as always difficult to disentangle. Schoenberg details both theoretical and empirical studies, showing that the latter in general confirm the assumptions of the former, that cultural difference is a problem, and that in general the more of such difference there is, the greater the problem. The work of Hofstede is a major theme in Schoenberg's chapter, because it is a major theme in the literature in general (see Hofstede, 1980). Hofstede's work has been enormously fruitful in stimulating research in cross-cultural issues in business. There is room for concern, however, that areas of difference which are not highlighted by the Hofstede framework are actually being neglected, even effaced, through the uncritical application of Hofstede's dimensions. It is a challenge to research in this area to find a way round this problem (see Chapman, 1997; d'Iribarne, 1977).

13 'Globalization' and the Convergence of National Business Systems[1]

Hugo Radice

INTRODUCTION

Recent debates about globalization have raised a wide range of fundamental issues about the contemporary world economy. The main purpose of this chapter is to examine the question of whether or not, among the advanced industrial countries, the various national political economies, or 'business systems', are becoming more alike through a process of convergence.[2] Broadly speaking, we can identify a 'strong' thesis of homogenization, according to which the irresistible social forces summarized in the term 'globalization' are breaking down national differences in economic institutions, practices and policies.[3] Against this stands the view that economic life remains firmly embedded in distinct national systems, and these will persist because either globalization is not happening, or, if it is, it has no necessary effect on national differences.

This chapter argues that there is evidence of economic and political processes occurring in common across different national economies, stemming from their closer integration. These processes result in part from the spread of transnational business, linking national production systems more and more closely, and in part from changes in government policies, which themselves are increasingly linked together. What they lead to is a recasting of national differences; some institutions, practices and policies are subject to convergence, while other differences – especially economic *outcomes* – are not.

Since our hypothesis is that globalization leads to convergence, the section that follows begins by defining and discussing 'globalization'. Sections three to five examine the evidence for convergence of national business systems by looking at three different areas currently under debate; section three looks at the growth of so-called global capital markets, section four at the global integration of R&D, and section five at corporate governance systems. The final section draws conclusions and suggests some directions for future work.

WHAT IS 'GLOBALIZATION'?

As a general focus of analysis in the study of international business, economics and political economy, the concept of globalization has only emerged in the last ten years (Waters, 1995, p. 2). Students of international business have, of course, used the term 'global' for many years to characterize firms or industries in which cross-border activities are especially extensive and significant, but in the 1990s a growing number of business people, social scientists and politicians have posited globalization as a universal and perhaps ineluctable socioeconomic trend, heralding a transition to a new type of world economic system. This new 'globalized' system is seen as differing in important respects from the traditional model of an 'inter-national' economy made up of *a priori* separate and autonomous nation-states, which interact with each other in world markets; globalization means the tendency for all national economies to become essentially component zones within a single integrated global economy – as prefigured most famously in Kindleberger's remark in 1969 that 'the nation-state is just about through as an economic unit' (1969, p. 207).

There is, however, no agreement at all in these wider debates about the real content and significance of this trend. Most writers have positioned themselves in one of two camps; those who confirm the existence of the trend can be designated as 'globalists', while those who deny or downplay it might best be termed 'nation-statists'. However, matters are enormously complicated by sharp disagreements over the *desirability* of globalization, which have led to a dangerous conflation of positive and normative arguments. Many 'globalists' strongly support the weakening of national barriers to economic exchange on traditional liberal grounds, and in recent years their views have typically extended to wholehearted support for privatization, deregulation, the dismanting of tariff and non-tariff barriers to trade and capital movements, and more generally the 'rolling-back' of the state associated with fiscal conservatism and other 'neoliberal' policies. In reaction to this, many 'nation-statists' argue that globalization is being exaggerated precisely for ideological and political effect, in order to support the view that (in Mrs Thatcher's immortal words) 'there is no alternative' to the neoliberal order.

It is not possible to resolve a debate of this kind by appealing simply to 'the evidence', since there is no agreement on the criteria to be applied. When globalists point to the rapid growth in foreign trade, direct and portfolio investment, and patenting, their critics argue that the *levels* of these activities, by comparison to intra-national activities, are no higher than they were before 1914 (Hirst and Thompson, 1996, chapters 2 to 4; Wade, 1996; Weiss, 1997). When globalists hail the emergence of regional integrations as evidence of economic activity outgrowing the nation-state (as in Ohmae's 'triad' concept), their critics present those same regional integrations as evidence of the durability and necessity of the nation-state as a political form, since the integrations are created by groups of nation-states acting, as always, in the national interest. Matters are made worse by the natural tendency of both sides to caricature their opponents; thus nation-statists are caricatured as the defenders of the special interests of state bureaucracies, small business and organized labour, while globalists are caricatured as defenders of big business and rapacious global speculators.

The hypothesis of convergence of national business systems does not escape from this crude confrontation of views. Much of the writing about such systems in sociology, political economy and political science has explicitly or implicitly sought to contrast the market-driven, individualistic 'Anglo-Saxon' model with the more community-based and solidaristic 'continental', 'Rhineland' or 'East Asian' model (see, especially, Albert, 1993; but also Hart, 1992; Whitley, 1992; Hollingsworth, Schmitter and Streek, 1994; and Hutton, 1995). Since supporters of the latter models see globalism as a modern version of Anglo-Saxon *laissez-faire* ideology, they are anxious to demonstrate the superiority of alternatives in which the state continues to play a dynamic and positive role in improving economic performance. They also argue that economic institutions evolve historically not on the basis of abstract (market-determined) economic efficiency, but on the basis of broad social choices, which are manifested through national political processes: to accept globalization as inevitable is thus to deny the value of political democracy.

On this view, convergence may take place towards a more 'organized' and state-centred model of business system, because people see it as yielding more socially-desirable outcomes, and vote in governments which organize appropriate changes in laws and policies. On the other hand, supporters of free-market capitalism argue that it is (at least in the present epoch) more dynamic and efficient, and especially that it offers a more realistic prospect of economic advance in less-developed countries and regions than the discredited protectionism and state socialism which dominated them from roughly 1930 to 1980. Again, if this proposition engenders widespread support, it may lead to convergence of systems, but in this case on the 'Anglo-Saxon' model.

If this way of looking at globalization and national business systems is accepted, then it suggests an obvious second hypothesis; as well as asking whether convergence is taking place, we can ask whether it is taking place towards a particular model.

However, there are important reasons why this whole approach should be questioned. In particular, the insistent counterposition of 'global economy' and 'nation-state'[4] has seriously impeded the analysis of economic and political change in recent years. From a historical standpoint, the two have evolved hand-in-hand since their common emergence in the sixteenth to the eighteenth centuries. Looking at the recent past, it seems quite apparent that transnational corporations[5] have sought to operate *economically* as freely as possible across national borders, and in that sense Kindleberger's dictum is borne out. However, this in no sense implies the homogenization of economic space; on the contrary, competition in increasingly integrated global markets keeps generating differential outcomes for the participant firms, new patterns of locational advantage, and new modes of organizing production and exchange – in short, fundamentally 'uneven' and heterogeneous economic change. What is more, corporations whatever their scope continue to rely no less than before on legitimate political authorities, including nation-states, to supply the legal and regulatory framework without which an economic system based on private property and exchange cannot function.[6]

The nation-state, meanwhile, takes on the scope and forms appropriate to the more global nature of economic life. It has always existed as a *global system* of nation-states, not as a political form immanent in a hypothetically-isolated economic community. In the period from roughly 1930 to 1970, the nation-state became, as it were, the refuge for both capital and labour against the crisis of world production and trade;[7] already by the late 1950s, capital (though not labour) chafed at the constraints of a system which limited its cross-border mobility, and in due course won changes in both national and international regulation which have transformed important areas of public policy. As cross-border trade and investments have increased, and have taken on increasingly complex and irreversible forms, so each nation-state acknowledges this fact by including the interests of foreign-owned firms when discharging its policy functions, and accepts in turn that 'its' firms will seek accommodation with host states to safeguard their interests abroad. Taken as a whole, however, this involves more than an 'accommodation' between distinct interests (namely, those of global business on the one hand and the nation-state on the other), but rather a mutual permeation of interests.

From this standpoint, our original hypothesis still stands, but the suggested second hypothesis about the direction of convergence takes on a different character. The mid-century period of 'relative national autonomy' may have been a period when national differences in business systems were accentuated, as business and political elites sought the most appropriate ways of building a national consensus. Since the 1970s, deeper cross-border integration of firms and markets brought national business systems increasingly into contact with each other. However, this results not in a competition between existing systems, but a process of partial fusion, in which the *common core* (that is, of a capitalist political economy) is reasserted, while national differences are to some degree eroded. This still leaves open, of course, the possibility that some models are more liable to erosion than others, while if a 'global business system' is discernible, it may owe more to one model than to another. We now turn to examine three different ways in which globalization may be reshaping national differences.

GLOBAL CAPITAL MARKETS AND NATIONAL MACROECONOMIC POLICIES

Perhaps the strongest case for convergence-through-globalization concerns macroeconomic policy-making. It is widely argued that globalization and deregulation have created a fully-integrated global capital market which imposes fiscal and monetary discipline on all governments, and indeed reconstructs government policies and institutions around a deflationary agenda (see, for example, Teeple, 1995). The counter-view is that alternative policies can still be pursued, because capital markets are not in fact really as global as they appear. In so far as policy autonomy has become constrained by markets, this has been the result of conscious policy choices by national governments, which can restore their powers through the re-regulation of capital markets on a national or transnational basis (for example, Helleiner, 1996).

The capital controls explicitly retained in the original articles of the International Monetary Fund (IMF) allowed national governments a measure of control over their macroeconomic policies, especially in the monetary area, under a regime of 'fixed-but-moveable' exchange rates. By the time the fixed-rate regime collapsed following the dollar devaluation of 1971, however, controls had been steadily eroded, while at the same time both international flows and the volume of 'stateless' eurodollars had expanded greatly. Speculative attacks on currencies judged by 'the markets' to be overvalued seemed to be increasing in frequency and severity, with floating rates failing to neutralize them as the neoclassical textbooks expected. However, despite occasional attempts to turn back the tide, notably in France in 1983, by the end of the 1980s controls on capital movements had effectively disappeared among the OECD countries.

In an ideal-type 'fully-integrated' global capital market,[8] the argument goes, marginal interest rates could not differ between countries, except on the basis of perceived risk; if governments are competing freely for capital with other borrowers, then their borrowing costs – and eventually their ability to borrow at all – will simply reflect the market's expectations about their capacity to repay. The free movement of capital will force a levelling of fiscal regimes, and therefore the continued ability of a government to pursue any sort of 'discretionary' monetary or fiscal policy will depend on its central bank's ability to defend the currency through intervention on foreign exchange markets. The message is clear; only those governments that achieve the Golden Rule of 'acceptable' levels of public borrowing, inflation and the balance of payments will have access to capital markets on the best terms.

The real world is, of course, a very different matter. In the first place, some states are more equal than others when it comes to borrowing, especially when their currencies are *de facto* reserve currencies. The US in particular continues to increase its aggregate level of foreign debt to unprecedented levels because the dollar is still in such demand. But more importantly, in order to understand the real circumstances that prevail today we have to ask *why* international capital movements have grown so massive, and *why* the erosion of controls took place. Despite the popular view of international capital markets as detached from the economic 'real world', their growth has been based on the rapid growth of world trade and *direct* investment flows since the war. The acceleration of this growth in the 1980s was based on the twin processes of financial deregulation and securitization, which have enormously widened and deepened the structures of financial asset-holding underlying world production and trade. Just as foreign direct investment (FDI) became a central part of the accumulation strategies of the US and the UK, and then European and Japanese big business, so the global expansion of financial services provision (through FDI, foreign lending and the offshore credit and securities markets) represented a strategic choice for banking and financial capital. The abolition of capital controls may have fitted in with an ideological shift among political elites back to pre-Keynesian economic thinking, but it was *brought about* by unrelenting pressure from domestic business and financial communities desperate for equal access to foreign markets (Goodman and Pauly, 1993).

In so far as the globalization thesis has provided ideological justification for the policy preferences of big business, it is not surprising that some have challenged the real extent and significance of the globalization of capital markets. It has been suggested that they are no more integrated than they were before 1914, because *net* mobility of capital between countries is no greater; because domestic savings and investment are still closely correlated; or because of substantial differences in risk-adjusted rates of return on financial assets (see reviews of evidence in Epstein, 1996, pp. 212–15; and in Hirst and Thompson, 1996, pp. 34–44). However, the generally-accepted conclusion is that global financial integration *is* qualitatively different today by comparison with the period from 1945 to 1970, and that this *does* have important consequences for the policy autonomy of national governments.

Critics of the globalization thesis seem on stronger ground in arguing that because global financial integration has been predicated upon explicit government support – not only through policy liberalization, but also through a web of intergovernmental measures designed to manage the markets – it is therefore reversible. Helleiner (1996) sees three factors at work to reverse global financial liberalization:

- firstly, a growing awareness at national level of the domestic economic and political costs;
- secondly, the fragility of governmental commitment to liberalization, apparent during the European Union's (EU's) currency crisis of 1992–93; and
- thirdly, an expected reduction in US and UK government support, once US and UK financial capital lose their 'first-mover' advantages.

On all three points, however, Helleiner provides no real evidence of any broad reversal of trend: he merely asserts that it *might* happen in certain circumstances, such as a deep global financial crisis. The problem is that throughout Helleiner's paper, government decision-making is identified with a presumed 'national interest', as in: 'Although Britain and the US have obtained special benefits from the financial liberalization trend . . .' (1996, pp. 203–4). Yet he himself accepts the importance of '. . . the growing demand for it from large financial firms and multinational businesses' (*ibid.*, p. 194), referring indeed to Goodman and Pauly's account.

Epstein (1996) offers a potentially stronger argument in developing an alternative theoretical understanding of global financial integration. He rejects the underlying Walrasian approach of orthodox neoclassical theory, returning to something closer to classical theories of the market, competition and price formation. For him, global capital markets are arenas of economic power and inequality, with imperfect information underlying the need for repayment enforcement mechanisms which can only be provided by states:

> Hence, the important issue is not whether there can and ought to be state intervention in international financial relations but, rather, what type of intervention is desirable. *Thus, the nation-state and capital mobility are not opposites; they go hand in hand.* (Epstein, 1996, p. 212, emphasis added)

If what matters for continued participation in global capital markets (especially as a net borrower) is not the interest rate that a government is willing to pay, but rather the confidence of lenders in its repayment of loans,[9] then *in principle* governments can choose between different institutions and practices for maintaining lender confidence. What matters then is whether it is possible to overturn current pressures from the 'investment communities' towards an institutional regime of 'independent' central banks, coupled with bureaucratically-managed 'free' trade and investment agreements at regional or global level.

However, if financial globalization does not stem from the strategies of a distinct 'globalist' component of financial capital in the major OECD countries, but rather is linked organically to the increasing internationalization of *production*, the mobilization of political support for financial re-regulation is much more problematic. To give two examples: first, the general support of the EU business communities for closer financial integration has not diminished at all, either after the 1992–93 crisis, nor in the face of growing popular opposition to Economic and Monetary Union (EMU) on the Maastricht terms; and, secondly, despite the apparent resurgence of organized labour in the US, Clinton has not wavered in his support for the North American Free Trade Agreement (NAFTA), and his post-reelection cabinet is even more Wall-Street-oriented than the previous one. Although the British case seems particularly clear, it now looks unlikely that in any major OECD country big business will be anything other than implacably opposed to re-regulation. This is not because of a wilful desire to enjoy the fruits of capital mobility, such as the leverage it provides against organized labour, although that is a powerful benefit; but because production and competition in the world economy *cannot* now be reshaped into national (or even regional) structures of accumulation *except at the cost of enormous material and financial disruption*. The two sections that follow will provide arguments in support of this proposition, by examining the extent to which the technological base of production has become itself 'globalized', and the way in which national business systems are tending to fuse together.

To conclude this section, while it is open to us to oppose global financial liberalization in pursuit of equity or democracy, it seems very likely to continue, or at least not to be reversed. This does not mean that it will not be subject to regulation, both national and transnational, since a truly free market in finance is impossible. But it does make it likely that governments will increasingly have to accept common rules of the game with regard to national macroeconomic policies, in the absence of dramatic changes in the balance of political power within the major states.[10]

TECHNOLOGY, NATIONAL INNOVATION SYSTEMS AND POLICIES FOR NATIONAL COMPETITIVENESS

If national governments are constrained in their macroeconomic policies by 'globalized' capital markets, then this points to the alternative of 'supply-side' policies aimed at accelerating economic growth through improving the availability and productivity of domestically-located factors of production. Policies as diverse as financial liberalization and the public funding of training have been lumped under the heading of 'supply-side' in recent years: here the focus will be on public support for research, development and innovation, both through direct funding and through the provision of an appropriate institutional and policy framework.

The literature on innovation suggests strongly that technological change is embedded in mixed public–private networks. It involves 'public good' activities in the generation and transmission of basic scientific and technical knowledge, but also the commercialization of this knowledge, typically in the private sector and in response to the profit motive. In principle, governments can exert policy leverage on these networks through a very wide range of instruments, including targeted public expenditure, fiscal discrimination through taxes and tariffs, and direct controls over access to resources and markets. The general presumption is that such measures can enhance the competitiveness of particular sectors and companies on world markets, and thus accelerate growth in gross domestic product (GDP) and/or increase the national share of global value-added (particularly exports of high-tech manufactures and services).

Much of the writing on industrial policies and innovation or technology policies is mercantilist in character, with a clear focus on national competitiveness; this has been sharply criticized from a classical free-trade standpoint by Krugman (1994). However, a more narrowly-focused literature on 'national innovation systems' (hereafter NISs) aims to provide more carefully-tailored policy advice by studying the historical and institutional context of innovation in individual countries (notably Nelson, 1993). For example, Pavitt and Patel (1988) distinguished broadly between 'myopic' and 'dynamic' innovation systems, exemplified by Britain and Germany respectively, rooted in national differences in (among other things) finance, management and education.

The question of globalization raises two main issues for the existence and development of national innovation systems: firstly, whether technology itself has become global, leading to the increasing interpenetration of NISs; and, secondly, whether national technology policies are effective in the context of deeper global integration.

Is technology still essentially national, or has it become global? The 'embedded' character of technology suggests, first, that cultural and institutional factors are vitally important for success in innovation. If this is coupled with economies of agglomeration based on specialized resources, and the importance of face-to-face contacts in transmitting informal knowledge, it is easy to see how distinctive 'innovation systems' can emerge which are locationally-based (for example, in so-called Marshallian industrial districts). The consolidation of national economies and strategies of national industrial development from the early nineteenth century then creates nationally-specific systems, reflecting not just pre-industrial national characteristics (including in politics and cultural life), but also patterns of resource endowment, trade specialization and the historical epoch in which the system is formed (Nelson, 1993). Global market integration in the form of trade specialization might be expected to lead to greater national differentiation by sector or product, which would maintain or even deepen differences in innovation systems.

However, the postwar growth of trade and FDI has been largely not only between countries at increasingly similar levels of industrialization, but also increasingly in the form of *intra-industry* trade and FDI; this is particularly true in many relatively technology-intensive sectors. If production is becoming globally-integrated, then surely the commercial elements of national innovation systems are too, since research, development, design, training and other activities will have to be integrated by transnational corporations (TNCs) across their subsidiaries in different countries. Given the intricate overlapping of private and public elements in each NIS, the process of cross-border integration must extend also to public-sector activities in research, training and so on.

This view has been challenged by a number of writers, particularly in a recent symposium in the *Cambridge Journal of Economics*. Archibugi and Michie (1995), in particular, argue that the globalization of technology has been exaggerated. They hold that while cross-border patenting and licensing has grown considerably, the growth in international technological collaboration has been limited to a few emerging 'high-tech' sectors. Furthermore, most TNCs *generate* their patents in their home country, apart from a limited degree of 'foreign' generation by European firms in other European countries. They also draw on a wider literature to support the view that national technological specialization has if anything increased, with TNCs investing in R&D abroad largely as a *consequence* of this, not a cause (in order to tap into local expertise).

There are, however, weaknesses in their argument. First, they rely on patent data, which emphasises precisely those elements of technology and innovation that are most formal, bounded and therefore immediately commercializable and transferable. Foreign production does not require the local production of *patentable* knowledge, but it does require localized *informal* knowledge. It also generates strong pressures for standardization of the *language* of technology – metrication, knowledge of English, International Standards Organization (ISO) standards, and so on – which in turn facilitates international knowledge transfers.[11] Secondly, the theoretical literature on the economics of innovation has repeatedly stressed the difficulty in drawing boundaries between the generation, transfer and application of technology. The degree of 'decentralization' may be lowest in the first of these, but the 'global' production organization of TNCs ensures that the wider application of innovations generates the revenues to reproduce them. Finally, greater national specialization in patenting by sector suggests the emergence of distinct *sectoral* innovation systems that are able to cluster in particular countries *precisely because* they are themselves embedded in *global* production systems: this would seem to fit in with Cantwell's evidence (Cantwell, 1995, pp. 171–2).

Is globalization making national technology policies less effective? If only product *markets* become more globally integrated, governments pursuing export success can simply seek relative improvements in any production costs that are national in character, that is, affect all nationally-located producers – for example, by investing in improved national training systems. On the other hand, if *production itself* is globally organized, in the sense that 'value chains' cross and recross national borders, then the effects of national policy measures are likely to be dispersed to non-nationals who obtain external benefits from national innovations (Nelson and Wright, 1992).

Fransman (1995) argues that Japanese national technology policies, widely regarded as especially effective in the past, have not become obsolete, despite rapid increases in Japanese outward and inward FDI, and technology alliances with foreign firms. After documenting the growing 'leakages' of Japanese technology, he shows that Japanese technology policy, located in Japan's Ministry of International Trade and Industry (MITI) and elsewhere, remains based on a market-failure approach; now that Japan has reached the 'frontier-sharing' stage of economic development, the focus of policies to correct market failure has shifted towards support for basic research. In particular, MITI is funding 'internationalized' cooperative R&D programmes including foreign companies, and even some established jointly with foreign R&D agencies. Fransman argues that despite leakages this is considered beneficial, because the tacit character of much basic research knowledge ensures that the benefits cannot easily be transferred outside the specific Japan-based programmes. In addition, the location of the programmes within Japan may give a short but commercially important lead to Japanese companies even if all the knowledge eventually 'leaked'. In any case, *inflow* leakages also occur in internationalized programmes.

The implication of this is that in other countries, too, the 'globalization' of technology still leaves room for national technology policy, but only in areas where tacit knowledge is important, and only given appropriate institutional structures for exploiting the results domestically; this returns us to Pavitt and Patel's distinction between myopic and dynamic systems. A similar conclusion is reached by Sharp (1993) in a wider review of technology policies: she concludes that such national policies should aim 'to promote the science and technology infrastructure and an efficient system for the diffusion of innovation ... and to promote competition' (*op. cit.*, p. 208), but that such policies need to be supplemented by intergovernmental policies to 'promote the global "level playing field"' (*loc. cit.*), in order to prevent measures of deliberate technological protectionism.

Three points come out of these debates:

- Firstly, the argument over whether technology is global or not is misplaced. While certain elements of knowledge production are subject to strong agglomeration tendencies, these are embedded in organizations and networks, both private and public, which increasingly extend across borders. There is, in some sectors in particular, a global innovation system centred on the activities of TNCs which is intertwined with different national systems.
- Secondly, this is causing the latter to be defined to a greater extent by sectoral characteristics of knowledge production. A strong national industry now attracts inward investment which transforms the geography of the 'supply chains' in knowledge and technology which are central to any innovation system; this in turn consolidates the host industry as a global leader.
- Thirdly, there remains a role for national technology policies, but they increasingly follow a *common* pattern of selectively promoting basic research and the technology infrastructure, with the aim of attracting largely transnational investments (and holding on to 'home' company investments) in those sectors where there is a realistic chance of establishing global leadership. Since it is the same population of TNCs that all governments seek to attract, and since the key sectors are less and less based on locationally-specific resources, it is likely that innovation systems will become less distinctively national, and that 'supply-side' technology policies will become more similar across countries.

CORPORATE GOVERNANCE

Systems of corporate governance (hereafter CG), channeling market forces through forms of business ownership and finance, make up the core institutions of all varieties of capitalism. They are central, therefore, to the debates on alternative models of capitalism referred to in the second section above. The dominant normative theme of this literature is active espousal of the merits of more 'organized' or 'social market' models, in which (by law or in practice) forms of social participation, 'stakeholding' or citizenship provide a real counterbalance to private property and the market. In Britain and the USA in particular, both Japanese and German models are seen as recognizing the necessary 'embeddedness' of market processes in social values and institutions, and as offering a more secure basis for economic dynamism on the basis of security, commitment and trust. The CG systems likewise fall into two broad categories: the Anglo-Saxon, which is dominated by owners, funded by the stock market, and short-termist in its contracts and investments; and the Rhenish/

Japanese, which includes other stakeholders, relies much more on bank finance, and invests for the long term (for recent reviews, see Clarke and Bostock, 1994; and Kay and Silberston, 1995).

The debates on the comparative merits of CG systems reveal a number of unsettled issues of fact and interpretation. In Britain, critics of the Anglo-Saxon model have focused on the apparent investment short-termism of British firms, starting from the assumption that in the long run, international competitiveness requires a long-term commitment to investments in innovation, training, and so on. They argue that British short-termism is sustained by financial reliance on a stock market dominated by investment institutions, which are obliged to compete on the basis of short-term performance in order to obtain and retain fund management contracts, and which therefore hold highly diversified portfolios managed by frequent buying and selling of stock. Meanwhile, banks obsessed by the need for liquidity stick to short-term secured lending, which further obliges their corporate borrowers to look for rapid and high returns on investments, and to maintain costly levels of liquidity themselves.

However, defenders of the present British system argue that it has encouraged a much wider range of savers into the provision of industrial finance; that it allows flows of funds to be switched much more rapidly towards more profitable emerging products and markets; that superior transparency and disclosure prevents the covering-up of strategic blunders by insider managers;[12] that as a matter of fact British firms rely almost as much on banks as their Rhenish rivals, and otherwise in any case mainly on internal funds; and that the banking system's lack of commitment to long-term industrial finance makes it less liable itself to failure.[13] While none of these arguments is necessarily convincing, they do suggest that, even abstracting from current pressures on CG systems, the balance of advantage is not entirely on the side of stakeholder-type systems (see also Jenkinson and Mayer, 1992).

In any case, there are strong arguments that globalization is eroding the non-Anglo-Saxon CG systems in important respects. Reliance on stakeholding and long-term relationships has not stopped large Japanese, German or French firms from steadily expanding their foreign direct investments over the last 25 years. Some important Japanese TNCs do seek to transplant certain features of their domestic business system to foreign subsidiaries, especially at the level of work organization, supply relations and management systems; in other respects, there is adaptation to local norms. In so far as the CG system is focused at the level of top management, strategic decision-making and sources of finance, there is no reason in principle why it should be particularly affected by expansion overseas. However, foreign firms wanting to raise funds in the USA or the UK have to conform to Anglo-Saxon expectations concerning disclosure and the rights of shareholders and creditors. This may not be unwelcome: if, for example, financial conservatism and the protection of big insider shareholders are imposed on German corporations by the structural power of German banks, the corporations may prefer to bring on board shareholders who will play a more passive role.[14]

At the same time, continental European banks have themselves been pursuing strategies of foreign direct investment, diversification (for example, into insurance) and securitization: this has led them, notably, to purchase most of the remaining UK merchant banks and investment houses. Competing in the market for managing global securities issuance and in global corporate banking in turn puts pressure on the continental banks to submit to the scrutiny of the Anglo-Saxon credit-rating agencies. All this suggests that greater global competition and integration is encouraging 'organised' corporate capitalists both to expand abroad and to modify their CG systems, and that these trends are mutually reinforcing.

On the other hand, the widespread movements to emulate Japanese production systems, German training systems, and so on in the USA and the UK suggest that if convergence is happening, it is not all one-way. In the area of corporate governance, the Cadbury and other enquiries in Britain have revealed a lack of confidence in big business in the Anglo-Saxon model. Activist institutional investors such as CalPERS in the USA have revealed the self-perpetuating and self-serving nature of the existing system of dominance by top internal managers. However, rather than moving towards a stakeholder model, the dominant voices in this movement are concerned solely with maximizing shareholders' net worth: they may be content to root out incompetent top executives and phoney 'outside' directors, but only to install typically ruthless Anglo-Saxon pursuers of the bottom line.[15]

A more promising line of argument is that institutions may seek to emulate the legendary long-termism of the most successful postwar US investor, Warren Buffett; it should also be remembered that highly-concentrated ownership and close corporate interlocks were common in US corporate capitalism at least until the 1950s. The spread of both domestic and foreign strategic alliances, especially in technology, also suggests a move away from excessive reliance on 'arm's-length' relations and clear-cut owner control, but if this is driven by a desire to cut risk by controlling markets and speeding up commercialization, it may just reflect the absence of patient, committed investors.

What, then is the most likely direction of change? Albert and Gonenc (1996), in their review of present trends, are not optimistic about the likelihood of convergence towards the 'Rhenish' model, although they argue its continuing superiority from the standpoint of dynamic efficiency. Perkin (1996) is more sanguine: he insists on the 'inexorable necessity' of some form of stakeholding for 'enduring success and survival in post-industrial society' (p. 202), and argues that convergence will 'have to be . . . on European and east Asian rather than Anglo-American terms' (p. 207).

Yet what is striking about these and many other writers in this field is the assumption that social change is based on a universal rationality in which efficiency and social justice are balanced on the basis of some social, technological or environmental necessity. More realistically, CG systems evolve largely through pragmatic adaptation by and for economic and political elites to the circumstances that surround them, including challenges from outside and from below. Rather than CG systems (or indeed alternative capitalisms more generally) being a *causal factor* in comparative national industrial performance, they may be just as much – or more – the *result* of it. If the 'national cake' is growing rapidly enough, whether on the basis of successful free-trade imperialism or mercantilist developmentalism, then potential threats to corporate capitalism can be contained through various forms of inclusion at little cost to competitiveness; if growth slows, and wage costs and taxation become perceived as an excessive burden on big business, then such compromises may eventually 'have to' be brought to an end. Certainly, this can help to explain the demise of the 'Fordist regime' in the USA, and Thatcher's abrupt abandonment in the 1980s of the corporatist experiments undertaken in 1960s and 1970s Britain.

In conclusion, it seems that the dominant view on corporate governance systems, which looks for a long-term 'institutional fix' to the problem of weak industrial and innovative performance at a national level, fails to grasp the real relationship between governance and performance in the context of globalization. First, rising levels of foreign direct and portfolio investment are eroding the sharp differences in forms of ownership and business finance found between the major industrial countries up to the 1980s. Secondly, if the world's CG systems have tended to become more 'Anglo-Saxon', this may have been a response to greater uncertainty, sharper distributional conflicts and more rapid structural change, rather than evidence of the intrinsically 'Anglo-Saxon' character of globalization.

CONCLUSIONS

- Firstly, globalization provides a powerful ideological framework within which big business pushes for a redistribution of income, wealth and power towards economic elites, under the slogan of 'there is no alternative' (to the market). But globalization is undoubtedly also a *real* process which is tending to integrate different national economies more and more deeply.

- Secondly, the growth of global finance narrows the scope for governments to adopt macroeconomic policies at variance with the norms of fiscal and monetary rectitude. This apparent loss of power results less from the naked exercise of power by 'external' financiers, than from the changing interests of the national business and financial community as it becomes more globally-integrated.
- Thirdly, the globalization of technology, although less intensive than might be expected, is sufficient to link together previously autonomous 'national innovation systems', and to generate a 'normal' set of innovation policies aimed at attracting high-quality investments which will build and sustain centres of global leadership.
- Fourthly, transnational ownership, corporate finance and production are eroding those national system differences which centre on corporate governance.

On balance, there is considerable evidence in support of our hypothesis that globalization is leading to convergence of national business systems. This relatively brief survey, however, has only encompassed a small part of the diverse literatures on globalization and national business systems. Important areas such as labour markets and industrial relations and education and training need to be included.[16] At the same time, it is important to develop agreed criteria, where feasible, for the quantitative assessment of convergence.

Notes

1. An earlier version of this paper was presented to a workshop held in Malaga, Spain in January 1997 on *Globalization and Industrial Transformation in Europe*, part of a series on 'European Management and Organizations in Transition' funded by the European Science Foundation. I am grateful to participants in that workshop, as well as those at the 1997 UK AIB conference, and to the editors of the present volume, for their comments.
2. Since this paper was written my attention has been drawn to Berger and Dore (1996), whose contributors address the same issue.
3. A more extreme version, associated with more orthodox neoclassical thinking, also postulates an equalization of economic *condition*, proposing that factor prices are equalizing as a result of the fusion of national markets into a single global market.
4. For example, Weiss begins a recent paper thus: 'The new globalist orthodoxy posits the steady disintegration of national economies and the demise of the state's domestic power' (Weiss, 1997, p. 3).
5. Including in this term banks and trading companies.
6. Note that Kindleberger's claim was only that the nation-state was 'about through' as an *economic* unit.
7. This 'refuge' form was brilliantly evoked by Keynes (1933) when he advocated 'national self-sufficiency'.
8. Such a world would, however, logically have only a single currency, and a single central bank.

9. Including, of course, confidence in the availability of acceptable currency for repaying *private* loans.
10. This does not mean that these 'rules of the game' will be the same for all players or all circumstances. Precisely because the capitalist world economy is subject to such sharp inequalities of wealth and power, departures from the rules can be made with impunity by the powerful, or indeed permitted (subject to conditions) for the peripheral and powerless.
11. On the importance of standards in business systems, see Lane (1997).
12. The recent cases of Daimler Benz and Metalgesellschaft come to mind, and Credit Lyonnais' disastrous funding of the MGM takeover.
13. Here the contrast is more with the French or Spanish experience than the German.
14. As well as tapping into Anglo-Saxon equity markets and bank finance, continental European firms are also looking to benefit from the growth in non-bank financial institutions in their home economies, which in turn has been fuelled by the growth in Anglo-Saxon-style private pensions and privatization programmes.
15. If institutions work closely together to control a board of directors, this looks a bit like the French *noyau dur* model.
16. See Stråth (1996) on labour markets, Bamber and Lansbury (1993) on industrial relations, and Ashton and Green (1996) on education and training.

14 Employee Ownership and Employment: The Case of Russian Privatized Firms

George Sharpley, Trevor Buck, Igor Filatotchev and Mike Wright

INTRODUCTION

There has been a long tradition of empirical work testing for the effects on enterprise behaviour and performance of employee control (EC) and employee ownership (EO). This research has focused on the separate effects of EC and EO as well as their combination in the producer co-operative or self-managed firm. Thus, their separate and combined effects have been assessed in terms of employee stock-ownership plans (ESOPs) within conventional capitalist firms, and in the 'islands' of producer cooperatives in the West (see Bonin, Jones and Putterman, 1993, for a review).

Since Ward's (1958) seminal paper, there has also been a stream of research concerned with so-called self-management in former-Yugoslavia, with examples as late as Prasnikar *et al.* (1994). While this research has enriched the discussion, it can be claimed that even at its peak in the former-Yugoslavia, 'self-management' only applied to about a sixth of its population at a time when a minimum of 40 per cent of product prices were centrally-controlled, industrial managers were usually political nominees, and local government (that is, the League of Communists) founded most firms and subsequently interfered with many of their decisions. In any case, EC through workers' councils was restricted to fairly minor, local decisions (see Buck, 1982, pp. 113–19). In addition, large firms in the former-Yugoslavia did not distribute tradeable stock to employees, giving 'employee ownership' a hollow ring.

On the face of it, the Russian privatization programme after 1991 provides researchers with a new laboratory in which to test their theoretical propositions concerning EC and EO, with employees ostensibly gaining majority ownership and control of most privatized industrial firms, with the liberalization of most product prices, the withdrawal of most state subsidies and some tradeability of enterprise stock on capital markets. However, the volatile Russian economic and political environment creates many research problems, and to date no hypothesis-testing has been published in relation to the performance of Russian manufacturing firms. Nevertheless, it seems worthwhile to try to overcome data problems and to consider theoretical propositions in this new context.

This chapter presents some results, concentrating on the level of enterprise employment as a crucial dependent variable that involves no valuation problems with a rapidly-inflating currency. It begins with a review of EC and EO in the determination of employment levels, including the derivation of hypotheses to be tested. Before reporting the results of tests, the chapter presents an account of the Russian privatization programme, the Nottingham survey and a description of the variables used.

EMPLOYEE CONTROL (EC)

In the tradition of the literature on self-management (or producer co-operatives), EC is given more weight than mere employee ownership (EO), which simply modifies the incentive regime within which EC operates (Bonin *et al.*, 1993, p. 1291). EC is defined in terms of the collective employee determination of major enterprise decisions such as the choice of output and employment levels, the output mix and important investment decisions.

As decision-controllers, employees can of course be considered as just one group among a whole range of enterprise stakeholders who could in principle exercise enterprise-decision-control, or corporate governance (Hansmann, 1996, p. 10). A complete list of candidates for a share of control would include outside investors, senior enterprise managers, suppliers, creditors, banks and the state.

In a conventional firm without EO, employees can be seen as recipients of rental payments (wages) that are relatively fixed compared with the dividends and capital gains received by conventional shareholders, and this may be expected to influence their utility functions as decision-controllers in a distinctive, and not always negative, way. Employee-determined enterprise decisions could be assumed to favour the preferences of the median worker, who may be expected to have a shorter time-horizon than outside investors, perhaps even shorter than the median employee's expected tenure with the firm (Pejovich, 1994). As a result, employees may introduce (Pejovich, 1994) '... a conservative bias in the firm's decisions that have longer-run consequences' (p. 227). In brief, employees as decision-makers may be expected to have current wages and manning levels as prominent arguments in their utility functions, which may lead to them blocking output restructuring and long-run investment programmes that have implications for long-run profitability, though this result must also be influenced by who owns the firm (see below).

Hansmann (1996, pp. 66–87) reinforces this negative view of decision-control by employees, especially in large firms where the communications costs of EC are high, where the labour force is so heterogeneous that the preferences of the median employee are costly to establish in terms of communications expense, and in capital-intensive industries where investment decisions are problematical. While employees may favour high wages and manning levels, however, there are differences between the preferences of the median and the marginal employee (Hansmann, 1996, p. 65). The interests of the median worker may be promoted by the exclusion or dismissal of peripheral workers who are outside a core group applying EC to enterprise decisions.

On the positive side, however, EC can be expected to improve enterprise decisions and labour productivity (and thus long-run profit and employment) if employees feel part of a team that agrees collectively to apply self- and horizontal monitoring to the contributions of themselves and each other on a reciprocal basis (Welbourne, Balkin and Gomez-Mejia, 1995, p. 883), in place of the vertical monitoring of conventional firms. From this perspective, the effectiveness of EC must be contingent upon the nature of the industries in which it is applied. Conventional vertical control may be expected to offer a comparative advantage in those industries where processes and products can be reduced to routines; that is, those with high programmability (Welbourne *et al.*, 1995, p. 883). In other industries, low programmability and a heavy reliance on the judgements of employees provides opportunities for EC.

Apart from certain possible cases (for example, the Mondragon community in Spain, former-Yugoslavia, the former-USSR), actual EC across many industries has been rare and EC has been restricted to certain industrial niches where the potential costs of EC have been reduced by the existence of small, homogeneous labour forces, low capital-intensity and an absence of mass-production techniques. For example, successful EC can be cited in professional partnerships (Hansmann, 1996, p. 58), and in taxicab firms and the printing industry (Bonin *et al.*, 1993, pp. 1293–4). In these industries, EC could be expected to be associated with employment generation, as superior governance provides an edge on product markets.

This is not to say that employee judgements in mass-production industries are unimportant if conventional firms are to compete in terms of build quality, product design and customization (Best, 1990). In many large firms, however, cooperative problem-solving or project teams amount to labour participation on a partial, temporary basis that falls well short of full EC, as defined at the beginning of this section. In addition to EC and employment generation, there is a large literature concerned with insider control and the appropriation of economic surplus as wages (see McCain, 1982, for a summary).

Given the limited adoption of full EC in most Western industries, therefore, this study will test in Russian industry the hypotheses that, after controlling for other influences, *variables representing EC will be associated with job-preservation and higher average real wages* in the face of a collapse in input and output markets.

In the case of Russia, the large size of privatized industrial firms provides a considerable barrier to the potentially positive effects of EC. The communications costs of EC are further increased by the extremely heterogeneous nature of the average Russian workforce, arguably united only by the economic crisis and a collapse in the demand for their firms' products. In these circumstances, the negative effects of EC are likely to be enhanced and tests on the proposed hypotheses seem appropriate. In general, however, the consequences of EC can be expected to be modified by the extent of employee ownership.

EMPLOYEE OWNERSHIP (EO)

Conventional property rights theory predicts that the efficiency of decisions relating to the uses of assets is likely to be maximized when those who determine asset-use are entitled to the fruits (or a share of the fruits) of those resource allocations, especially when these rights to control and to a share of residual income can be alienated (that is, transferred to other owners, Hansmann, 1996, p. 9). In the context of this study, this implies that a combination of EO (and hence profit-sharing) with EC can be expected to enhance the quality of enterprise decisions, though paradoxically the literature on self-management has often concentrated on the way in which profit-sharing among employees may reinforce the potentially negative properties of EC in relation to manning levels (see above). These issues are addressed below after a consideration of share tradeability.

The ownership of enterprise shares conveys the right, which may be exercised or not at the discretion of the shareholder, to contribute to the control of enterprise decisions. Shareholders may be formally polled on key decisions (for example, the appointment of directors or the decision to approve a take-over of the firm), or they may influence decisions more informally (for example, institutional investors in the West are often consulted informally on market-influencing decisions). This influence amounts to shareholder *voice* (Hirschman, 1970), and, in the context of share ownership by employees, this is the process by which EC is conferred (see above).

In addition, the tradeability of shares adds to the control of the shareholder through the effect of share *exit* (Hirschman, 1970), and the perceived threat of exit, on share price and the security of managers making decisions. In the case of EO, however, severe limits are often placed on the tradeability of stock, through the reluctance of employees to sell stock to outsiders who might threaten their wages and tenure with the firm, and through practical restrictions on share transfers imposed by managers, often with the connivance of employees in general.

If shares are virtually untradeable, however, EO reduces to EC through voice plus a right to a share of current profits, and this profit share will tend to take the form of current dividends rather than capital gain, since the market in shares is severely constrained (Bonin *et al.*, 1993, p. 1308). In this case, theoretical propositions concerning the relative risk-aversion of undiversified employee-owners (Hansmann, 1996, p. 69) and arguments about the alleged bias in Western economic institutions against risk-bearing employees (Doucouliagos, 1995) become virtually irrelevant. This is not to say that employee ownership is infeasible and inefficient. Indeed, Blasi and Kruse (1992) emphasize that by the year 2000, employee-shareholders should outnumber trade union members in US industry, though the contribution of state subsidies to the apparent success of ESOPs is undeniable (Kaufman and Russell, 1995).

If individual employees are unable to sell their shares on an open capital market, this creates serious problems for investment decisions, especially in capital-intensive industries, since employees with truncated time-horizons will vote for high levels of externally-financed investment but will be biased against all self-financed investment (Bonin *et al.*, 1993 p. 1308), with the exception of investments with short-term pay-offs, which immediately protect jobs. As already noted, the existence of untradeable enterprise shares reduces EO to just EC (though without the exit threat) plus current profit-sharing through dividend distributions. In this case, all sorts of positive and negative theoretical possibilities arise.

On the positive side, there are good reasons why profit-sharing should enhance the quality of EC (Ben-Ner and Jones, 1995), and empirical support has been found for the positive effects of combined EC and profit-sharing on productivity (Bonin *et al.*, 1993, p. 1307). In the long-term, higher productivity should be reflected in employment-creation through product market effects, though in the short-run, higher labour productivity may eliminate jobs. Paradoxically, however, the positive interaction of EC and profit-sharing suggested by property rights theory in terms of the sharing of decisions *and* outcomes has been seen as a major source of weakness, and a massive literature on Ward–Vanek effects (see a review in Bonin *et al.*, 1993, pp. 1297–1302) has emphasised the possibility of perverse decisions concerning employment levels that may reinforce the prediction of EC being associated with job-preservation (see above).

The Ward–Vanek literature assumes that, in the absence of tradeable shares, bodies of employee-owners influenced by the median employee will rationally choose employment (and therefore output) levels that maximize not absolute profit, but average variable product per worker (AVP), or total wages plus profit per worker. If demand (and therefore price) for an enterprise's product falls, AVP falls, but the variable product of the marginal worker (MVP) is now above AVP. Despite the fall in demand, therefore, employee-owners can raise their assumed maximand (AVP) by employing more workers, or at least resisting dismissals.

This literature has attracted widespread criticism. Product demand uncertainty makes a difference, and it is now recognized that firms with EO can change output through variations in the intensity of employee effort and hours worked, and by switching outputs in multi-product firms (Buck, 1982, pp. 85–96). In any case, long-run equilibrium could eliminate perverse supply responses through the entry of new firms. Conventional capitalist firms could even be expected to generate perverse supply responses if shares were not tradeable and shareholders maximized profits per share. Indeed, tradeable employee shares would eliminate Ward–Vanek effects, with any consideration paid for shares acquired modifying the calculation of MVP.

For the purpose of this study, however, a combination of EC with barriers to share tradeability can provide new opportunities for testing for Ward–Vanek effects. Without a significant degree of share tradeability, it is hypothesized that measures of EO will be associated with perverse employment responses to changes in product demand, and Meade (1972, p. 406) explains that high average capital costs per employee (or capital-intensity) can in theory amplify any perversity in employment decisions, encouraging job-preservation in the middle of a collapse in demand, though relatively risk-averse employees may be more effective decision-makers where capital costs are a low proportion of value-added and AVP is high (Buck and Chiplin, 1983, p. 277). On the other hand, EO without share tradeability produces under-investment problems (Hansmann, 1996, p. 70) that reduce job-creation, so the impact of capital-intensity is not straightforward.

The point of this consideration of Ward–Vanek effects in the context of Russia is that since 1991 there has been a dramatic overall collapse in product demand. While employment increases in this context would be quite absurd, the maximization of AVP is not inconceivable as an enterprise objective, and a modified hypothesis can be employed which predicts, if not actual perverse supply responses, *a positive association between EO and job-preservation and real average wages*, other things equal. This hypothesis parallels and complements a similar prediction for EC variables alone (see above). As a supplementary hypothesis, *in firms enjoying an increase in product demand, EO and EC should be associated with less employment creation than conventional firms.*

Where some limited share tradeability is permitted (for example, upon flotation or at the auction stage in privatization programmes) and conventional outside shareholders are able to obtain enterprise shares at the expense of employees who have current wages and job-preservation as prominent arguments in their utility functions, outsiders can be assumed to seek only maximum shareholder value. In this case, it is hypothesized that after controlling for other independent variables, *control by outside investors will be associated with employment reduction and lower real average wages.*

The next section reviews the relevant aspects of the Russian privatization process with a view to testing these hypotheses, paying particular attention to the transferability of shares.

RUSSIAN INDUSTRIAL PRIVATIZATION

A study of the effects of EC, EO and outside ownership on employment change in Russian privatized firms requires a brief review of the institutional background. This section summarizes the privatization process in Russia, making reference to some of the descriptive features of the Nottingham survey (see below) that are not part of the formal hypothesis testing. This review concentrates on EO, EC and share tradeability.

The first phase of a 'top-down' programme of Russian privatization ran from late 1992 until mid-1994, and ended with over 80 per cent of industrial output in private firms. However, an unknown number of firms became privatized in a spontaneous, or 'bottom-up' process which was dominated by the conversion of enterprises that were previously 'leased' into closed partnerships and joint-stock companies, and open companies after mid-1993. 'Direct' privatization buy-outs could also arise from the process of enterprise liquidation. The unknown quantity of such spontaneous privatizations contributes to the sampling problems for researchers in Russia (see next section below).

The formal programme had two 'variants' that proved significant in practice. Variant 2 turned out to be the dominant form, accounting for 77 per cent of the variant privatizations in the sample reported below. With this variant, managers and other employees were able to buy 51 per cent of shares upon privatization, and then compete with any outsiders for the remaining 49 per cent at auction, using cash and/or vouchers which were available virtually free to each adult citizen. Under variant 1 (20 per cent of the sample), managers and other employees could acquire shares more cheaply than under variant 2, but risked losing majority control of the company to outsiders. In practice, the Nottingham survey found inside/outside ownership patterns upon privatization broadly consistent with other studies (Blasi, 1994; Boycko, Shleifer and Vishny, 1993), with 66.7 per cent of shares held on average by managers and other employees (in about a 1:2 ratio), 13.5 per cent with private outsiders and 20.3 per cent with the state. State ownership was destined to decline quickly after privatization as State Property Funds disposed of remaining shares.

As a case of EO, it must be emphasised that Russian managers and other employees differed from Western shareholders in one major respect: their shares were obtained in what amounted to a 'give-away' distribution, with vouchers freely distributed and shares often sold at nominal prices at the pre-auction stage. This could have implication for EC and corporate governance, since Western shareholders must make significant financial sacrifices to acquire shares. This could make shareholder value maximization (including loss minimization) less important to Russian employee-shareholders than their short-run objectives as employees concerned with wages and job-preservation. This leads to a more general consideration of EC. On the face of it, majority EO should imply effective EC of Russian firms, with employees able to voice their preferences at board level, in formal consultations, at workers' assemblies or informally. In practice, however, reality proved more complex. The survey described below found (see Table 14.1) that employee representation on boards actually fell after privatization, and only existed in about one-quarter of companies.

Although formal and informal employee consultations remained steady after privatization, they still only existed in about half the companies, and the lower part of Table 14.1 shows that adverse market conditions far outweighed employee influence through EO and employee meetings as a constraint on enterprise decisions.

At the same time, however, EO should not be dismissed as irrelevant in the Russian context. Many enterprise managers still have paternalistic attitudes towards their workers, and while the present authors agree with most researchers (see, for example, Earle and Estrin, 1996, p. 22 for an account of 'managerially controlled, employee-owned' firms) that managers are the dominant stakeholders in most firms, they also concur with Webster *et al.* (1994) that employees give managers a fairly free hand in enterprise decisions until wage reductions or redundancies are threatened, whereupon employee influence becomes very important (for example, in relation to the election of directors). In addition, Clarke (1993) distinguishes generally weak employee influence from the sometimes important influence of 'core' established workers who may collude with managers in the dismissal of their more 'peripheral' colleagues (for example, female employees, working pensioners and part-timers).

It is argued here, therefore, that EO and EC should at least be retained as independent variables in tests on the determination of employment levels in Russian industry. Of course, the nature of the influence of EO

Table 14.1   Channels of employee control

(a) Please indicate whether employees with shares participate in decision-making through the following channels (percentage of 171-firm sample responding in the positive).

	Year before privatization	*Year after privatization*
Active employee board representation	30.5	25.7
Passive or no board representation	68.9	74.3
Formal consultation with workers' assemblies on strategic issues	54.0	57.6
Formal consultation with workers' assemblies on operational issues	35.5	37.3
Informal consultation with workers' assemblies on strategic and operational issues	44.8	48.5

(b) What factors constrained senior managers' ability to manage the company?

	Year before privatization	*Year after privatization*
State control	45.6	32.3
Employee shares/assemblies	13.9	15.4
Trading relationships with customers and suppliers	7.8	16.5
Adverse market conditions	57.1	88.1

on decisions depends crucially on the tradeability of enterprise shares (or shareholders' ability to 'exit' their shares). It is maintained here that there are very severe limitations on the tradeability of shares in most Russian privatized firms, with the exception of 'blue-chip' firms (see below); and that these limitations change the nature of employee influence through EO. It should be emphasized that this conclusion applies to the bulk of Russian privatized firms but not to the minority of 'blue-chip' firms (about one hundred at the time of writing), whose shares are traded on the Russian Trading System (RTS), which approximates to the NASDAQ system in the USA. Most shares in the RTS are in resource-based firms, however, largely outside manufacturing industry, which is the subject of this chapter.

The main barrier to systematic research on the tradeability of shares in Russian privatized firms is a presidential decree that makes restrictions placed by managers on the free sale and transfer of shares illegal. This means that managers are unlikely to volunteer information to researchers on the restrictions they deploy. Nevertheless, it is clear that important restrictions are prevalent, based on managerial control of shareholder registers and the transfer process. For example, one of the authors spent three days in Nizhny Novgorod at the GAZ motor-works, the subject of the largest privatization buy-out in the world with over 100 000 employees. In this company, employees could only offer their shares to a company set up by the GAZ president for the purpose of keeping GAZ shares away from outsiders. The significance of the single case of GAZ to this study lies in the fact that GAZ is one of the very few Russian manufacturing firms with a stock-market quotation in Moscow, based on the very small proportion of total shares that have reached the outside market. Despite being one of the most liberal Russian manufacturing firms in this respect, GAZ maintains significant controls on share tradeability.

Restrictions on share sales applied (illegally) by managers mean that share-sale proceeds for employees are likely to be much lower than on a market where outsiders are free to bid. In the case of Gazprom, the world's largest natural gas producer, shares sold in the West in October 1996 attained a value four times higher than the price of supposedly equivalent shares held in Russia by employees. This is because Gazprom restricts the ownership of its domestic shares to insiders so far as is possible (*Financial Times*, 7 October 1996).

Restrictions on share tradeability, and thus low share prices, may have a subtle effect on EO, with employees encouraged to think more like employees with short-run objectives than as shareholders with freely convertible stakes at prices that reflect a realistic valuation of long-run dividend prospects. Such a short-run bias and its implications for investment decisions is consistent with those parts of the Nottingham survey which are not part of the formal tests reported below, where it was found that, in relation to investment for example, Russian firms after privatization have behaved rather like textbook labour-managed firms, with negligible investment out of retained earnings, and extensive external borrowing to finance working capital investments, and hence job-preservation. Share-trading restrictions can therefore be expected to reinforce the restrictive effects of EO on employment change, hypothesized above.

THE SURVEY AND VARIABLES

The Russian economy in general, and Russian privatized firms in particular, present formidable barriers to scientific enquiry. Some of these difficulties are considered here, not in an apologetic way but in order to explain the nature of the sample and the choice of measures of the main variables. Research problems seem likely to grow rather than diminish in the foreseeable future.

In terms of the general economic situation, very rapid inflation at the time of the survey, in 1994, and a general unfamiliarity in Russia with the estimation of real changes in rouble variables using a price index, meant that variables had to be expressed either in volume terms or as ratios with roubles in the numerator and the denominator (for example, the wage-bill as a percentage of sales). Given the rather complicated calculations needed for such ratios for respondents, it was decided to ask for categorical responses on most variables, using a five-point Likert scale.

In relation to the privatized firms themselves, and in common with all other Russian surveys (Webster *et al.*, 1994; Blasi and Shleifer, 1996; Boycko *et al.*, 1993; Earle and Estrin, 1996), all survey responses were based on a single enterprise director's perceptions and no triangulation was feasible. Since programmed privatization was regionally decentralized and was in any case supplemented by a large number of spontaneous privatizations outside the formal programme (see above), no statistics were (or are) available on the industry and size characteristics of the population of Russian privatized firms. This effectively rules out structured samples.

Particular problems were experienced in relation to the ownership of shares by enterprise managers and other employees. While it is estimated that shares in industrial privatized firms are held roughly in the proportion of one managerial share for every two held by other employees, in practice it was found that enterprise directors defined 'senior manager' very flexibly. It was therefore decided to concentrate on total (managerial and other) employee ownership as an independent variable. Support for this procedure comes from the presumption that it is the sum of all employee shares that can be expected to influence dependent variables (Earle and Estrin, 1996, p. 22). Furthermore, it was found from case-studies that managers have been adept at hiding their real stakes in the hands of 'friendly' outsiders, giving percentage managerial stakes a spurious accuracy.

The survey was carried out by professional interviewers directed by the Working Center for Economic Reform of the Russian Government, between March and August 1994, approximately one year after privatization. Given the impossibility of structured samples, it was decided to aim for as large a sample as possible, covering large and medium-sized industrial firms in four main industrial regions: St Petersburg, Moscow, Nizhny Novgorod and Ekaterinburg. A sample of 171 usable responses was collected from enterprises privatized spontaneously (29.9 per cent of the sample), and from enterprises privatized through vouchers (14.0 per cent variant 1, 53.8 per cent variant 2, and only four cases of variant 3).

The main dependent variable used in the survey was *employment change* since privatization, on a five-point scale (from a 'decline of more than 10 per cent' through 'an increase of more than 10 per cent'). Because only very few firms (11 out of 171) reported any increases in employment, increases of more than 10 per cent and increases up to 10 per cent were merged, effectively creating a four-point scale for this variable.

The employment change variable is the net outcome of voluntary quits, formal redundancies and gross hirings, and was preferred to a decision variable based on formal redundancies, which are rare in Russia, representing the outcome of a long and rarely used legal procedure. Employment change does not distinguish employees who are unpaid or who are on paid leave, since managers were unlikely to disclose their magnitude. Similarly, this variable cannot identify the gender of employees or their hours of work. As a supplementary independent variable, *average wages* were surveyed as a percentage of sales, on a five-point scale.

In accordance with the hypotheses developed above, *employee ownership* (EO) and *employee control* (EC) were the main independent variables. EO was measured in terms of percentages of voting shares held. Although they were estimated separately, managers' shares were aggregated with those of other employees as total 'insider equity', for reasons explained above. This procedure seems justified by the wide variations in managerial shareholdings estimated in different surveys. Although they all reported broadly the same pattern of inside/outside shareholdings, in the Nottingham survey, managers were reported as holding 19.3 per cent of shares and other employees 44.4 per cent, but Blasi (1994) showed the respective proportions in his sample as 9 per cent and 56 per cent. According to a 1994 decree in Russia, a 51 per cent stake gives shareholders the power to replace an entire slate of board directors, so, given the potentially inaccurate nature of managerial holdings (see above) and the crucial importance of a 50 per cent holding, the EO variable was entered as dummies representing total insider equity ownership above/below 50 per cent.

Given the problems of defining the extent and frequency of formal and informal EC in operational and strategic decisions within the enterprise, it was decided to measure EC simply in terms of the number of employees on the main board. To test for the influence of active outside shareholders (see hypotheses above), the number of board members nominated by outside investment funds was also surveyed. As with EO, EC and outsider control were represented as dummies denoting boards with/without board membership for employees and outside investment funds, respectively.

In addition to these dependent and independent variables, it was decided to include two *control variables* in the estimating equations. It is widely recognized that the general economic collapse after 1991 had major sectoral variations (EBRD, 1995, pp. 77–84), and this could give a spurious significance to the estimated effects of corporate governance (such as EC and EO) on employment change and average real wages. Since a collapse in output sales and in the availability of inputs can both contribute to employment reduction in the enterprise, the survey asked for five-point responses to a question concerning the importance of 'adverse market conditions' to enterprise decisions.

Besides the uneven impact of general market collapse, it was decided to control for the degree of capital-intensity of an enterprise's sector, as there are theoretical grounds (see above) for supposing that capital-intensity modifies the influence of EO and EC on employment levels, both directly through Ward–Vanek effects and through the investment decisions upon which job-creation depends. Measures of capital-intensity for the former USSR, based on historic investments, provide only a very coarse measure of capital-intensity, so, as with other variables, dummies were introduced denoting above/below-average degrees of capital-intensity. The sample was further partitioned in the final stages of the analysis (see below) into two sub-samples according to whether real changes in sales since privatization were negative (in most cases) or positive. Again, dummies indicating negative/positive real sales change were derived from five-point Likert responses.

RESULTS

Data from the Nottingham survey were used to test hypotheses that, controlling for adverse market conditions and capital-intensity, EC and EO should be positively (and investment-fund board-representation negatively) associated with job-preservation and real average wages in Russian privatized firms, particularly in firms with increasing sales volume.

The nature of the data (involving categorical observations on the main dependent variable, employment change) indicated the estimation of ordered probit models, which can handle discrete and ordered responses. An ordered probit model estimates the probabilities for each of the possible values that a dependent variable may take for given values of the regressors. Estimated coefficients on the regressors do not, however, directly represent the marginal responsiveness of dependent to independent variables. These are obtained for continuous regressors by differentiating each of the probabilities of the dependent variable with respect to the regressor, while holding other regressors constant. The marginal effects of dummy variables are obtained by comparing the probabilities for each value of the dependent variable when the dummy variable takes on its

Table 14.2 Change in employment since privatization, ordered probit model

Variable	Coefficient	(t-stat)
Constant	0.88**	(2.77)
Adverse market conditions	0.68*	(2.36)
Employees on board	0.43*	(1.99)
Capital-intensive	0.39*	(2.01)
Inside equity $>$ 50%	−0.17	(−0.88)
Investment funds on board	0.86**	(3.34)
μ_1	1.30**	(7.44)
μ_2	2.09**	(11.1)
Log L	−191.16	
Restricted log L	−204.30	
χ_5^2	26.28**	

Note:
**significant at 1% level; *significant at 5% level.

different values while holding other variables constant (Greene, 1993, p. 706). Other continuous variables are held constant at their sample means, while other dummies are generally held at zero.

In order to test the impact of EO, EC and investment fund representation on changes in employment levels and wages, an ordered probit model estimated these relationships while controlling for adverse market conditions and capital intensity.

Table 14.2 shows the standard diagnostics for the ordered probit model. All right-hand-side variables appear as statistically significant with the exception of EO as measured by insider equity exceeding 50 per cent, but any realistic interpretation should be based on the marginal effects reported in Table 14.3.

As with Table 14.2, all the right-hand-side variables shown in Table 14.3 appear as having a significant impact on employment change, again with the exception of inside equity (EO). Both control variables proved significant. Adverse market conditions were associated with less employment increase and more employment decline, as expected. Higher capital-intensity also made matters worse for firms, and the significance of this result supports the inclusion of this control, although the theoretical expectations for this variable were not straightforward (see above).

Turning to the independent variables, the influence of an outside investor, as measured by the presence of an investment fund nominee on the company's board, has the effect of encouraging employment-decline and discouraging employment-increase. For example, the presence of an investment fund on the board is associated with a 25 per cent increase in the probability of a decrease in employment of more than 10 per cent. These results are consistent with predictions.

Table 14.3 Marginal effects on the probability of employment change, ordered probit model

Variable	Increase in employment	No change in employment	Decrease in employment < 10%	Decrease in employment > 10 %
Adverse market conditions	–0.13*	–0.14*	0.08*	0.18*
Employees on board	–0.09*	–0.07*	0.06*	0.10*
Capital intensity	–0.09*	–0.06*	0.06*	0.09*
Inside equity > 50%	0.05	0.01	–0.03	–0.03
Investment funds on board	–0.15**	0.19**	0.08**	0.25**

Note:
**significant at 1% level; *significant at 5% level.

The results in relation to the main independent variables, EC (as measured by employees on the board) and EO (inside equity above 50 per cent) were less straightforward, though interesting. The impact of EO in Table 14.3 is statistically insignificant and there is no uniform evidence of EO being associated with job preservation. This result is not inconsistent with the possibility that EO in Russian industry is just window-dressing in relation to enterprise variables such as employment.

At the same time, EC is statistically significant but can be seen to have a similar impact to adverse market conditions in that greater EC is associated with less employment creation and more employment decline. This result is quite the opposite of the predictions developed above.

At this stage of the analysis, the hypothesis that EC and EO should be associated with job-preservation receives no support, and greater EC is found to be consistent with enterprise rationalization and restructuring that require job-reduction. On the face of it, pessimism concerning the impact of EC in Russia seems misplaced, though employment-reduction may have been at the expense of peripheral workers as insiders preserve core jobs (Clarke, 1993, p. 235). Besides employment change, it was decided to analyse real wages to embrace the possibility that EC and EO may have raised the wages of remaining incumbents, despite employment decline.

Table 14.4 reports the aggregate results, but discussion is again restricted to the marginal effects of right-hand-side variables reported in Table 14.5.

Table 14.5 shows all right-hand-side variables to be statistically insignificant in relation to wage determination with the exception of EO,

Table 14.4 Change in real wages since privatization, ordered probit model

Variable	Coefficient	(t-stat)
Constant	0.36	(1.14)
Adverse market conditions	0.18	(0.62)
Employees on board	−0.35	(−1.59)
Capital-intensive	−0.14	(−0.76)
Inside equity > 50%	−0.41**	(2.17)
Investment funds on board	−0.26	(−0.88)
μ_1	0.94	(8.51)
μ_2	1.38	(9.50)
Log L	−188.83	
Restricted log L	−193.97	
χ^2_5	10.29*	

Note:
**significant at 5% level; *significant at 10% level.

Table 14.5 Marginal effects on the probability of average real wage change, ordered probit model

Variable	Increase in real wage	No change in real wage	Decrease in real wage < 10%	Decrease in real wage > 10 %
Adverse market conditions	−0.07	0	0.02	0.05
Employees on board	0.14	−0.03	0.04	−0.07
Capital intensity	0.05	−0.01	−0.01	0.03
Inside equity > 50%	0.16*	−0.04*	−0.04*	−0.08*
Investment funds on board	0.10	−0.02	0.03	0.05

Note:
**significant at 1% level; *significant at 5% level.

which is shown to be associated with higher probabilities of an increase in real wages, and lower probabilities of reductions. This is consistent with our hypothesis and suggests that employee-owners (or managers under their influence) may be willing to accept reductions in employment provided it is accompanied by wage increases for incumbents remaining with the firm. Again, it would be interesting to distinguish changes for core and peripheral workers and to compare dividend payments to employees as an alternative to wages. Unfortunately, Russian

Table 14.6 Change in employment when firms reported increased sales volume, ordered probit model

Variable	Coefficient	(t-stat)
Constant	1.00*	(1.69)
Adverse market conditions	0.60	(1.08)
Employees on board	1.00*	(1.72)
Capital-intensive	0.96	(1.72)
Inside equity > 50%	−1.30**	(1.97)
Investment funds on board	−4.47	(0.00)
μ_1	1.06***	(3.11)
μ_2	1.89***	(4.15)
Log L	−33.70	
Restricted log L	−41.25	
χ^2_5	15.10***	

Note:
***significant at 1% level
**significant at 5% level
*significant at 10% level

enterprise managers are unwilling to disclose this information.

In addition to these results in relation to the main predictions developed in this chapter concerning employment and wage levels in the whole sample of 171 firms, it was decided to partition the sample into two segments. One segment (31 firms) reported increased sales volume in the year after privatization, and the remaining segment (of 140 firms) comprised those firms with unchanged or reduced sales volume. This segmentation was made to test the Ward–Vanek prediction of an association of less job-creation with higher levels of EC and EO in firms with increased demand for their products.

The aggregate results for those 31 firms who managed to increase their sales volume, even in the middle of a general collapse in demand, are shown in Table 14.6, although commentary is restricted to the marginal effects of right-hand-side variables on employment-change, reported in Table 14.7.

For these successful firms, only inside equity (EO) had a significant effect on employment, with EC becoming insignificant, implying that employee board nominees faced with buoyant sales and employment levels did not add significantly to job-creation. In Table 14.7 however, EO did contribute significantly to job-creation, and the significant coefficient of 0.46 reflected an increase in the probability of employment-increase from 16 per cent when insider equity was below 50 per cent to a 62 per cent probability when insider equity was above 50 per cent. Firms with declining sales volumes only showed an 18 per cent probability of increasing employment when incumbents held over half of the equity. These results

Table 14.7 Marginal effects on the probability of the change in employment when sales volume increased, ordered probit model

Variable	Increase in employment	No change in employment	Decrease in employment < 10%	Decrease in employment > 10 %
Adverse market conditions	−0.10	−0.12	0.03	0.20
Employees on board	−0.14	−0.21	0.01	0.36
Capital intensive	−0.13	−0.21	0	0.34
Inside equity > 50%	0.46*	−0.07*	−0.22*	−0.17*
Investment funds on board	0.84	−0.36	−0.29	−0.19

Note:
*significant at 5% level.

do imply that Ward–Vanek effects have not been strong for firms enjoying increases in product-demand, and the influence of EO is consistent with employees influencing decisions as if they were shareholders wishing to maximize shareholder value than as self-interested employees.

There remains, however, the possibility that firms with growing demand are by definition firms with low outsider stakes and high EO and EC because growing sales are related to insiders' perceptions of company prospects. There is undoubtedly an element of self-selection at play here; of the 31 firms with increased sales volume, only three had insider equity below 50 per cent, and investment funds were virtually shut out of these successful firms, defined in terms of growing sales.

This brings us to those (140) firms with declining sales volume. These declining firms were studied in order to examine the possibility that the extent of employee-ownership and control (EO and EC) upon privatization may stand as proxies for incumbents' perceptions of their company's prospects in the years after privatization. This possibility was not developed as a formal hypothesis, but is considered here in the spirit of one stage in the inductive generation of new hypotheses in the future.

In this regard, the segmentation was prompted by responses to case-study investigations made by two of the authors with Moscow investment funds in November 1996. Investment funds reported that it was almost impossible for them to acquire shares in the manufacturing firms with the best prospects, thanks to the restrictions placed by managers on share sales to outsiders discussed above. In fact, the general director at Togl'iatti was quoted to the effect that '... privatized firms in Russia only release shares to outsiders if they are in serious trouble'. By the same token,

Table 14.8   Change in employment when sales volume decreased, ordered probit model

Variable	Coefficient	(T-stat)
Constant	0.76***	(1.79)
Adverse market conditions	1.16*	(2.79)
Employees on board	0.39	(1.22)
Capital-intensive	0.17	(0.62)
Inside equity > 50%	0.15	(0.54)
Investment funds on board	0.69**	(2.28)
μ_1	1.00*	
μ_2	2.11*	
Log L	−95.32	
Restricted log L	−103.92	
χ^2_5	17.19*	

Note:
***significant at 1% level
**significant at 5% level
*significant at 10% level

any influence from EC and EO on job-preservation could be expected to be stronger under duress (that is, in firms with declining sales volumes).

Table 14.8, therefore, first presents the aggregate results for the segment of 140 firms in the sample without increases in sales volume, to see if the impact of right-hand-side variables differs between the segments.

Table 14.9 reports the more interesting marginal results. Compared with Table 14.3, EO continues to be insignificant, but EC also loses its significance, indicating that, in declining firms, EC and EO did not contribute significantly to job-preservation. Investment-fund board-membership continues to have the predicted impact in reducing employment, and the marginal effect on employment of adverse market conditions on declining firms is increased dramatically, with an increase of one-third in the probability of employment reductions in excess of 10 per cent.

Declining firms therefore appear as firms with poor prospects upon privatization, where outsider board membership can significantly add to employment reduction, but where EO and EC do not seem to have had the effect of blocking employment reduction. This result for declining firms thus repeats the conclusions concerning growing firms and the sample as a whole: other things equal, EC and EO do not seem to have led significantly to job-preservation or to a reluctance to increase employment when sales increase.

Table 14.9 Marginal effects on the probability of the change in employment when sales volume decreased, ordered probit model

Variable	Increase in employment	No change in employment	Decrease in employment < 10%	Decrease in employment > 10 %
Adverse market conditions	−0.20**	−0.22**	0.08**	0.34**
Employees on board	−0.10	−0.06	0.07	0.09
Capital intensive	−0.05	−0.02	0.04	0.03
Inside equity > 50%	0.04	−0.02	0.03	0.03
Investment funds on board	−0.15**	−0.12**	0.10**	0.17**

Note:
**significant at 1% level; *significant at 5% level.

CONCLUSIONS

In the literature, EO and EC are pessimistically associated with job and real wage preservation in the face of aggregate economic decline. Ownership by outside owners, however, is expected to promote the maximization of shareholder value rather than the advancement of immediate employee interests. Russian privatization has effectively produced management/ employee buy-outs imposing severe restrictions on the sale of shares to outsiders (or 'exit'); such circumstances would seem to favour the maximum restrictive impact of EC and EO. In short-term (or 'reactive') restructuring (EBRD, 1995, p. 133), Russian privatized firms could be expected to react slowly or even perversely as a result of EC and EO, especially since the large labour forces of many Russian firms represent a barrier to effective EC.

In line with expectations, this study consistently associated outside ownership with more employment-decline in firms with reductions in sales volume, and more employment-growth in firms with an increasing volume of sales. At the same time, however, investment funds as major outside investors have been virtually shut out from firms with growing sales volume.

With regard to EO and EC, the survey reported here was unable to produce any consistent evidence of restrictive behaviour by employees in terms of short-term restructuring as evidenced by employment change. Indeed, employees on firms' boards were found to have a similar impact on employment levels to outsider representation. In growing firms, EC and EO were not found to add significantly to growth in employment, and neither did they seem to act as a barrier to reduction in employment in declining firms.

It needs to emphasised, however, that these conclusions were derived in the context of total employment change, which did not distinguish between core/peripheral workers or between workers who were being paid regularly or not. Underlying trends may have been hidden by core employees placing the burden of adjustment on peripheral workers, and evidence elsewhere supports this possibility (Clarke, 1993). Such an interpretation is consistent with our findings on average real wages, where the level of EO is positively associated with the level of wages for employees retained by the firm.

In addition, extensive short-term restructuring may have been associated with EC and EO because the firms in which EC and EO prevailed were the very same firms with the best prospects that offered the best returns to restructuring. In this sense, employment reduction may have occurred despite EC and EO, rather than as a result of it.

Although these conclusions relate to the short-term, the evidence reported here may have helped to dispel some of the pessimism concerning EC, EO and short-run employment, and management/employee buy-outs may have provided a suitable vehicle for reactive restructuring in Russian industry. In the longer term, however, employees and managers (and probably indigenous Russian financial institutions, too) seem unlikely to prove capable of supplying the investable funds needed to raise the product design and build-quality of Russian industrial output towards world standards. Without substantial amounts of import protection, the management/employee buy-out may prove a necessary though transitional form of corporate governance.

15 Trust and Enforcement in Emerging Business Systems

Chong Ju Choi, Soo Hee Lee and Carla Millar

INTRODUCTION

A substantial amount of social science research on economic institutions and organizations has been unprepared for the major turbulence, structural change and intensifying competition in today's global business environment. While the role of trust and other relational attributes in international business arrangements have been recognized, there is a lack of knowledge on governing and facilitating business transactions in emerging-economy contexts. Also, there is an increasing need to reexamine the issue of national competitiveness (Porter, 1990) and economic institutions in light of the recent transformation, particularly in the context of emerging economies. According to Nelson (1992), there are three clusters of analysis concerning the determinants of national competitiveness. The first views firms as the main competitive unit; the second considers the macroeconomic performance of national economies; and the third looks at microeconomic policies at the level of industries. International business studies need a conceptual framework that takes into account all three levels of analysis, while addressing the importance of the interactions between institutions and organizations.

North's (1990, 1991) research on economic institutions is especially relevant for such a multiple-level analysis. North (1990) has shown how the combination of formal and informal constraints determines the rules of exchange and change in national economies (Hirsch and Lounsbury, 1996), and also analysed how organizations influence and change the institutions. North (1990) acknowledges the considerable increase of measurement and enforcement costs in the current economic system, and their role in shaping the patterns of interdependence between organizations and institutions. His analysis can be seen as an attempt to reconcile the political and ideological aspects of behavioural theories and the rational theories of organizational economics.

Studies on change and success of national business systems have tended to focus on two areas. The first is the analyses of the evolution of dynamic markets over time, which originated from Schumpeter and the Austrian economists. This area has traditionally merited no more than a footnote in textbooks and is only now being revived as an important approach for economics and management (Kogut, 1993; Choi, Lee and Kim, 1996a; Roe, 1993; Whipp and Pettigrew, 1994; Teece and Pisano, 1994; North, 1990).

The second is the study of the history of certain economies and industries, the province of economic and business history (North, 1990; Chandler, 1990; Bell and Pavitt, 1994; Dosi, Freeman and Fabiani, 1994; Langlois, 1992; Grief, 1993, 1994; Grief, Milgrom and Weingast, 1994; de la Mothe and Paquet, 1996). This approach of comparing the social organization or institutional foundations of individualist versus collectivist societies has been associated with new institutional economics, especially that of North (1990), which originated from the seminal work of Coase (1937). Williamson's (1985) analysis, in parallel to the historical and comparative approach, has further articulated the underlying logic of transaction-cost economics by examining institutional arrangements, observable attributes of economic transactions, and optimal organizational forms. In their comparison of North and Williamson, Hirsch and Lounsbury (1996) point out that one major difference between them is their relative emphasis on measurement and enforcement costs.

Dunning (1996), in his reexamination of the eclectic paradigm, also recognizes that the socio-institutional structure of market-based capitalism is undergoing changes characterized principally by innovation-led growth, a 'voice' (Hirschman, 1970) reaction to market failure, and cooperation as a competitiveness-enhancing measure. The ability of a society to express voice is dependent on shared identity and cultural beliefs. In this sense, the role of the state and other non-market mechanisms have become increasingly important to research on comparative business systems as analysed in, for example, Stopford and Strange (1991), Buckley and Casson (1985), Boddewyn (1988), Brewer (1992, 1993), Boddewyn and Brewer (1994), Hillman and Keim (1995), Orru, Biggart and Hamilton (1997), Hill (1995), Doz and Prahalad (1984) and Brahm (1995). The catalysts for structural economic change and the blurring of national boundaries, as well as their various consequences for firm-activities and performance, have led to an urgent need to reassess the traditional frameworks of national business systems. As discussed by Stopford (1996), there is an increasing paradox in the global business environment between the forces of globalization and standardization, versus the forces of nationalism and domestic institutional constraints.

However, what has been much less understood are the patterns of institutional and organizational mechanisms and processes that have emerged in the absence of strong legal regimes or binding social norms, particularly in the context of transition or emerging economies in Eastern Europe and Asia. As these countries have recently undergone a massive economic transformation, many radical solutions on privatization, investment and international trade have been prescribed, often without taking their social, historical and institutional conditions into full consideration. An alternative approach could be formulated by asking what type of trading and international business systems, under what conditions, have existed in these countries, and to clarify their implications for international business strategy.

As noted by North (1990), and with a few exceptions (Barzel, 1982; Bernstein, 1992; Choi, 1994), the vast amount of literature on transaction-costs analysis since Coase's (1937) seminal work has not fully addressed the role of measurement and enforcement costs in creating institutional arrangements. As these costs are fundamental to understanding the nature of institutional and organizational variance, we set out here a research agenda which seeks to fill this gap in the area of comparative business systems by pursuing an analysis of enforcement mechanisms across different business settings, particularly in the context of emerging economies. Although measurement costs can have a significant impact upon the emergence and design of optimal exchange arrangements, our substantive discussions focus more on the issue of enforcement costs and institutions, since our aim here is to develop an analytical framework for national-level comparison.

The purpose of this chapter is threefold. First, we analyse the growing importance of the emerging market phenomenon in relation to national business systems (Gerlach and Lincoln, 1992; Child and Markoczy, 1993; Choi, 1994; Choi *et al.*, 1996a; Lazonick, 1994; Whitley, 1990; Peng and Heath, 1996; Hill, 1995; Mueller, 1994; Sorge, 1991). According to North (1990), the relative success of national business systems is largely dependent on different configurations of the interaction between formal and informal institutions on the one hand, and the four major types of organizations – economic, social, political and educational on the other. The individualist, Anglo-Saxon countries such as the United States and United Kingdom tend to rely on formal relative to informal institutions, such as common law, statute law and regulations, where the overlapping interests and direct links among the four types of organization are relatively weak.

By contrast, in the emerging business systems, especially in the more collectivist countries of Asia, there is a greater reliance on informal institutions such as social norms, collective thinking, codes of conduct and conventions. In Asia, personnel-linkage, interest-coordination and information-sharing across the four types of organization also tend to be much greater. This type of comparative perspective allows us to better understand why establishing or transplanting certain formal institutions such as common law, statute law and regulations in an emerging business system is not sufficient for national economic or business success. Thus, further articulating North's (1990) basic research agenda, we argue that the interaction of cultural foundations with national institutions and organizations determines the success or failure of national business systems.

Second, we develop a conceptual framework of business cooperation to analyse the relative configuration of institutions and organizations within which transaction costs in their entirety can be experienced and understood. Further elaborating on the institutionalist rationale (Williamson, 1985; North, 1990), we develop here a typology of business exchange and enforcement, pertinent to the study of emerging economies: namely contract, trust and hostage. Schelling's (1960) analysis of cooperative strategy under uncertainty is highly applicable to international business transactions involving emerging economies, in that the creation of mutual commitments through hostage exchange can help overcome the weaknesses of implicit trust, reputation or ethics in very uncertain and unpredictable environments.

Third, we analyse countertrade arrangements, offsets in particular, to illustrate the effectiveness of hostage-based exchange, and argue that the persistence of international countertrade in emerging markets can be understood as an organizational response to institutional deficiency in transaction governance rather than foreign exchange shortage (Fletcher, 1996; Caves and Marin, 1992; Marin and Schnitzer, 1995). Our analysis will show that in the context of emerging economies, countertrade-type arrangements may be more effective than trust or contract-based exchange in facilitating transactions and enforcing collaborative agreements.

TRANSACTION COSTS, INSTITUTIONAL DIVERSITY AND COOPERATIVE STRATEGY

One of the continuing phenomena in international business practice is the proliferation of international strategic alliances and other types of business partnerships. There is an extensive literature in this area proposing various new frameworks of cooperative strategy in global competition, addressed in works such as Arthur (1994), Rugman (1982), Casson (1995), Levinthal (1992), Langlois (1992), Landa (1994) and Shan and Hamilton (1991). Past research on cooperative interorganizational relationships has identified their main determinants, such as reciprocity, trust, opportunism and forbearance, and analysed its developmental processes in contrast to the formal and legal aspects of contractual exchange (Ring and van de Ven, 1992, 1994). Beamish and Banks (1987), Buckley (1990), Parkhe (1991) and Madhok (1995), among others, have emphasized the role of trust and other relational attributes in international business arrangements.

In this section, we analyse how cooperative exchange or transactions can occur in various types of societies and how transaction costs may influence the emergent forms of institutional arrangements and cooperative strategy.

The proliferation of international joint ventures, alliances and networks, coupled with a heightened interest in Japanese industrial organization (Fruin, 1992; Gerlach and Lincoln, 1992), have also led to a reappraisal of the core theories of international business in the age of alliance capitalism (Dunning, 1996). On the other hand, the continuing debate on transaction-costs analysis indicates that both market and non-market-based exchanges within and between organizations are crucial for the choice and design of efficient transaction governance structures (Williamson, 1996). However, what has been much less understood is the patterns of institutional and organizational mechanisms and processes that have emerged in the absence of strong legal regimes or binding social norms, particularly in the context of transition economies in Eastern Europe and Asia. Therefore, there is an urgent need to develop knowledge on governing and facilitating business exchange in the context of emerging economies.

Williamson (1975, 1985, 1996) has further elaborated on the underlying logic of Coase's (1937) original work on transaction-costs economics by analysing the relative merits of alternative organizational arrangements. Williamson's (1975) basic thesis was that transactions should be governed by a regime or institutional arrangement which best economizes on the costs imposed by bounded rationality and opportunism. The existing management research based on Williamson's transaction-costs theory has therefore tended to explain the emergence and boundaries of organizations with recourse to various concepts of market failure, thus conceptualizing the alternative modes of transaction governance in a continuum.

Williamson's operationalization led to a considerable body of conceptual and empirical research on the validity of transaction-cost propositions that has studied issues of organizational structure, including vertical supply arrangements, structure of the multinational firm and joint ventures. However, North (1990) has recently pointed out that past research on organizations or comparative institutions has not incorporated the full implications of enforcement (Choi, 1994) and measurement costs (Barzel, 1982; Bernstein, 1992). Measurement costs refer to the costs incurred by the difficulty of measuring the value of products in a transaction and pricing each item individually. Enforcement costs are associated with the impediments to enforcing and safeguarding agreements. Such costs are especially important in international business settings where the level of complexity and uncertainty tends to be particularly high.

Contractual arrangements may be influenced by the need to reduce excessive or duplicative sorting, searching and measurement costs, especially when product intangibility is high, and it is difficult for producers to control their quality or for buyers to ascertain their value. As illustrated by the cases of first-run entertainment products or uncut diamonds, parties to a transaction can thus gain benefits by not measuring the exact value of what is being exchanged at every transaction, which would otherwise raise the transaction costs significantly. Therefore, organizational arrangements designed to reduce the time and effort spent in redundant search and re-pricing leave more gains from trade to be retained among the principle parties.

With respect to enforcement costs, past research on comparative institutions has often contrasted institutionalized forms of trust relationships in Japan with legal contracts in the United States. In Japan, the organization-oriented system is seen as being owned by the entire community and various stakeholders, and therefore is underlined by strong social trust. By contrast, the market-oriented Anglo-Saxon system in the United States is driven mainly by self-interested shareholders. These two extremes of achieving enforcement of agreements do not address the transactional problems prevalent in business situations where neither mechanism is reliable. An alternative can be derived from what Schelling (1960) described as the tendency for parties to mutually exchange a hostage in order to ensure cooperation and enforcement of agreements in environments with highly problematic outcomes.

Global competition can be seen from the viewpoint of what motivates and constrains firm strategy and behaviour in today's business environment. Such constraints include national culture, the legal and regulatory environment, the business–government relationship, the role of financial institutions, and the corporate governance system in the home market as well as in the host countries of multinational firms. Porter (1990) has noted the importance of home-market conditions in terms of the pressure placed on firms to innovate and improve product quality. The importance of the national business environment in influencing the organizing principles and competitive strategies of firms has also been analysed, in Stopford and Strange (1991), Kogut (1993), Lodge and Vogel (1987) and Albert (1991). According to their analysis, domestic institutions play as important a role in determining corporate behaviour as the pressures of globalization. For example, in many parts of continental Europe and Asia it is still not the financial markets but various government ministries that monitor corporate performance and control financial allocation, although this practice has been heavily criticized as being the main cause of the recent financial crisis. In many continental European countries, such as Germany and Switzerland, the banking sector as institutional shareholders monitors corporate performance and investment decisions.

Firm behaviour and strategy, especially investment decisions such as new market entry, diversification, and innovation and new product development can be significantly constrained by the differences of home-market institutions, while at the same time providing sources of competitive advantage. However, the competitive advantage of firms endowed by home-market institutions may not be so easily transferred across national boundaries as organizational capabilities. The effects of home-market institutions in turn constrain the scale and scope of collaborative activities across national boundaries. Thus, in spite of the global nature of today's competition, the political, economic and sociocultural effects of home-market institutions can have both positive and negative influences on firm capabilities and competitive advantages.

Research in game theory (Camerer, 1991) has suggested that cooperation is difficult to sustain when the game is not repeated, when there is little information known on the other players, and when there are large number of players. Conversely, cooperative behaviour is usually observed when individuals interact repeatedly, when they have a great deal of information about each other and when the number of players is limited. However, in a world of rapidly-changing technology, specialization and division of labour, as well as constantly shifting boundaries of management, organization and markets, there arises an increasing necessity to establish cooperative arrangements without the benefit of repeat transactions, clearly identifiable counterparts, or limits on the number of participants. Thus, various types of cooperative arrangements have proliferated over the past decade, both within the Western world and in other international contexts. This phenomenon of increasing cross-border networks raises several important questions on the validity of the conventional wisdom on cooperative behaviour and strategy. Fundamental questions raised for international business and organization research is how cooperation is made possible under severe constraints, and how is it sustained over time.

In an attempt to explain why certain national business systems are more successful than others, North (1990) has shown how the combination of formal and informal institutional constraints determines the rules of exchange in national economies and their differential performance, combining the political and ideological aspects of behaviouralist theories with the rationalist theories of organizational economics. This type of macro-institutional analysis, combined with the transactional-level analysis based on a theory of cooperative exchange and enforcement, can not only provide crucial insights in explaining the relative success or failure of national business systems, but also has significant practical implications for developing effective cooperative strategies across different business systems.

COMPARATIVE BUSINESS SYSTEMS: INTERPLAY BETWEEN INSTITUTIONS AND ORGANIZATIONS

The importance of national business systems has been raised recently in various works that emphasize the role of social contingency or cultural foundations of economic organization, as opposed to macroeconomic conditions (Mueller, 1994; Whitley, 1990; Sorge, 1991; Child and Markoczy, 1993; Choi, 1994; Casson, 1996; Choi *et al.*, 1996a). However, the distinction between institutions and organizations was not clearly made in these works. This distinction is crucial to understanding why the mere adaptation of certain formal institutions or rules such as common or statute law, or regulations that are prevalent in the Anglo-Saxon business systems such as the United States and United Kingdom, does not necessarily warrant a similar level of performance elsewhere (North, 1990). In this section, we compare the collectivist business systems with the individualist business systems, paying particular attention to the enforcement of business cooperation.

North (1990, 1991) defines institutions as a set of rules that establish the basis and stable structure for production, exchange and distribution in a society, and distinguishes between formal and informal institutions. The formal institutions such as common law and market regulations are very important in Anglo-Saxon countries such as the United States, the United Kingdom, Australia and Canada. Informal institutions include codes of conduct, social norms, conventions and other rules that the society has developed over time. Such informal institutions, which are closely linked to the values of collectivism and personal exchange, are crucial for most Asian business systems. Thus, the institutional differences also indicate that the preferred mode of governance, the means of contracting and enforcing agreements, will be different. As North (1990) points out, the existence of either or both formal and informal institutions is no guarantee of economic efficiency. One distinction between formal and informal institutions can be made by certain specialized roles; a Supreme court judge who safeguards the administration of justice as defined by the constitutional law would be an example of a formal institution.

Organizations are the players within a national business system that take advantage of, or are constrained by, the formal and informal institutions. There are four major types of organizations: economic organizations (such as firms, cooperatives, stockmarkets, banks and trade unions); political organizations (such as political parties and city councils); social organizations (such as clubs, churches and sporting groups); and educational organizations (such as universities and vocational schools). Members of an organization often have common objectives, founded on shared beliefs and ideologies. Through this cultural process, organizations can

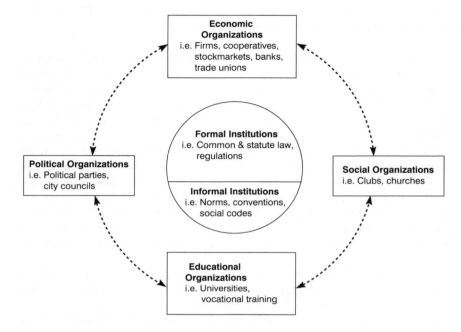

Figure 15.1　National business systems: institutions and organizations

also change the rules or institutions in a national business system. Developing North's (1990) distinction between institutions and organizations, we present in Figure 15.1 a framework for their symbiotic relationship.

We believe that this interaction between formal and informal institutions, and, in turn, their interactions with the four types of organizations, fundamentally determine the success of national business systems. This basic framework of national business systems can help to explain the differences between the more mature or developed economies and those that are emerging. As countries develop and emerge economically, the balance between formal and informal institutions may tip more towards formal institutions, such as common law and regulations. However, it is not certain that the formal institutions will dominate over the informal institutions as emerging countries reach a mature economy status such as that of Japan.

In the Anglo-Saxon business systems that rely on formal institutions, there exist relatively weaker interconnections across the four types of organizations. Thus, economic organizations such as firms, stockmarkets and central banks (like the US federal reserve) are quite separate from political organizations and the government (Roe, 1993). There is also a

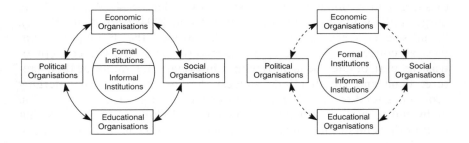

Figure 15.2 Collectivist vs individualist business systems

clear differentiation between public and private domains. Working for a firm, or performing job-related activities, is seen as a public aspect of life which is separate from private activities associated with social organizations like clubs and churches. In many emerging business systems, and especially in Asia, the linkages across these organizations are stronger, and are thus similar to communitarian, continental European countries such as Germany and Sweden (Choi *et al.*, 1996a).

In Figure 15.2, which compares the two ideal types of individualist and collectivist business systems, we try to characterize, using dotted versus solid lines, the potential differences between the formal, legal and market-driven Anglo-Saxon business systems and the informal, emerging business systems, especially of Asia.

In the diagram to the left of Figure 15.2, the solid lines indicate the strong links among the four types of organizations in the emerging business systems of Asia, while showing a larger ratio of informal institutions relative to formal institutions. The diagram to the right of Figure 15.2 is more characteristic of the Anglo-Saxon business systems, and shows, using dotted lines, the much weaker links among these four organizations, with a relatively larger ratio of formal relative to informal institutions. Our intention in presenting a graphic description of national business systems is to delineate the basic elements and issues before moving on to the more complex dimensions of comparative institutions.

TRUST AND ENFORCEMENT INSTITUTIONS

International business literature has shown the diversity of national business systems and their paths towards success and failure (Melecki, 1985; Stopford, 1996; Casson, 1995; Buckley and Casson, 1985; Lazonick, 1994; Levinthal, 1994; Porter, 1990). On the other hand, a stream of comparative management literature has analysed the role of trust in emerging national business systems and how trust can be linked to success or lack of success in national business systems (Mueller, 1994; Whitley, 1990; Sorge, 1991; Child and Markoczy, 1993; Choi, 1994; Choi *et al.*, 1996a). Social science research has often tended to view the developing countries as collectivist societies, and, therefore, perceives the concept of trust as part of the social norms and informal constraints in their culture. Peng and Heath (1996) suggest that organizations in emerging economies tend to absorb market uncertainties either by internalization or by the formation of networks. Dunning (1996) also recognizes that relationships fill in the gap created by market failures in facilitating transactions. Thus, the idea that economic transactions and institutions are significantly influenced by trust relationships or other informal ties has often been linked more to traditional societies or developing countries.

However, the recent revival of interest in the concept of trust (Kramer and Tyler, 1996) has tended to look at the developed or individualist countries. There are some important reasons why the role of informal attributes and social norms has also become an important issue for organizations in mature business systems. The concept of trust has recently received growing attention in organization and management theory due to the major environmental and organizational changes characterized by the breakdown of hierarchical structures, the impact of re-engineering and downsizing on employment practices, and the proliferation of interorganizational alliances and networks. Trust is of paramount importance to organization and management theory, since its presence or absence will have significant effect on the preferred or emergent mode of coordination and cooperation, both within and between organizations. The increasing concern with trust, therefore, has been advanced not just for the sustainability and effective management of cooperative interorganizational relationships (Ring and van de Ven, 1994; Beamish and Banks, 1987; Parkhe, 1991; Madhok, 1995) but also for the meta-level explanation of the very nature of the organization as a distinctive mode of economic coordination and as a value-creating entity (Simon, 1991).

The academic debate on the relevance of transaction costs and the market-failure reasoning for organization theory has continued with issues ranging from whether markets provide an alternative to failures of organizations (Simon, 1991), to the assumption of risk-neutrality in transaction costs (Chiles and McMackin, 1996), and to the importance of measurement and enforcement costs (North, 1990; Bernstein, 1992; Choi, 1994). Throughout these debates, the concept of trust often surfaces as a factor of mediation. It is not surprising, given the general increase in uncertainty in the global business environment, that trust emerges as a more important factor in most types of exchange and cooperation. We suggest that the tremendous recent interest in the concept of trust (Kramer and Tyler, 1996) and other informal cooperative mechanisms, is linked to the enforcement aspects of international transactions or cooperative arrangements. In other words, organizations faced with environmental uncertainty and complexity may prefer, or actively seek to design, a governance arrangement that would either capitalize on the existing level of social trust, or enhance the perceived level of partner-specific trust.

Grief (1994), in an historical comparison of Genoese and Maghribis merchants in the eleventh century, has shown that, although they used a similar technology, faced a similar international business environment and sold similar products, for social and political reasons the Genoese became individualist and the Maghribis became collectivist. Grief suggested two major reasons for this. First, the Genoese adopted Christianity, which emphasized the individual rather than the social group as the centre of exchange and interaction, in contrast to the Maghribis traders, who were Muslim immigrants from Iraq to Tunisia and relied on personal and social networks and norms (Hughes, 1974; Grief, 1994). Second, the increased migration of people to Genoa at the time lead to a diverse population. In such heterogeneous population, or where there is less shared identity among the members, there are often advantages in having enforcement institutions based on an individualist style of exchange, or formal contracts. Greif, Milgrom and Weingast, (1994) have shown how the merchant guilds and champagne fairs of the twelfth and thirteenth centuries provided the formal enforcement and protection mechanisms that facilitated business and trade. In time, this third-party role was replaced by the state and by courts and the legal enforcement of contracts.

In collectivist societies, the enforcement of cooperation is done by the group members themselves. Thus, this could be called second party enforcement (North, 1990). In the case of individualist societies, if the enforcement is done by a third party, this is usually the formal, legal courts of the state. This important role played by a third party is an issue analysed in detail by Burt and Knez (1996), who have considered whether the third party is passive or active in a given situation. While the coordination of economic activities tends to be strongly influenced by cultural beliefs in collectivist societies, individualist approaches to coordination can also be due to games driven by 'focal points' or salience (Schelling, 1960), along with other social and political events.

Although trust is a crucial concept to the nature of economic exchange, it needs to be assessed along with other mechanisms and costs underlying cooperative relationships. Measurement costs are especially important in transactions involving intangible resources and assets, such as knowledge. The intangibility of the product or service being exchanged can in turn increase the role of trust in such transactions. For example, if the content of the item being exchanged is intangible, difficult to measure, or it takes time to ascertain its value, then the identity of the parties undertaking the transaction and the level of trust between them can have considerable influence on their cooperation. Thus, in a situation with low enforcement costs, parties may have an incentive to deliberately increase measurement costs in order to develop long-term trust.

One important issue in the current context of the debate is the causal relationship between trust and competitive advantage (Barney and Hansen, 1994). Thus, our analysis of national business systems has some implications for the advantages and disadvantages of relational exchange structures and network forms of transaction governance, in the sense that the limitations of trust-based exchange are also expounded at the national level. Our view is also in line with some historical studies (Hughes, 1974; Grief, 1994) as well as more recent discussion on the success and failure of industrial clusters, a type of industrial network (Pouder and St John, 1996; Porter, 1990; Harrison, 1992). Thus, we suggest that there are limits to trust, and that trust can eventually lead to the failure of such closed networks. This provides an important lesson as to why the mere effect of changing formal institutions, such as law and regulations, without taking into account their relationship with informal institutions such as trust, social norms and conventions, does not guarantee the competitiveness of a national business system.

ENFORCEMENT OF COOPERATION IN EMERGING MARKETS

Williamson (1985) has defined the term 'opportunism' as the 'threat of one party by not trading to appropriate a greater share of the surplus after specific investments have been made'. Opportunism is reduced by contracting, by obligations of an ethical or trusting nature, or by reputation. At one extreme is the explicit contract, and unfortunately, as discussed by King (1988), Beale and Dugdale (1975), Ellickson (1991) and Macauly (1963), certain societies have tended to overemphasize litigation, laws and regulations, at the cost of institutionalizing trust throughout society. At the other extreme are societies where trust and reputation are more important, for example in Asia. The differences between the two societies and approaches have been analysed in works such as Fruin (1992), Choi (1994) and Choi *et al.* (1996a, b). Casson (1995, 1996) and Buckley and Chapman (1996) have also recently highlighted the important intersection between economics and social anthropology, and the need to compare the relative importance of formal and informal alternatives to the legal system.

Eastern Europe, and the developing world, does not often have recourse to such mechanisms. This can be because of factors such as the randomness of the environment, or the unpredictable discretion of the institutions of government. As noted by Olson (1992), legal enforcement of contracts and property may be key factors in future business arrangements with Eastern Europe:

Table 15.1   Three types of cooperation and enforcement

Type of cooperation and enforcement	Characteristics of business environment
Formal, legal contracts	Free markets; relatively perfect information availability; strong formal institutions such as law; separation among different types of organizations such as banking, stock markets and industries
Informal, trust and reputation	Relatively regulated markets by government intervention; strong informal institutions such as social norms, conventions and traditions; close connections in organizations
Mutual commitment and hostages	High uncertainty and volatility in economic and industry indicators; inefficiency of market mechanisms; weak legal system; arbitrary use of power by political organizations; lack of organizational development

. . . many of the gains from trade cannot, however, be attained through spot transactions. They require legal and governmental institutions that guarantee, among other things, individual rights to impartial enforcement of contracts and property . . . the order in Soviet-type societies came from administration – from official discretion – rather than from the rule of law. (Olson, 1992)

Such official discretion from government administration can of course discourage parties from trying to form more long-term relationships based on trust or reputation, while legal enforcement and explicit contracts are also not reliable. In this sense, certain business environments, such as Eastern Europe, may be characterized by neither the formal, legal systems of Anglo-Saxon countries, nor the informal systems of Asian countries, such as Japan. Thus, an alternative form of cooperation based on hostages and mutual commitment may be more efficient in certain business environments. Table 15.1 introduces a typology of frameworks for achieving enforcement and cooperation.

In this typology, we have tried to move beyond the traditional distinction made, among others, by Fruin (1992) that compares the trust-based systems (such as Japan) with the legalistic systems in many Anglo-Saxon countries (such as the United States). Many societies do not have the stable business environment for either trust or contract-based cooperation. In such societies, a hostage-based, or mutual-commitment approach may be more appropriate. This is especially true in the 'emerging' business systems of the world such as Eastern Europe, Asia and Latin America. However, a greater reliance on informal cooperation mechanisms such as trust and hostages, relative to formal cooperation mechanisms such as legal contracts, is not necessarily linked to the relative stage of emergence that a national business system may evolve through.

The two extremes of achieving cooperation through either trust or contracts does not address the situation of business environments where neither enforcement mechanism is possible; this is further magnified by the difficulties of measurement costs (Barzel, 1982; Choi, 1994). The extent of measurement costs in turn depends on the nature of the product; for example, services tend to have higher measurement costs than more tangible products such as commodities. Enforcement costs are fundamental to achieving cooperation, since the perceived level of enforcement costs will not only determine the choice of transaction governance form, but also can discourage parties from exploring potential opportunities. Regions of the world such as Eastern Europe, certain parts of Asia, Latin America and Africa all provide environments where neither contracts nor trust-type enforcement mechanisms may be effective (Choi and Maldoom, 1992; Choi *et al.*, 1996a, b). An alternative to either may be similar to what Schelling, as early as 1960, described as the tendency for parties to mutually exchange a hostage in order to ensure cooperation and enforcement of agreements in environments with highly problematic outcomes:

> ... the ancients exchanged hostages, drank wine from the same glass to demonstrate the absence of poison, met in public places to inhibit the massacre of one by the other, and even deliberately exchanged spies to facilitate transmittal of authentic information ... in a lawless world that provides no recourse to damage suits for breach of unwritten contracts, hostages may be the only device for partners to strike a bargain. (Schelling, 1960)

This approach overcomes the weaknesses of implicit trust, reputation or ethics as enforcement guarantors in very uncertain and unpredictable environments, by creating a situation where both parties must lose if they do not cooperate. Deals based on hostaging are endemic in some business environments, for example in Eastern Europe. In this sense, we suggest that the enforcement mechanism of countertrade arrangements provides critical hints on how effective cooperation can be achieved in potentially high transaction-cost environments, typical of emerging economies. The nature of cooperation and strategic behaviour has always been at the foundations of game theory (Schelling, 1960). The influence of game-theory reasoning on economics and other social sciences is analysed in more detail by Camerer (1991), Casson (1995, 1996) and Buckley and Casson (1993).

Various type of countertrade have been the norm rather than the exception in many cases of international business agreements involving developing countries (Choi and Maldoom, 1992; Marin and Schnitzer, 1995; Choi *et al.*, 1996b). The four types of countertrade that utilize hostaging or artificial creation of mutual commitments are as follows: barter (the direct exchange of goods between two parties without foreign exchange); counterpurchase (the promise of one party to purchase goods at a later date in return for accepting goods at the present time); offsets (a seller partially offsets the costs of the buyer by agreeing to subcontract or produce together with the buyer); and buybacks (one party provides an input into the production process of another party, in return for promising to purchase a proportion of the resulting output). All these types of exchange have elements of mutual commitment as an enforcement mechanism.

An important point raised by the continuing prevalence of such countertrade agreements is whether they arise due to the lack of institutional development in a society, or are they efficient institutional arrangements in their own right? For example, Buckley and Chapman (1996) and Casson (1996) have analysed the important linkages between economics-oriented formal reasoning and informal and substantive ideas of social anthropology. Although countertrade is seen to be rooted in primitive societies, its current variety may be due to the particular mix of institutions and organizations in such countries and regions (North, 1990). Thus, at this point it is possible to suggest that countertrade arrangements often involve highly-complex exchange relations and evolve into different forms of exchange over time (Fletcher, 1996).

COUNTERTRADE AS AN ENFORCEMENT INSTITUTION

The interactions between organizations and institutions, both formal and informal, can be clearly illustrated by the existence of countertrade arrangements (or linked or tied business agreements). We examine the potential advantages of countertrade agreements in emerging business environments, which rely on hostage exchange. Such business practices are common in various parts of the world, but especially in Eastern Europe, Asia and Latin America.

Hennart (1989, 1990) showed the importance of unconventional trade practices through a detailed analysis of various types of countertrade. His analysis differentiated between two types of countertrade: barter (based on clearing arrangements and switch trading, which are used to avoid money-based exchange); and buybacks, offsets and counterpurchase (which are used to impose reciprocal commitments) (Hennart, 1990). Therefore, the latter category of countertrade can be conceived as an organizational response to contractual uncertainty in the context of emerging economies. The concept of reciprocal commitments articulated by Schelling (1960) has been further analysed in recent applications of countertrade and other non-conventional trade practices (Casson and Chukujama, 1988; Choi and Maldoom, 1992; Hennart and Anderson, 1993; Lecraw, 1989; Mirus and Yeung, 1986; Yoffie, 1984; Choi *et al.*, 1996b; Williamson, 1985; Kogut, 1986).

Legal enforcement requires a developed legal system that can ensure and secure title for individuals to both property and rights. This explicit system of policing clearly does not yet exist in many emerging business systems, such as in Eastern Europe. The state had title over property within its national boundaries and could, therefore, trade with the outside world. However, states can be arbitrary in their actions. In consequence, the amount of commerce that could occur was restricted to that which could be negotiated at the level of the state. This meant that external trade with enterprises within these countries and internal trading conducted on behalf of foreign firms was not possible. However, internal trade and business did occur within these countries, conducted both legally and illegally by the countries' own nationals. Olson (1992) notes that the Eastern European countries had many of the characteristics of societies at the beginning of history. There were no courts or governmental systems to facilitate trade, and power was often exercised arbitrarily by a leadership beyond the normal social pressures of group membership. But, as Olson notes, trade and business did nevertheless take place even without an apparent context for trade; trade was irrepressible in the centrally-planned economies and is likely to be so again in the transition economies because:

> ... the gains from trade are substantial, if not colossal; some trades, and especially those that can be consummated on the spot, are essentially self-enforcing in that the interests of the parties are by themselves sufficient to make the transactions happen. (Olson, 1992)

Imperfections that ameliorate the alternatives to legal enforcement have been in evidence. One such is social norms and sanctions. As noted by Olson (1992), the former Eastern European countries faced a context where neither social nor legal norms existed, certainly from the perspective of foreign companies wishing to do international business with them. Olson (1992) points out that establishing or strengthening legally enforceable contracts and property rights may be key factors in developing business with Eastern European countries. Historically, in Eastern Europe, enforcement of business contracts has been at the discretion of the government. This has been enforced by dicta rather than by the rule of law. Cooter and Landa (1984) showed that when the legal framework for enforcing contract law is underdeveloped, transactions tend to be based on the alternate of long-term social relationships between the parties with implicit enforcement. Such long-term relationships take time to develop. In the short and medium term, foreign companies may therefore find the investment required to establish such relationships so costly that trade with such societies is unattractive.

We now analyse in more depth offsets, a major type of countertrade, to illustrate the reciprocal elements of countertrade such as mutual hostages and mutual commitment. Hall and Markowski (1993) summarize the definition of offsets provided by Udis and Maskus (1991):

> In general, an offset is a contract imposing performance conditions on the seller of a good or service so that the purchasing government can recoup, or offset, some of its investment. In some way, reciprocity beyond that associated with normal market exchange of goods and services is involved such as licensed production or subcontractor production. Indirect offsets involve goods and services unrelated to the exports referenced in the sales agreement and may include some forms of foreign investment, technology transfer. (Udis and Maskus, 1991)

The credibility of such deals, in the case of indirect offsets, is almost certainly sustainable since the state is a prime contracting party – the existing authority in the state often has a clearly-vested interest in sustaining the deal. This shows the potentially important role of the state and political organizations in working closely with economic organizations such as foreign corporations to ensure that a cooperative business relationship can be developed. By accepting the deal, a hostage is created by the purchasing government. This hostage may take the form of political leverage, in providing domestic corporations access to otherwise unavailable foreign sales, or as technology, which the government can use in the future. Reneging, or acting opportunistically, on the deal in either case will damage the interests of the purchasing government.

Both direct and indirect offsets are examples of agreements where the selling corporations voluntarily enter complex arrangements with foreign governments, agreeing to undertake trade in a linked manner. The nature of offsets, like countertrade in general, is that both parties have something to lose from breaking off the agreement. This provides strong incentives to maintain mutual commitment. An example of a typical offset contract was the purchase of civilian aircraft from Mcdonnell-Douglas by Yugoslavia. This was offset by the purchase by McDonnell-Douglas of Yugoslav ham. In this example, the Yugoslavian ham was the hostage. Yugoslavia as a state generated additional benefit for its citizens from ham sales, which it would lose if it reneged on the contract. Thus, the offset contract provided incentives to the purchaser to abide by the agreement despite the lack of legal enforceability. This type of agreement similarly does not depend on any implicit, informal relationships based on moral norms, trust or reputation; if indeed there is trust, it is trust that is compelled by the mutual investment and commitment to the co-operative relationship.

CONCLUSIONS

This chapter has analysed the relative configuration of institutions and organizations engendered by different conditions of transaction-cost requirements, and the implications of such variance for international business cooperation. Although the role of trust and other relational attributes in international business arrangements have been recognized, there is a general lack of knowledge on governing and facilitating business transactions in the context of the emerging economies. Thus, our main concern here has been to examine how cooperative exchange or transactions can occur in various types of societies, and how enforcement costs may influence the emergent forms of institutional arrangements and cooperative strategy, while taking into account the major structural shifts in today's global business environment, particularly the rise of the emerging markets.

First, relying on North's (1990) theory of institutions, we examined the role of transaction costs in economic organization and the diversity of national business systems with reference to trust and enforcement institutions (Mueller, 1994; Whitley, 1990; Sorge, 1991; Child and Markoczy, 1993; Choi, 1994). We argue that enforcement costs and mechanisms are fundamental to understanding the nature of national business systems in that they have significant influence on the emergent configurations of interrelationships between organizations and institutions. We also show that the individualist, Anglo-Saxon countries tend to rely on formal institutions such as common law, statute law and regulations, where the overlapping interests and direct links among organizations are relatively weak. In contrast, emerging business systems with personnel linkage, interest coordination and information sharing across different types of organizations tend to rely more on informal institutions. This type of comparative perspective better explains why transplanting certain formal institutions from an advanced country into an emerging business system does not provide sufficient conditions for national economic success. In this sense, it is worthwhile to look into the patterns of institutional and organizational mechanisms and processes that have emerged in the absence of strong legal regimes or binding social norms, particularly in the context of transition or emerging economies in Eastern Europe and Asia.

Second, and further elaborating on the institutionalist rationale (Williamson, 1985; North, 1990), we develop a conceptual framework for business exchange and enforcement, pertinent to the study of emerging economies: namely, contract, trust and hostage. The interrelationship between these types of enforcement and transaction costs in turn leads to the problem of identity and the role of intermediaries in facilitating cooperative exchange. These alternative types of enforcement have their particular strengths and weaknesses with respect to the degree of uncertainty and one party's ability to discover the identity of the other party. While contracts facilitate anonymous market transactions, trust is crucial to the formation and sustainability of cooperative relationships. Where neither contracts nor institutionalized trust in social relationships provide viable enforcement, hostages can impose mutual commitment in interlinked or reciprocal exchanges. The optimal choice between the enforcement mechanisms that should reduce transaction costs is largely dependent on the level of emergence of the business system, as well as the dynamics of interaction between its organizations and institutions. However, in terms of operational purpose, they are not necessarily mutually-exclusive or unchanged over time since in our discussion they have been treated as ideal-types that constitute our framework of cooperative strategy.

Third, we have analysed countertrade arrangements and offsets in detail to illustrate the effectiveness of hostage-based exchange, and argue that the persistence of international countertrade in emerging markets can be understood as an organizational response to contractual uncertainty and institutional deficiency in transaction governance rather than foreign exchange shortage. Schelling's (1960) analysis of cooperative strategy under uncertainty is highly applicable to international business transactions involving emerging economies, in that the creation of mutual commitments through hostage exchange can help overcome the weaknesses of implicit trust, reputation or ethics in very uncertain and unpredictable environments. However, the business environments in emerging countries may vary considerably in terms of culture and politics. The countries can be categorized into different stages of emergence according to their relative economic, institutional and organizational development. Therefore, future research on this topic requires a further elaboration of key concepts, and empirical works to test the similarities and differences among emerging business systems, for example between Asia and Eastern Europe (Child and Markoczy, 1993).

16 Segmenting the Market: An 'Old' Approach that Holds 'New' Promise for the FDI-Attraction Process in Developing Countries

Edward Coyne

INTRODUCTION

Research published to date on the issue of investment attraction conditions, policies and practices required or expected of those developing countries wishing to attract foreign direct investment (FDI) has arrived at contradictory conclusions and recommendations. There seems to be little accepted wisdom or consensus surrounding the key issue – the priorities of the *investor* when assessing potential investment locations. Nor is there agreement as to which policies and incentives, if any, are the more helpful to developing countries. Developing countries, especially small developing countries with limited resources to expend on investment-attraction programmes, may be spending their scarce funds inefficiently. With recommendations to developing countries potentially being based on overly aggregated research data, the result may be that these countries may be overpaying to attract some investors, while missing other investors by not providing sufficient enticement (and forcing multinational corporations, or MNCs, into second-best economic alternatives). Moreover, incentives given to those MNCs who would have invested anyway represent a squandering of assets by the provider and windfall profits to the receiver. Valued incentives withheld, or onerous restrictions applied to specific investor groups can represent missed opportunities for the overly-cautious provider and force second-best locations on the would-be recipient.

This study contributes to the debate regarding the effectiveness of investment incentives by analysing distinct categories of FDI. It presents a model for segmenting FDI into discrete units associated with groups of investing corporations possessing relatively homogeneous attributes. A survey was conducted to test this model by analysing the location preferences of MNCs investing in Barbados, Jamaica, and Trinidad and

Tobago. By segmenting inward FDI to these countries in terms of investment timing, strategic objectives and investment size, this survey reveals some significant variations in the investment incentives preferred by discrete groups of corporations. Thus, the research model proposed can be used to develop an appropriate database so that investment-attraction codes can be articulated which target identified investment types.

AIMS AND OBJECTIVES

The study reported here is an attempt to respond to the growing call for research that distinguishes between different types of FDI in terms of its timing (initial investment), its strategic objectives (motivation), and its size (quantum). The objective of this study was to construct a framework to search for discrete sub-sets of FDI investors possessing relatively homogeneous attributes and investment preferences. The segmental analysis model used in this study provides evidence that homogenous groups of investors (or micro-groups) can be identified. Once identified, the variation in the importance attached to individual elements of a host country's investment-attraction package (IAP) by such micro-groups can be studied and addressed – to the benefit of the host developing country itself, the investing multinational corporation, or both.

An analysis of the strength of reaction of investor micro-groups to the various elements of a country's investment-attraction package was carried out by subdividing this package into those elements in which the government exercised direct control of the element, and those elements wherein the government's ability to directly effect a desired change was more indirect, or virtually non-existent. The objective of this further segmentation of MNC preferences was to attempt a constructive contribution to the ongoing debate on the effectiveness, if any, of investment incentives.

ATTRACTION OF FOREIGN INVESTMENT

Governments and international lending institutions are likely to fashion their actions and recommendations to developing countries regarding their policy towards attracting inward FDI based upon the best available evidence as supplied by researchers in the field. Research into what attracts MNCs to invest in developing countries appears to have followed a discernible path that broadly corresponds to the predominant thrust of FDI being experienced during the period of the research effort. For example, from the mid-1960s through the mid-1980s research seems to have focused on the overpowering strategic motivation of the times – host-country market opportunities and the effective mechanisms and conditions for attracting MNCs so motivated. Other strategic motivations for FDI, if mentioned at all, were treated as an aside.

In the main, the research analysed data that effectively treated all FDI as being monolithic and motivated by market-oriented concerns. Researchers such as Aharoni (1966), Usher (1977), Shaw and Toye (1978), Lim (1983), Rolfe and White (1992), among others, concluded that investment incentives have little impact on the location of FDI. These researchers generally take the view that incentives are unnecessary, since the key attractors of a potential host country are such things as its market size and political stability. Others, like Rueber *et al.* (1973); Root and Ahmed (1978), and the Group of Thirty (1984) also agree that market size, gross national product (GNP) and stability factors are probably more important than investment incentives. Still others, including Cable and Persaud (1987), partially agree but express an unwillingness to write off the value of incentives. Evans and Doupnik (1986) assert that profit repatriation has the highest priority, regardless of investment incentives.

Strategic Motivation

Since the late 1980s, there has been a rapid rise in FDI motivated by cost-reduction (frequently referred to as export-oriented FDI), and this was duly discussed in the academic literature. Brewer (1993) has observed that the distinction between market and cost-reduction motives for investing has been largely overlooked in the internationalization literature. He advocates that the distinction becomes important in analysing the effects of government policies on FDI because 'government subsidies and restrictions that effect market imperfections and FDI flows vary according to the strategic nature of the FDI projects'. Empirical research findings on this issue did not begin to be available until the early 1990s (for example, Woodward and Rolfe, 1993; Kumar, 1994).

The task of segmenting FDI by its strategic motivation becomes more important when read in the context of Beamish *et al.* (1991) and Miller (1993), who predicted that fewer and fewer foreign investments would be motivated by market-seeking behaviour. Miller, in particular, notes that the current strategic interests of investing firms is to build plants whose output will be internationally competitive in cost and quality.

Timing

Original investment and expansion investment are likely to respond to different incentives. Guisinger (1985), Wells (1986), Contractor (1991) and Woodward and Rolfe (1993) point out that the effectiveness of incentives may depend upon the specific investor's circumstances. For example, they draw particular attention to the probable positive benefits of incentives in export-oriented investments. They highlight the potential that MNCs making expansion investments may have differing reactions to the various elements of a host country's investment-attraction package than those making initial investments. Although the different investment-attraction requirements of initial investment and expansion investment have received attention from researchers, evidence of empirical study of either investment-timing group is rare. Most researchers appear to aggregate these distinct categories of investment in their analyses.

Size

In 1993, Rolfe *et al.* reported introductory work on the role of investment size in their study of the preferred FDI incentives of US firms with operations in the Caribbean region. Their analysis shows size to be an important variable. For example, they conclude that small firms place more emphasis on the relaxation of restrictions on dividends and on intercompany payments, while larger firms place more emphasis in the areas of capital gains, tax and subsidies. These results show the need for greater effort to incorporate the specific situation of an investing MNC in an appraisal of the effectiveness of incentives on inward investment activity.

MODEL FOR SEGMENTING FDI ATTRACTION PREFERENCES OF MNCS

This study uses a framework for identifying discrete sub-sets of FDI investors with relatively homogeneous attributes and investment preferences. Once identified, the varying importance that such discrete micro-groups attach to individual elements of an investment-attraction package can be studied and addressed. The model used in this study to analyse MNCs preferences for host-country incentives and disincentives relies on two critical theories. The first is Williamson's (1986) transaction-costs theory, which assigns a key role to three capital risk elements; namely non-trivial investment, the redeployability of assets and the transaction-specificity of assets. The second theoretical approach is that of Buckley (1989), who categorizes the firm's strategic motivations for FDI as the search for (host) markets, for raw materials or for cost reductions (including export-oriented markets).

The model presented here assumes that governance-concerns interact continually with the firm's strategic motivation for investment, and that the decision tree is actualized by reference to specific location candidates, which, in turn, produces a specific 'make or buy' decision. When

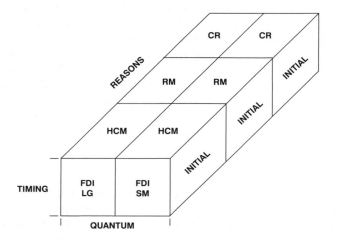

Figure 16.1   FDI attraction: initial framework

Notes:
CR = cost reduction; RM = raw materials; HCM = host-country market;
LG = large-scale; SM = small-scale.

the 'make' decision involves the ownership and control of facilities in another country, FDI occurs. The specific reference points of our model were formed by the intersections of non-trivial (or quantum) investment along one axis, and the elements of the strategic motivation for FDI – that is, host-country market (HCM), raw materials (RM) and cost reduction (CR) – along the other axis (see Figure 16.1). The capital-risk element of 'quantum' was employed as a single surrogate for the three transaction-cost capital-risk elements. Quantum was further sub-divided into 'large' and 'small' to indicate the relative size of investment. These reference points are set in the *single* investment-timing plane of our model represented by the MNC's *initial* investment into the focus host countries. This is because investors must be attracted into the host country for an initial investment before an expansion opportunity exists.

SURVEY OF MNC INVESTMENT PREFERENCES

To test our segmented analysis model, a survey was undertaken of MNCs investing in three Caribbean countries. The focus countries were selected and the survey instrument designed to facilitate a realistic study of the factors that influence corporate investment decisions. Statistical analysis of the survey results yielded useful information for the development of effective investment incentives.

Focus Countries

As the ability to attract foreign investment is especially critical for small developing countries, this study focused on three English-speaking Caribbean countries: Barbados, Jamaica, and Trinidad and Tobago. The World Bank (1992) classifies Barbados and Trinidad and Tobago as upper-middle income countries (with a GNP per capita of between $2466 and $7619), while Jamaica is classified as lower-middle income (between $611 and $2465). Each of these independent island-states of the Caribbean are relatively stable politically, have good telecommunications infrastructures, are open democratic societies, and have high levels of education and literacy. Thus, despite their small populations (264 000 for Barbados; 1 265 000 for Trinidad and Tobago; and 2 469 000 for Jamaica), they each potentially represent attractive investment opportunities for MNCs. By any standard, though, even the largest is considered small among the potential markets of the world. All three host countries present small economies with a limited range of export alternatives and a large diversity of import requirements.

Survey Instrument

The survey instrument was designed to provide: (i) the information required to place the subsidiary firm on the analytical model grid (see Fig. 16.1); and (ii) the relative preference and strength of preference of the parent corporation for each element of the investment-attraction package of the three focus countries.

The investment-attraction package constitutes that compendium of incentives and disincentives presented by a host country to potential foreign direct investors. The potential components of this package listed in the survey instrument were derived from the following works: the draft of a proposed 1992 'The World Bank Direct Investment Survey', which sought information on investment levels as well as the reaction of investors to host-country conditions; Guisinger's (1985) study, which provided an extensive listing of incentives and disincentives, together with an estimate of their effect on after-tax MNC returns; Contractor's (1990) categorization of FDI policy changes (into seven principle attributes); Bradberry's (1986) listing of incentives and disincentives and the motivation for investment; and, finally, Wallace's (1990) survey of the critical conditions faced by direct investors in developing countries. Our survey instrument identified 49 specific elements that potentially can comprise an investment-attraction package. They include provisions established by developing countries for the purpose of affecting FDI within their borders, or represent some of the more common services or conditions which can exist within developing countries and which may affect FDI within their borders.

The survey divided these elements of an investment-attraction package into two groups (see Table 16.1). The direct control group contained 28 elements over which the government can exercise direct control, either by imposing restrictions or by offering incentives. Restrictions (that is, laws and regulations whose application tends to limit FDI) were examined in the 'financial' and 'investment and ownership' areas, while incentives (that is, laws and regulations generally regarded as favourable to FDI) were examined in the 'taxes and subsidies' area.

For the 21 elements included in the indirect-control group, government capability for control is either indirect or non-existent. These indirect-control items covered the economic, legal, political, labour, infrastructure and administrative conditions in the subject countries. For these six indirect-control areas, firms were asked to rate the potential effect on the location-decision should the listed items be deemed uncompetitive with those of other developing countries. Table 16.1 shows the specific groups, classifications and elements included in the survey.

Survey Sample

The survey sample included all US and UK firms believed to have undertaken foreign direct investment in Barbados, Jamaica, and/or Trinidad and Tobago. This primary research measured the reactions of MNCs to the elements presumed to be of potential importance to the firms in making FDI location decisions. The surveyed firms were asked to rank each element of the investment-attraction package both relatively, within classification, and absolutely, in terms of its overall location-decision effect. The survey instrument was sent to the chief executive officer of the parent corporation, on the assumption that the occupant of this position would either have final decision responsibility or be the key location-advocate in any required board of director action.

A total of 72 useable questionnaires were returned, giving a raw response rate of 32 per cent. The valid mailing-adjusted response rate is estimated at 40 per cent (45 per cent for US firms and 27 per cent for UK firms). Most (81 per cent) of the survey respondents were corporate officers, whose approval and recommendations are likely to have been required for a corporate 'go-ahead' decision.

Study Assumptions and Limitations

According to Grubert and Mutti (1991), 'Economic theory suggests that a multinational corporation will allocate capital internationally so that its risk-adjusted marginal after-tax rate is equal across all alternatives'. An assumption of this study is that individual MNCs have investment parameters for judging the comparative desirability of potential FDI

Table 16.1 Investment attraction package: classification and elements

Direct government control	Indirect or no government control
Financial restrictions	*Economic conditions*
Mandated minimum exports	Exchange rate fluctuation
Foreign exchange controls	Inflation growth rate and trends
Capital repatriation limitations	GDP growth rate
Foreign personnel and input limits	Level of tariffs and/or quotas
Profit repatriation limitations	
Mandated local R&D minimums	*Legal conditions*
Mandated local content minimums	Expropriation guarantees
Dividend repatriation/utilization	Host country dispute resolution
Foreign exchange balancing	required
required	Clarity/simplicity of laws and
Financing from abroad required	procedures
Investment and ownership restrictions	*Political considerations*
Equity ownership limitations	Political leadership turnover
Diversification/expansion restricted	Political stability of country
profit	Potential for civil disturbance
Reinvestment restrictions	
Divestiture of ownership required	*Labour conditions*
Appointments to board restricted	Availability of skilled labour
Certain sectors of economy denied	Education facilities
Intellectual property rights limited	'Hire/fire' restrictions
Right to own land/business premises	Local wage rates
Taxes and subsidies	*Infrastructure*
Accelerated depreciation schedules	Transportation system adequacy
Subsidies (including below market	Telecommunications facilities
loans)	Electricity reliability
Low corporate income tax	
Protection against imports	*Administration conditions*
Low rent 'free trade zone' facilities	FDI screening procedures
Government tender preferences	Investment 'red tape'
Withholding tax	Public safety provisions
Tax holidays	Integrity of officials and level of
Capital grants	corruption
Duty free importation of inputs	Effectiveness of host-country
	administration

locations, and that these parameters are applied in a reasonably uniform manner across potential host countries. The study also assumes that the investment-attraction preferences of MNCs domiciled in the US and the UK are essentially similar, and that the response of US MNCs investing in one of the subject countries is not significantly different from the response of US MNCs to the other two countries. Since the study population is vital to the confidence level to be placed in the various statistical techniques utilized in the study, tests to confirm the validity of these assumptions were performed.

Table 16.2   Summary of findings

Research hypothesis	Direct control group		Indirect-control group	
	Support for hypothesis	No support for hypothesis	Support for hypothesis	No support for hypothesis
1 Motivation for FDI				
1A Host-country market-seeking (HCM) vs raw-materials seeking (RM)	X			X
1B Host-country market-seeking vs cost-reduction seeking (CR)	X			X
1C raw-materials seeking vs cost-reduction seeking	X			X
2 FDI quantum and motivation				
2A Total survey (large and small)		X		X
2B Host-country market size (large vs small)		X		X
2C Cost reduction (large vs small)	X		X	
2E Small quantum (HCM vs CR)	X		X	
2F Large quantum (HCM vs CR)	X		X	

Hypotheses and Test Criteria

Hypothesis 1 proposes that the investment-attraction packages preferred by MNCs making their initial investment in the specified countries will *differ* depending upon the MNC's strategic *motivation* for undertaking the investment. To test this hypothesis, we first grouped together those MNCs that indicated the same strategic motivation for entry – market, raw materials or cost-reduction – according to FDI motivation theory. This hypothesis was then tested in three sub-parts (A, B and C), each of which tested two of the motivations for statistically-significant differences in their reaction to elements of the investment-attraction process (see Table 16.2).

Hypothesis 2 proposes that the investment-attraction packages preferred by MNCs making their initial investment in the specified countries will *differ* depending upon the size (or quantum) of MNC investment undertaken – both *within* the same motivation and *between* motivations. Hypothesis 2 utilizes the full transaction-cost/strategic motivation framework for segmenting the reaction of MNCs to the elements of the investment-attraction package. This is accomplished by dividing into micro-groups those MNCs holding the same quantum level of investment and the same motivation for investment. Sub-parts A, B, C, E and F of hypothesis 2 each test two of these micro-groups. Sub-part D was not tested as there were insufficient responses from small-quantum investors with a raw-materials motive for investment.

Null hypotheses were formulated for hypothesis 1, hypothesis 2, and their sub-parts. Statistical tests of significance at the .05 level were conducted to test these null hypotheses. These tests included *t*-tests, Anova procedures and Duncan's multiple range tests. Since the investment-attraction package itself is a collection of 49 elements, each divided into nine classifications, which themselves were split into two groups, the determination of significant differences in each classification and group is more a matter of judgement than of science. Effort was made to present findings that have a substantive as well as a technical foundation.

FINDINGS AND INTERPRETATIONS

A finding concerning the null hypothesis was made under each of the nine broad classifications making up the investment-attraction package. These classifications were then brought together under the two groupings; the direct-control group and the indirect-control group. As stated before, the distinguishing characteristic separating these two groups is the host-country government's unilateral ability to successfully take action to achieve a change in an element of the package that it desires to change.

FDI Motivation and MNC Preferences

For hypothesis 1, the findings for the direct-control group was one of rejection of the null hypothesis, supporting the hypothesis that MNCs with different motivations for FDI (host market, raw materials and cost-reduction-seeking) also have significantly different preferences regarding the various financial performance-effecting elements of the host country's investment-attraction package. Guisinger (1985), Contractor (1991), and Cable and Persaud (1987), speculate that firms in export-oriented industries, for example, probably attach greater importance to legislation affecting financial performance than do investors seeking access to host-country markets. Thus, for the direct-control group, acceptance of the research hypothesis confirms in practice the speculation of these researchers.

The findings for the indirect-control group, however, led to acceptance of the null hypothesis, indicating that different motivations for FDI do not influence the MNC's preference for those elements of the host country's investment-attraction package that are less related to financial performance (see Table 16.2). The indirect-control group is a collection of elements that focus on conditions existing within a prospective host country. Root and Ahmed (1978), the Group of Thirty (1984) and Lim (1983) suggest that it is country conditions such as change (and the direction of change) in factors such as GNP, inflation and market size that determine where MNCs locate their FDI. For the indirect control group, this study confirms the implications of that prior research that MNCs emphasize host-country conditions regardless of their strategic motivation.

The delineation of the findings of this study into direct-control and indirect-control groups may also help to explain the inconsistent findings of prior researchers. The 'split decision' regarding the significance of strategic motivations in evaluating investment-attraction packages demonstrates the dangers inherent in generalizations based on observations of amalgamations of similar yet distinctly different entities. This reinforces Contractor's (1991) caution concerning the appropriateness of general statements regarding the effectiveness of FDI policies.

Although Williamson (1986), Brewer (1987) and Woodward and Rolfe (1993), among others, have advocated that the raw materials-seeking motive for investment should be considered as being included in the strategic category of cost-reduction, the data in the present study finding points to significant differences between raw material-seeking and cost-reduction/export-oriented investors regarding their preferences towards elements of an investment-attraction package.

Quantum and FDI Motivation

As with hypothesis 1, findings were made separately for both the direct-control and the indirect-control groups. However, in the case of the hypothesis 2 'micro-groups', the independently evaluated direct and indirect-control groups showed the same results for each (see Figure 16.2). The evidence tends to support an overall finding that the size (or *quantum*) of an investment influences the MNC's preferences for elements of a country's investment attraction package under two circumstances: (i) when the *motivation* for investing differs (that is, either host-country market or cost-reduction seeking), and (b) when the *motivation* for the investment is *cost-reduction seeking*.

Specific Preferences

Table 16.2 reveals no consistent pattern in the findings regarding the MNC's preference for elements of the investment attraction package in terms of the quantum of investment made and the motivation for investment. It is in the inconsistency itself wherein the significance of 'micro-groups' (with homogeneous attributes and investment-attraction preferences) can be found. Examination of the results for the sub-hypotheses appears to confirm a key premise of this study; that the segmentation of investor parameters along the lines suggested by transactions-cost theory and MNC strategic motivations for conducting FDI

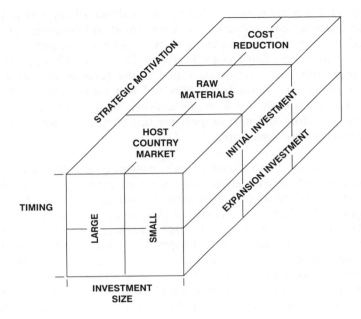

Figure 16.2   FDI attraction: segmented analysis

can lead to the identification of micro-groups possessing homogeneous attributes and unique investment attraction preferences. Considering these specific preferences in turn:

Protected markets. Whereas Rueber *et al.* (1973) considered a protected market of major importance for market development projects, host-country market-seeking MNCs ranked this factor quite low in the present study.

Tax holidays. Guisinger (1985), Helleiner (1973), Bond and Samuelson (1986), Wells (1986), and Rolfe and White (1992) reported tax holidays to be important to export-oriented investors. The testing, in hypothesis 1, of undifferentiated host-country market-seeking and cost-reduction-seeking motivations found no greater preference for tax holidays among export-oriented investors. In the micro-groups of hypothesis 2, tax holidays were held in higher regard by the 'initial investor, cost-reduction seeking, small' group, but in lower regard by the 'initial investor, cost-reduction seeking, large' group.

Subsidies. The study offers no support for the finding in Rolfe *et al.* (1993) that export-oriented firms making initial investments place high value on cash grants and subsidies.

Foreign exchange restrictions. There is no evidence of support in the 'initial investment, cost-reduction seeking, small' micro-group that profit repatriation and foreign exchange restrictions is of the highest concern, as found by Evans and Doupnik (1986). However, this concern is evident in *all* other micro-groups. Stated in the reverse, the survey found weak support for Contractor (1990) and Rolfe and White (1991), that profit repatriation is not a major concern with 'small, cost-reduction seeking' investors and non-support for this contention with 'large, cost-reduction seeking' investors.

Taxes and wages. In this study, small investors, both host-country market-seeking *and* cost-reduction seeking, are attracted by low income taxes, low wage levels and fiscal and financial incentives. Shaw and Toye (1978), Lim (1983), Rueber (1973), Root and Ahmed (1978), the Group of Thirty (1984), and Cable and Persaud (1987) characterized these elements as being relatively unimportant and support is found in this study for that contention with the other micro-groups. Although their sample population was heavily weighted towards expansion investors and quantum was unreported in a form segmented for motivation, Rolfe *et al.* (1993) reported that small firms placed emphasis on the relaxation of restrictions on dividends and on intercompany payments. On the other hand, these researchers found that larger firms placed more emphasis in the capital grants, tax and subsidy areas. The present study provides no support for these conclusions among small, host-country market-seeking investors and contrasting findings among small, cost-reducing investors. When strategic motivations are aggregated, however, the present study generally *supports* the Rolfe *et al.* (1993) findings.

Duty-free concessions. Rolfe *et al.* (1993) found the duty-free concession to be more highly prized by export-oriented investors than by host-country market-seeking investors. This study strongly supports this conclusion for the 'initial, cost-reduction seeking, small' micro-group, but, equally as well among the 'initial, host-country market-seeking' sub-groups (both 'large' and 'small') and the 'initial, cost-reduction seeking, large' sub-group.

Major MNC Concerns

This study revealed significant variation in preferences for elements of the investment-attraction package between different sub-groups of potential investors (see Table 16.3).

The table lists by group the most important initial-investment preferences of MNCs in Barbados, Jamaica, and Trinidad and Tobago. Survey respondents ranked these items highest on the absolute importance scale.

Table 16.3 Most important preferences of MNCs

	Investment incentives	
Micro-group	Direct control	Indirect control
Host-Country Market-Seeking Small Investors	• Profit repatriation • Dividend repatriation • Capital repatriation • Foreign exchange controls • Equity limits • Profit reinvest limits • Divest ownership required • Income tax – low	• Civil disturbance • Country stability • Law clarity
Host-Country Market-Seeking Large Investors	• Profit repatriation • Foreign exchange control • Dividend repatriation • Capital repatriation • Equity limits • Profit reinvest limits • Divest ownership required • Expand/diversify limits • Ownership of land and buildings limited	• Country stability • Civil disturbance • Integrity of officials • Law clarity • Expropriation protection • Skills available
Raw-Materials Seeking Investors	• Profit repatriation • Dividend repatriation • Intellectual property (IP) protection	• Country stability • Integrity of officials • Transportation system
Cost-Reduction Seeking Small Investors	• Duty-free import	• Tariff levels • Clarity of laws • Country stability • Civil disturbance • Wage levels • Electricity reliability
Cost-Reduction Large Investors	• Profit repatriation • Capital repatriation • Foreign exchange control • Dividend repatriation • Foreign personnel • Equity limits • Board appointments limited • Divest ownership required • Ownership of land and buildings limited • IP protection	• Civil disturbance • Telecommunications facilities • Foreign exchange fluctuations • Tariff levels • Transport system

Table 16.3 summarizes the means of responses, segmented by quantum of investment and strategic motivation, as calculated from the returns of surveyed MNCs in these countries. Even casual inspection reveals the differing priorities of various segments of investors. Although the differences in findings could be attributed to the uniqueness of the subject countries, the uniqueness of the responding MNCS, or other uniqueness that could tend to invalidate the results, the more likely explanation for differences in the findings of this study from those of prior researchers is that similar questions were addressed to dissimilar audiences. While the questions put to the respondents appear broadly similar to those of prior studies, the harmony with prior researchers began to dissolve as the responses were segmented into micro-groups of unique and homogeneous identity.

CONCLUSIONS

At the very least, the evidence from this and other studies suggests that FDI investors constitute a *market* for host countries seeking to attract FDI, while host countries offer a *'product'* to this market. Identifiable market niches for FDI investors do exist, and these market niches have *unique* needs to be met by host countries. In particular, the logic behind the speculations of Guisinger (1985), Evans and Doupnik (1986), Cable and Persaud (1987) and Contractor (1990), among others, seems overpowering – that expansion investment and initial investment are likely to require *different* investment-attraction approaches on the part of host-country policy-makers.

Figure 16.2 sets forth a proposed new model that categorizes FDI investors by their strategic motivation (host market, raw materials and cost-reduction seeking motives), the quantum of investment (large or small), and the investment timing (initial or expansion). It is suggested that acquisition-investment be treated in accordance with the MNC's country-investment timing: initial investment *or* expansion investment. Should further research reveal that acquisition-investment nets a significantly different set of needs and/or tax effects for the MNC, then the model can be modified to add this dimension.

Segmenting MNCs into relatively homogeneous and discrete microgroups reveals that the preferences of MNCs towards the various elements making up the investment-attraction packages of host countries are not uniform. This study demonstrates that these preferences depend upon the specific reason (the strategic motivation) for the investment, the scale of investment undertaken by the MNC, and the timing of the investment. Additional factors suggesting potential differences among investors, such as industry groupings, could also be considered for inclusion in the segmentation. However, care needs to be given to the potential for excessive fragmentation of sample size, especially in developing countries.

Knowledge of the differing needs and preferences of unique microgroups of investors may permit host-country authorities to target specific groups of MNCs whose unmet needs have been masked by their inclusion in larger groups of investors. Developing countries, especially the small economy, poorly-endowed countries, need to be sure that they retain the MNCs they have, expand the activities of these firms where they can, and seek both large and small investments of market-seekers, cost-reducers, and natural-resource consumers. The segregation of potential investors into reasonably homogeneous groups can lead to a closer 'up-front' approximation of fitting the needs of the individual investor into a framework of 'equal particulars/equal treatment' or 'like things for like projects'. Such a policy does not eliminate the need for bargaining on a case-to-case basis to 'fine tune the fit', but it can reduce the scope of such bargaining, which leads to the benefit of increased transparency.

Among other things, transparency would improve the likelihood that interested developing countries would be included in the potential candidate-group surviving the investing MNC's first-cut scanning process. Towards this end, developing countries may wish to consider the establishment of articulated investment-attraction codes. Specifically targetted incentives, regulations and laws could be fashioned for specific groups of investors possessing homogeneous attributes, and which display unique sets of needs and bring unique sets of benefits and costs. Such targetting potentially represents more effective use of resources – with the beneficiaries being the host country, investing MNCs or both.

17 Cultural Compatibility in International Acquisitions

Richard Schoenberg

INTRODUCTION

Recent years have seen a marked increase in international acquisition activity (Hamill and Castledine, 1996) as firms pursue a simultaneous strategy of business consolidation and geographical diversification (Taggart and McDermott, 1993). Indeed, cross-border acquisitions by UK firms have shown a rising trend over the past five years in terms of both numbers and values (see Figure 17.1). In 1996, Corporate UK invested £35 billion in such deals, accounting for over half of our total acquisition activity (data source: *Acquisitions Monthly*).

Yet, empirical studies continue to highlight the low success rates associated with such acquisitions. Recent research reveals that 43 per cent of international acquisitions fail to produce a financial return in excess of the acquirer's cost of capital (Bleeke and Ernst, 1993), and 45 per cent fail to meet their initial strategic objectives (Rostand, 1994). Disturbingly, these figures show only a marginal improvement over Kitching's 1974 study which found that 46 to 50 per cent of European acquisitions were considered failures or not worth repeating by acquiring managements.

There has been a considerable volume of literature published on acquisitions in both the academic and practitioner media, three main bodies of such literature can be identified that discuss the determinants of acquisition performance. The 'Strategic Fit' literature focuses on the link between performance and the strategic attributes of the combining firms, in particular the extent to which a target company's business should be related to that of the acquirer. While no consensus emerges as to the importance of relatedness and relative size between bidder and target (Kusewitt, 1985; Chatterjee, 1986; Lubatkin, 1987; Singh and Montgomery, 1987; Seth, 1990; Nayyar, 1992), this body of literature does identify a set of generic criteria for value-creation based on the transfer of strategic capabilities (Porter, 1987; Dixon and Wright, 1990).

The 'Process' literature focuses on the important role that the choice of acquisition process itself can play. These scholars highlight that

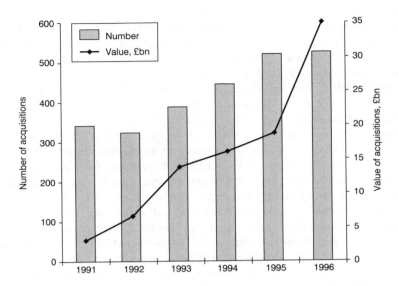

Figure 17.1 International acquisitions made by UK companies, 1991–96

Source: *Acquisitions Monthly*.

inappropriate decision-making, negotiation and integration processes can impede adequate consideration of strategic fit and organizational-fit issues and so lead to inferior acquisition outcomes (Jemison and Sitkin, 1986; Hunt, 1990; Haspeslagh and Jemison, 1991). A key contribution of this approach has been the contingent frameworks for the form of post-acquisition integration that take into account both the strategic and organizational requirements of a particular acquisition (Shrivastava, 1986; Haspeslagh and Jemison, 1991).

The 'Organizational Fit' acquisitions literature attempts to understand how the organizational and human resource aspects of an acquisition influence the subsequent performance of the union. This literature stream has diverse origins in the human resource, organizational behaviour and strategic management disciplines that in combination provide both theoretical and empirical perspectives on the factors influencing organizational and cultural compatibility (Buono and Bowditch, 1989; Napier, 1989; Schweiger and Walsh, 1990; Cartwright and Cooper, 1992).

The 1990s have seen a growing practitioner focus on the latter issue. Many column inches have appeared in the recent financial press which argue that acquiring across borders can bring clashes of different management styles, philosophies and ways of dealing with customers. For example, the *Financial Times* (29 October 1994) highlights the cultural challenge that the 'traditional, risk-averse, and consensus-minded' Deutsche Bank has taken on in its acquisition of the 'innovative and freewheeling' Morgan Grenfell. Similarly, the declining performance of the Metal Box-Carnaud merger was attributed to conflicts between the autocratic management style of the French and the more participative orientation of the British (*Financial Times*, 12 September 1991). Management consultants, too, caution of the cultural risks. Ernst & Young (1996) identify cultural differences as a primary cause of the higher perceived risk that European acquirers associate with cross-border acquisitions. Coopers and Lybrand (1993) report that differences in management attitudes are a significant cause of failure in 85 per cent of unsuccessful UK acquisitions.

Against this background, this chapter presents a critical review of the prior cultural-compatibility research. How much do we really know about the determinants and consequences of cultural compatibility in international acquisitions? The chapter is presented in three sections. First, the theoretical models and empirical lessons available from the literature on organizational cultural compatibility are reviewed. The next section addresses the relatively limited number of empirical studies that have investigated the influence of national culture compatibility in cross-border acquisitions. Finally, the results from these two literature streams are integrated to provide conclusions relevant to both practitioners and future researchers.

COMPATIBILITY OF ORGANIZATIONAL CULTURES

Compatibility of Organizational Cultures: Theoretical Studies

Culture has been defined as 'the beliefs and assumptions shared by members of an organization' (Nahavandi and Malekzadeh, 1988, p. 80) and 'the collective programming of the mind which distinguishes the members of one group or category of people from another' (Hofstede, 1991, p. 5). Organizational culture has been shown to be an important determinant of organizational behaviour (Handy, 1985), and a strong and coherent culture has been linked to superior performance (Peters and Waterman, 1982; Deal and Kennedy, 1982). Given that an acquisition involves the coming together of two separate organizational cultures, a large part of the Organizational Fit acquisitions literature has been concerned with the issue of cultural compatibility. What factors determine cultural compatibility and how does it affect acquisition outcomes? The former question has been addressed largely by theoreticians, while the latter has been investigated in a variety of empirical studies. The theoretical contributions to this stream are described below, followed by a review of the empirical studies.

Acculturation describes the process by which members from one culture adapt to another culture. Acculturation in acquisitions has been framed in terms of the struggle between human and property rights (Walter, 1985), a force-field analysis between the forces of cultural differentiation and organizational integration (Elsass and Veiga, 1994), and, perhaps most usefully, from an anthropological perspective which identifies four distinct modes of acculturation (Nahavandi and Malekzadeh, 1988, 1994):

- *Assimilation* in which the acquired firm willingly relinquishes its own culture and adopts that of the acquiring firm. Assimilation implies willingness rather than coercion and therefore is associated with low degrees of conflict.
- *Integration* where the basic assumptions and practices of both organizations are accepted and preserved. There is an element of both relative cultural autonomy and the exchange of selected cultural elements.
- *Separation* occurs where the acquired firm wishes to maintain all aspects of its culture in an autonomous manner and rejects the other's culture. The desire to remain separate is likely to cause a relatively high degree of conflict and be difficult to implement.
- *Deculturation* in which members of the acquired company no longer value the culture of their previous organization but do not wish to be assimilated into that of the acquiring firm. In effect, such employees find themselves outcasts and deculturation is associated with the highest levels of conflict and difficulties.

Nahavandi and Malekzadeh (1988) further identify the factors that influence the choice of acculturation mode and postulate an overall model for the acculturation process in acquisitions (see Figure 17.2). They argue that the level of potential post-acquisition conflict, or 'acculturative stress', rises both as a function of the acculturation mode adopted and the degree of congruence between the modes favoured by the merging firms. For the acquired firm, the favoured acculturation mode will depend on their perception of how attractive the acquirer's culture is relative to their own. In the case of the acquiring firm, the acculturation mode will depend on the extent to which cultural diversity is tolerated and accepted within the parent company.

The acquiring firm will also be influenced by its acquisition strategy, in particular the extent to which the acquirer has to impose its culture and practices on the target company in an attempt to achieve operating synergies. In their 1988 paper, Nahavandi and Malekzadeh suggest acquisition relatedness as the best proxy for cultural imposition, although, in the light of the recent work of Haspeslagh and Jemison (1991), the form of integration is likely to describe more accurately the strategic influences on the acculturation mode. This is because the form of

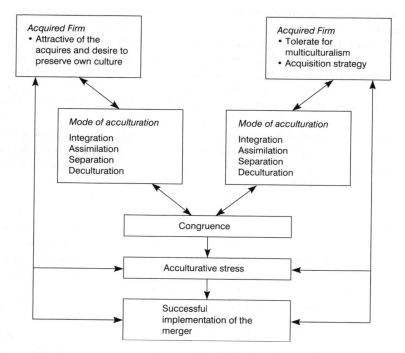

Figure 17.2 Model of acculturation in acquisitions

Adapted from A. Nahavandi and A.R. Malekzadeh, 'Acculturation in mergers and acquisition', *Academy of Management Review*, 13, 79–90, p. 85.
Reproduced by permission of the publisher via Copyright Clearance Center.

integration takes into account not only the degree of strategic interdependence necessary between the firms post-acquisition, but also the degree of organizational autonomy that is to be granted to the target company.

It should be noted also that the acculturation process is a dynamic one and the acculturation mode and level of perceived stress may change over time, for example as a result of familiarization with the other organization's culture and behaviour (Nahavandi and Malekzadeh, 1994). Multiple subcultures may also exist within a single organization, and therefore more than a single mode of acculturation may be operating post-acquisition (Elsass and Veiga, 1994).

Implicit in the model is the link between acculturative stress and conflict behaviour to the eventual acquisition outcome, a link which has received wide empirical support as detailed below. Therefore, the acculturation model provides a useful theoretical framework to understand the factors that influence the overall relationship between cultural differences and acquisition performance.

Compatibility of Organizational Cultures: Empirical Studies

To date there have been four major empirical contributions to the literature on acculturation in domestic acquisitions. Three of these are case-study based, undertaken from a phenomenological perspective (Sales and Mirvis, 1984; Buono and Bowditch, 1989; Cartwright and Cooper, 1992), and one is based on a positivist quantitative survey (Chatterjee *et al.*, 1992).

Sales and Mirvis (1984) provide a detailed exploration of the acculturation process in an agreed acquisition of a medium-sized US manufacturing firm by a large US conglomerate. They detail the clear differences that existed between the philosophies and behaviours of the two companies, and document the miscommunication, misunderstanding and conflict that arose as a result of these cultural differences during the first year. Although no attempt at performance evaluation is made, Sales and Mirvis's description reinforces the acculturation modes identified by Nahavandi and Malekzadeh (1988, 1994), as well as highlighting the dynamic nature of the process. Early actions of 'separation' were seen to give way over a period of three years to 'integration' of management styles and 'assimilation' of reporting and control practices.

Cartwright and Cooper (1992) also lend support to Nahavandi and Malekzadeh's framework. Their study of four UK acquisitions led them to confirm the proposition that culture clashes will be minimized when acquired employees are both willing to abandon their old culture and perceive the acquirer's culture as attractive. Cartwright and Cooper argue that this is achieved where the acquiring company has a culture that gives individuals a similar or greater degree of participation and autonomy than was granted within the acquired company's culture. Employees within the acquired company were seen to display greater commitment to achieving successful post-acquisition integration when they perceived that the acquisition would at least maintain, if not increase, their level of participation and autonomy.

Although Cartwright and Cooper suggest a general applicability of their conclusion, concerns of ethnocentric interpretation can be raised following the warnings of Ajiferuke and Boddewyn (1970). For example, the work of Hofstede (1991) points to the cultural specificity of a desire for greater participation and autonomy: such a desire is consistent with the mental programming of the average UK employee but is not universally applicable across all nations. Care may therefore be required in extending Cartwright and Cooper's findings to cross-national acquisitions, or those outside the UK.

Buono and Bowditch's (1989) longitudinal study of three service industry acquisitions documents the acculturative stress that can occur on the marriage of incompatible organizational cultures. In a bank merger, the planned vision of complete integration was initially reflected in the choice of the new name, locations and systems. However, within a year it had become clear that in reality the values, philosophy and personnel of one partner were dominating the merged organization. This led to significant voluntary resignations from target company employees, and resentment from those that remained, who ultimately adopted 'a series of behaviours that attempted to undermine the merger . . . and presented a significant barrier to successful integration of the firms during the first four years following the merger' (Buono and Bowditch, 1989, p. 183).

Similarly, although to a lesser degree, the acquisition of a fast-food chain by a large conglomerate was seen to lead to negative acculturative stress, despite the fact that the fast-food chain was being positioned as a stand-alone subsidiary within the new organization. The marked difference between the family-business style of the fast-food chain and the systematized high-growth orientation of the conglomerate parent led to feelings of intense pressure and frustration for the senior executives of the acquired firm, as they came to terms with the skills necessary to master the new formal planning systems and procedures. The result was an underachievement of the strategic growth targets set for the new subsidiary along with the planned voluntary exit of its chief executive officer.

These qualitative reports of the negative impact of cultural differences have been confirmed statistically in a data-set of 30 US acquisitions by Chatterjee, *et al.* (1992). These researchers found a strong negative relationship between perceived cultural differences and shareholder gains resulting from the acquisitions. Importantly, and against the prediction of Nahavandi and Malekzadeh's model, the introduction of a measure of the multicultural tolerance of the acquiring firm did not moderate the relationship. Although indicative of the negative impact that cultural differences can have on overall performance, the study is limited by the *ex-ante* nature of the stock price performance variable. Parallels can be drawn with the early relatedness studies in that shareholder expectations of future operating performance, here measured as the abnormal returns over the 15-day period surrounding the acquisition announcement, may not reflect accurately the *ex-post* reality (Nayyar, 1992).

In summary, the empirical studies confirm that differences in organizational culture can lead to acculturative stress which results in negative human resource implications and, in turn, inferior acquisition performance. Empirical support has been forthcoming for Nahavandi and Malekzadeh's (1988, 1994) model of the acculturation process, and in particular for how the impact of cultural differences can be moderated by perceptions of the relative attractiveness of the new culture and by the chosen form of integration strategy.

COMPATIBILITY OF NATIONAL CULTURES

National culture has been defined as the collective programming of the mind which distinguishes members of one nation from another (Hofstede, 1991). In contrast to organizational culture, the mental programmes that make up one's national culture are learned through early socialization with one's family and reinforced during schooling. These 'national' mental programmes reside primarily at the level of values about what is normal versus abnormal (Hofstede, 1991), and define one's basic assumptions concerning relationships with people, time and nature (Trompenaars, 1996).

Hofstede (1980, 1991) and more recently Trompenaars (1993, 1996) have produced classifications of national culture based on extensive survey data, which both define the dimensions embodied by the concept and allow a country's national culture to be operationalized in numerical form.

National culture, at least as defined by Hofstede's dimensions, has been found empirically to influence many aspects of a firm's organization and systems; for example, the success of organizational development interventions (Johnson and Golembiewski, 1992), managers' responses to strategic issues (Schneider and De Meyer, 1991), decision-making styles (Tayeb, 1988), the choice of foreign market entry mode (Kogut and Singh, 1988; Shane, 1994) and reactions to strategic alliance formation (Schoenberg, Denuelle and Norburn, 1995). Given these influences on organizational life and the link between organizational compatibility and acquisition performance reviewed above, several authors from the cultural school have posited that the compatibility of national cultures between firms combining in cross-border acquisitions will be an important determinant of the eventual outcome of the union (Hofstede, 1980, 1991; Smith, 1992; Larsson, 1993; Napier, Schweiger and Kosglow, 1993; Olie, 1994; Hoecklin, 1995).

The cross-national acculturation process is similar to that for the intra-national circumstances (Tung, 1993). Accordingly, and in line with the results of the organizational culture studies, Olie (1994) postulates that the cultural difficulties experienced within a cross-border acquisition will be contingent upon not only the degree of differences in organizational and national cultures, but also the level of integration achieved and the perceived attractiveness of the new identity.

These concepts have been investigated in two major pieces of empirical research to date. The most significant contribution has been made by the team of Calori, Lubatkin and Very based at Groupe ESC Lyon. These researchers collected data from 117 French and British firms that had been acquired by French, British or American companies between 1987 and 1989. The sample design provided for comparative data on cross-border and domestic acquisitions, and captured acquisition performance two to four years post-acquisition using perceptual measures which aggregated earnings, sales and market share variables. Importantly, data was collected from top managers of the *acquired firm*. This raises some concerns regarding the validity of the perceptual performance measure, as the acquired firm managers will not necessarily have been in a position to accurately assess performance relative to the acquisition's original objectives as set by the acquiring firm.

Their work provides two main empirical results. First, in line with Hofstede's (1980, 1991) national-culture dimensions, French acquirers were found to exercise more centralized formal control over the strategy and operations of their acquired businesses (high power-distance and uncertainty-avoidance), while American acquirers relied to a greater extent on informal communication and cooperation (lower uncertainty-avoidance). Further, aspects of these differing control mechanisms were found to correlate with acquisition performance, suggesting that the national culture of the acquirer does have an impact on the outcome of its cross-border acquisitions. Higher performance was associated with acquirers that exhibited high levels of informal personal efforts and imposed a low level of operational control (Calori, Lubatkin and Very, 1994). This result is noteworthy in that it reinforces Cartwright and Cooper's (1992) finding on relative cultural attractiveness, even within a sample that includes France, a high power-distance nation.

The second set of results focused on the level of acculturative stress felt by managers in target companies (Very, Calori, and Lubatkin, 1993; Very, Lubatkin, and Calori, 1996). Cross-border and domestic acquisitions were found to cause different levels of acculturative stress, particularly where expectations differed from reality with regard to 'performance and reward objectiveness' (British targets) and 'personal and societal response' (French targets). Greater levels of acculturative stress along these dimensions were associated with inferior acquisition performance. However, the cross-border acquisitions did not always result in higher acculturative stress than their domestic counterparts. The latter result suggests that national cultural differences may elicit perceptions of attraction as well as stress in acquired firms, although it also raises questions concerning the relative influence of organizational culture differences over national culture differences.

In total, Calori, Lubatkin and Very's work substantiates the influence that national culture can exert on cross-border acquisition performance, in particular through the formative effect it can have on the control mechanisms adopted by an acquirer. However, the researchers also note the complexity surrounding the impact of national culture, concluding that:

cross-national mergers are a complex phenomenon, sometimes influenced by national cultural differences, sometimes by organizational influences, sometimes by both, and sometimes by neither. (Very, Calori, and Lubatkin, 1993, p. 343)

Similar conclusions are reached by Morosini and Singh (1994), who in related work investigate how target-firm national culture influences the success of different post-acquisition integration strategies. In a sample of 65 Italian cross-border acquisitions completed between 1987 and 1992, three classes of post-acquisition strategy were identified: integration, (cf. absorption), independence (cf. preservation) and restructuring (cf. holding/symbiosis). The interaction between the strategy adopted and Hofstede's national culture scores was regressed against changes in acquired firm performance, controlling for relatedness and relative size. The researchers found that the performance of a particular strategy was related to Hofstede's (1980) uncertainty-avoidance score for the target firm; targets in high uncertainty-avoidance nations gave the highest one-year profit-margin increase when an independence strategy was adopted, while integration led to highly favourable results in countries with low uncertainty avoidance (Morosini and Singh, 1994).

Of interest is that no statistically significant results are reported for Hofstede's other three dimensions of national culture, pointing to the particular influence of the uncertainty-avoidance dimension. However, it is also noteworthy that two-year performance measures did not show the same strength of relationship, which suggests that further study is warranted on the time-dependence of any national-culture effect. Finally, some caution may be needed in interpreting these particular results as the performance measure again focused specifically on the acquired firm with the added complication here of accurate disaggregation in the full-integration cases.

The two empirical studies outlined above have confirmed theoretical reasoning that links the relative national cultures of buyers and sellers to the eventual outcome of an international acquisition. Yet, both studies also note strongly in their conclusions that the interaction between national and organizational culture must not be ignored. Indeed, Morosini and Singh (1994) recognize as a limitation their failure to simultaneously take account of the role of organizational culture.

Management style is a central element of a firm's culture (Sales and Mirvis, 1984; Sathe, 1985), which simultaneously reflects the influence of both organizational culture (Sathe, 1983; Sales and Mirvis, 1984) and national culture (Tayeb, 1988; Hofstede, 1991; Smith, 1992). In an extension of the cultural compatibility work on international acquisitions, Schoenberg (1996) found that a composite measure of management-style differences exhibited a statistically-significant negative relationship to acquisition performance in a sample of 124 European cross-border acquisitions. Interestingly, and in contrast to the findings of Morosini and Singh (1994), the negative relationship held regardless of the degree of post-acquisition integration. These results parallel those of a similar study conducted earlier on a sample of domestic US acquisitions (Datta, 1991).

CONCLUSION

Although cultural differences have sometimes been seen as a second-order effect (Haspeslagh and Jemison, 1991), the academic literature reviewed above shows that their impact is both measurable and meaningful: cultural differences, both organizational and national, can lead to marked difficulties in the post-acquisition period which in turn can significantly reduce acquisition performance. This broad conclusion confirms the often cited need for practitioners to make an assessment of cultural compatibility as part of their pre-bid planning and evaluation activities. However, the issue remains as to which particular factors should be the focus of attention in such an assessment. It is here that our present body of knowledge is not so definite. Theoretical models of the acculturation process in acquisitions predict that the underlying determinants of cultural compatibility will be the acquirer's tolerance of multiculturism, the relative attractiveness of the acquirer's culture, and the post-acquisition integration strategy. The actual influence of each of these factors has been tested separately in one or more empirical studies, but with varied results.

The tolerance for multiculturism has been found not to moderate the impact of organizational cultural differences (Chatterjee *et al.*, 1992). This result might be explained as follows. The tolerance for multiculturism can be seen as an individual rather than organizational trait, and an international acquirer frequently will allocate responsibility for the integration of each of its acquisitions to a different manager or set of managers. Thus, there may be wide variations in the tolerance for multiculturism present within any given acquirer, making this a problematical variable to operationalize and use in a predictive mode at the organizational level. In the absence of further research, the implication for practitioners is that, if anything, an assessment should be made of the fit between the individual managers' tolerance for multiculturism and the cultural dynamics of the particular acquisition for which they will be responsible.

The influence of the form of integration has received mixed empirical support. While one study established that the integration approach can moderate the impact of any cultural differences present (Morosini and Singh, 1994), three other studies have concluded that the relationship between cultural differences and acquisition performance is independent of the form of integration (Buono and Bowditch, 1989; Datta, 1991; Schoenberg, 1996). Further research is undoubtedly needed in this area, but the implication for practitioners is that it is dangerous to assume that managing an international acquisition at 'arm's length' (preservation integration) will soften the impact of any cultural differences.

The relative attractiveness of the acquirer's culture is supported as a key determinant of how readily two cultures will merge following acquisition. Superior acquisition performance has been reported in two studies to occur where the bidder's culture endorses a higher level of delegated autonomy and participation relative to that of the target (Cartwright and Cooper, 1992; Calori, Lubatkin and Very, 1994). Other studies point also to the influence of the firms' relative attitudes towards tolerance for ambiguity and informality (Calori, Lubatkin and Very, 1994; Morosini and Singh, 1994). These results suggest that prospective acquirers should focus particularly at their targets' attitudes towards participation and formality.

Unfortunately, the established methodological problems of separating the individual contribution of national and organizational culture within a given firm (Hofstede, 1991; Very, Calori and Lubatkin 1993; Olie, 1994) make it difficult to differentiate whether these attributes are based in the organizational or national cultures of the firms concerned. Certainly, the attributes do correspond to Hofstede's national culture dimensions of Power Distance and Uncertainty Avoidance, which suggests that a generic country effect may play a role in determining cultural compatibility in international acquisitions. However, these two dimensions are closely associated with decision-making routines and choices of organizational structure (Hofstede, 1980) that are open also to the influence of organizational culture, and establishing the size and importance of any purely national effect is likely to prove difficult in practice.

In summary, the research to date points to three statements. Clashes of culture do impact acquisition performance negatively. They are unlikely to be overcome by managing the newly-acquired company as a stand-alone subsidiary. The key cultural dimensions that appear to drive compatibility are participation and formality. That these statements are relatively limited in scope highlights the need for further research on the topic. The paucity of firm conclusions to date on the influence of the form of post-acquisition integration and the exact dimensions of culture that exert a critical influence on eventual performance suggests the potential value of more extensive work in these areas. Future researchers should also continue to investigate the presence of any country-specific patterns within the results of such studies to establish the precise influence of national culture over organizational culture. There is also widespread agreement amongst scholars that studies are required now to investigate the relationship between cultural compatibility and performance under a wider variety of post-acquisition strategies (Chatterjee *et al.*, 1992; Larsson, 1993; Schweiger, 1993; Morosini and Singh, 1994; Olie, 1994). For example, are particular acquisition rationales more susceptible to the impact of cultural differences? Do high rates of executive turnover in the acquired firm post-acquisition have a moderating influence? Continuing research on this important topic will assist future international acquirers to focus on the key dimensions of cultural compatibility and to understand the circumstances under which they are likely to exert a primary influence on ultimate acquisition success.

Bibliography

Adler, N.J. (1983) 'A typology of management studies involving culture', *Journal of International Business Studies*, 29–47.

Adler, N.J. (1986) *International Dimensions of Organisational Behaviour* (Boston, Mass.: Kent Publishing).

Agarwal, S. and S.N. Ramaswami (1992) 'Choice of foreign market entry mode: Impact of ownership, location and internalization factors', *Journal of International Business Studies*, 23(1), 1–27.

Aharoni, Y. (1966) *The Foreign Investment Decision Process* (Boston, Mass.: Harvard University Press).

Ajiferuke, M. and J. Boddewyn (1970) 'Culture and other explanatory variables in comparative management studies', *Academy of Management Journal*, 13, 153–6.

Albert, M. (1991) *Capitalisme Contre Capitalisme* (Paris: Seuil).

Albert, M. (1993) *Capitalism against Capitalism* (London: Whurr).

Albert, M. and R. Gonenc (1996) 'The future of Rhenish capitalism', *Political Quarterly*, 67(3), 184–93.

Aldrich, H.E. and D.A. Whetten (1981) 'Organization-sets, action-sets, and networks: Making the most of simplicity', in P.C. Nystrom and W.H. Starbuck (eds), *Handbook of Organizational Design* (London: Oxford University Press), 385–408.

Alsegg, R.J. (1971) *Control Relationships between American Corporations and their European Subsidiaries* (New York: American Management Association).

Anderson, E. (1990) 'Two firms, one frontier: On assessing joint venture performance', *Sloan Management Review*, 31(2) (Winter), 19–30.

Anderson, E. and A.T. Coughlan (1987) 'International market entry and expansion via independent or integrated channels of distribution', *Journal of Marketing*, 51, January, 71–82.

Anderson, E. and H.A. Gatignon (1986) 'Modes of foreign entry: A transaction cost analysis and propositions', *Journal of International Business Studies*, 17(3), 1–26.

Andersson, U. and M. Forsgren (1996) 'Subsidiary embeddedness and control in the multinational corporation', *International Business Review*, 5(5), 487–508.

Andersson, U. and C. Pahlberg (1997) 'Subsidiary influence on strategic behaviour in MNCs: An empirical study', *International Business Review*, 6(3), 319–334.

Ansoff, H.I. and P. Sullivan (1993) 'Optimizing profitability in turbulent environments: A formula for strategic success', *Long Range Planning*, 26(5), 11–22.

Archibugi, D. and J. Michie (1995) 'The globalisation of technology: A new taxonomy', *Cambridge Journal of Economics*, 19(1), 121–40.

Ariño, A. and J. de la Torre (1996) 'Learning from failure: The evolution of cooperative behavior in inter-firm ventures', paper presented at the AOM 1996 Annual Meeting, Cincinnati.

Arthur, B. (1994) *Increasing Returns and Path Dependency in the Economy* (Michigan: University of Michigan Press).

Ashton, D. and F. Green (1996) *Education, Training and the Global Economy* (London: Edward Elgar).

Aylmer, R.J. (1970) 'Who makes marketing decisions in the multinational firm?', *Journal of Marketing*, October, 25–39.

Badaracco, J.L. (1991) *The Knowledge Link: How Firms Compete Through Strategic Alliances* (Boston, Mass.: Harvard Business School Press).

Baden-Fuller, C.W.F. and J.M. Stopford (1992) *Rejuvenating the Mature Business* (London and New York: Routledge).

Bamber, G.J. and R.D. Lansbury (eds) (1993) *International and Comparative Industrial Relations* (London: Routledge).

Barber, B.R. (1995) *Jihad vs. McWorld* (New York: Times Books).

Barkema, H.G., O. Shenkar, F. Vermeulen and J.H.J. Bell (1997) 'Working abroad, working with others: How firms learn to operate international joint ventures', *Academy of Management Journal*, 40(2), 426–442.

Barney, J.B. and M.H. Hansen (1994) 'Trustworthiness as a source of competitive advantage', *Strategic Management Journal*, 15, 175–90.

Bartlett, C.A. (1981) 'Multilateral structural change: Evolution versus reorganization', in Lars Otterbeck (ed.), *The Management of Headquarters–Subsidiary Relationships in Multinational Corporations* (Aldershot: Gower).

Bartlett, C.A. (1986) 'Building and managing the transnational: The new organizational challenge', in M.E. Porter (ed.), *Competition in Global Industries* (Boston, Mass.: Harvard Business School Press).

Bartlett, C.A. and S. Ghoshal (1987) 'Managing across borders: New strategic requirements', *Sloan Management Review*, Summer, 6–17.

Bartlett, C.A. and S. Ghoshal (1989) *Managing Across Borders: The Transnational Solution* (Boston, Mass.: Harvard Business School Press).

Bartlett, C.A. and S. Ghoshal (1990) 'Matrix management: Not a structure, a frame of mind', *Harvard Business Review*, July–August, 138–47.

Bartlett, C. and S. Ghoshal (1990) 'Managing innovations in the transnational corporation' in C. Bartlett, Y. Doz and G. Hedlund (eds), *Managing the Global Firm* (London: Routledge).

Bartlett, C.A. and S. Ghoshal (1992) 'What is a global manager?', *Harvard Business Review*, 92, 124–32.

Bartlett, C.A. and S. Ghoshal (1993) 'Beyond the M-form: Towards the managerial theory of the firm', *Strategic Management Journal*, 14(1), 23–46.

Bartlett, C.A. and S. Ghoshal (1995) *Transnational Management*, 2nd edn (Richard D. Irwin).

Barzel, Y. (1982) 'Measurement cost and the organisation of markets', *Journal of Law and Economics*, 25, 27–48.

Baumol, W.J. and R.E. Quandt (1964) 'Rules of thumb and optimally imperfect decisions', *American Economic Review*, 54(1), 23–46.

Beale, H. and T. Dugdale (1975) 'Contracts between businessmen: Planning and the use of contractual remedies', *British Journal of Law and Society*, 60, 45–60.

Beamish, P.W. (1985) 'The characteristics of joint ventures in developed and developing countries', *Columbia Journal of World Business*, 20(3), 13–19.

Beamish, P.W. (1987) 'Joint ventures in less developed countries: Partner selection and performance', *Management International Review*, 27(1), 23–37.

Beamish, P.W. (1988) *Multinational Joint Ventures in Developing Countries* (London: Routledge).

Beamish, P.W. and J.C. Banks (1987) 'Equity joint ventures and the theory of the multinational enterprise', *Journal of International Business Studies*, Summer, 1–16.

Beamish, P.W. and A. Inkpen (1995) 'Keeping international joint ventures stable and profitable', *Long Range Planning*, 28(3), 26–36.

Beamish, P.W. and J.P. Killing (1996) 'Introduction to the special issue', *Journal of International Business Studies*, 27(5), iv–xxxi.

Beamish, P.W., J.P. Killing, D.J. Lecraw and H. Crookell (1991) *International Management: Text and Case* (Homewood, Ill.: Irwin).

Beechler, S. and J.Z. Yang (1994) 'The transfer of Japanese-style management to American subsidiaries: Contingencies, constraints, and competencies', *Journal of International Business Studies*, 25, 467–91.

Behrman, J.N. and W.A. Fischer (1980) *Overseas R & D Activities of Transnational Companies* (Cambridge, Mass.: Oelgeschlager, Gunn & Hain).

Bell, M. and K. Pavitt (1994) 'Technological accumulation and industrial growth: Contrasts between developed and developing countries', *Industrial and Corporate Change*, 2, 157–205.

Belsley, D., E. Kuh and R. Welsh (1980) *Regression Diagnostics* (New York, John Wiley).

Ben-Ner, A. and D.C. Jones (1995) 'Employee participation, ownership, and productivity: A theoretical framework', *Industrial Relations*, 34(4), 532–54.

Benito, G.R. and G. Gripsrud (1992) 'The expansion of foreign direct investments: Discrete rational location choices or a cultural learning process?', *Journal of International Business Studies*, 23(3), 461–76.

Berg, S.V., J. Duncan and P. Friedman (1982) *Joint Venture Strategies and Corporate Innovation* (Cambridge, Mass.: Oelgeschlager, Gunn & Hain).

Berger, S. and R. Dore (eds) (1996) *National Diversity and Global Capitalism* (Ithaca, N.Y.: Cornell University Press).

Bernstein, L. (1992) 'Opting out of the legal system: Extralegal contractual relations in the diamond industry', *Journal of Legal Studies*, 21, 115–57.

Best, M. (1990) *The New Competition* (Oxford: Polity Press).

Bettis, R.A. and V. Mahajan (1985) 'Risk/return performance of diversified firms', *Management Science*, 31(7), 785–99.

Bettis, R.A. and W.K. Hall (1982) 'Diversification strategy, accounting determined risk and accounting determined return', *Academy of Management Journal*, 25, 254–64.

Birkinshaw, J.M. (1996) 'How multinational subsidiary mandates are gained and lost', *Journal of International Business Studies*, 27(3), 467–96.

Birkinshaw, J.M. and A.J. Morrison (1995) 'Configurations of strategy and structure in subsidiaries of multinational corporations', *Journal of International Business Studies*, 26(4), 729–54.

Birkinshaw, J.M. and J. Ridderstrale (1996) 'Fighting the corporate immune system: A process study of peripheral initiatives in multinational corporations', in *Innovation and International Business, Proceedings of the European Business Academy*, 1, 105–27.

Blasi, J.R. (1994) *Corporate Governance in Russia*, paper presented to the Joint Conference of the World Bank and the Central European University Privatization Project, 15–16 December 1994, World Bank, Washington DC.

Blasi, J.R. and A. Shleifer (1996) 'Corporate governance in Russia: An initial look', in *Corporate Governance in Central Europe and Russia*, volume 2, *Insiders and the State* (London: Central European University Press), 78–108.

Blasi, J.R. and D.L. Kruse (1992) *The New Owners* (New York: HarperCollins).

Blau, P.M. (1968) 'Social exchange', in D.L. Sills (ed.), *International Encyclopedia of the Social Sciences*, 7, 452–8.

Blaug, M. (1992) *The Methodology of Economics: Or How Economists Explain* (Cambridge: Cambridge University Press) (2nd ed.).

Bleeke, J. and D. Ernst (1993) 'The death of the predator', in J. Bleeke and D. Ernst (eds), *Collaborating to Compete: Using Strategic Alliances and Acquisitions in the Global Marketplace* (New York: John Wiley).

Bleeke, J. and D. Ernst (eds) (1993) *Collaborating to Compete: Using Strategic Alliances and Acquisitions in the Global Marketplace* (New York: John Wiley & Sons).

Blodgett, L.L. (1992) 'Factors in the instability of international joint ventures: An event history analysis', *Strategic Management Journal*, 13(6), 475–81.

Blyton, P. and P. Turnbull (1992) *Reassessing Human Resource Management* (London: Sage).

Boddewyn, J.J. (1988) 'Political aspects of MNE theory', *Journal of International Business Studies*, 19(3), 341–63.

Boddewyn, J.J. and T.L. Brewer (1994) 'International-business political behaviour: New theoretical directions', *Journal of International Business Studies*, 19, 119–43.

Boddewyn, J.J., M.B. Halbrich and A.C. Perry (1984) 'Service multinationals: Conceptualization, measurement and theory', paper presented at the Annual Meeting of the Academy of International Business, Cleveland, Ohio, October.

Boersma, M.F. (1995) 'Managing transferred technology in former Soviet international joint ventures', unpublished masters thesis, Gröningen: University of Gröningen.

Boersma, M.F. and P.N. Ghauri (1997) 'Measuring my corn by your bushel: How trust may be built and sustained in International Joint Ventures', *Proceedings of the 23rd Annual Conference of the European International Business Academy* (Stuttgart: Universität Hohenheim, December), 849–72.

Bond, E.W. and L. Samuelson (1986) 'Tax holidays as signals', *The American Economic Review*, 76(4), 820–6.

Bonin, J.P., D.C. Jones and L. Putterman (1993) 'Theoretical and empirical studies of producer cooperatives – will ever the twain meet', *Journal of Economic Literature*, 31(3), 1290–320.

Bower, J. (1970) *Managing the Resource Allocation Process* (Boston: Harvard Business School Division of Research).

Bowman, E.H. (1980) 'A risk/return paradox for strategic management', *Sloan Management Review*, Spring, 17–31.

Boycko, M., A. Shleifer and R. Vishny (1993) 'Privatizing Russia', *Brookings Papers on Economic Activity*, 2, 139–92.

Boyer, R. and D. Drache (1996) *State against Markets: The Limits of Globalization* (London: Routledge).

Bradberry, W.J. (1986) 'U.S. multinational corporate managers' response to investment incentives and performance requirements', unpublished research dissertation, University of Texas at Dallas.

Bradford, C.I. (1994) *The New Paradigm of Systemic Competitiveness: Toward More Integrated Policies in Latin America* (Paris: OECD).

Brahm, R. (1995) 'National targeting policies, high-technology industries, and excessive competition', *Strategic Management Journal*, 16, 71–91.

Brandt, W.K. and J.M. Hulbert (1976) 'Patterns of communications in the multinational corporation: An empirical study', *Journal of International Business Studies*, 7(1), 56–64.

Brandt, W.K. and J.M. Hulbert (1977) 'Headquarters guidance in marketing strategy in the multinational subsidiary', *Columbia Journal of World Business*, Winter, 7–14.

Braunerhjelm, P. and R. Svensson (1995) *Host Country Characteristics and Agglomeration in Foreign Direct Investment* (Stockholm: Industrial Institute for Economic and Social Research), mimeo.

Breusch, T. and A. Pagan (1979) 'A simple test for heteroscedasticity and random coefficient variation', *Econometrica*, 47, 1287–94.

Brewer, T.L. (1992) 'An issue-area approach to the analysis of MNC-government relations', *Journal of International Business Studies*, 23(2), 295–309.

Brewer, T.L. (1993) 'Government policies, market imperfections, and foreign direct investment', *Journal of International Business Studies*, 24(1), 101–20.

Brooke, M.Z. and P.J. Buckley (1988) *Handbook of International Trade* (London: Macmillan).

Brooke, M.Z. and H. Remmers (1978) *The Strategy of Multinational Enterprise: Organisation and Finance* (2nd ed.) (London: Longman).

Brooke, M.Z. and J.M. Skilbeck (1994) *Licensing: The International Sale of Patents and Technical Knowhow* (Aldershot: Gower).

Buck, T. (1982) *Comparative Industrial Systems* (Oxford: Macmillan).

Buck, T. and B. Chiplin (1983) 'Risk-bearing and self-management', *Kyklos*, 36(2), 270–84.

Buckley, P.J. (1989) *The Multinational Enterprise* (London: Macmillan).

Buckley, P.J. (1990) 'Problems and developments in the core theory of international business', *Journal of International Business Studies*, 21, 657–65.

Buckley, P.J. (1995) *Foreign Direct Investment and Multinational Enterprises* (London: Macmillan).

Buckley, P.J., F. Burton and H. Mirza (1998) 'Introduction', in P.J. Buckley, F. Burton and H. Mirza (eds), *The Strategy and Organization of International Business* (Basingstoke: Macmillan).

Buckley, P.J. and M.C. Casson (1976) *The Future of the Multinational Enterprise* (London: Macmillan).

Buckley, P.J. and M.C. Casson (1981) 'The optimal timing of foreign direct investment', *Economic Journal*, 91, 75–87.

Buckley, P.J. and M.C. Casson (1985) *The Economic Theory of The Multinational Enterprise* (London: Macmillan).

Buckley, P.J. and M.C. Casson (1988) 'A theory of co-operation in international business', in F.J. Contractor and P. Lorange (eds), *Co-operative Strategies in International Business* (Lexington, Mass.: Lexington Books).

Buckley, P.J. and M.C. Casson (1993) 'Economics as an imperialist social science', *Human Relations*, 46, 1035–52.

Buckley, P.J. and M.C. Casson (1996) 'An economic model of IJV strategy', *Journal of International Business*, 27(5), 849–76.

Buckley, P.J. and M. Chapman (1996) 'Economics and social anthropology – reconciling differences', *Human Relations*, 49, 1123–50.

Buckley, P.J. and M. Chapman (1997) 'The measurement and perception of transaction costs', *Cambridge Journal of Economics*, 21, 127–45.

Buckley, P.J., L.J. Clegg and N. Forsans (1998) 'Globalisation, FDI and trade blocs', paper presented at the International Economics Study Group, 23rd Annual Conference on Globalization and Regionalization, 18–20 September 1998, Oxford.

Buckley, P.J. and S. Young (1993) 'The growth of global business: Implications and research agendas for the 1990s', in H. Cox, J. Clegg and G. Ietto-Gilles (eds), *The Growth of Global Business* (London: Routledge).

Buckley, P.J., C.L. Pass and K. Prescott (1992) 'The internationalization of service firms: A comparison with the manufacturing sector', *Scandinavian International Business Review*, 1(1), 39–56.

Buono, A. and J. Bowditch (1989) *The Human Side of Mergers and Acquisitions* (San Francisco: Jossey-Bass).

Burack, E.H. and R.D. Smith (1982) *Personnel Management: A Human Resource System Approach* (New York: Wiley).

Burt, R. and M. Knez (1996) 'Trust and third-party gossip', in R. Kramer and T. Tyler (eds), *Trust in Organisations* (California: Sage).

Burton, F.N. and A.R. Cross (1993) 'A reappraisal of franchising across national boundaries in foreign market entry mode analysis', in M. Levy and D. Grewal (eds), *Developments in Marketing Science*, 16, 638–42.

Business Week (1994) 'Tearing up today's organization chart', 12 December, 46–53.

Cable, V. and B. Persaud (1987) 'New trends and policy problems in foreign investment: The experience of Commonwealth developing countries', in V. Cable and B. Persaud (eds), *Developing With Foreign Investment* (Kent: The Commonwealth Secretariat; London: Croom Helm), 1–27.

Calori, R., M. Lubatkin and P. Very (1994) 'Control mechanisms in cross-border acquisitions: an international comparison', *Organisation Studies*, 15, 361–79.

Camerer, C. (1991) 'Does strategy research need game theory?' *Strategic Management Journal*, 12, 137–52.

Cantwell, J. (1989) *Technological Innovations and Multinational Corporations* (Oxford: Blackwell).

Cantwell, J. (1995) 'Multinational corporations and innovatory activities: Towards a new, evolutionary, approach', in J. Molero (eds.), *Technological Innovation, Multinational Corporations and International Competitiveness: The case of Intermediate Countries* (London: Harwood Academic Publishers).

Cantwell, J. (1995) 'The globalisation of technology: What remains of the product cycle model?', *Cambridge Journal of Economics*, 19 (1), 155–74.

Cartwright, S. and C. Cooper (1992) *Mergers and Acquisitions: The Human Factor* (Oxford: Butterworth-Heinemann).

Casson, M.C. (1982) 'Transaction costs and the theory of multinational enterprise', in A.M. Rugman (ed.), *New Theory of the Multinational Enterprise* (London: Croom Helm), 24–43.

Casson, M.C. (1987) *The Firm and the Market: Studies on Multinational Enterprise and the Scope of the Firm* (Oxford: Basil Blackwell).

Casson, M.C. (1989) 'The economic theory of multinational banking: An internalisation approach', University of Reading Discussion Papers in International Investment and Business Studies, no. 133.

Casson, M.C. (1990) 'Evolution of multinational banks: a theoretical perspective', in G. Jones (ed.), *Banks as Multinational* (London: Routledge), 14–29.

Casson, M.C. (1995) *Entrepreneurship and Business Culture* (Aldershot: Edward Elgar).

Casson, M.C. (1996) 'Economics and anthropology – reluctant partners', *Human Relations*, 49, 1151–80.

Casson, M.C. and F. Chukujama (1988) 'Countertrade: Theory and evidence', unpublished manuscript, University of Reading, UK.

Casson, M.C. and N. Wadeson (1996) 'Information strategies and the theory of the firm', *International Journal of the Economics of Business*, 3(3), 307–30.

Casson, M.C. and N. Wadeson (1997) 'Communication costs and the boundaries of the firm', *International Journal of the Economics of Business*, 5(1), 5–27.

Casson, M.C. and N. Wadeson (1998) 'Bounded rationality, meta-rationality and the theory of international business', *University of Reading Discussion Papers in International Investment and Business Studies*.

Caves, R.E. (1971) 'Industrial corporations: The industrial economics of foreign investment', *Economica*, 38, February, 1–27.

Caves, R.E. (1982) *Multinational Enterprise and Economic Analysis* (Cambridge: Cambridge University Press).

Caves, R.E. (1990) 'Exchange rate movements and foreign direct investment in the United States', in D.R. Audretsch and M.P. Claudon (eds), *The Internationalization of US Markets* (New York: New York University Press).

Caves, R.E. (1996) *Multinational Enterprise and Economic Analysis*, 2nd edn (Cambridge: Cambridge University Press).

Caves, R.E. (1998) 'Research on international business', *Journal of International Business Studies*, 29 (1), 5–19.

Caves, R.E. and D. Marin (1992) 'Countertrade transactions: Theory and evidence', *Economic Journal*, 102, 1171–83.

Chandler, A. (1990) *The Dynamics of Industrial Capitalism* (Cambridge, Mass.: Harvard Business School Press).

Chang, H.-J. and R. Rowthorn (eds) (1995) *The Role of the State in Economic Change* (Oxford: The Clarendon Press).

Chapman, M. (1997) 'Social anthropology, business studies, and cultural issues', *International Studies of Management and Organisation*, Winter, 26 (4), 3–29.

Chatterjee, S. (1986) 'Type of synergy and economic value: The impact of acquisitions on merging and rival firms', *Strategic Management Journal*, 7, 119–39.

Chatterjee, S., M. Lubatkin, D. Schweiger, and Y. Weber (1992) 'Cultural differences and shareholder value in related mergers: Linking equity and human capital', *Strategic Management Journal*, 13, 319–34.

Chesnais, F. (1986) 'Technical cooperation agreements between firms', *STI Review*, 4.

Child, J. and L. Markoczy (1993) 'Host country managerial behaviour and learning in Chinese and Hungarian joint ventures', *Journal of Management Studies*, 30, 611–31.

Chiles, T.H. and J.F. McMacklin (1996) 'Integrating variable risk preferences, trust, and transaction cost economics', *Academy of Management Review*, 21(1), 73–99.

Cho, K.R. (1985) *Multinational Banks: Their Identities and Determinants* (Ann Arbor, Mich.: UMI Research Press).

Choi, C.J., S.H. Lee and J.B. Kim (1996a) 'Collaborating across business systems', British Academy of Management conference Proceedings, Birmingham, UK.

Choi, C.J., S.H. Lee and J.B. Kim (1996b) 'Countertrade and international business enforcement', paper presented at the Academy of International Business annual conference, Banff, B.C., Canada.

Choi, C.J. and D. Maldoom (1992) 'A simple model of buybacks', *Economic Letters*, 34, 77–82.

Choi, C.J. (1994) 'Contract enforcement across cultures', *Organisation Studies*, 15, 673–82.

Churchill, G.A., Jr. (1995) *Marketing Research: Methodological Foundations*, 6th edn (Fort Worth: Dryden Press).

Clarke, S. (1993) 'Privatisation and the development of capitalism in Russia', in S. Clarke, P. Fairbrother, M. Burawoy and P. Krotov (eds), *What About the Workers?* (London: Verso).

Clarke, T. and R. Bostock, (1994) 'International corporate governance: Convergence and diversity', T. Clarke and E. Monkhouse (eds), *Rethinking the Company* (London: Routledge).

Clegg, L.J. (1987) *Multinational Enterprise and World Competition: A Comparative Study of the USA, Japan, the UK, Sweden, and West Germany* (London: Macmillan).

Clegg, L.J. (1993) 'Investigating the determinants of service sector foreign direct investment', in H. Cox, L.J. Clegg and G. letto-Gillies (eds), *The Growth of Global Business* (London and New York: Routledge), 85–104.

Coase, R. (1937) 'The contractual nature of the firm', *Journal of Law and Economics*, 4, 386–405.

Coase, R. (1960) 'The problem of social cost', *Journal of Law and Economics*, 3, 1–44.

Coase, R.H. (1988) *The Firm, the Market, and the Law* (Chicago, Ill.: The University of Chicago Press).

Cole, R.E. (1973) 'Functional alternatives and economic development: An empirical example of permanent employment in Japan', *American Sociology Review*, 38, 424–38.

Collie, D. (1992) 'Export subsidies, entry deterrence and countervailing tariffs' *The Manchester School*, LX (2), 136–51.

Commission on Global Governance (1995) *Our Global Neighbourhood* (Oxford and New York: Oxford University Press).

Contractor, F.J. (1990) 'Contractual and cooperative forms of international business: Towards a unified theory of modal choice', *Management International Review*, 30 (1), 31–54.

Contractor, F.J. (1990) 'Do government policies towards foreign investment matter? An empirical investigation of the link between national policies and FDI flows', Working paper series, Rutgers University.

Contractor, F.J. (1991) 'Government policies and foreign direct investment', *UNCTC Studies Series*, no. 17 (New York: United Nations).

Contractor, F.J. (1997) 'The Compleat executive: The state of international business education and some future directions', in I. Islam and W. Shepherd (eds), *Current Issues in International Business* (Cheltenham: Edward Elgar).

Contractor, F.J. and P. Lorange (1988) 'Why should firms cooperate? The strategy and economic basis for cooperative ventures', in Contractor, F.J. and P. Lorange (eds), *Cooperative Strategies in International Business* (Lexington, Mass.: Lexington Books).

Coopers & Lybrand (1993) *A Review of the Acquisitions Experience of Major UK Companies* (London: Coopers and Lybrand).

Cooter, R. and J. Landa (1984) 'Personal versus impersonal trade and the optimal size of clubs', *International Review of Law and Economics*, 4, 15–22.

Cowdell, J. and C.C. Farrance (1993) *Marketing of Financial Services* (Bankers Workbook Series, The Chartered Institute of Bankers in association with Sheffield Hallam University).

Crozier, M. (1964) *The Bureaucratic Phenomenon* (London: Tavistock).

Culem, C.G. (1988) 'The locational determinants of direct investments among industrialised countries', *European Economic Review*, 32(4), 885–904.

Cyert, R.M. and J.G. March (1963) *A Behavioural Theory of the Firm* (Englewood Cliffs, N.J.: Prentice: Hall).

D'Iribarne, P. 1997 'The importance of an ethnographic approach to the study of organisations', *International Studies of Management and Organisation*, Winter, 26(4), 30–49.

Dahlman, C.J. (1979) 'The problem of externality', *The Journal of Law and Economics*, 22(1), April.

Datta, D. (1991) 'Organisational fit and acquisition performance: Effects of post-acquisition integration', *Strategic Management Journal*, 12, 281–97.

Davidson, W. (1980) 'The location of foreign direct investment activity, country characteristics and experience effects', *Journal of International Business Studies*, 11, 9–22.

De Meyer, A. (1992) 'Management of international R&D Operations', in O. Granstrand, L. Hakanson and S. Sjolander (eds), *Technology Management and International Business* (London: Wiley & Sons).

De Meyer, A. (1993) 'Management of an international network of industrial R&D laboratories', *R&D Management*, 23(2), 109–20.

de la Mothe, J. and G. Paquet (eds) (1996) *Evolutionary Economics and the New International Political Economy* (London: Pinter).

de Meza, D. (1979) 'Commercial policy towards multinational monopolies: Reservations on Katrak', *Oxford Economic Papers*, 31(2), 334–7.

Deal, T. and A. Kennedy (1982) *Corporate Cultures: The Rites and Rituals of Corporate Life* (Reading, Mass.: Addison-Wesley).

Deutsch, M. (1973) *The Resolution of Conflict* (New Haven: Yale University Press).

Diamond, D. (1991) 'Debt maturity structure and liquidity risk', *Quarterly Journal of Economics*, 709–37.

Dillman, D.A. (1978) *Mail and Telephone Surveys: The Total Design Method* (New York Wiley).

Dillman, D.A., J.J. Dillman and C.J. Makela (1984), The importance of adhering to details of the total design method (TDM) for mail surveys', in D.C. Lockhart (ed.), *Making Effective Use of Mailed Questionnaires* (San Francisco: Jossey-Bass).

Dixon, P. and M. Wright (1990) 'Creating value through acquisition', *Acquisitions Monthly*, 31–32.

Dosi, G., C. Freeman and S. Fabiani (1994) 'The process of economic development: Introducing some stylised facts and theories on technologies, firms and institutions', *Industrial and Corporate Change*, 3, 1–43.

Doucouliagos, C. (1995) 'Institutional bias, risk and workers' risk aversion', *Journal of Economic Issues*, 29(4), 1097–117.

Doz, Y.L. (1976) *National Policies and Multinational Management*, DBA dissertation, cited in J. Roure, J.A. Alvarez, C. Garcia-Pont and J. Nueno (1993) 'Managing international dimensions of the managerial task', *European Management Journal*, 11, 485–92.

Doz, Y.L. (1986) *Strategic Management in Multinational Companies* (Oxford: Pergamon).

Doz, Y.L. and C.K. Prahalad (1984) 'Patterns of strategic control within multinational corporations', *Journal of International Business Studies*, Fall, 55–72.

Doz, Y.L. and C.K. Prahalad (1991) 'Managing MNCs: A search for a new paradigm', *Strategic Management Journal*, 12, 145–64.

Dunning, J.H. (1958) *American Investment in British Manufacturing Industry* (London: George Allen & Unwin).

Dunning, J.H. (1977) 'Trade, location of economic activity and the multinational enterprise: A search for an eclectic approach', in B. Ohlin, P.-O. Hesselborn and P.M. Wijkman (eds), *The International Allocation of Economic Activity* (London: Macmillan).

Dunning, J.H. (1981) *International Production and the Multinational Enterprise* (London: George Allen & Unwin).

Dunning, J.H. (1988) *Explaining International Production* (London: Unwin Hyman).

Dunning, J.H. (1993) *Multinational Enterprise and the Global Economy* (Workingham: Addison-Wesley).

Dunning, J.H. (1993b) 'The globalization of service activities', in *The Globalization of Business: The Challenge of the 1990s* (London: Routledge).

Dunning, J.H. (1993c) 'Internationalising Porter's Diamond', *Management International Review*, 33(2), 7–15.

Dunning, J.H. (1994) *Globalization: The Challenge for National Economic Regimes* (Dublin: The Economic and Social Research Council).

Dunning, J.H. (1996) 'Reappraising the eclectic paradigm in an age of alliance capitalism', *Journal of International Business Studies*, 26(3), 461–91.

Dunning, J.H. (1996) 'The geographical sources of the competitiveness of firms: Some results of a new survey', University of Reading, *Discussion Papers in International Investment and Business Studies*, no. 218.

Dunning, J.H. and R. Nurala (1994) 'The R&D activities of foreign firms in the US', University of Reading, *Discussion Papers in International Investment and Business Studies*, no. 189.

Earle, J.S. and S. Estrin (1996) 'Employee in transition', in *Corporate Governance in Central Europe and Russia*, Volume 2, *Insiders and the State* (London: Central European University Press), 1–63.

Eaton, J. and G.M. Grossman (1986) 'Optimal trade and industrial policy under oligopoly', *Quarterly Journal of Economics*, 101(2), 383–406.

Ebers, M. (ed.) (1997) *The Formation of Inter-Organizational Networks* (Oxford: Clarendon Press).

Egelhoff, W.G. (1991) 'Information-processing theory and the multinational enterprise', *Journal of International Business Studies*, 22(3), 341–68.

Ellickson, R. (1991) *Order without Law* (Cambridge: Harvard University Press).

Elsass, P.M., and J.F. Veiga (1994) 'Acculturation in acquired organisations: A force-field perspective', *Human Relations*, 47, 431–53.

Elster, J. (ed.) (1986) *Rational Choice* (Oxford: Blackwell).

Elster, J. (1989) *The Cement of Society* (Cambridge: Cambridge University Press).

Enderwick, P. (1989) 'Some economics of service-sector multinational enterprises', in P. Enderwick (eds.), *Multinational Service Firms* (London and New York: Routledge), 3–34.

Epstein, G. (1996) 'International capital mobility and the scope for national economic management', in R. Boyer and D. Drache (eds), *State against Markets: The Limits of Globalization* (London: Routledge).

Ernst & Young (1996) *European Acquisitions: Getting it Right* (Ernst & Young/ Warwick Business School).

Erramilli, M.K. (1990) 'Entry mode choice in service industries', *International Marketing Review*, 7(5), 50–63.

Erramilli, M.K. (1991) 'The experience factor in foreign market entry behaviour of service firms', *Journal of International Business Studies*, 22(3), 479–501.

Erramilli, M.K. (1996) 'Nationality and subsidiary ownership patterns in multinational corporations', *Journal of International Business Studies*, 27(2), 225–48.

Euromoney (various issues, 1993–94), *Country Risk* (London: Euromoney Publications).

European Bank for Reconstruction and Development (1995), *Transition Report 1995* (London: EBRD).

Evans, T. and T. Doupnik (1986) 'Foreign exchange risk management under Standard 53–83 (Stamford, Conn.: Financial Accounting Standards Board).

Feldman, M.P. (1994) *The Geography of Innovation* (Dordrecht: Kluwer).

Fletcher, R. (1996) 'Network theory and countertrade transactions', *International Business Review*, 5, 167–89.

Florida, R. (1995) 'Towards the learning region', *Futures*, 27(5), 527–36.

Form, W. (1979) 'Comparative industrial sociology and the convergence hypothesis, *Annual Review of Sociology*, 5, 1–25.

Forsgren, M. (1990) 'Managing the international multi-centre firm: Case studies from Sweden', *European Management Journal*, 8(2), 261–7.

Forsgren, M., U. Holm and J. Johanson (1992) 'Internationalisation of the second degree: The Emergence of European-based centres in Swedish firms', in S. Young and J. Hamill (eds), *Europe and the Multinationals* (Aldershot, Hants: Edward Elgar).

Fortune (1994) 'McDonald's conquers the world', October 17, 59–70.

Franko, L.G. (1971) *Joint Venture Survival in Multinational Corporations* (New York: Praeger).

Fransman, M. (1995) 'Is national technology policy obsolete in a globalised world? The Japanese response', *Cambridge Journal of Economics*, 19(1), 95–119.

Freeman, C. and J. Hagedoorn (1994) 'Catching up or falling behind: Patterns in international interfirm technology partnering', *World Development*, 22, 771–80.

Fruin, M. (1992) *The Japanese Enterprise System* (Oxford: Oxford University Press).

Gannon, M. (1993) 'Towards a composite theory of foreign market entry mode choice: The role of marketing strategy variables', *Journal of Strategic Marketing*, 1(1), 41–54.

Gardner, M. and G. Palmer (1992) *Employment Relations* (Melbourne: Macmillan).

Garnier, G.H. (1982) 'Context and decision making autonomy in the foreign affiliates of U.S. multinational corporations', *Academy of Management Journal*, 25(2), 893–908.

Gates, S.R. and W.G. Egelhoff (1986) 'Centralization in headquarters–subsidiary relationships', *Journal of International Business Studies*, 17(2), 71–92.

Gatignon, H.A. and E. Anderson (1988) 'The multinational corporation's degree of control over foreign subsidiaries: An empirical test of a transaction cost explanation', *Journal of Law, Economics and Organization*, 4(2), 305–36.

Geringer, J.M. (1988) *Joint Venture Partner Selection: Strategies for Developed Countries* (Westport, Conn.: Books Quorum).

Geringer, J.M. (1991) 'Strategic determinants of partner selection criteria in international joint ventures', *Journal of International Business*, 22(1), 41–62.

Geringer, J.M. and L. Hebert (1989) 'Control and performance of international joint ventures', *Journal of International Business Studies*, 20(2) 235–54.

Geringer, J.M. and L. Hebert (1991) 'Measuring performance of International joint ventures', *Journal of international Business Studies*, 22(2), 249–63.

Gerlach, M. and J. Lincoln (1992) 'The organisation of business networks in the U.S. and Japan', R. Eccles and N. Nohria (eds), *Networks and Organisations* (Boston: Harvard Business School Press).

Ghauri, P.N. (1983) *Negotiating International Package Deals*, doctoral thesis, Upsala.

Ghoshal, S. and C.A. Bartlett (1988) 'Creation adoption and diffusion of innovations by subsidiaries of multinational corporations', *Journal of International Business Studies*, 19(3), 365–88.

Ghoshal, S. and C., Bartlett (1993) 'The multinational corporation as an interorganisational network', in S. Ghoshal and E. Westney (eds), *Organisational Theory and the Multinational Corporation* (New York: St Martin's Press).

Ghoshal, S. and C.A. Bartlett (1990) 'The multinational corporation as an interorganizational network', *Academic Management Review*, 15(4), 603–25.

Ghoshal, S. and C.A. Bartlett (1995) 'Changing the role of top management: Beyond structure to processes', *Harvard Business Review*, January–February, 86–96.

Ghoshal, S. and N. Nohria (1989) 'Internal differentiation within multinational corporations', *Strategic Management Journal*, 10(2), 323–37.

Ghoshal, S. and N. Nohria (1993) 'Horses for courses: Organizational forms for multinational corporations', *Sloan Management Review*, 34(2), 23–35.

Gilman, M.G. (1981) *The Financing of Foreign Direct Investment: A Study of the Determinants of Capital Flows in Multinational Enterprises* (London: Frances Pinter).

Glaister, K.W. and P.J. Buckley (1994) 'UK international joint ventures: An analysis of patterns of activity and distribution', *British Journal of Management*, 5(1), 33–51.

Glaister, K.W. and P.J. Buckley (1996) 'Strategic motives for international alliance formation', *Journal of Management Studies*, 3(3), 301–32.

Glaister, K.W. and P.J. Buckley (1997) 'Tasks-related and partner-related selection criteria in UK international strategic alliances', *British Journal of Management*, 8(3), 199–222.

Gomes-Casseres, B. (1987) 'Joint venture instability: Is it a problem?' *Columbia Journal of World Business*, Summer.

Goodman, J.B. and L.W. Pauly (1993) 'The obsolescence of capital controls? Economic management in an age of global markets', *World Politics*, 46(1), 50–82.

Goold, M., A. Campbell and M. Alexander (1994) *Corporate Level Strategy: Creating Value in the Multibusiness Company* (New York: John Wiley).

Graddy, D.B. and A.H. Spencer (1990) *Managing Commercial Banks: Community, Regional, and Global* (London: Prentice-Hall).

Granovetter, M. (1985) 'Economic action and social structure: The problem of embeddedness', *American Journal of Sociology*, 91(3), 481–510.

Granovetter, M. and R. Swedberg (1992) *The Sociology of Economic Life* (Boulder: Westview Press).

Gray, H.P. and J. Gray (1981) 'A multinational bank: A financial MNC', *Journal of Banking and Finance*, 5, 33–63.

Greene, W.H. (1993) *Econometric Analysis* (London: Collier–Macmillan).

Greiber, W. (1997) *One World, Ready or Not* (New York: Simon & Schuster).

Gresser, C. and P. Gaskell (1993) 'Business environment: Intangibles and invisibles', *Corporate Location*, August, 14–15.

Grief, A. (1993) 'Contract enforceability and economic institutions in early trade: The Maghribi traders' coalition', *American Economic Review*, 83, 525–48.

Grief, A. (1994) 'Cultural beliefs and the organisation of society: A historical and theoretical reflection on collectivist and individualist societies'. *Journal of Political Economy*, 102, 912–50.

Grief, A., P. Milgrom and B. Weingast (1994) 'Coordination, commitment, and enforcement: the case of the Merchant Guild', *Journal of Political Economy*, 102, 745–76.

Griffiths, G. (1993) 'Powerful selling point', *Investors Chronicle*, 106(1349), November, 102.

Group of Thirty (1984) *Foreign Direct Investment 1973–87* (New York: Group of Thirty).

Grubel, G.H. (1977) 'A theory of multinational banking', *Banca Nazionale del Lavoro Quarterly Review*, 123, December, 349–63.

Grubel, G.H. (1989) 'Multinational banking', in P. Enderwick (ed.), *Multinational Service Firms* (London and New York: Routledge), 61–78.

Grubert, H. and J. Mutti (1991) 'Taxes, Tariffs, and Transfer Pricing in Multinational Decision Making', *The Review of Economics and Statistics*, 285–93.

Guisinger, S.E. (1985) *Investment Incentives and Performance Requirements: Patterns of International Trade, Production and Investment* (Westport, Conn.: Greenwood Press).

Hagedoorn, J. (1993) 'Understanding the rationale of strategic technology partnering: Interorganisational modes of co-operation and sectoral differences', *Strategic Management Journal*, 14, 371–85.

Hagedoorn, J. and J. Schakenraad (1991) *The Role of Interfirm Cooperation Agreements in the Globalisation of Economy and Technology* (Brussels, Commission of the European Communities: The MONITOR-FAST Programme.

Hall, P. and S. Markowski (1993) 'On the normality and abnormality of offsets obligations', logistics and project management discussion papers, University College, the University of New South Wales.

Hamel, G. (1991) 'Competition for competence and inter-partner learning with international strategic alliances', *Strategic Management Journal*, 12, 83–103.

Hamel. G. and C.K. Prahalad (1996) 'Competing in the new economy: Managing out of bounds', *Strategic Management Journal*, 14(1), 23–46.

Hamill, J. and G. Hunt (1993) 'Joint venture in Hungary: Key success factors', *European Management Journal*, 11(2), 238–47.

Hamill, J. and P. Castledine (1996) 'Foreign acquisitions in the UK: Impact and policy', in F. Burton, M. Yamin and S. Young (eds), *International Business and Europe in Transition* (London: Macmillan).

Handy, C. (1985) *Understanding Organizations* (New York: Penguin).

Hannan, M. and J. Freeman (1977) 'The population ecology of organisations', *American Journal of Sociology*, 82, 929–64.

Hansmann, H. (1996) *The Ownership of Enterprise* (Cambridge, Mass.: Harvard University Press).

Hargreaves Heap, S. (1989) *Rationality in Economics* (Oxford: Blackwell).

Harrigan, K.R. (1985) *Strategies for Joint Ventures* (Lexington, Mass.: Lexington Books).

Harrigan, K.R. (1987) 'Strategic alliances: Their new role in global competition', *Colombia Journal of World Business*, 67–9.

Harrigan, K.R. (1988) 'Joint ventures and competitive strategy', *Strategic Management Journal*, 9, 141–58.

Harrison, B. (1992) 'Industrial districts: Old wine in new bottles', *Regional Studies*, 26, 5–20.

Hart, J.A. (1992) *Rival Capitalists: International Competitiveness in the US, Japan and Western Europe* (Ithaca: Cornell University Press).

Hart, O. (1995) *Firms, Contracts, and Financial Structure* (Oxford: Oxford University Press).

Haspeslagh, P. and D. Jemison (1991) *Managing Acquisitions* (New York: Free Press).

Häusler, J. H.W. Hahn and S. Lütz (1994) 'Contingencies of innovation networks: A case study of successful interfirm R&D collaboration', *Research Policy*, 23, 153–70.

Hedlund, G. (1981) 'Autonomy of subsidiaries and formalization of headquarters–subsidiary relationships in Swedish MNCs', in L. Otterbeck (ed.), *The Management of Headquarters–Subsidiary Relationships in Multinational Corporations* (Aldershot, Hants: Gower).

Hedlund, G. (1986) 'The hypermodern MNC: A heterarchy?' *Human Resource Management*, 25, 9–36.

Hedlund, G. (1993) 'Assumptions of hierarchy and heterarchy: An application to the multinational corporation', in S. Ghostal and E. Westney (eds), *Organization Theory and the Multinational Corporation* (London: Macmillan), 211–36.

Hedlund, G. (1994) 'A model of knowledge management and the N-form corporation', *Strategic Management Journal*, 15, 73–90.

Hedlund, G. (1996) 'Organization and management of transnational corporations in practice and research', in United Nations, *Transnational Corporations and World Development*, UNCTAD Division on Transnational Corporations (London: International Thomson Business Press).

Hedlund, G. and D. Rolander (1990) 'Actions in heterarchies', in C.A. Bartlett, Y.L. Doz and G. Hedlund (eds), *Managing the Global Firm* (London: Routledge).

Hedlund, G. and J. Ridderstrale (1992) 'Towards the N-form corporation: Exploitation and creation in the MNC', paper presented at the Conference on Perspectives on International Business: Theory, Research and Institutional AItangements, University of South Carolina, Columbia, SC.

Helleiner, E. (1996) 'Post-globalization: Is the financial liberalization trend likely to be reversed?', in R. Boyer and D. Drache (eds), *State against Markets: The Limits of Globalization* (London: Routledge).

Helleiner, G.K. (1987) 'Direct foreign investment and manufacturing for export: A review of the issues', in V. Cable and B. Persaud (eds), *Developing with Foreign Investment* (Kent: the Commonwealth Secretariat; London: Croom Helm).

Hennart, J-F. (1989) 'Can the "new forms of investment" substitute for the "old forms?" A transaction costs perspective', *Journal of International Business Studies*, 20(2), 211–33.

Hennart, J-F. (1989) 'The transaction costs rationale for countertrade', *Journal of Law, Economic and Organisation*, 5, 127–53.

Hennart, J-F. (1990) 'Some empirical dimensions of countertrade', *Journal of International Business Studies*, 21, 243–70.

Hennart, J-F. and E. Anderson (1993) 'Countertrade and the minimization of transaction costs: An empirical examination', *Journal of Law, Economics and Organisation*, 9, 290–313.

Hennart, J.F. (1982) *A Theory of Multinational Enterprise* (Ann Arbor: University of Michigan Press).

Hennart, J.F. (1988) 'A transactions cost theory of equity joint ventures', *Strategic Management Journal*, 9, 361–74.

Hennart, J.F. (1991) 'The transaction cost theory of the multinational enterprise', in C.N. Pitelis and R. Sugden (eds), *The Nature of the Transnational Firm* (London: Routledge), 81–116.

Hennart, J.F. (1991) 'The transaction costs theory of joint ventures: An empirical study of Japanese subsidiaries in the United States', *Management Science*, 37(4), 483–97.

Herbert, T.T. (1984) 'Strategy and multinational organisation structure: An interorganisational relationships perspective', *Academy of Management Review*, 9(2), 259–71.

Hergert, M. and D. Morris (1988) 'Trends in international collaborative agreements', in F.J. Contractor and P. Lorange (eds), *Co-operative Strategies in International Business* (Lexington, Mass.: Lexington Books).

Hickson, D.J., C.R. Hinnings, C.J.M. McMillan and J.P. Schwitter 'The culture-free context of organisation structure: A tri-national comparison', *Sociology*, 8, 59–80.

Hill, C. (1995) 'National institutional structures, transaction cost economizing and competitive advantage', *Organisation Science*, 6, 119–31.

Hill, C.W.L., P. Hwang and C.W. Kim (1990) 'An eclectic theory of the choice of international entry mode', *Strategic Management Journal*, 11, 117–28.

Hillman, A. and G. Keim (1995) 'International variation in the business–government interface – institutional and organisational considerations', *Academy of Management Review*, 20, 193–214.

Hirsch, P. and M. Lounsbury (1996) 'Rediscovering volition: The institutional economics of Douglas C. North', *Academy of Management Review*, book review essay, 21, 872–84.

Hirschman, A. (1970) *Exit, Voice and Loyalty* (Cambridge: Harvard University Press).

Hirst, P. and G. Thompson (1996) *Globalization in Question* (London: Polity Press).

Hobsbawm, E. (1995) *Age of Extremes* (London: Abacus).

Hoecklin, L. (1995) *Managing Cultural Differences* (Wokingham: Addison-Wesley).
Hofstede, G. (1980) *Culture's Consequences: International Differences in Work-Related Values* (Beverly Hills, Cal.: Sage).
Hofstede, G. (1991) *Cultures and Organisations* (London: McGraw-Hill).
Hofstede, G., B. Neuijen and F. Ohavy (1990) 'Measuring organizational cultures: A qualitative and quantitative study across twenty cases', *Administrative Science Quarterly*, 35, 286–316.
Hollingsworth, J.R., P.C. Schmitter and W. Streeck (eds) (1994) *Governing Capitalist Economies: Performance and Control of Economic Sectors* (Oxford: Oxford University Press).
Homans, G. (1974) *Social Behavior: Its Elementary Forms*, 2nd edn (New York: Harcourt Brace Jovanovich).
Hood, N. and S. Young (1979) *The Economics of Multinational Enterprise* (London: Longman).
Hood, N. and S. Young (1982) *Multinationals in Retreat: The Scottish Experience* (Edinburgh: University Press).
Hood, N., S. Young and D. Lal (1994) 'Strategic evolution within Japanese manufacturing plants in Europe: UK evidence', *International Business Review*, 3, 97–122.
Howells, J. (1990a) 'The location and organisation of research and development: New horizons', *Research Policy*, 19, 133–48.
Howells, J. (1990b) 'The internationalisation of R&D and the development of global research networks', *Regional Studies*, 24, 495–512.
Hughes, D. (1974) 'Toward historical ethnography: Notarial records and family history in the middle ages', *Historical Methods Newsletter*, 7, 61–71.
Hunt, J.W. (1990) 'Changing pattern of acquisition behaviour in takeovers and the consequences for acquisition processes', *Strategic Management Journal*, 11, 69–77.
Hunter, J.E. and F.L. Schmidt (1990) *Methods of Meta-analysis: Correcting Error and Bias in Research Findings* (Newbury Park: Sage).
Huntington, S. (1993) 'The clash of civilizations', *Foreign Affairs*, 72, Summer, 22–49.
Hutton, W. (1995) *The State We're In* (London: Cape).
Hymer, S.H. (1976) *The International Operations of National Firms: A Study of Direct Foreign Investment*, doctoral dissertation, MIT, 1960 (published by NUT Press, 1976).
Iannaccone, L. (1992) 'Sacrifice and stigma in cults, communes and other collectives', *Journal of Political Economy*, 100, 271–92.
Inkpen, A.C. and J. Birkinshaw (1994) 'International joint ventures and performance: An inter-organizational perspective', *International Business Review*, 3(3), 201–17.
International Monetary Fund (various years) *International Financial Statistics* (Washington, DC: IMF).
Jaffe, A., M. Trajtenberg and R. Henderson (1993) 'Geographical localisation of knowledge spillovers, as evidenced by patent citations', *Quarterly Journal of Economics*, 108, 577–98.
Jarillo, J.C. and J.I. Martinez (1990) 'Different roles for subsidiaries: The case of multinational corporations in Spain', *Strategic Management Journal*, 11, 501–12.
Jemison, D. and S. Sitkin (1986) 'Corporate acquisitions: A process perspective', *Academy of Management Review*, 11, 145–63.
Jenkinson, T. and C. Mayer (1992) 'The assessment: Corporate governance and corporate control', *Oxford Review of Economic Policy*, 8(3), 1–10.

Jensen, M. (1988) 'Takeovers: Their causes and consequences', *Journal of Economic Perspective* , 2(1), 21–48.

Johanson, J. and F. Wiedersheim-Paul (1975) 'The internationalisation of the firm – four Swedish cases', *Journal of Management Studies*, October, 305–22.

Johanson, J. and J.E. Vahlne (1977) 'The internationalization process of the firm – a model of knowledge development and increasing foreign commitments', *Journal of International Business Studies*, 8(1), 23–32.

Johnson, K.R. and R.T. Golembiewski (1992) 'National culture in organizational development: A conceptual and empirical analysis', *International Journal of Human Resource Management*, 3, 71–84.

Jones, G. (1990) 'Banks as multinationals', in G. Jones (ed.), *Banks as Multinationals* (London: Routledge), 1–13.

Jones, G. (1993) 'British multinational banking strategies over time', in H. Cox, J. Clegg and G. Ietto-Gillies (eds), *The Growth of Global Business* (London and New York: Routledge), 85–104.

Jong, G. de (1998) *Long-term Supply Relationships: Theory and Evidence from the United States, Japan, and Europe* (Doctoral thesis, Gröningen: University of Gröningen).

Jorde, T.M. and D.J. Teece (1989) 'Competition and cooperation: Striking the right balance', *California Management Review*, 25–7.

Kamoche, K. (1997) 'Knowledge creation and learning in international HRM', *The International Journal of Human Resource Management*, 8(3), 213–23.

Kaufman, R.T. and R. Russell (1995) "Government support for profit sharing, gainsharing, ESOPs and TQM', *Contemporary Economic Policy*, 13(2), 38–48.

Kay, J.A. and A. Silberston (1995) Corporate governance', *National Institute Economic Review*, August.

Kennedy, P.M. (1993) *Preparing for the Twenty-First Century* (New York: Random House).

Kerr, C.J., J.T. Dunlop, F.H. Harbison and C.A. Myers (1952) *Industrialism and Industrial Man: The Problem of Labour and Management in Economic Growth* (Cambridge Mass.: Harvard University Press).

Keynes, J.M. (1933) 'National self-sufficiency', *The Yale Review*, XXII(4).

Khoury, S.J. (1980) *Dynamics of International Banking* (New York: Praeger).

Killing, J.P. (1983) *Strategies for Joint Venture Success* (New York: Praeger).

Kim, W.C. and P. Hwang (1992) 'Global strategy and multinationals' entry mode choice', *Journal of International Studies*, 23(2), 29–53.

Kim, W.C., P. Hwang and W.P. Burgers (1993) 'Multinationals' diversification and the risk/return trade-off', *Strategic Management Journal*, 14, 275–86.

Kindleberger, C.P. (1969) *American Business Abroad: Six Lectures on Direct Investment* (New Haven: Yale University Press).

King, J.B. (1988) 'Prisoner's paradoxes', *Journal of Business Ethics*, 8, 475–87.

Kirman, A.P. and M. Salmon (eds) (1995) *Learning and Rationality in Economics*(Oxford: Blackwell).

Kitching, J. (1974) 'Winning and losing with European acquisitions', *Harvard Business Review*, March–April, 124–36.

Knickerbocker, F.T. (1973) *Oligopolistic Reaction and Multinational Enterprise* (Boston, Mass.: Harvard University Press).

Kogut, B. (1986) 'On designing contracts to guarantee enforceability: Theory and evidence from East–West trade', *Journal of International Business Studies*, 17, 47–62.

Kogut, B. (1988) 'Joint ventures: Theoretical and empirical perspectives', *Strategic Management Journal*, 9, 319–32.

Kogut, B. (1990) 'International sequential advantages and network flexibility', in C. Bartlett, Y. Doz and G. Hedlund (eds), *Managing the Global Firm* (London: Routledge).

Kogut, B. (1993) *Country Competitiveness: Technology and the Organising of Work* (New York: Oxford University Press).

Kogut, B. and H. Singh (1988) 'The effect of national culture on the choice of entry mode', *Journal of International Business Studies*, 413–31.

Kogut, B. and U. Zander (1993) 'Knowledge of the firm and the evolutionary theory of the multinational corporation', *Journal of International Business Studies*, 24(4), 625–45.

Kotler, P., D.H. Haider and I. Rein (1993) *Marketing Places* (New York: The Free Press).

Kozul-Wright, R. (1995) 'The myth of Anglo-Saxon capitalism: Reconstructuring the history of the American state', in H.-J. Chang and R. Rowthorn (eds) (1995), *The Role of the State in Economic Change* (Oxford: The Clarendon Press).

Kramer, R.M. and T.R. Tyler (eds) (1996) *Trust in Organisations: Frontiers of Theory and Research* (London: Sage).

Krugman, P. (1994) 'Competitiveness: A dangerous obsession', *Foreign Affairs*, 73(2).

Kumar, N. (1994) 'Determinants of export orientation of foreign production by U.S. multinationals: An inter-country analysis', *Journal of International Business Studies*, 25(1), 141–56.

Kusewitt, J.B. (1985) 'An exploratory study of strategic acquisition factors relating to performance', *Strategic Management Journal*, 6, 151–69.

Landa, J. (1994) *Trust, Ethnicity and Identity* (Michigan: University of Michigan Press).

Lane, C. (1997) 'The social regulation of interfirm relations in Britain and Germany: Market rules, legal norms and technical standards', *Cambridge Journal of Economics*, 21, 197–215.

Lane, H.W. and P.W. Beamish (1990) 'Cross-cultural cooperative behavior in joint ventures in LDCs', *Management International Review*, 30, special issues, 87–102.

Langlois, R. (1992) 'Transaction-cost economics in real time', *Industrial and Corporate Change*, 1, 99–127.

Larsson, R. (1993) 'Barriers to acculturation in Mergers and acquisitions: Strategic human resource implications', *Journal of European Business Education*, 2, 1–18.

Laurent, A. (1983) 'The cultural diversity of western management conceptions', *International Studies of Management and Organizations*, 8, 75–96.

Laurent, A. (1986) 'The cross-cultural puzzle of international human resource management', *Human Resource Management*, 25, 91–102.

Lawrence, P. and J. Lorsch (1967) *Organizations and Environment* (Cambridge, Mass.: Harvard University Press).

Lazonick, W. (1994) 'Industry clusters versus global webs: Organisational capabilities in the American economy', *Industrial and Corporate Change*, 2, 1–24.

Lecraw, D. (1989) 'The management of countertrade: Factors influencing success', *Journal of International Business Studies*, 20, 41–59.

Lee, C. and P.W. Beamish (1995) 'The characteristics and performance of Korean joint ventures in LDCs', *Journal of international Business Studies*, 26(3), 637–54.

Legge, K. (1989) 'Human resource management: A critical analysis', in J. Storey, (ed.), *New Perspectives on Human Resource Management* (London: Routledge, 19–55).

Leung, S. and C. Tan (1993) 'Managing Across Bordes: An Empirical Test of the Batlett and Ghoshal (1989) Typology', *Journal of International Business Studies*, 24(3), 449–464.

Levinthal, D. (1991) 'Organisational adaptation and environmental selection: Interrelated processes of change', *Organisation Science*, 2, 140–5.

Levinthal, D. (1992) 'Surviving Schumpeterian environments: An evolutionary perspective', *Industrial and Corporate Change*, 1, 427–43.

Lewis, M.K. and K.T. Davis (1987) *Domestic and International Banking* (Deddington: Philip Allan).

Lim, D. (1983) 'Fiscal incentives and foreign direct investment in less developed countries', *Journal of Development Studies*, January, 207–12.

Lincoln, J., M. Hanada and J. Olson (1981) 'Cultural orientations and individual reactions to organizations: A study of employees of Japanese-owned firms', *Administrative Science Quarterly*, 26, 93–115.

Lippman, S.A. and J.J. McCall (eds) (1979) *Studies in the Economics of Search* (Amsterdam: North-Holland).

Lodge, G.C. and E. Vogel (1987) *Ideology and National Competitiveness: an Analysis of Nine Countries* (Cambridge: Mass.: Harvard University Press).

Lubatkin, M. (1987) 'Merger strategies and stockholder value', *Strategic Management Journal*, 8, 39–53.

Lundvall, B. (1988) 'Innovation as as interactive process: From user–producer interaction to national systems of innovation', in Dosi, G. *et al.* (eds), *Technical Change and Economic Theory* (London: Pinter).

Lunn, J. (1983) 'Determinants of US direct investment in the EEC: Revisited again', *European Economic Review*, 21(3), 391–3.

Luo, Y. (1995) 'Business strategy, market structure and performance of international joint ventures: The case of joint ventures in China', *Management International Review*, 35(3), 241–64.

Lyles, M.A. and I.S. Baird (1994) 'Performance of international joint ventures in two Eastern European countries: The case of Hungary and Poland', *Management International Review*, 34(4), 313–29.

Macaulay, S. (1963) 'Non-contractual relations in business: A preliminary study', *American Sociological Review*, 50, 55–70.

Madhok, A. (1995a) 'Revisiting multinational firms' tolerance for joint ventures: A trust-based approach', *Journal of International Business Studies*, 26, 117–37.

Madhok, A. (1995b) 'Opportunism and trust in joint venture relationships: An exploratory study and a model', *Scandinavian Journal of Management*, 11, 57–74.

Madura, J. (1992) 'Portfolio diversification for international lenders: A risk analysis of the Pacific Rim and Eastern European nations', *International Journal of Commerce and Management*, 2(1&2), 17–27.

Malerba, F. (1992) 'Learning by firms and incremental technical change', *Economic Journal*, 2, 845–59.

March, J. (1991) 'Exploration and exploitation in organisational learning', *Organisation Science*, 2, 71–87.

Marin, D. and M. Schnitzer (1995) 'Tying trade flows: a theory of countertrade with evidence', *American Economic Review*, 85, 1047–64.

Mariotti, S. and L. Piscitello (1995) 'Information costs and location of FDI within the host country: Empirical evidence from Italy', *Journal of International Business Studies*, 26(4), 815–41.

Mariti, P. and R.H. Smiley (1983) 'Co-operative agreements and the organisation of industry', *Journal of Industrial Economics*, 31(4), 437–51.

Markusen, A. (1994) *Sticky Places in Slippery Spaces: The Political Economy of Post-War Fast Growth Regions*, New Brunswick Center for Urban Policy Research, Rutgers University Working Paper no. 79.

Marschak, J. and R. Radner (1972) *The Economic Theory of Teams* (New Haven, Conn.: Yale University Press).

Mattesini, F. (1993) *Financial Markets, Asymmetric Information and Macroeconomic Equilibrimu* (Aldershot: Dartmouth).

McCain, R.A. (1982) 'Empirical implication of worker participation in management', in D.C. Jones and J. Svejnar (eds), *Participatory and Self-Managed Firms* (Lexington, Mass.: Lexington Books).

McDonald's Corporation (1994) *Annual Report*.

McManus, J.C. (1972) 'The theory of the multinational firm', in G. Paquet (ed.), *The Multinational Firm and the Nation State* (Don Mills, Ontario: Collier–Macmillan).

Meade, J.E. (1972) 'The theory of labour-managed Finns and of profit-sharing', *Economic Journal*, 82 (special issue), 402–28.

Melecki, E.J. (1985) 'Industrial location and corporate organisation in high-tech industries', *Economic Geography*, 61, 345–69.

Meyer, J.W. and B. Rowan (1977) 'Institutionalized organizations: Formal structure as myth and ceremony', *American Journal of Sociology*, 83, 340–63.

Miles, R.E. and C.C. Snow (1984) 'Fit, failure and the hall of fame', *California Management Review*, 26(3), 10–28.

Miller, R. (1993) 'Determinants of U.S. manufacturing abroad', *Finance and Development* March, 118.

Mirus, R. and B. Yeung (1986) 'Economic incentives for countertrade', *Journal of International Business Studies*, 17, 27–40.

Mody, A. (1993) 'Learning through alliances', *Journal of Economic Behavior and Organisation*, 20, 151–70.

Mohr, J. and R. Spekman (1994) 'Characteristics of partnership success: Partnership attributes, communication behavior and conflict resolution technique', *Strategic Management Journal*, 15, 135–52.

Morosini, P. and H. Singh (1994) 'Post cross-border acquisitions: Implementing national culture compatible strategies to improve performance', *European Management Journal*, 12, 390–400.

Moss, S. and J. Rae (1992) *Artificial Intelligence and Economic Analysis: Prospects and Problems* (Aldershot: Edward Elgar).

Moutinho, L. (1991) 'Problem 9.1: The four I's of services', *Problems in Marketing Analysis and Applications* (London: Paul Chapman Publishing).

Mudambi, R. (1995a) 'The MNE investment location decision: Some empirical evidence', *Managerial and Decision Economics*, 16, 249–57.

Mudambi, R. (1995b) 'Output tradability and the regulation of a multinational firm', in A. van Witteloostuijn (ed.) *Market Evolution: Competition and Cooperation* (Dordrecht/Boston: Kluwer).

Mudambi, R. and L.W. Taylor (1995) 'Some non-parametric tests for duration dependence: An application to UK business cycle data', *Journal of Applied Statistics*, 22(1), 163–77.

Mueller, F. (1994) 'Societal effect, organisational effect, and globalization', *Organisation Studies*, 15, 407–28.

Nahavandi, A. and A.R. Malekzadeh (1988) 'Acculturation in mergers and acquisitions', *Academy of Management Review*, 13, 79–90.

Nahavandi, A. and A.R. Malekzadeh (1994) 'Successful mergers through acculturation', in G. von Krogh, A. Sinatra and H. Singh (eds), *The Management of Corporate Acquisitions* (London: Macmillan).

Naisbitt, J. (1994) *Global Paradox, the Bigger the World Economy, the More Political its Smallest Players* (New York: William Morrow).

Napier, N.K. (1989) 'Mergers and acquisitions, human resource issues and outcomes: A review and suggested typology', *Journal of Management Studies*, 21, 271–89.

Napier, N.K., D.M. Schweiger and J.J. Kosglow (1993) 'Managing organizational diversity: Observations from cross-border acquisitions', *Human Resources Management*, 32, 505–23.

Nayyar, P.R. (1992) 'On the measurement of corporate diversification strategy: Evidence from large US service firms', *Strategic Management Journal*, 13, 219–35.

Negandhi, A.R. (1979) 'Convergence in organizational practices: an empirical study of industrial enterprise in developing countries', in C.J. Lammers and D.J. Hickson (eds), *Organizations Alike and Unlike* (London: Routledge & Kegan Paul), 323–45.

Negandhi, A.R. (1985) 'Management in the Third World', in P. Joynt and M. Warner (eds), *Managing in Different Cultures* (Oslo: Universitetsforlaget), 69–97.

Nelson, R. (1992) 'Recent writings on competitiveness: Boxing the compass' *California Management Review*, 20, 117–25.

Nelson, R. (1988) 'Institutions supporting technical change in the United States', in G. Dosi, C. Freeman, R.R. Nelson, G. Silverberg and L.G.G. Soete (eds), *Technical Change and Economic Theory* (London: Frances Pinter).

Nelson, R.R. (ed.) (1993) *National Innovation Systems: A Comparative Analysis* (Oxford: Oxford University Press).

Nelson, R. and S.G. Winter (1982) *An Evolutionary Theory of Economic Change* (Cambridge: Mass.: Harvard University Press).

Nelson, R.R. and G. Wright (1992) 'The rise and fall of American technological leadership: The postwar era in historical perspective', *Journal of Economic Literature*, 30(4), 1931–64.

Netherlands Economic Institute (in cooperation with Ernst & Young) (1992) *New Location Factors for Mobile Investment in Europe* (Rotterdam/London, April).

Nohria, N. and N. Venkatraman (1987) 'Interorganizational information systems via information technology: A network analytic perspective', working paper no. 1909–87 (Cambridge: Mass.: Massachusetts Institute of Technology, Sloan School of Management).

Nohria, N. and S. Ghoshal (1994) 'Differentiated fit and shared values: Alternatives for managing headquarters–subsidiary relations', *Strategic Management Journal*, 15(6), 491–502.

Nooteboom, B. (1993) 'Trust, opportunism and governance: A process and control model', *Organisation Studies*, 17, 985–1010.

Nooteboom, B. (1994) *Management van Partnerships* (Schoonhoven: Academic Service).

North, D.C. (1990) *Institutions, Institutional Change and Economic Performance* (Cambridge: Cambridge University Press).

North, D.C. (1991) 'Institutions', *Journal of Economic Perspectives*, 5, 97–112.

Ohmae, K. (1995) *The End of the Nation State: The Rise of Regional Economies* (London: HarperCollins).

Olie, R. (1994) 'Shades of culture and institutions in international mergers', *Organisation Studies*, 15(3), 381–405.

Olson, M. (1992) 'The hidden path to a successful economy', in C. Clague and G. Rausser (eds) *The Emergence of Market Economies in Eastern Europe* (Cambridge: Blackwell).

Orru, M., N. Biggart and G. Hamilton (1997) *The Economic Organization of East Asian Capitalism* (New York: Sage).

Osborn, R.N. and C.C. Baughn (1987) 'New patterns in the formation of US/ Japanese co-operative ventures: The role of technology', *Colombia Journal of World Business*, 57–65.

Otterbeck L. (1981) (ed.) *The Management of Headquarters–Subsidiary Relationships in Multinational Corporations* (Aldershot: Gower).

Pan, Y., W.R. Vanhonacker and R.E. Pitts (1995) 'International joint ventures in China: Operations and potential close-down', *Journal of Global Marketing*, 8(3/4), 125–49.

Panic, M. (1995) 'International economic integration and the changing role of national governments', in H.-J. Chang and R. Rowthorn (eds), *The Role of the State in Economic Change* (Oxford, the Clarendon Press).

Papanastassiou, M. (1995) *Creation and Development of Technology by MNEs' Subsidiaries in Europe: The Cases of UK, Greece, Belgium and Portugal*, PhD Thesis, Department of Economics, University of Reading.

Papanastassiou, M. and R. Pearce (1994) 'Host-country determinants of the market strategies of US companies' overseas subsidiaries', *Journal of the Economics of Business*, 1, 199–217.

Papanastassiou, M. and R. Pearce (1996a) 'The creation and application of technology by MNEs' subsidiaries in Europe', in F. Burton, M. Yamin and S. Young (eds), *International Business and Europe in Transition* (London: Macmillan).

Papanastassiou, M. and R. Pearce (1996b) 'Individualism and interdependence in the technological development of MNEs: The strategic positioning of R&D in overseas subsidiaries', paper presented at EIBA conference, Stockholm.

Papanastassiou, M. and R. Pearce (1997a) 'Cooperative approaches to strategic competitiveness through MNE subsidiaries: Insiders and outsiders in the European market', in P.W. Beamish and P.J. Killing (eds), *Cooperative Strategies: European Perspectives* (San Francisco: The New Lexington Press).

Papanastassiou, M. and R. Pearce (1997b) 'Technology sourcing and the strategic roles of manufacturing subsidiaries in the UK: Local competencies and global competitiveness', *Management International Review* 37(1), 5–25.

Park, S.H. and M.V. Russo (1996) 'When competition eclipses cooperation: An event history analysis of joint venture failure', *Management Science* 42(6), 875–90.

Parkhe, A. (1991) 'Interfirm diversity, organisational learning, and longevity in global strategic alliances', *Journal of International Business Studies*, 22(4) 579–601.

Parkhe, A. (1993) '"Messy" research, methodological predispositions, and theory development in international joint ventures', *Academy of Management Review*, 18(2), 227–68.

Patel, P. and K. Pavitt (1991) 'Large firms in the production of the world's technology: An important case of "neo-globalisation"', *Journal of International Business Studies*, 22(1), 1–21.

Pavitt, K. (1987) 'International patterns of technological accumulation', in N. Hood and H. Vahne (eds), *Strategies in Global Competition* (London: Croom Helm).

Pavitt, K. and P. Patel (1988) 'The international distribution and determinants of technological activities', *Oxford Review of Economic Policy*, 4.

Pearce, R. (1989) *The Internationalisation of Research and Development by Multinational Enterprises* (London: Macmillan).

Pearce, R. (1992) 'World product mandates and MNE specialisation', *Scandinavian International Business Review*, 1, 38–58.

Pearce, R. (1995) 'Creative subsidiaries and the evolution of technology in multinational enterprises', University of Reading, Department of Economics, Discussion Papers in International Business and Investment Studies, no. 194.

Pearce, R. and M. Papanastassiou (1996a) *The Technological Competitiveness of Japanese Multinationals: The European Dimension* (Michigan: University of Michigan Press).

Pearce, R. and M. Papanastassiou (1996b) 'R&D networks and innovation: Decentralised product development in multinational enterprises', *R&D Management*, 26, 315–33.

Pearce, R. and S. Singh (1992) *Globalising Research and Development* (London: Macmillan).

Pecchioli, R.M. (1983) *The Internationalization of Banking – The Policy Issues* (Paris: Organisation for Economic Cooperation and Development).

Pejovich, S. (1994) 'A property rights analysis of alternative methods of organizing production', *Communist Economies and Economic Transformation*, 6(2), 219–30.

Peng, M. and P. Heath (1996) 'The growth of the firm in planned economies in transition: Institutions, organisations and strategic choice', *Academy of Management Review*, 21, 492–528.

Penrose, E.T. (1959) *The Growth of the Firm* (Oxford: Basil Blackwell).

Perez, C. (1983) 'Structural changes and the assimilation of new technologies on the economic and social system,' *Futures*, 15, 357–75.

Perkin, H. (1996) 'The third revolution and stakeholder capitalism: Convergence or collapse?', *Political Quarterly*, 67(3), 198–208.

Perlmutter, H.V. (1969) 'The tortuous evolution of the multinational corporation', *Columbia Journal of World Business*, 4, 9–18.

Peters, L.S., (1994) 'Multinational corporate investment in universities as a resource for industrial innovation', paper presented at The Globalisation of Business in 1990s: Implications for Trade and Investment, conference, reading.

Peters, T.J. and R.H. Waterman (1982) *In Search of Excellence* (New York: Harper & Row).

Pfeffer, J. and P. Nowak (1976) 'Joint ventures and interorganisational interdependence', *Administrative Science Quarterly*, 21, 398–418.

Pisano, G. (1991) 'The governance of innovations: Integration and collaborative arrangements in biotechnology', *Research Policy*, 3, 237–50.

Poole, M. (1990) 'Human resource management in an international perspective', *International Journal of Human Resource Management*, 1, 1–15.

Porcano, T.M. (1993) 'Factors affecting the foreign direct investment decision of firms from and into major industrialized countries', *Multinational Business Review*, Fall, 26–36.

Porter, M.E. (1987) 'From competitive advantage to corporate strategy', *Harvard Business Review*, May–June, 43–59.

Porter, M.E. (1980) *Competitive Strategy: Techniques for Analyzing Industries and Competitors* (New York: The Free Press).

Porter, M.E. (1986) 'Changing patterns of international competition', *California Management Review*, 28, 9–40.

Porter, M.E. (1990) *The Competitive Advantage of Nations* (New York: The Free Press).

Porter, M.E. and M.B. Fuller (1986) 'Coalitions and global strategy', in M.E. Porter (ed.), *Competition in Global Industries* (Boston, Mass.: Harvard Business School Press).

Pouder, R. and C. St John (1996) 'Hot spots and blind spots: Geographical clusters of firms and innovation', *Academy of Management Review*, 21, 1192–225.

Powell, W.W. (1990) 'Neither market nor hierarchy: Network forms of organization', *Research in Organizational Behavior*, 12, 295–336.

Prahalad, C.K. (1976) 'Strategic choices in diversified MNCs', *Harvard Business Review*, July–August, 67–78.

Prahalad, C.K. and Y.L. Doz (1987) *The Multinational Mission: Balancing Global Demands and Global Vision* (New York: Free Press).

Prasnikar, J., J. Svejnar, D. Mihaljek and V. Prasnikar (1994) 'Behavior of participatory firms in Yugoslavia: Lessons for transforming economies', *Review of Economics and Statistics*, 76(4), 728–41.

Prospective Dossier no. 2, *Globalisation of Economy and Technology*, vol. 8.

Ray, E.J. (1989) 'The determinants of foreign direct investment in the United States: 1979–85', in R. Feenstra (ed.), *Trade Policies for International Competitiveness* (Chicago: University of Chicago Press).

Rifkin, J. (1995) *The End of Work* (New York: G.P. Putnam's Sons).

Ring, P. and A. van de Ven (1992) 'Structuring cooperative relationships between organisations', *Strategic Management Journal*, 13, 483–98.

Ring, P. and A. van de Ven (1994) 'Developmental processes of cooperative inter-organisational relationships', *Academy of Management Review*, 19, 90–118.

Roe, M. (1993) 'Some differences in corporate structure in Germany, Japan and the United States', *Yale Law Journal*, 102, 1927–2003.

Rolfe, R. and R. White (1992) 'The influence of tax incentives in determining the location of foreign direct investment in developing countries', *Journal of the American Taxation Association*, 13(2), 39–57.

Rolfe, R.J., D.A. Ricks, M.M. Pointer and M. McCarthy (1993) 'Determinants of FDI preferences of MNEs', *Journal of International Business Studies*, 24(2), 335–56.

Root, F.R. (1987) *Entry Strategies for International Markets* (Lexington: Mass.: D.C. Heath).

Root, F.R. and A.A. Ahmed (1978) 'The influence of policy instruments on manufacturing foreign direct investment in developing countries', *Journal of International Business Studies*, 9(3), Winter, 81–94.

Rosenweig, P. and J. Singh (1991) 'Organisational environments and the multinational enterprise', *Academy of Management Review*, 16(2), 340–61.

Rostand, A. (1994) 'Optimizing managerial decisions during the acquisition integration process', paper presented to the 14th Annual Strategic Management Society International *Conference*, Paris.

Rowland, K.M. and S.L. Summers (1981) 'Human resource planning: A second look', *Personnel Administrator*, 26, 73–80.

Rueber, G., H. Crookell, M. Emerson and G. Gallais-Hamono (1973) *Private Foreign Investment in Development* (Oxford: Clarendon Press).

Rugman, A.M. (1976) 'Risk reduction by international diversification', *Journal of International Business Studies*, 7, 75–80.

Rugman, A.M. (1979) *International Diversification and the Multinational Enterprise* (Lexington, Mass.: Lexington Books).

Rugman, A.M. (1981) *Inside the Multinationals: The Economics of Internal Markets* (New York: Columbia University Press).

Rugman, A.M. (1982) 'Internalization and non-equity forms of international involvement', in A.M. Rugman (ed.), *New Theory of the Multinational Enterprise* (London: Croom Helm), 9–23.

Rugman, A.M. and J. Bennett (1982) 'Technology transfer and world product mandating in Canada', *Columbia Journal of World Business*, 17(4), 58–62.

Sagari, S.B. (1992) 'United States foreign direct investment in the banking industry', *Transnational Corporations*, 1(3), December, 93–124.

Sah, R.K. and J.E. Stiglitz (1986) 'The architecture of economic systems: Hierarchies and polyarchies', *American Economic Review*, 76(4), 716–27.

Sako, M. (1992) *Prices, Quality and Trust: Inter-firm Relations in Britain and Japan* (Cambridge: Cambridge University Press).

Sales, A. and P. Mirvis (1984) 'When cultures collide: Issues in acquisition', in J. Kimberly and R. Quinn (eds), *New Futures: The Challenge of Managing Corporate Transition* (Homewood, Ill.: Irwin).

Sathe, V. (1983) 'Some action implications of corporate culture: A manager's guide to action', *Organisational Dynamics*, 4–23.

Sathe, V. (1985) *Culture and Related Corporate Realities* (Homewood, Ill.: Irwin).

Scaperlanda, A.E. (1967) 'The EEC and US foreign investment: Some empirical evidence', *Economic Journal*, 77, 22–6.

Schaan, J.L. (1983) 'Parent control and joint venture success: The case of Mexico', unpublished doctoral dissertation, University of Western Ontario, London, Ontario, Canada.

Schelling, T.C. (1960) *The Strategy of Conflict* (Cambridge: Harvard University Press).

Schneider, S. and A. De Meyer (1991) 'Interpreting and responding to strategic issues: The impact of national culture', *Strategic Management Journal*, 12, 307–20.

Schoenberg, R. (1996) 'European cross-border acquisitions: The impact of management style differences on performance', in F. Burton, M. Yamin and S. Young (eds), *International Business and Europe in Transition* (London: Macmillan).

Schoenberg, R., N. Denuelle and D. Norburn (1995) 'National conflict within European alliances', *European Business Journal*, 7, 8–16.

Schuler, R.S., P.J. Dowling and H. De Cieri (1993) 'An integrative framework of strategic international human resource management', *Journal of Management*, 19, 419–59.

Schwab, K. and C. Smadja (1996) *Start Taking the Backlash Against Globalization Seriously*, address given to Davos Forum, January.

Schweiger, D.M. (1993) 'Commentary on an investigation of national and organisational culture influences in recent European mergers', *Advances in Strategic Management*, 9, 347–51.

Schweiger, D.M. and J.P. Walsh (1990) 'Mergers and acquisitions: An interdisciplinary view', *Research in Personnel and Human Resource Management*, 8, 41–107.

Seth, A. (1990) 'Value creation in acquisitions: A reexamination of performance issues', *Strategic Management Journal*, 11, 99–116.

Shamdasani, P.N. and Sheth, J.N. (1995) 'An experimental approach to investigating satisfaction and continuity in marketing alliances', *European Journal of Marketing*, 29(4), 6–23.

Shan, W. and W. Hamilton (1991) 'Country-specific advantage and international cooperation', *Strategic Management Journal*, 12, 419–32.

Shane, S. (1994) 'The effect of national culture on the choice between licensing and direct foreign investment', *Strategic Management Journal*, 15, 627–42.

Sharp, M. (1993) 'Industrial policy and globalisation: What role for the nation state?', in K. Hughes (ed.) *The Future of UK Competitiveness and the Role of Industrial Policy* (Policy Studies Institute).

Shaw, S.M.S. and J.F.T. Toye (1978) 'Fiscal incentives for firms in some developing countries: Survey and critique', in J.F.T. (ed.), *Taxation and Economic Development* (London: Frank Cass).

Shrivastava, P. (1986) 'Postmerger integration', *Journal of Business Strategy*, 7, 65–76.

Simon, H.A. (1991) 'Organisations and markets', *Journal of Economic Perspectives*, 5, 25–44.

Simon, H.A. (1947) *Administrative Behaviour* (New York: Macmillan).

Simon, H.A. (1982) *Modes of Bounded Rationality* (Cambridge: Mass.: MIT Press).

Simon, H.A. (1992) *Economics, Bounded Rationality and the Cognitive Revolution* (with M. Egidi, R. Marris and R. Viale) (Aldershot: Edward Elgar).

Simons, R. (1994) 'How new top managers use control systems as levers of strategic renewal', *Strategic Management Journal*, 15, 169–89.

Singh, H. and C. Montgomery (1987) 'Corporate acquisition strategies and economic performance', *Strategic Management Journal*, 8, 377–86.

Smith, P. and J. Misumi (1994) 'Japanese management – A sun rising in the West?', in C.L. Cooper and I.T. Robertson (eds), *Key Reviews in Managerial Psychology* (London: Wiley).

Smith, P.B. (1992) 'Organisational behaviour and national cultures', *British Journal of Management*, 3, 39–51.

Sölvell, O. and I. Zander (1995) 'Organization of the dynamic multinational enterprise', *International Studies of Management and Organization*, 25(1–2), 17–38.

Sorge, A. (1991) 'Strategic fit and the societal effect: Interpreting cross-national comparisons of technology, organisation, and human resources', *Organisation Studies*, 12, 161–90.

Spekman, R.E., L.A. Isabella, T.A. Macavoy and T. Forbes (1996) 'Creating alliances that endure', *Long Range Planning*, 29(3), 346–57.

Stafford, E.R. (1995) 'Opportunities for alliance research in marketing: An argument for a multimethod case research strategy', *American Marketing Association*, Summer.

Stevens, G.V.G. (1993) 'Exchange rates and foreign direct investment: A note', International Finance Discussion Papers no. 444 (April), Washington DC, Board of Governors of the Federal Reserve System.

Stewart J.C. (1976) 'Linkages and foreign direct investment', *Regional Studies*, 10, 245–58.

Stopford, J.M. (1996) 'The globalization of business', in J. de la Mothe and G. Paquet (eds), *Evolutionary Economics and the new International Political Economy* (London: Pinter).

Stopford, J.M. and L. Turner (1985) *Britain and the Multinationals* (London: Wiley).

Stopford, J.M. and L.T. Wells (1972) *Managing the Multinational Enterprise* (New York: Basic Books).

Stopford, J.M. and S. Strange (1991) *Rival States, Rival Firms* (Cambridge: Cambridge University Press).

Storey, J. (1989) *New Perspectives on Human Resource Management* (London: Routledge).

Storey, J. (1992) *Developments in the Management of Human Resources* (Oxford: Blackwell).

Storper, M. (1997) *The Regional World* (London: Guilford Press).

Stråth, B. (1996) *The Organization of Labour Markets: Modernity, Culture and Governance in Germany, Sweden, Britain and Japan* (London: Routledge).

Sullivan, J., R.B. Peterson, N. Kumeda and J. Shimada (1981) 'The relationship between conflict resolution approaches and trust: A cross cultural study', *Academy of Management Journal*, 24(4), 803–15.

Taggart, J.H. and M. McDermott (1993) *The Essence of International Business* (London: Prentice Hall).

Taggart, J.H. (1996) 'Multinational manufacturing subsidiaries in Scotland: Strategic role and economic impact', *International Business Review*, 5(5), 447–68.

Taggart, J.H. (1997) 'An evaluation of the integration–responsiveness grid: MNC manufacturing subsidiaries in the UK', *Management International Review*, 37(4).

Taggart, J.H. (1997) 'Autonomy and procedural justice: A framework for evaluating subsidiary strategy', *Journal of International Business Studies*, 28(1), 51–75.

Tayeb, M.H. (1988) *Organizations and National Culture* (London: Sage).

Tayeb, M.H. (1994) 'Japanese managers and British culture: A comparative case study', *International Journal of Human Resource Management*, 5, 145–66.

Tayeb, M.H. (1996) *The Management of a Multicultural Workforce* (Chichester: Wiley).

Tayeb, M.H. (1998), 'Transfer of HRM policies and practices across cultures: An American company in Scotland', *International Journal of Human Resource Management*, 9, 332–58.

Taylor, W. (1991) 'The logic of global business: An interview with ABB's Percy Barnevik', *Harvard Business Review*, March–April, 90–105.

Teece, D.J. (1981) 'The market for know-how and the efficient international transfer of technology', in R.D. Lambert and A.W. Heston (eds), *The Annals of the American Academy of Political and Social Science* (London: Sage).

Teece, D.J. (1983) 'Technological and organisational factors in the theory of the multinational enterprise', in M.C. Casson (ed.), *The Growth of International Business* (London: Allen & Unwin), 51–62.

Teece, D.J. (1987) 'Profiting from technological innovation: Implications for integration collaboration, licensing and public policy', in Teece, D.J. (ed.) *The Competitive Challenge* (Cambridge, Mass.: Ballinger Publishing).

Teece, D.J. and G. Pisano (1994) 'The dynamic capabilities of firms and introduction', *Industrial and Corporate Change*, 3, 537–56.

Teeple, G. (1995) *Globalization and the Decline of Social Reform* (Toronto: Garamond Press).

Thompson, R.S. (1985) 'Risk reduction and international diversification: an analysis of large UK multinational companies', *Applied Economics*, 17, 529–41.

Trompenaars, F. (1993) *Riding the Waves of Culture* (London: Economist Books).

Trompenaars, F. (1996) 'Resolving international conflict: Culture and business strategy', *Business Strategy Review*, 7, 51–68.

Tung, R.L. (1993) 'Managing cross-national and intra-national diversity', *Human Resource Management*, 32, 461–77.

Udis, B. and K.E. Maskus (1991) 'Offsets as industrial policy: lessons from aerospace', *Defence Economics*, 20, 151–64.

UNCTAD (1996) *Incentives and Foreign Direct Investment* (Geneva and New York: United Nations).

Usher D. (1977) 'The economics of tax incentives to encourage investment in developing countries', *Journal of Development Economics*, June, 119–61.

Vernon, R. (1966) 'International investment and international trade in the product cycle', *Quarterly Journal of Economics*, 80, 190–207.

Very, P., M. Lubatkin and R. Calori (1996) 'A cross-national assessment of acculturative stress in recent European mergers', *International Studies of Management and Organizations*, 26, 59–86.

Very, P., R. Calori and M. Lubatkin (1993) 'An investigation of national and organisational cultural influences in recent European mergers', *Advances in Strategic Management*, 9, 323–46.

Vismer, B.E. (1994) 'Industry and location standard index models', *American Association of Cost Engineers Transactions (AEE)*, CE2.1–CE2.5.

Von Hippel, E. (1987) 'Co-operation between rivals: Informal know-how trading', *Research Policy*, 16, 291–302.

Von Hippel, E. (1988) *The Sources of Innovations* (Oxford: Oxford University Press).

Wade, R. (1995) 'Resolving the state–market dilemma in East Asia', in H.-J. Chang and R. Rowthorn (eds) (1995), *The Role of the State in Economic Change* (Oxford, The Clarendon Press).

Wade, R. (1996) 'Globalization and its limits: Reports of the death of the national economy are greatly exaggerated', in S. Berger and R. Dore (eds), *National Diversity and Global Capitalism* (Ithaca, New York: Cornell University Press).

Wallace, C.D. (1990) *Foreign Direct Investment in the 1990s. A New Climate in the Third World* (Dordrecht, Netherlands: Martinus Nijhoff).

Walter, G.A. (1985) 'Culture collisions in mergers and acquisitions', P.J. Frost, L.F. Moore, M.R. Louis, C.C. Lundberg and J. Martin (eds), *Organisational Culture* (Beverly Hills: Sage).

Ward, B. (1958) 'The firm in Illyria: Market synicalism', *American Economic Review*, 48(4), 566–89.

Waters, M. (1995) *Globalization* (London: Routledge).

Webster, L.M., J. Franz, I. Artimiev and H. Wackman (1994) *Newly Privatized Russian Enterprises*, World Bank Technical Paper, no. 241 (Washington, DC: The World Bank).

Weiss, L. (1997) 'Globalization and the myth of the powerless state', *New Left Review*, 225, September/October, 3–27.

Welbourne, T.M., D.B. Balkin and L.R. Gomez-Mejia (1995) 'Gainsharing and mutual monitoring: A combined agency–organizational justice interpretation' *Academy of Management Journal*, 38(3), 881–99.

Welch, D. (1994) 'Determinants of international human resource management approaches and activities: A suggested framework', *Journal of Management Studies*, 32, 139–64.

Wells, L.T. (1986) 'Investment incentives: an unnecessary debate', *CTC Reporter*, Autumn, 58–60.

Wernerfelt, B. (1984) 'A resource-based view of the firm', *Strategic Management Journal*, 5, 171–80.

Westney, D.E. (1990) 'Internal and external linkages in the MNC: The case of R&D subsidiaries in Japan', in C.A. Bartlett, Y. Doz and G. Hedlund (eds), *Managing the Global Firm* (London: Routledge).

Westney, E. (1993) 'Institutional theory and the multinational corporation', in S. Ghoshal and E. Westney (eds), *Organisational Theory and The Multinational Corporation* (New York: St Martin's Press).

Whipp, R. and A. Pettigrew (1994) 'Managing change for competitive success: Bridging the strategic and the operational', *Industrial and Corporate Change*, 2, 205–33.

White, R. and T. Poynter (1984) 'Strategies for foreign-owned subsidiaries in Canada', *Business Quarterly*, Summer, 59–69.

White, R. and T. Poynter, (1990) 'Organising for world-wide advantage', in C. Bartlett, Y.L. Doz and G. Hedlund (eds), *Managing the Global Firm* (London: Routledge).

Whitley, R. (1990) 'Eastern Asian enterprise structures and the comparative analysis of forms of business organisations', *Organisation Studies*, 11, 47–70.

Whitley, R. (ed.) (1992) *European Business Systems: Firms and Markets in their National Contexts* (London: Sage).

Wilhelm, W.R. (1990) 'Revitalizing the human resource management function in a mature, large corporation', *Human Resource Management*, 29, 129–44.

Bibliography

Williamson, O.E. (1975) *Markets and Hierarchies: Analysis and Antitrust Implications* (New York: Free Press).
Williamson, O.E. (1985) *The Economic Institutions of Capitalism* (New York: Free Press).
Williamson, O.E. (1986) *Economic Organisation: Firms, Markets and Policy Control* (New York: University Press).
Williamson, O.E. (1996) 'Economic organisation: The case for candor', *Academy of Management Review*, 21, 48–57.
Woodward, D.P. and R.J. Rolfe (1993) 'The location of export oriental foreign direct investment in the Caribbean Basin', *Journal of International Business Studies*, 24(1), 121–44.
World Bank (1992) *World Development Report 1992: Development and the Environment* (Oxford: Oxford University Press).
World Bank (1997) *The World Development Report 1997: The State in a Changing World* (Oxford and New York: Oxford University Press).
Yannopoulos, G.N. (1983) 'The growth of transnational banking', in M.C. Casson (ed.), *The Growth of International Business* (London: Allen & Unwin), 236–57.
Yip, G.S. (1994) 'Industry drivers of global strategy and organization', *The International Executive*, 36(5), 529–56.
Yoffie, D.B. (1984) 'Profiting from countertrade', *Harvard Business Review*, 62(3), 8–18.
Yoshino, M. and U.S. Rangan (1995) *Strategic Alliances: An Entrepreneurial Approach to Globalization* (Boston, Mass.: Harvard Business School Press).
Young, S., N. Hood and A. Wilson (1994) 'Targeting policy as a competitive strategy for European inward investment agencies', *European Urban and Regional Studies*, 1(2), 143–59.
Young, S., N. Hood and S. Dunlop (1988) 'Global strategies, multinational subsidiary roles and economic impact in Scotland', *Regional Studies*, 22(6), 487–97.
Young, S.J. Hamill, C. Wheeler and J.R. Davies (1989) *International Market Entry and Development* (Hemel Hempstead: Harvester Wheatsheaf).
Zand, D.E. (1972) 'Trust and managerial problem solving', *Administrative Science Quarterly*, 17(2), 229–39.
Zeira, Y., W. Newburry and O. Yeheskel (1995) 'Equity joint ventures (EIJVs) in Hungary: Factors affecting their effectiveness', paper presented at the 3rd annual conference on Marketing Strategies for Central and Eastern Europe, Vienna.

Index

DATE DUE

HIGHSMITH #45230

Printed in USA